MEDICAL DECISION-MAKING ON BEHALF OF YOUNG CHILDREN

In the wake of the *Charlie Gard* and *Alfie Evans* cases, there emerged a wide-ranging international conversation about the courts' role in disputes between parents and medical professionals over the treatment of young children. Central issues in this debate include the question of the appropriate threshold for judicial intervention, the different balances that can be struck in weighing up the rights and interests of the child, the parents' rights and responsibilities, and the relative roles of medical professionals and the courts.

This collection provides a comparative perspective on these issues by bringing together analyses from a range of jurisdictions across Europe, North and South America, Africa and Asia. This is particularly important as parents are increasingly seeking treatment abroad when overseas doctors are prepared to offer the child a treatment that domestic doctors will not. By contextualising the differences and similarities, and drawing out the cultural and social values that inform the approach in different countries, this volume will be highly valuable to scholars across jurisdictions, not only to inform their own local debate on how best to navigate such cases, but also to foster interjurisdictional debate on these issues.

Medical Decision-Making on Behalf of Young Children

A Comparative Perspective

Edited by
Imogen Goold
Cressida Auckland
and
Jonathan Herring

•HART•
OXFORD • LONDON • NEW YORK • NEW DELHI • SYDNEY

HART PUBLISHING

Bloomsbury Publishing Plc

Kemp House, Chawley Park, Cumnor Hill, Oxford, OX2 9PH, UK

1385 Broadway, New York, NY 10018, USA

HART PUBLISHING, the Hart/Stag logo, BLOOMSBURY and the Diana logo are trademarks of Bloomsbury Publishing Plc

First published in Great Britain 2020

A catalogue record for this book is available from the British Library.

Library of Congress Cataloging-in-Publication data

Names: Goold, Imogen, editor. | Auckland, Cressida, 1992- editor. | Herring, Jonathan, editor.

Title: Medical decision-making on behalf of young children : a comparative perspective / edited by Imogen Goold, Cressida Auckland and Jonathan Herring.

Description: Oxford, UK ; New York, NY : Hart Publishing, Bloomsbury Publishing Plc, 2020. | Includes bibliographical references and index.

Identifiers: LCCN 2020018669 (print) | LCCN 2020018670 (ebook) | ISBN 9781509928569 (hardcover) | ISBN 9781509928576 (ePDF) | ISBN 9781509928583 (Epub)

Subjects: LCSH: Parent and child (Law) | Children with disabilities—Medical care—Law and legislation. | Children with disabilities—Legal status, laws, etc. | Child health services—Law and legislation. | Informed consent (Medical law)

Classification: LCC K705 .M43 2020 (print) | LCC K705 (ebook) | DDC 346.01/7—dc23

LC record available at https://lccn.loc.gov/2020018669

LC ebook record available at https://lccn.loc.gov/2020018670

ISBN: HB: 978-1-50992-856-9
ePDF: 978-1-50992-857-6
ePub: 978-1-50992-858-3

Typeset by Compuscript Ltd, Shannon

TABLE OF CONTENTS

LIST OF CONTRIBUTORS

Cressida Auckland Assistant Professor in Medical Law at the London School of Economics, England.

Ingrid Boone Associate Professor at KU Leuven, Belgium.

Jeffrey Botkin Professor of Paediatrics and Adjunct Professor of Human Genetics, University of Utah, USA.

Lydia Bracken Lecturer in Law at the University of Limerick, Ireland.

Alan Brown Lecturer in Private Law at the University of Glasgow, Scotland.

Andrea Büchler Professor for Private and Comparative Law at the University of Zurich, Switzerland.

Daisy Cheung Assistant Professor at the Faculty of Law, University of Hong Kong, Hong Kong.

Douglas S Diekema Professor of Paediatrics at the University of Washington School of Medicine and Director of Education at the Treuman Katz Center for Paediatric Bioethics at the Seattle Children's Research Institute, USA.

Chunyan Ding Associate Professor at the School of Law of City University of Hong Kong, Hong Kong.

Mariana Dobernig Students' Ombudsman and the Professor of Bioethics & Law and Family Law at Iberoamericana University, Mexico City, Mexico.

Leslie Francis Distinguished Alfred C Emery Professor of Law and the Distinguished Professor of Philosophy at the University of Utah and the Director of the Center for Law and Biomedical Sciences at the University of Utah, USA.

Roy Gilbar Senior Lecturer at the School of Law, Netanya Academic College, Israel.

Imogen Goold Associate Professor in Law at the University in Oxford and a Fellow of St Anne's College, University of Oxford, England.

Ben Gray Senior Lecturer, Primary Health Care and General Practice at the University of Otago Wellington, New Zealand.

Jonathan Herring Professor of Law at the University of Oxford and a Fellow of Exeter College, University of Oxford, England.

Calvin WL Ho Associate Professor at the Faculty of Law, University of Hong Kong, Hong Kong.

Sharon Kaur Senior Lecturer at the Faculty of Law, University of Malaya, Malaysia.

Fabiola Lathrop Professor of Civil Law at Universidad de Chile, Chile.

Pernilla Leviner Professor in Public Law at the Centre for the Rights of the Child, Faculty of Law, Stockholm University, Sweden.

John Lombard Lecturer in Law at the University of Limerick, Ireland.

Constance MacIntosh Viscount Bennett Professor of Law, Schulich School of Law, Dalhousie University, Canada.

Jean-Frédéric Ménard Lecturing Professor at the Université de Sherbrooke, Canada.

Rosalind McDougall Senior Lecturer in Health Ethics at the University of Melbourne, Australia.

Admark Moyo Senior Researcher at the Centre for Human Rights of the University of Pretoria and a Senior Law Lecturer, the Great Zimbabwe University, Zimbabwe.

Monica Navarro-Michel Professor of Private Law at the University of Barcelona, Spain.

Paula Siverino Bavio Member of the International Bioethics Committee of the UNESCO.

Karl Harald Søvig Professor at the Faculty of Law, University of Bergen, Norway.

Cameron Stewart Professor of Health Law and Ethics at Sydney Health Law, Sydney Law School, University of Sydney, Australia.

Thitinant Tengaumnuay Law Lecturer at Chulalongkorn University, Thailand.

Theodoros Trokanas Scientific Collaborator, Hellenic Open University and at the Department of Accounting and Finance at the University of Macedonia, Greece.

Samuel Ujewe Research Fellow at the Canadian Institute for Genomics and Society, Canada.

1

Introduction

IMOGEN GOOLD, CRESSIDA AUCKLAND
AND JONATHAN HERRING

In recent years, a number of cases involving a dispute between parents and doctors over the continued treatment of a seriously ill child have come before the courts of England and Wales. The cases of Charlie Gard, Alfie Evans and Tafida Raqeeb all concerned an application by the treating hospital to confirm the lawfulness of no longer providing life-sustaining treatment to a child, all applications which the parents of the children strongly resisted. In *Gard*,[1] Charlie's parents hoped to take him to the United States, where an alternative treating team were willing to trial an extremely experimental treatment which might have, if successful, extended his life and produced some improvement in his condition. In both *Evans* and *Raqeeb* meanwhile,[2] the parents wished to travel to Italy, where in each case, there was a hospital willing to perform a tracheotomy on the child and continue artificial ventilation to extend their life a little longer. Although all parties involved in the cases believed they were doing what was best for the child, agreement could not be reached between the parents and medical professionals. In the face of such disagreement, the English courts were clear that in disputes of this kind, wherever the welfare of a child is affected, they have the authority to make medical decisions on behalf of the child, on the basis of what they consider to be in the child's best interests.[3]

The courts' approach, while highly orthodox from a legal perspective, grabbed the attention of media from across the world, prompting a wide-ranging

[1] *Great Ormond Street Hospital v Yates and Gard* [2017] EWHC 972 (Fam).

[2] *Alder Hey Children's NHS Foundation Trust v Mr Thomas Evans, Ms Kate James, Alfie Evans (A Child by his Guardian CAFCASS Legal)* [2018] EWHC 953 (Fam); *Raqeeb v Barts NHS Foundation Trust & Anors* [2019] EWHC 2531 (Admin).

[3] *In the matter of Charlie Gard (Permission to Appeal Hearing)*, Thursday 8 June 2017; *Judgment of the UK Supreme Court in the Case of Charlie Gard*, 19 June 2017, [13].

international conversation about when courts ought to be able to override the wishes of parents, and who should have the final say over a child's medical treatment. Public feeling ran high at the time of both the *Gard* and *Evans* decisions, particularly following the court's ruling in each case in favour of the medical team's position. One reason for this was a fundamental disagreement about the authority of the state to intervene in private, family matters, and this was evident not just in England and Wales, but across the globe. Thousands marched in protest at the children's treatment worldwide,[4] while high-profile figures such as US President Donald Trump and Pope Francis openly condemned the decisions and offered to assist the parents in securing treatment for the children elsewhere. In Tafida Raqeeb's case, the court took the view that continued life-sustaining treatment was in her best interests, and she was in fact permitted to be moved to Italy for this to be provided.

One interesting dimension to the international media's response to the cases was the widespread speculation about whether or not a similar scenario could unfold in other countries.[5] Much of the commentary, particularly in the United States, showed a propensity to regard the court's treatment of the children in these cases as peculiarly British. Responses such as that of Father Tad Pacholczyk, Director of Education at the National Catholic Bioethics Center in the United States, were common:

> In the US we don't have the same kind of despotic hospital system that we see in Great Britain. Not only a hospital system, but a judicial system that seems to be weighed in the direction of not allowing parents to make decisions for their own children. … So, this kind of thing, in the US, we don't see routinely.[6]

The reasons given by commentators for why these cases were unlikely to arise in their respective countries related not only to the difference in legal position (with many speculating that the 'best interests' standard did not apply in the same way elsewhere in the world), but also to the United Kingdom's 'despotic' National Health

[4] R Bishop, 'Alfie Evans' Supporters Take to the Streets in Protests Worldwide over Parents' Wishes Being Rejected by Courts' *Mirror* (26 April 2018) www.mirror.co.uk/news/uk-news/people-across-london-northern-ireland-12433984.

[5] See eg S Scutti, 'Could Charlie Gard's Case Happen in the United States?' *CNN* (6 July 2017) https://edition.cnn.com/2017/07/06/health/charlie-gard-us-laws/index.html; S Scott and R Armitage, 'Charlie Gard: Could a Personal and Legal Tragedy of a Terminally Ill Baby Happen in Australia?' *ABC News* (24 July 2017) www.abc.net.au/news/2017-07-24/could-a-charlie-gard-case-happen-in-australia/8735900; WJ Smith, 'Charlie Gard Has Happened Here Too' *National Review* (4 July 2017) www.nationalreview.com/corner/charlie-gard-has-happened-here-too/.

[6] S Foley, 'Could an Alfie Evans Case Happen in the US?' *Relevant Radio* (26 April 2018) https://relevantradio.com/2018/04/could-an-alfie-evans-case-happen-in-the-united-states/.

System (as compared with privately funded systems),[7] its 'moral decline'[8] and its lack of religious conviction.[9] As one US commentator confidently expressed:

> We do not yet have cases of children or incompetent adults being captured and detained in hospitals by force of law, and the breath-taking vehemence and sweep of the British court in the case of Alfie Evans is not going to happen here soon, especially in setting out the rights of parties in such cases. We are not there yet. Even with Obamacare, we do not yet have the comprehensive government-controlled medical system that provided the foundation for the decision in Alfie's case. There is no national legally enforceable standard for the 'best interests of the child'.[10]

Whether any of these factors really do give rise to a difference of approach is open to debate. However, it was speculation of this nature about how such cases might have unfolded in other countries that prompted us to produce this collection. Its purpose is twofold. Firstly, it seeks to examine the legal position of other jurisdictions and to explore whether similar situations have arisen elsewhere and how the courts in other countries have responded to them. Understanding how disputes of this kind play out in other countries is more than simply a question of what the legal position is in that jurisdiction. The likelihood of such a dispute emerging, the prospect of it being litigated and the court's eventual resolution will all be influenced by numerous factors, and this collection seeks to explore what these are, including how a country's medical culture, cultural heritage, religious conviction, and understanding of the role of the family and the state may all affect how disputes unfold. The book therefore brings together analyses from a range of jurisdictions across Europe, North and South America, Africa and Asia, in order to produce a volume that not only shows the breadth of approaches to this issue, but contextualises these differences and similarities by drawing out the cultural and social values that inform the approach in different countries.

Secondly, given both the opposition to the current law in England and Wales revealed by the public response to *Gard* and *Evans*, and the legislative efforts that have followed them (most notably the campaign for 'Charlie's Law', which would permit the court to intervene in such cases only where the parent's decision exposes their child to a risk of significant harm[11]), there is clearly a need to

[7] ibid.
[8] J Cimmino, 'Charlie Gard and the Moral Decline of Europe' *National Review* (5 July 2017).
[9] D French, 'Alfie Evans Foreshadows a Dark American Future' *National Review* (26 April 2018) www.nationalreview.com/2018/04/alfie-evans-case-americas-future/.
[10] T Ascik, 'Can an Alfie Evans Case Happen in the United States?' *The Imaginative Conservative* (17 March 2018) https://theimaginativeconservative.org/2018/05/alfie-evans-case-united-states-thomas-ascik.html.
[11] The Charlie Gard Foundation, 'Charlie's Law', www.thecharliegardfoundation.org/charlies-law/.

critically appraise the current law. It is hoped that the experiences of other countries will provide a lens through which to evaluate the approach of the English courts, and to inform the UK's approach to navigating this issue. There remains considerable debate across the globe over how to balance the rights and interests of the child with the responsibilities and authority of the parents; the role of medical professionals in such disputes; and the extent to which it is legitimate for the courts to intervene in private, familial decisions. Through exploring how different jurisdictions strike this balance and what thresholds for intervention they adopt, this collection therefore provides a framework for examining how the law of England and Wales should regulate disputes of this kind. This collection includes chapters from six continents, covering more than twenty-five jurisdictions, and it is hoped that this will be valuable for scholars not only in England, but across jurisdictions, to inform their own local debate on how best to navigate such cases, and to foster interjurisdictional debate on the issues.

2

Identifying Who and What, then How: Attending to the Role of the Decision-Maker in the Normative Debate about the Best Interests Standard

ROSALIND McDOUGALL

I. Introduction

Amongst countries, diverse approaches exist to the question of when the state should intervene in parental decisions. As the chapters in this collection demonstrate, one aspect of this diversity is the use of different key concepts to justify state intervention.[1] A central point of contention in some countries is the role of the concept of harm, and specifically whether a harm threshold should replace the best interests test as the appropriate approach to court intervention in parents' medical decision-making for their children. In chapter 9, Francis and colleagues highlight this issue in the US context; in chapter 11, Goold and colleagues evaluate the merits of English courts moving to a harm threshold. In this chapter I explore recent debate about these concepts in the bioethics literature, to provide insights from an ethical perspective for the collection's exploration of how different jurisdictions approach medical decision-making on behalf of young children.

[1] eg the concept of unreasonableness is the focus in some countries, as discussed by J-F Menard, 'Offering a Reasonable Future: Withdrawal of Life-Sustaining Treatment From Infants in French Law with Illustrations from a Parisian Neonatal Resuscitation Unit'; and A Moyo, 'Parental Responsibility and Medical Decision-Making in Southern Africa: A Comparative Analysis of South Africa and Botswana', both in this book. The concept of best interests is the focus in other places: see A Brown, '"Parental Rights", "Best Interests" and the Withdrawal of Life-Sustaining Medical Treatment of Children in Scotland: A Lack of Authority'; D Cheung, 'Medical Decision-Making on Behalf of Minors: The Hong Kong Context', all in this book.

Across jurisdictions, bioethics writing on conflicts between doctors and parents often implies that there should be the same decision-making standard for courts and clinicians. The recent ethical debate has primarily been framed as 'best interests standard' versus 'harm threshold', with an underlying assumption that one framework fits all.[2] In this chapter, I argue that by focusing on the decision-making standard, inadequate ethical attention has been directed to the *role* of the decision-maker. Given that the notion of role-relative obligations is fundamental to medical ethics, we need to attend closely to the type of agent making the decision in order to better understand the ethics of intervention in parental decision-making.

II. The 'Who' Question and the 'How' Question

Bioethics debate during and after the Charlie Gard case focused both on the appropriate principle for deciding this type of dispute, and on the appropriate forum for doing so. In his editorial of an issue of the *Journal of Medical Ethics* focused on the Charlie Gard case, Pope writes:

> Perhaps a quasi-judicial multimember tribunal would be a better dispute resolution mechanism than a court. That determines *who* adjudicates these disputes. But we must also determine *how* the decision-maker adjudicates these disputes.[3]

I will refer to the question of the appropriate principle as the *how* question, and the question of the appropriate forum or decision-maker as the *who* question. Several chapters in this volume indicate the different approaches taken to the who question in different jurisdictions, for example the role of ethics committees in determining disputes in some countries.[4] Elsewhere, Paris and colleagues reflect that these '[q]uestions of "who should decide" and "on what standard" are as old as the reflections on the role of medicine'.[5]

[2] For a review of bioethics work on conflicts between doctors and parents prior to Charlie Gard, see R McDougall and L Notini, 'Overriding Parents' Medical Decisions for Their Children: A Systematic Review of Normative Literature' (2014) 40 *Journal of Medical Ethics* 448. Following Charlie Gard, see D Wilkinson and J Savulescu, *Ethics, Conflict and Medical Treatment for Children: From Disagreement to Dissensus* (London, Elsevier, 2019). See also special issues in 2018 of the *Journal of Medical Ethics* 44(7) and the *American Journal of Bioethics* 18(8).

[3] TM Pope, 'Charlie Gard's Five Months in Court: Better Dispute Resolution Mechanisms for Medical Futility Disputes' (2018) 44 *Journal of Medical Ethics* 436.

[4] See R Gilbar, 'Withholding and Withdrawal of Life-Prolonging Treatment from Young Children in Israel'; and F Lathrop Gomez 'Decisions About Their Body: Children's Rights and Parental Responsibility in Chile', both in this book, who outline the role of ethics committees in Israel and Chile respectively.

[5] JJ Paris, BM Cummings, MP Moreland et al, 'Approaches to Parental Demand for Non-Established Medical Treatment: Reflections on the Charlie Gard Case' (2018) 44 *Journal of Medical Ethics* 443.

> The *who* question: who is the appropriate decision-maker when there is an entrenched disagreement between doctors and parents about a child's medical treatment?
>
> The *how* question: how should their decision be made?

While there has been some bioethics work on the who question, particularly in the UK,[6] a great deal of ethical attention has been paid to the how question. Alongside the substantial body of work on conflicts between doctors and parents that preceded the Charlie Gard case,[7] there have recently been special issues of both the UK-based *Journal of Medical Ethics* and the *American Journal of Bioethics* that included various articles exploring these questions. For example, the *American Journal of Bioethics* issue contains two extended articles and twenty-two commentaries primarily focusing on the appropriate normative basis for decision-making when doctors and parents disagree.[8]

Recent discussion of the how question has primarily been framed as a binary: the best interests standard (BIS) versus the harm principle. Is the child's best interests the appropriate standard for decision-making, or the lower threshold of lack of harm? Article titles such as 'The Harm Principle Cannot Replace the Best Interest Standard'[9] and 'Harm Is All You Need?'[10] exemplify this framing. Ethicists from various parts of the globe have driven forward this discussion, with contributions from particularly the USA, the UK, Canada, Australia and New Zealand. The ethical debate about the how – ie the appropriate principle for decision-making in this type of case – has been essentially binary.

However, the discussion has lacked exploration of the potential *connection between the who and the how*. Perhaps there are different *hows* for different *whos*: different principles for decision-making depending on the role of the decision-maker. In this chapter, I will explore this possibility. I will not assume, as some writing in this area does, that the key issue is whether the BIS is superior to the harm principle or vice versa. Rather I will argue that the role of the decision-maker

[6] See eg R Huxtable, 'Clinic, Courtroom or (Specialist) Committee: In the Best Interests of the Critically Ill Child?' (2018) 44 *Journal of Medical Ethics* 471. Also, L Austin, 'UK Processes for Resolution of Disagreements about the Care of Critically ill Children' (September 2018) www.nuffieldbioethics.org/wp-content/uploads/Austin-L-2018-UK-processes-for-resolution-of-disagreements-in-care-of-critically-ill-children.pdf.

[7] For a review, see McDougall and Notini (n 2).

[8] *American Journal of Bioethics* 18(18) Contents, www.tandfonline.com/toc/uajb20/18/8?nav=tocList.

[9] JC Bester, 'The Harm Principle Cannot Replace the Best Interest Standard: Problems with Using the Harm Principle for Medical Decision Making for Children' (2018) 18 *American Journal of Bioethics* 9.

[10] G Birchley, 'Harm Is All You Need? Best Interests and Disputes About Parental Decision-Making' (2016) 42 *Journal of Medical Ethics* 111.

matters. In my view, continuing a binary debate about best interests versus harm is an insufficiently nuanced approach to the issue of conflicts between doctors and parents about a child's medical treatment. In this chapter, I will suggest that identifying who and what, then how is essential to rigorous ethical decision-making in these situations of conflict between doctors and parents.

III. Candidate Principles: Best Interests Standard and Harm Threshold

In exploring conflicts between doctors and parents, the ethical discussion to date has come to focus on two concepts: best interests and harm. There are, of course, nuanced bioethical and legal debates about defining each of these concepts in the context of paediatric healthcare more generally and as approaches to decision-making in the specific context of entrenched disagreements between clinicians and parents. Much of the recent ethics discussion focuses on conceptual clarification and definitions. Increasing conceptual precision around both the BIS and the harm threshold has been a feature of this literature,[11] with defenders and critics of the respective standards often failing to align on the conceptual content of the principles being debated.[12] I will not detail these debates here, but rather provide a brief outline of current definitions of the two main candidate answers to the how question, in order to point to the potential ethical significance of the role of the decision-maker in conflict cases.

Kopelman describes the BIS as 'a guidance principle used in medicine, law and elsewhere instructing surrogates making decisions for individuals lacking decision-making capacity to maximally promote their good'.[13] The notions of maximising and objectivity are two elements of the BIS that have been controversial and increasingly nuanced from a definitional perspective. Kopelman highlights that 'duties generated under the BIS … to maximize benefits and minimize harms for someone … can be overridden by equal or higher duties, such as those relating to the rights, needs, and interests of others'.[14] In the paediatric context, on this understanding, the BIS requires the decision-maker to maximise the child's well-being within the constraints of other ethical obligations.

[11] See eg TM Pope, 'The Best Interest Standard for Health Care Decision Making: Definition and Defense' (2018) 18 *American Journal of Bioethics* 36; DM Hester et al, 'Agreed: The Harm Principle Cannot Replace the Best Interest Standard … But the Best Interest Standard Cannot Replace the Harm Principle Either' (2018) 18 *American Journal of Bioethics* 38; LM Kopelman, 'The Best-Interests Standard as Threshold, Ideal, and Standard of Reasonableness' (1997) 22 *Journal of Medicine and Philosophy* 271.

[12] LM Kopelman, 'Why the Best Interest Standard is Not Self-Defeating, Too Individualistic, Unknowable, Vague or Subjective' (2018) 18 *American Journal of Bioethics* 34.

[13] ibid; see also Kopelman (n 11).

[14] Kopelman (n12).

In terms of objectivity, Bester has described the BIS as requiring the decision-maker to 'weigh different available health care options and choose the option that best promotes the welfare of the child'.[15] This type of interpretation has been seen as assuming an objective measure of best interests. However, as Gray argues in chapter 26, assuming that an objective best interests assessment can be made is problematic. Pope, including in response to Bester, argues that the BIS does not involve this notion of an objectively best option. He writes that the BIS 'does not require that surrogates choose objectively "literally best" options for the patient. Instead the BIS requires only that surrogates choose what *they themselves think is best* for the patient.'[16] Kopelman similarly argues that there are both subjective and objective components to the BIS. She writes that:

> The BIS has subjective features because they are, in part, shaped by the surrogates' values, views, and perceptions about what is best. It also has objective components when judgments about what is likely to benefit or harm others are grounded in sound logic, good information and scientific findings.[17]

Further, the way in which a child's individual interests relate and combine to generate an overall best interests option remains far from settled,[18] and thus currently involves a degree of subjective judgement.

Diekema's harm principle is often framed as the opposing candidate to the BIS. It is discussed in greater detail in the chapter by Francis, Botkin and Diekema in this collection. In his 2004 paper putting forward this principle, Diekema critiques the BIS as a threshold for state intervention when parents refuse medical treatment for a child. He writes that: 'The real question is not so much about identifying which medical alternative represents the best interest of the child, but rather about identifying a harm threshold below which parental decisions will not be tolerated.'[19] Drawing on the philosophy of Mill and Feinberg, Diekema puts forward eight conditions for justified state interference with parental decision-making:

1. By refusing to consent are the parents placing their child at *significant risk of serious harm*?
2. Is the harm *imminent*, requiring immediate action to prevent it?
3. Is the intervention that has been refused *necessary* to prevent the serious harm?
4. Is the intervention that has been refused of *proven efficacy*, and therefore, likely to prevent the harm?

[15] Bester (n 9).

[16] TM Pope, 'The Best Interest Standard for Health Care Decision Making: Definition and Defense' (2018) 18 *American Journal of Bioethics* 37 (emphasis added).

[17] Kopelman (n 12) 35–6.

[18] R McDougall, L Gillam, N Kerruish and J Snelling, 'Within the ZPD: Focusing on Harm and Children's Interests' in R McDougall, C Delany and L Gillam (eds), *When Doctors and Parents Disagree: Ethics, Paediatrics and the Zone of Parental Discretion* (Sydney, Federation Press, 2016) 25–40.

[19] DS Diekema, 'Parental Refusals of Medical Treatment: The Harm Principle as Threshold for State Intervention' (2004) 25 *Theoretical Medicine and Bioethics* 249.

5. Does the intervention that has been refused by the parents not also place the child at significant risk of serious harm, and do its *projected benefits outweigh its projected burdens* significantly more favourably than the option chosen by the parents?
6. Would any other option prevent serious harm to the child in a way that is *less intrusive* to parental autonomy and more acceptable to the parents?
7. Can the state intervention be *generalized* to all other similar situations?
8. Would *most parents* agree that the state intervention was reasonable?[20]

Also focused on harm is the concept of the zone of parental discretion (ZPD).[21] This concept arose through clinical ethics case consultation within the paediatric hospital context.[22] Gillam defined the ZPD as

> the ethically protected space where parents may legitimately make decisions for their children, even if the decisions are sub-optimal for those children. … In this space, 'good enough' parental decisions should be tolerated, until the point where they would cause harm to the child.[23]

The key idea is that in situations of entrenched disagreement, clinicians can accept parental decisions that are suboptimal for the child (from the clinician's perspective), so long as the decisions do not involve probable harm to the child.[24] This framework directs clinicians to consider both the potential harm to the child associated with the parents' decision, *and* the potential harm to the child if the parents' decision is overridden.

For brevity, throughout the rest of this chapter, I will use term 'harm threshold' to refer to Diekema's harm principle and Gillam's ZPD together – as answers to the 'how' question that centre on harm to the child. I will also refer to them separately where necessary.

IV. Clarifying the Decision at Hand: The 'What' Question

Both the harm principle and the ZPD are defined as relating to a particular type or types of situation. The concepts include specification of the kind of decision to which they apply. The harm principle, as originally described, is for 'determining

[20] ibid 252 (emphasis added). See B Gray, 'The Relevance of Cultural Competence to Resolving Disputes in Relation to Medical Decisions for Children' in this book for an argument that condition 8 inevitably disadvantages parents from minority communities.

[21] L Gillam, 'The Zone of Parental Discretion: An Ethical Tool for Dealing with Disagreement Between Parents and Doctors About Medical Treatment for Children' (2016) 11 *Clinical Ethics* 1; R McDougall, L Gillam and H Gold, 'The Zone of Parental Discretion' in McDougall et al (n 18) 14–24.

[22] R McDougall, C Delany and L Gillam, 'Introduction' in McDougall et al (n 18) 3–5.

[23] Gillam (n 21) 2.

[24] McDougall, Gillam and Gold (n 21) 14.

whether state intervention might be necessary', specifically in situations where parents are refusing consent for a medical intervention.[25] As Hester, Diekema and colleagues write more recently:

> The role of the harm principle is not to replace the BIS, but to supplement it, charged with one specific task: determining when parental refusal of a medical recommendation should be challenged through state action.[26]

The harm principle is posited as applicable when a decision needs to be made about state intervention when parents refuse treatment.

The ZPD is for the broader category of 'situations of entrenched disagreement'.[27] It applies to both parental refusals of treatment and parental requests for treatment, and to the range of ways in which clinicians might override parental decisions, not limited to seeking state intervention:

> With the ZPD framework, we are extending the idea of the harm principle to those many situations of disagreement between parents and clinicians that may never get near court but which are somehow resolved or managed in the clinical setting.[28]

So, the scope of situations to which the ZPD is relevant is importantly different to those in which the harm principle is relevant in at least two respects: the ZPD applies to both parental refusals and parental requests for treatment, and the ZPD applies to overriding parental decisions in the clinical setting in ways that do not necessarily involve state intervention.[29]

In terms of applicability, the BIS is much less specific than either the harm principle or the ZPD. Best interests, as a concept, is put forward as applicable to a far wider set of decisions and situations. Kopelman, for example, outlines diverse uses of the BIS: as an ideal expressing what we want for children, as a way of testing the reasonableness of a paediatric clinician's decision, and in the context of decision-making by state actors in cases of child abuse and neglect.[30] The BIS is posited as applying across multiple different types of decisions and situations both in paediatric healthcare and more broadly.

The importance of the BIS in paediatric healthcare is a crucial area of agreement among writers who have differing views about the ethically appropriate answer to the how question. Advocates of the BIS and supporters of the harm threshold both see a role for the BIS in paediatrics – the point of contention is the applicability of this standard to the specific situation of disagreements between doctors and parents about a child's medical treatment. Advocates of the harm threshold do

[25] Diekema (n 19) 246.
[26] Hester et al (n 11) 39.
[27] McDougall, Gillam and Gold (n 21) 14. See also Gillam (n 22).
[28] McDougall, Gillam and Gold (n 21) 17.
[29] McDougall, Delany and Gillam (n 22) 3.
[30] Kopelman (n 12). See also Kopelman (n 11).

see a role for the BIS, just a more limited one than advocates of the BIS perceive. For example, in describing the ZPD

> [w]e are not suggesting that the ZPD is an appropriate framework for guiding clinicians when they are making their own assessment of treatment options for their patients. The best interests standard is still appropriate for medical decision-making by the clinician about the child's treatment in the first instance. … The ZPD is to guide clinicians once there is an entrenched disagreement with parents, not to guide clinical decision-making overall.[31]

Hester, Diekema and colleagues make a similar point in relation to the harm principle, encapsulated in the title of the relevant paper: 'Agreed: The Harm Principle Cannot Replace the Best Interest Standard … But the Best Interest Standard Cannot Replace the Harm Principle Either'.[32] Many writers who support the harm threshold as the ethically appropriate approach to entrenched disagreements also see the BIS as ethically appropriate for other situations in paediatric healthcare.

Attending to this issue of applicability highlights that a third question is necessary when we are thinking through the ethics of decision-making when doctors and parents disagree. Alongside the who question and the how question, there is also a what question: what is the decision that needs to be made? Is it a clinical decision about the best medical treatment for the child? Is it a decision about the justifiability of state intervention? Or about the justifiability of clinicians overriding a parent's decision? While the who question and the how question are normative questions, the what question is a descriptive one. It directs us to attend to the specific type of situation and identify the kind of decision that needs to be made.

The *what* question: what is the specific type of *decision* that needs to be made?

- Is state intervention justified?
- Should clinicians override the parents' decision?
- What is the best medical treatment for this child?

This *what* question has been addressed in the BIS versus harm threshold ethics literature primarily in terms of a distinction between a 'guiding' standard and a 'limiting' principle.[33] Medical decision-making (What is the best medical

[31] McDougall, Gillam and Gold (n 21) 21.

[32] Hester et al (n 11).

[33] See eg DS Diekema, 'Revisiting the Best Interest Standard: Uses and Misuses' (2011) *Journal of Clinical Ethics* 22, 128; TM Pope, 'The Best Interest Standard: Both Guide and Limit to Medical Decision Making on Behalf of Incapacitated Patients' (2011) 22 *Journal of Clinical Ethics* 134.

treatment for this child?) needs a guiding standard, and conflict decision-making (Should clinicians override the parents' decision? Is state intervention justified?) requires a limiting principle. Other similar framings that are sometimes used are whether the harm principle is 'augmenting' versus 'replacing' the BIS,[34] and 'aspirational or minimal standards'.[35] Defenders of the harm principle use these distinctions to clarify the scope of the harm principle, answering critics by arguing that there are different tools for different tasks. Hester, Diekema and colleagues, for example, emphasise the need to 'articulate … carefully the difference between an aspirational guidance principle (which the BIS serves as, admirably) and a "lower interference threshold" that is, in part, what Diekema's work seeks to identify'.[36] Paquette and Ross similarly write that 'by recognizing the distinction between guidance and intervention, there is room for both best interests and harm'.[37] These writers are essentially positing a relationship between the what and the how – that the type of situation determines the appropriate principle for decision-making. What has not yet been adequately attended to is the relationship between the who and the how – that the type of decision-maker has an impact on the appropriate principle for decision-making.

V. Role-Specificity

Bioethics often posits role-specific ethical principles. One obvious example is Beauchamp and Childress's four principles,[38] outlined in their hugely influential bioethics text. Their framework of principles is particular to healthcare. They are principles of *biomedical* ethics specifically, put forward as a set of obligations that health professionals have towards patients by virtue of their professional role. More broadly, the whole field of professional ethics is based on the notion that particular roles involve particular ethical obligations. As Oakley and Cocking write, ethics need to 'do justice to the responsibilities and sensitivities proper to various professional roles'.[39] In professional ethics, ethical approaches and principles are put forward aiming to guide the decision-making of a specific type of agent.[40]

[34] See eg Bester (n 9).
[35] See eg G Birchley, 'The Harm Principle and the Best Interests Standard: Are Aspirational or Minimal Standards the Key?' (2018) 18 *American Journal of Bioethics* 32.
[36] Hester et al (n 11) 39.
[37] ET Paquette and LF Ross, 'Pediatric Decision Making Requires Both Guidance and Intervention Principles' (2018) 18 *American Journal of Bioethics* 44.
[38] TL Beauchamp and JF Childress, *Principles of Biomedical Ethics*, 7th edn (New York, Oxford University Press, 2013).
[39] J Oakley and D Cocking, *Virtue Ethics and Professional Roles* (Cambridge, Cambridge University Press, 2001) 2.
[40] See eg C Martin, W Vaught and RC Solomon (eds), *Ethics Across the Professions*, 2nd edn (New York, Oxford University Press, 2017).

Detailed and consistent attention to roles is lacking in the normative thinking about conflicts between doctors and parents to date. In discussions of the harm principle and BIS, there is sometimes an assumption that one principle fits all. The focus has been on the candidate principles for decision-making, and much less so on the decision-maker and the obligations associated with his or her specific role. Much of the discussion takes a principle as applying across a range of decision-makers, often without explicit justification. There are many examples where a principle is described (or assumed) to apply across a number of different decision-making roles. For example, Winters writes of the 'several existing frameworks that *clinicians, ethics committees, mediators, and arbiters* use to resolve entrenched disagreements for children too young to participate in decision making'.[41] Diekema similarly invokes a wide range of different types of decision-makers: courts, physicians, parents, ethicists and ethics committees.[42] There are many instances of this lack of role clarity in the normative debate about the BIS and the harm threshold, particularly writing that moves between doctors and judges as the relevant decision-maker, without explicit attention to professional role obligations.[43] While it might be the case that a particular principle applies to various types of professional roles, this is an argument that needs to be made based on each of the specific professions rather than simply assumed.

It seems likely that doctors and judges have different role-specific obligations to children in the context of entrenched disagreements about medical treatment. For clinicians, there may be a prima facie ethical obligation to maintain a therapeutic relationship with the family, which does not exist for a judge. For clinicians, in order to promote the child's well-being, it may be necessary to ensure that the family remains engaged with the hospital and clinical team. Situations such as those of Ashya King in the UK and Tovia Laufau in New Zealand indicate that, in the context of entrenched disagreements about a child's medical treatment, parents sometimes remove their families from the hospital's care entirely. Gray, in chapter 26, cites his empirical findings that around one-third of families fled in the context of a court order imposing cancer treatment on a child when cultural or religious reasons were at stake. Ensuring that the child receives medical attention (including, for example, pain management) means that clinicians are obliged to try and maintain a functional relationship with parents and this might mean that greater compromise is ethically appropriate for clinicians than for judges. Both roles involve promoting the child's well-being, but the prima facie ethical obligations associated with the roles might be different. Attending to the ethical obligations associated with a particular role is even more important given

[41] JP Winters, 'When Parents Refuse: Resolving Entrenched Disagreements Between Parents and Clinicians in Situations of Uncertainty and Complexity' (2018) 18 *American Journal of Bioethics* 20 (emphasis added).

[42] See eg Diekema (n 33).

[43] See eg Wilkinson and Savulescu (n 2) 92–93; Hester et al (n 11).

recent calls for new types of decision-makers in this space, such as tribunals, independent ethics committees, etc.[44] There would be a great deal of work to be done to establish the ethical role and related obligations of these new types of decision-makers.

Recognising that role-specificity is fundamental to ethical decision-making has important theoretical and practical implications for this area. It suggests that identifying the role of the decision-maker is the first step in thinking through the appropriate normative basis for decision-making when doctors and parents disagree, and for reasoning about these conflicts in practice. As a first step, we need to answer a descriptive version of the who question: not the broader question of 'who *should* be the decision-maker?', but 'who *is* the decision-maker?' Who, in the current situation, is in fact faced with making a decision about what to do? Is it clinicians or a court or another type of decision-maker? We then need to clarify the decision at hand, ie answer the what question. Is it a decision about medical treatment or about overriding parents in the context of entrenched disagreement? On a practical level, it is necessary to identify the decision-maker and the specific question at hand, in order to identify the appropriate role-specific principle for the decision.

Attending to role in conflict decision-making: who and what, then how:

- Who is making a decision? That is, specifying the decision-maker's professional role.
- What is the specific type of decision that needs to be made?
- How should this kind of decision-maker make this type of decision?

VI. Moving Beyond Best Interests Standard Versus Harm Threshold

Across jurisdictions, a great deal of ethicists' time and journals' space has been consumed with the debate between the BIS and the harm threshold. In my view, continuing scholarship in this area would be most fruitful if we could move past this overly dichotomous approach. There is a lot that writers in this area in fact agree on. One key area of agreement is that there is a role for the BIS in paediatric healthcare. Another area of agreement is on the need for multiple ethical concepts in paediatrics: that neither best interests nor harm is the only conceptual tool needed by decision-makers. Other considerations – such as the interests

[44] Pope (n 3) 436.

of others,[45] decision-making capacity[46] and distributive justice[47] – will have an impact on an ethically justifiable decision, either as a component of an overarching approach or principle, or as part of a set of principles.

We need to move past this BIS versus harm threshold thinking in two ways. Firstly, as I have argued in this chapter, greater clarity is required when we are thinking about and employing concepts such as the BIS and the harm principle. The role of the decision-maker and the type of decision at hand are both important in determining the appropriate principle for decision-making. If we are clear about the role of the decision-maker and the nature of the question that the decision-maker is answering, we can more deftly employ the most appropriate conceptual tool or tools. We can also more precisely identify points of disagreement amongst scholars in this area, and thus target our discussions most productively.

Secondly, we need to start exploring the issue of conflicts between doctors and parents in ways that are more conceptually creative. Pitting one approach against the other ultimately stifles innovative thinking in this area. It also invites simplification and straw-manning of the non-favoured view. Continuing to frame the discussion simply in terms of BIS versus harm threshold may be distracting us from exploring other potentially useful concepts that may be very important to addressing these conflicts ethically. Some scholars have recently made several useful suggestions for different focal concepts in this space. These concepts include reasonableness[48] and children's interests.[49] Gray, in this collection, suggests cultural competence as a more appropriate focal concept. The bioethics debate to date between the BIS and the harm threshold has shown us that there are points of agreement and some of seemingly intractable disagreement. So, instead of continuing to think in terms of this BIS versus harm threshold contest, investigating these other concepts seems to offer greater potential for new insights and fruitful outcomes for the complex challenges faced by all types of decision-makers involved in situations of conflict about children's medical treatment

[45] See eg Kopelman (n 12).

[46] See eg J Massie, 'Parents Seeking Treatment That Health Professionals Consider Burdensome' in McDougall et al (n 18) 157.

[47] See eg Wilkinson and Savulescu (n 2).

[48] Wilkinson and Savulescu (n 2). See also R Rhodes and IR Holzman, 'The Not Unreasonable Standard for Assessment of Surrogates and Surrogate Decisions' (2004) 25 *Theoretical Medicine and Bioethics* 367.

[49] Birchley (n 10); R McDougall, 'Indeterminacy and the Normative Basis of the Harm Threshold for Overriding Parental Decisions: A Response to Birchley' (2016) 42 *Journal of Medical Ethics* 119.

3

Parental Rights, Best Interests and Significant Harm: Medical Decision-Making on Behalf of Children in Belgium

INGRID BOONE

I. Introduction

The long-running, tragic case of Charlie Gard received extensive attention in the Belgian media.[1] Although medical treatment disputes of this nature have not yet been brought before Belgian courts, end-of-life decisions, such as withholding or withdrawing potentially life-prolonging treatment, are nevertheless an integral part of medical practice for critically ill minors. A study on medical end-of-life decisions in neonates and infants in Flanders found that 74 per cent of all non-sudden deaths were preceded by an end-of-life decision. Non-treatment decisions made up the largest proportion of end-of-life decisions.[2] A study on deaths of minors during an 18-month period spanning 2007 and 2008 showed that 36.4 per cent of all deaths were preceded by a medical end-of-life decision. The main reasons for taking such a decision were the absence of real survival chances and the prognosis of a very poor quality of life. In the physicians' opinion, life was shortened by less than a day in 70 per cent of the cases. In fewer than

[1] See eg 'Ruim 350.000 Mensen Eisen Experimentele Behandeling voor Doodzieke Charlie Gard', www.demorgen.be/nieuws/ruim-350-000-mensen-eisen-experimentele-behandeling-voor-doodzieke-charlie-gard~b102f279; 'Geen Zinnig Rechter Houdt Charlie in Leven', www.standaard.be/cnt/dmf20170711_02966818; 'Ouders Staken Strijd om Doodzieke Baby Charlie', www.nieuwsblad.be/cnt/dmf20170724_02984961; 'De Zaak Charlie Gard', www.knack.be/nieuws/wereld/de-zaak-charlie-gard/article-opinion-883349.html.

[2] V Provoost, F Cools, F Mortier, J Bilsen, J Ramet, Y Vandenplas and L Deliens, 'Medical End-of-Life Decisions in Neonates and Infants in Flanders' (2005) 365 *Lancet* 1315.

10 per cent of the cases was life shortened by more than a week.[3] In most cases the physician discussed the end-of-life decision with the parents and the decision was taken together with them.[4] This practice of shared decision-making between doctors and parents might explain why end-of-life medical decisions for minors generally do not end up before court.

The medical literature reports several situations in which conflict has arisen with regard to older children. Not uncommonly in these cases, the physician runs into conflict with the parents about the question of who has the right to give consent for a medical treatment, the minor or his parents.[5] Medical interventions on young children rarely seem to give rise to conflict between parents and physicians. The cases that are mentioned most often are those in which parents refuse a blood transfusion on religious grounds.[6]

This chapter examines the Belgian legal framework concerning decisions about children in the context of medical care. It focuses specifically on very young children who cannot speak for themselves. How does Belgian law balance between the rights and interests of the child, the parents' rights and responsibilities, and the role of medical professionals and the courts?

II. Exercise of Minor Patients' Rights

A. The Minor Child's Representation in the Context of Medical Care

According to the Belgian civil law rules on the legal status of children, anyone under the age of eighteen is a minor (Article 388 Civil Code). The general rule is that minors are legally incompetent and need to be represented by their parents or legal guardian. As long as the child is a minor, the child's parents[7] hold parental responsibilities[8] (Article 372 Civil Code), which they should exercise in the best interests of the child (Article 374 § 1 Civil Code). Parental responsibilities

[3] G Pousset, 'Incidentie van Levensbeeïndiging bij Minderjarigen in Vlaanderen: Onderzoeksresultaten en Ethisch Perspectief' (2018) 4 *Tijdschrift voor Jeugd en Kinderrechten* 387, 390–91.

[4] ibid 392.

[5] M Deneyer, C Clybouw, E De Groot, A De Backer, P Van den Brande and Y Vandenplas, 'The Surgeon and the Law on Patient's Rights for Minors' (2011) 111 *Acta Chirurgica Belgica* 119.

[6] M Deneyer, D Matthys, J Ramet, L Michel, D Holsters and Y Vandenplas, 'Legislation and Refusal of Blood Transfusion by a Minor Jehovah-Witness in Belgium' (2011) 111 *Acta Chirurgica Belgica* 355. See below.

[7] The term 'parent' is used in the meaning of 'legal parent', ie parenthood established according to filiation laws or through adoption.

[8] The Belgian Civil Code uses the term 'parental authority'.

encompass the right to make decisions concerning the child's health and medical treatment. Although incompetence of minors is the general principle, Belgian law recognises, following the UN Convention on the Rights of the Child, that minors have evolving capacities and are entitled to participation and autonomy, according to the level of their capacity. This is reflected in the Patients' Rights Act of 22 August 2002.[9]

The Patients' Rights Act applies to all people receiving healthcare from a health professional.[10] The exercise of patients' rights for children is regulated by Article 12.[11] The first paragraph of Article 12 reiterates the general principle of incompetence of children: minor patients cannot exercise their patients' rights themselves, as those rights are exercised by their parents or legal guardian.[12] This principle applies to all rights enumerated in the Act.[13] Thus, parents are entitled to information about the health situation of their child.[14] They have the right to consent to medical treatment[15] and the right to access their child's medical records.[16] Parents also have the right to choose the doctor who will treat their child. According to Article 6 of the Patients' Rights Act, the patient has the right to free choice of healthcare professional and to change his or her choice.[17] This right, which is exercised by the parents on behalf of their child, is also guaranteed by social security legislation.[18] There are nevertheless legal restrictions on the right to free choice, for instance in case of an emergency.[19]

[9] 'Wet Betreffende de Rechten van de Patiënt' *Belgisch Staatsblad* (26 September 2002). See section II.B below.

[10] Art 3(1) Patients' Rights Act. The Patients' Rights Act is a *lex generalis*. It also applies to healthcare services that are governed by a specific act, insofar as the specific act does not deviate from the Patients' Rights Act (T Vansweevelt, 'Wet Patiëntenrechten: Definities en Toepassingsgebied' in T Vansweevelt and F Dewallens (eds), *Handboek Gezondheidsrecht*, vol II: *Rechten Van Patiënten: Van Embryo tot Lijk* (Antwerp, Intersentia, 2014) 291, 299 and 301–02). Examples of specific legislation pertaining to minors are the Act of 13 June 1986 on the Removal and Transplantation of Organs and the Act of 28 May 2002 on Euthanasia.

[11] See generally G Genicot, *Droit Médical et Biomédical* (Brussels, Larcier, 2016) 234–47; C Lemmens, 'De Handelings- en Wilsonbekwamen' in Vansweevelt and Dewallens (n 10) 825–32; G Schamps, 'The Minor Child's Degree of Autonomy and the Measures Taken to Protect Him or Her Within the Health Care Sector in Belgium' (2001) 30 *Medicine & Law* 345; S Tack and T Balthazar, *Patiëntenrechten. Informed Consent in de Zorgsector: Recente Evoluties* (Brussels, De Boeck & Larcier, 2007) 19–26.

[12] F Ang, 'The Implementation of Participation Rights in the Field of Flemish Child Mental Health' in F Ang, E Berghmans and L Cattrijsse et al (eds) *Participation Rights of Children* (Antwerp, Intersentia, 2006) 123, 130.

[13] H Nys, *Geneeskunde. Recht en medisch handelen* (Mechelen, Kluwer, 2016) 257.

[14] Art 7 Patients' Rights Act.

[15] Art 8 Patients' Rights Act.

[16] Art 9 Patients' Rights Act.

[17] See generally F Dewallens and P Schoukens, 'Het Recht op Vrije Keuze van Beroepsbeoefenaar' in Vansweevelt and Dewallens (n 10) 311–29.

[18] Art 127 of Coordinated Act 14 July 1994 on compulsory insurance for medical care and benefits.

[19] Act of 8 July 1964 on emergency medical assistance.

B. The Minor Child's Evolving Capacities and Participation in Medical Decision-Making

The second paragraph of Article 12 of the Patients' Rights Act nuances the general principle in a twofold way. First, children who are considered to be able to have a reasonable judgement of their interests can exercise their patients' rights themselves, without involvement of their parents or legal guardian. This is an important exception to the legal incompetence of children in Belgian law.[20] A child who is considered to have a reasonable judgement of his or her interests can consent to medical treatment or refuse a therapy, even against the will of the parents.[21] The Patients' Rights Act does not use a strict age limit to determine whether a minor patient can exercise his or her rights autonomously. The ability of the child to have a reasonable judgement of his or her interests is assessed *in concreto* by the health professional who treats the child.[22] The capacity of children to exercise their patients' rights autonomously is assessed more strictly when very high risks are at stake.[23]

Second, in between the extremes of, on the one hand, children not being able to exercise their rights, and on the other hand, children exercising their rights autonomously, Article 12 § 2 of the Patients' Rights Act provides for a buffer zone.[24] The minor patient is involved in the exercise of his or her rights, in accordance with age and maturity. The Patients' Rights Act thus recognises that minors have evolving capacities and should be involved in medical decision-making according to the level of their capacity.[25] The child can be involved in the decision-making process in various ways: helping the child to understand his or her health condition; informing the child about the details and options regarding medical procedures; or encouraging the child to express his or her views.[26]

The proper level of participation of a particular child is determined case by case, based on their emotional and intellectual development, their health condition, the nature and scope of the treatment, their experience with illness, and their

[20] Lemmens (n 11) 826.

[21] H Nys, 'De Weigering van een Levensverlengende Behandeling door een Wilsbekwame Minderjarige in het Belgisch en Nederlands Gezondheidsrecht' (2017) 4 *Tijdschrift voor Jeugd en Kinderrechten* 357, 362; Tack and Balthazar (n 11) 20–21; J Verbruggen, M Deneyer and D Matthys, 'Ethische Aspecten bij Weigering van Therapie bij Minderjarigen met een Chronische Pathologie: is er een Rol voor Juridische Interventie?' (2015) 71 *Tijdschrift voor Geneeskunde* 1081, 1083.

[22] Genicot (n 11) 239–40; C Lemmens, *De minderjarige en de Wet Patiëntenrechten* (Antwerp, Intersentia, 2013) 12–13; Schamps (n 11) 347–48.

[23] eg refusal of a life-saving therapy. See P Borry, 'Minderjarigen en Medische Besluitvorming' (2016) 3(17) *Tijdschrift voor Jeugd en Kinderrechten* 221, 228–29; Raadgevend Comité voor Bio-Ethiek, *Advies no 16 Betreffende het Weigeren van Bloedtransfusie door de Getuigen van Jehova* (2002).

[24] Ang (n 12) 131.

[25] Lemmens (n 11) 825.

[26] Borry (n 23) 227.

particular family and sociocultural milieu.[27] Most children of preschool age do not possess a sufficient level of comprehension to meaningfully participate in decision-making.[28] Since the focus of this book is on very young children, this chapter will only elaborate on those situations in which parents exercise patients' rights on behalf of their children.

III. Parents' Right to Consent to a Medical Intervention

A. Presumption of Agreement of the Other Parent

Parents of children who are not considered to possess reasonable judgement of their interests exercise patients' rights on their children's behalf (Article 12 § 1 Patients' Rights Act). Parents are viewed as the key decision-makers on behalf of their children, primarily because they are considered to be best placed to know what is in their children's best interests.[29] In principle, for any medical intervention on a minor patient, the informed consent of the parents is required.

According to the Belgian rules on parental responsibilities, the parents jointly exercise parental responsibilities, even if they live separately (Articles 373 and 374 § 1 Civil Code). Only exceptionally may one of the parents be entrusted with sole exercise of parental responsibilities (Article 374 § 1 Civil Code). Joint exercise implies that the parents should agree with each other before making a decision. Nevertheless, when one parent acts individually, it is presumed with regard to a third party acting in good faith that this parent acts with the agreement of the other parent (Articles 373 and 374 § 1 Civil Code). As a result of this presumption, the health professional who is not informed of a disagreement between the parents may intervene having obtained the consent of only one of the parents.[30]

When the health professional is informed of a disagreement between the parents, he or she may not intervene without having obtained the consent of both parents. If the disagreement between the parents persists, it is not for the health professional, but for the court, to settle the dispute.[31] Each of the parents or the

[27] V Jeremic, K Sénécal, P Borry, D Chokoshvili and D F Vears, 'Participation of Children in Medical Decision-Making: Challenges and Potential Solutions' (2016) 13 *Bioethical Inquiry* 524, 530; Lemmens (n 22) 16–19.

[28] Jeremic et al (n 27) 524.

[29] ibid 529.

[30] Genicot (n 11) 237–38; Schamps (n 11) 348. However, the National Council of the Order of Physicians recommends that, in cases of non-urgent irreversible medical interventions, physicians should proceed with caution and should request the consent of both parents. See Nationale Raad Orde der Artsen, *Advies Betreffende Medische Zorg Verstrekt aan Minderjarigen – Instemming van Beide Ouders* (2011).

[31] Nys (n 13) 258.

public prosecutor may refer the matter to the family court (Article 373 alinea 3 and 387bis Civil Code). The court may authorise one of the parents to act alone for the specific matter (Article 373 alinea 4 Civil Code). The court may also decide, instead of the parents, whether a medical intervention on the child can take place. Except when the child's life is in danger or when there is a risk of severe health damage, the physician must await the decision of the court.[32] The criterion on which the court should base its decision is the best interests of the child (Article 387bis Civil Code).[33]

In Belgium, it is very rare for courts to decide on disputes between parents concerning medical interventions on their child. In the court's assessment of the best interests of the child, the nature and consequences of the medical intervention are taken into account. This is illustrated by a recent case in which a father asked the family court to grant him permission to have his ten-year-old son circumcised in hospital, against the will of the mother. The court noted that there was no medical indication for this intervention and that circumcision would have an irreversible impact on the child's body. The court rejected the father's request.[34]

B. Situations in which Consent of the Parents is Not Required

In some specific situations Belgian law allows health professionals to perform a medical intervention on a child without prior consent of the parents. When in an emergency there is no parental decision, the health professional should immediately perform any necessary intervention in the interests of the child's health. The health professional must record this in the child's medical records. As soon as the parents can be consulted, the normal procedure of consent applies again.[35]

Restrictions on the parents' right to consent to medical intervention on their child can also result from legislation that serves the public interest. An example of this is the regulation that makes vaccination against poliomyelitis compulsory.[36] Parents who refuse to have their children vaccinated risk criminal prosecution.[37] The doctor has to inform the parents about the possible consequences of their refusal. The Belgian Cour de cassation decided that compulsory vaccination

[32] Art 15 § 2 Patients' Rights Act; see below. Lemmens (n 22) 44.

[33] M Mallien, *Le contentieux judiciaire parental à propos de l'éducation de l'enfant. Hiérarchie et inventaire des principaux critères d'appréciation retenus par les juges* (Brussels, Larcier, 2017) 112–14.

[34] 'Familierechtbank Brussel' [29 March 2016] *Revue Trimestrielle de Droit Familial* 1093.

[35] Art 8 § 5 Patients' Rights Act.

[36] Royal Decree of 26 October 1966 whereby the vaccination against poliomyelitis is made compulsory, *Belgisch Staatsblad* (6 December 1966).

[37] Ibid Art 8; Arts 1, 1° and 5 Health Act of 1 September 1945, *Belgisch Staatsblad* (10 October 1945). See Hof van Cassatie [25 March 2014] *Arresten van het Hof van Cassatie* (2014) 870; Hof van Cassatie [16 May 2017] *Rechtskundig Weekblad* (2017) 1109.

against poliomyelitis does not constitute an unlawful interference in the private life of the child.[38]

IV. Disagreement between Parents and Medical Professionals

Perspectives on what constitutes the best interests of the child may differ between medical professionals and parents. Disagreement between parents and medical professionals can occur when the parents refuse to consent to the medical treatment proposed by the professional, or when the professional does not want to start treatment the parents request or wants to stop treatment against the will of the parents. How does Belgian law handle these conflict situations?

A. Acceptance of Parents' Decision

Parents are entrusted with making medical decisions on behalf of their children, because the legislator assumes that they are in principle best placed to assess what is in the interests of their children. Therefore, medical professionals must in principle respect the decisions of the parents. If the parents refuse the proposed treatment, the physician may not perform this treatment. Otherwise, the physician could be prosecuted for causing intentional injury (Article 398 Criminal Code). In the reverse case that the physician refuses to perform a treatment that the parents request, especially a potentially life-prolonging or life-saving treatment, he or she could also risk criminal prosecution (Article 422bis Criminal Code: failure to provide assistance to a person in great danger). Moreover, not respecting the parents' decision may lead to civil liability and disciplinary sanctions.[39]

In most cases, the requirement of parental consent for interventions on a minor patient does not cause any problems in medical practice.[40] Parents are usually closely involved in the medical decision-making process and in most cases the decision is taken together.[41] However, if the parents refuse a life-saving therapy,

[38] Hof van Cassatie [18 December 2013] *Arresten van het Hof van Cassatie* (2013) 2806. See S Dalessandro, 'La vaccination obligatoire: l'analyse de l'exception de légalité au principe du consentement et l'examen du régime des restrictions aux droits et libertés individuelles' [2013–14] *Tijdschrift voor Gezondheidsrecht* 306.

[39] See E Delbeke, 'Staken of Niet Instellen van een Medische Behandeling' in Vansweevelt and Dewallens (n 10) 1433, 1435–38.

[40] Lemmens (n 11) 848.

[41] A study of deaths of minors during an eighteen-month period in 2007 and 2008 found that, in all of the reported cases where a medical non-treatment decision preceded death, this decision was discussed with the parents. In 66.7% of these cases the doctor involved the parents with the intention of reaching a decision together. In 33.3% of the cases the non-treatment decision was taken at the request of

which is very exceptional in Belgium, this decision is generally not accepted by the medical professional.[42] The parents' refusal is more likely to be respected if the chances for survival or healing are limited or if a treatment involves serious risks or side effects.[43]

B. Overruling a Parent's Decision to Refuse Treatment: Risk of Significant Harm

The parents' right to give or to refuse their consent to a medical treatment for their child is indeed not absolute. Article 15 § 2 of the Patients' Rights Act states that the health professional should overrule the parents' decision, where appropriate in multidisciplinary consultation, when the child's life is in danger or when there is a risk of severe health damage. This so-called 'escape clause' provides the legal basis for deviating from the parents' decision in certain cases. The health professional who appeals to the escape clause must add a written justification to the child's medical records (Article 15 § 3 Patients' Rights Act).

A risk of significant harm constitutes the threshold for the application of Article 15 § 2 of the Patients' Rights Act. The escape clause firstly applies when the parents refuse a life-saving therapy for their child.[44] A typical case is the refusal of blood transfusion by Jehovah's Witnesses while their child is in a critical situation. In order to prevent the child from dying, the physician must intervene, even if it is against the will of the parents.[45] A case reported in medical literature can serve as an illustration.

> Jehovah's Witnesses refuse a blood transfusion for their four year old son, despite a Hb of 3 g/dl due to a spleen rupture as a consequence of a bicycle accident. After the parents kept persisting in spite of the degree of emergency and an extreme attempt to persuade them, a blood transfusion and a splenectomy were carried out.[46]

The escape clause not only applies in life-threatening emergencies, but in all cases in which a decision of the parents to refuse a medical intervention can have very adverse consequences for the minor patient.[47] The words 'risk of severe health

the parents (Pousset (n 3) 392–93). A study of attitudes of physicians towards end-of-life decisions in neonates and infants in Flanders showed that a large majority (93%) of the physicians agreed that the parents' wishes can be taken into account in deciding on non-treatment (Provoost et al (n 2) 1318–19).

[42] See D Matthys and R Rubens, 'Wanneer Ouders een Levensreddende Therapie Weigeren voor hun Kind' (2013) 69 *Tijdschrift voor Geneeskunde* 1125.

[43] Borry (n 23) 225; Lemmens (n 11) 860; Verbruggen et al (n 21) 1081, 1084.

[44] Nys (n 13) 259; Tack and Balthazar (n 11) 24.

[45] S De Prycker, R Rubens and D Matthys, 'Jehova-Patiënten: Niet Allemaal Gelijk? Ethische, Legale en Medische Dilemma's bij het Behandelen van Jehova-Patiënten' (2013) 69 *Tijdschrift voor Geneeskunde* 795, 797.

[46] Deneyer et al (n 5) 121. For further case reports in medical literature that illustrate the problems encountered with Jehovah's Witnesses, see Deneyer et al (n 6) 355–59.

[47] Nationale Raad van Orde der Artsen, *Advies Patiëntenrechtenwet* (2003).

damage' in Article 15 § 2 of the Patients' Rights Act are interpreted broadly, so that they also include situations where the physical or the mental health of the child is seriously threatened. To assess whether the physician can overrule the parents' decision, multiple criteria are taken into account: the chances of success of the proposed treatment; the severity of the potential harm in the absence of treatment; and the extent of the risks and side effects of the treatment. If the prognosis is positive and if the potential harm in case of non-treatment is very significant, while the risks of the treatment are limited, the solution should be clear.[48] Overruling the parents' decision can thus be justified if the treatment aims at avoiding significant future harm to the child.[49] An application of Article 15 § 2 of the Patients' Rights Act in this context is the treatment of newborn babies with a seropositive mother. Even if the parents oppose the treatment, the child should receive the necessary treatment, given the chance of the child being HIV positive and the significant threat that this entails for the child.[50]

C. Overruling a Parent's Request to Initiate or Continue Treatment

It is not only the parents' decision to refuse a medical treatment that can entail a severe risk to the health of the child. A treatment requested by the parents can also be harmful to the health of the child. If there is a risk of significant harm, the medical professional should refuse to provide the requested treatment. For example, a physician must refuse to respond to a request by parents to perform female genital mutilation on their daughter.[51]

It is less obvious to apply the escape clause of Article 15 § 2 of the Patients' Rights Act when parents request a potentially life-prolonging treatment for their child. In that case, the parents' request does not endanger the child's life; quite the contrary.[52] However, the National Council of the Order of Physicians advises stopping, or not starting, treatment if it is scientifically established that there is no longer any hope for a reasonable improvement, and life-prolonging treatments would not increase the patient's comfort but only cause him or her more discomfort.[53] The National Council also recommends that physicians refuse

[48] Lemmens (n 22) 52.
[49] Verbruggen et al (n 22) 1082.
[50] Nationale Raad Orde der Artsen, *Advies Hiv-Positieve Moeder* (2006).
[51] Art 409 Criminal code; Lemmens (n 11) 862.
[52] Lemmens (n 11) 863.
[53] Nationale Raad van Orde der Artsen, *Advies Stopzetten en Weigeringen van Behandelingen* (2015). The National Council of the Order of Physicians determines the Code of Medical Deontology. It is also the task of the National Council to issue advice about rules of medical deontology (Art 15 Royal Decree of 10 November 1967 on the Order of Physicians). Advice of the National Council does not in itself constitute a deontological rule, but it can be taken into account when assessing whether or not

to resuscitate an extremely premature baby who is in a hopeless situation and where death would only be delayed or would entail unacceptable risks of serious damage.[54] If the parents do not agree to the cessation or non-initiation of treatment, the physician should act against the will of the parents, in the interest of the minor patient, in application of Article 15 § 2 of the Patients' Rights Act.[55]

These recommendations of the National Council of the Order of Physicians are in line with the majority opinion that a physician can never be obliged to start or continue a treatment that he or she feels is medically useless.[56] However, some authors argue that the decision as to whether a certain treatment is useless often implies a value judgement and that it is not for the physician but for the patient or their representative to decide on that.[57] According to these authors, the parents' request for a treatment of their critically ill child cannot simply be put aside for the reason that this treatment would be useless. In the first place, it is for the parents to make a decision about whether or not the treatment is useless. They should make this decision according to principle of serving the child's best interests.[58] The physician should in principle respect the parents' decision. Only if the treatment would cause significant harm to the child, such as severe suffering, could the treatment requested by the parents be refused on the grounds of the escape clause (Article 15 § 2 Patients' Rights Act).[59] This approach respects the balance that the Belgian legislator has pursued between the interests of the child, the rights and responsibilities of the parents and the role of medical professionals.

D. Overruling a Parents' Decision as an Ultimate Remedy

Performing or refusing a medical treatment on a child against the will of the parents should be an *ultimum remedium*. To the extent possible, the physician must try to obtain cooperation from the parents, through information, persuasion and, if possible, by offering alternatives.[60] If the parents and the physician continue to disagree, a multidisciplinary consultation can be held, or an appeal can be made

a physician's actions are in accordance with medical deontology. See R Van Goethem 'De Orde van Geneesheren' in T Vansweevelt and F Dewallens (eds), *Handboek Gezondheidsrecht*, vol I: *Zorgverleners: Statuut en Aansprakelijkheid* (Antwerp, Intersentia, 2014) 535, 555–56.

[54] Nationale Raad van Orde der Artsen, *Advies Reanimatie bij Extreem Vroeg Geboren Kinderen* (2010).

[55] Nationale Raad van Orde der Artsen, *Advies Stopzetten en Weigeringen van Behandelingen* (2015).

[56] See eg Genicot (n 11) 769–70; T Goffin, *De professionele autonomie van de arts* (Bruges, die Keure, 2011) 395 et seq; T Vansweevelt, 'De Euthanasiewet: De Ultieme Bevestiging van het Zelfbeschikkingsrecht of een Gecontroleerde Keuzevrijheid?' (2003) *Tijdschrift voor Gezondheidsrecht* 216, 229.

[57] Delbeke (n 39) 1451–53; Lemmens (n 11) 863.

[58] Delbeke (n 39) 1452–53.

[59] C Lemmens (n 11) 863–64.

[60] Nys (n 13) 259.

to the ombudsman service or to the hospital's ethics committee.[61] If the parents continue to resist, the physician can – as a last resort – inform the public prosecutor, who can then bring the case to court. At the request of the public prosecutor, the juvenile court can order juvenile protection measures when the child is in a situation that threatens his or her development.[62] The juvenile court can temporarily divest the parents from their parental authority on the ground of abuse, manifest misconduct or gross negligence that jeopardises the health or safety of the child.[63]

In an emergency, an appeal to the court is of course not always feasible. Moreover, an appeal to the court is not necessary when the child's life or health is seriously threatened, as the physician's actions receive legal support in Article 15 § 2 of the Patients' Rights Act.[64] However, if there is any doubt about whether Article 15 § 2 is applicable in a specific case, or if the parents physically object, the physician should proceed with caution and should inform the public prosecutor, provided there is sufficient time. A case reported in medical literature can serve as an illustration.[65] In this case, the parents refused a blood transfusion for their son for religious reasons. They physically resisted administration of the transfusion. The physician informed the public prosecutor and a court order was swiftly procured that temporarily divested the parents of their parental authority. The boy was saved.

V. Conclusion

According to the Belgian Patients' Rights Act, parents exercise patients' rights for their minor child if the child is not considered to have a reasonable judgement of his or her interests. Parents are entrusted with making medical decisions on behalf of their children, because the legislator assumes that they are in principle best placed to assess what is in the interest of their children. Therefore, medical professionals must in principle respect decisions made by parents.

However, the parents' right to give or to refuse their consent to a medical treatment for their child is not absolute. According to Article 15 § 2 of the Patients' Rights Act, a health professional should overrule the parents' decision when the child's life is in danger or when there is a risk of severe health damage. A risk of significant harm constitutes the threshold for the application of this so-called 'escape clause'. Overruling the parents' decision to refuse a medical intervention

[61] Lemmens (n 11) 857.
[62] Arts 2, 54° and 47 Decree of 12 July 2013 on integral youth care, *Belgisch Staatsblad* (13 September 2013).
[63] Art 32 Youth Protection Act of 8 April 1965, *Belgisch Staatsblad* (15 April 1965).
[64] Genicot (n 11) 241–42; Matthys and Rubens (n 42) 1126; Nys (n 13) 259.
[65] See Deneyer et al (n 6) 356–57.

can be justified not only in life-threatening emergencies, but also in situations where the physical or the mental health of the child is seriously threatened. If the parents continue to resist, the physician can – as a last resort – inform the public prosecutor who can then bring the case to court. In extreme cases, the juvenile court can temporarily divest parents of their parental authority. There is no unanimity in legal doctrine about whether a physician can overrule a request by parents for a potentially life-prolonging treatment on their critically ill child only because he or she feels that the treatment would be medically useless. It remains to be seen what position the courts would take on this.

4

'Parental Rights', 'Best Interests' and the Withdrawal of Life-Sustaining Medical Treatment of Children in Scotland: A Lack of Authority

ALAN BROWN

> Parents may know their children best, and their decision may be motivated by love, hope, and compassion, but the decision may still conflict with the best interests of the child.[1]

The story of Charlie Gard, and the dispute between his parents and the medical professionals at Great Ormond Street Hospital over whether or not to withdraw his life-sustaining treatment,[2] captured media and public attention throughout the UK (and indeed other parts of the world) in a manner that far exceeded the level of public interest ordinarily associated with proceedings of the English High Court or Court of Appeal.[3] This attention has been reflected in a variety of academic articles which have considered the underlying legal issues raised by this dispute.[4]

This public interest was no less present in Scotland, but it is notable that no similar cases have come before the Scottish courts.[5] As such, there is no direct

[1] E Cave and E Nottingham, 'Who Knows Best (Interests)? The Case of Charlie Gard' (2018) 26 *Medical Law Review* 513.

[2] *In re Gard (A Child) (Child on Life Support: Withdrawal of Treatment)* [2017] EWCA Civ 410; [2018] 4 WLR 5(2–5), the Court of Appeal judgment summarises the factual background at [1]–[16].

[3] Indeed, the case was commented upon by both President Donald Trump and Pope Francis.

[4] See eg J Bridgeman, '*Gard and Yates v GOSH*, the Guardian and the United Kingdom: Reflections on the Legal Process and the Legal Principles' (2017) 17 *Medical Law International* 285; C Fenton-Glynn, 'Life-Sustaining Treatment and the Best Interest of the Child: *Re Charlie Gard*' (2017) 47 *Family Law* 810; Cave and Nottingham (n 1).

[5] It is not possible to ascertain whether this reflects differences in healthcare practice between NHS Scotland and NHS England or whether it is simply a reflection of the significantly smaller size of Scotland's population.

judicial authority in Scots law on the issue of disputes between parents and medical professionals regarding the withdrawal of treatment from a child in a minimally conscious state.[6] This lack of authority arises more broadly, as AB Wilkinson and Kenneth Norrie observe, because 'there is little in Scottish case law to indicate how the parental power in relation to medical treatment is to be exercised over a child who does not have legal capacity to determine his or her own medical treatment'.[7] This lack of case-law reflects the position in Sweden, described by Pernilla Leviner in this collection, who notes that '[n]o similar cases have been tried in a Swedish court'.[8] Consequently, unlike in England and Wales, there has not been an authoritative judicial interpretation of how the relevant statutory provisions[9] relate to the medical treatment of children. In Scotland, disputes regarding all aspects of 'parental responsibilities' and 'parental rights'[10] are determined on the basis of the 'welfare test', set out in section 11(7)(a) of the Children (Scotland) Act 1995 ('the 1995 Act'), which provides that the court, 'shall regard the welfare of the child concerned as its paramount consideration'.[11] The consistently asserted position of textbooks and academic writers, when considering how this provision would be interpreted in the context of medical treatment, is that the approach adopted by the English courts to determining the 'best interests' of the child would likely be followed in Scotland. Joe Thomson observes that the 'English decisions are instructive',[12] Wilkinson and Norrie comment that 'there seems little doubt that the approach to welfare adopted in these English cases is likely to commend itself to the Scottish court also',[13] and Sarah Elliston suggests that 'while there may be procedural differences, it seems likely Scottish courts would follow the same approach as in England and Wales'.[14] This is unsurprising, because the

[6] This contrasts sharply with England and Wales, where these issues have been the subject of various reported cases over the past 25–30 years. See eg *Re J (A Minor) (Wardship: Medical Treatment)* [1991] Fam 33, and *Re A (A Child) (Withdrawal of Medical Treatment)* [2016] EWCA Civ 759; [2016] 7 WLUK 303, both cited by McFarlane LJ in his judgment in the *Gard* case.

[7] AB Wilkinson and KMcK Norrie, *The Law Relating to Parent and Child in Scotland*, 3rd edn (Edinburgh, W Green & Son, 2013) 233. See eg *Docherty v McGlynn* 1983 SLT 645; *Finlayson, Applicant* 1989 SCLR 601; and *Houston, Applicant* 1996 SCLR 943 for three pre-1995 Act cases where the issue is considered in very specific factual circumstances.

[8] P Leviner, 'Who Has the Final Word? On Trust and Legal Uncertainty Within the Swedish Health Care System' in this book.

[9] Which, as set out below, differ substantively between Scots law (Children (Scotland) Act 1995) and English law (Children Act 1989) despite underlying conceptual similarities between the legal regimes.

[10] s 11 of the Children (Scotland) Act 1995 sets out the court's powers in relation to parental responsibilities and rights; in particular s 11(2) provides that '[t]he court may make such order … as it thinks fit'.

[11] This standard contrasts with the position in other jurisdictions considered in this book. See eg I Boone, 'Parental Rights, Best Interests and Significant Harm: Medical Decision-Making on Behalf of Children in Belgium' in this book, who notes that in Belgium, under Art 15(2) of the Patients' Rights Act, '[a] risk of significant harm constitutes the threshold for the application of this so called "escape clause"'.

[12] JM Thomson, *Family Law in Scotland*, 7th edn (London, Bloomsbury Professional, 2014) 276.

[13] Wilkinson and Norrie (n 7) 235.

[14] S Elliston, *The Best Interests of the Child in Healthcare* (London, Routledge, 2007) 146.

approach of Scots and English law to the substantive content of the 'welfare test' is substantially similar in other contexts.[15]

To that end, section I will set out the legislative regime concerning parental responsibility and parental rights in Scots law, how this applies to decisions regarding the medical treatment of children, and the differences and similarities between Scots law and English law in this context. Thereafter, section II will consider how the differences in statutory provisions are combined with significant differences in court procedure between the two jurisdictions. To conclude, section III will discuss the substantive issues raised by these cases within the context of paucity of judicial authority in Scotland, focusing upon whether the reasoning of the English cases would be followed.

I. The Legislative Framework

In Scotland, the legal framework governing parental responsibilities[16] and parental rights[17] is set out in the 1995 Act.[18] While this legislation is underpinned by similar principles[19] to the Children Act 1989 ('the 1989 Act'),[20] which governs these issues in English law,[21] the 1995 Act employs a different approach to the definition of 'parental responsibilities' and 'parental rights' than that adopted by the 1989 Act. However, what is apparent is that in both regimes the central concept

[15] See eg the approach of both jurisdictions to the significance of contact with the non-resident parent in the welfare of the child: in Scotland in *White v White* 2001 SLT 485 and in England and Wales in *Re O (Contact: Imposition of Conditions)* [1995] 2 FLR 124, and *Re W (Children) (Direct Contact)* [2012] EWCA Civ 999, [2013] 1 FLR 494.

[16] s 1.

[17] s 2.

[18] For the background to the reforms of the 1995 Act, see Scottish Law Commission, 'Report on Family Law' no 135 (May 1992) particularly pts II–V, www.scotlawcom.gov.uk/files/5912/8015/2668/Report%20on%20family%20law%20Report%20135.pdf; and the White Paper, 'Scotland's Children: Proposals for Child Care Policy and Law' (The Scottish Office, August 1993) www.gov.uk/government/uploads/system/uploads/attachment_data/file/271973/2286.pdf.

[19] Indeed, the 'best interests' standard is utilised for decisions regarding medical treatment in many jurisdictions throughout the world, particularly those where the influence of English law is felt, as set out in various chapters of this book (see eg C MacIntosh, 'Decisionally Incapable Children and Medical Treatment Choices in Canada'; SJ Uweje, 'Making Decisions for Children in Healthcare and Medical Research: African Communal Responsibility or Individual Rights?'; A Moyo, 'Parental Responsibility and Medical Decision-Making in Southern Africa: A Comparative Analysis of South Africa and Botswana'; and L Francis, J Botkin and D Diekema, 'Decision-Making on Behalf of Children in the Research and Clinical Context: A United States Perspective', all in this book).

[20] Both legislative regimes are underpinned by the paramountcy of the 'welfare of the child'. To that end, s 11(7)(a) Children (Scotland) Act 1995 provides that the court, 'shall regard the welfare of the child concerned as its paramount consideration'. Similarly, s 1(1) Children Act 1989 provides that, 'the child's welfare shall be the court's paramount consideration'.

[21] Scottish Law Commission, 'Report on Family Law' [2.1] at 3 states: 'We were aware that the increased emphasis on parental responsibilities, rather than parental rights, in English law under the Children Act 1989 had met with very wide support and approval.'

is that of 'parental responsibilities'. Indeed, in English law, the 1989 Act adopts a relatively wide and imprecise definition of 'parental responsibilities' – 'all the rights, duties, powers, responsibilities and authority which by law a parent of a child has in relation to the child and his property'.[22] While this definition leaves the specific content of the concept to be considered by the courts, it expressly defines any 'rights' of the parent as being part of the 'parental responsibilities'.

In Scots law, the 1995 Act provides more detailed definitions of both 'parental responsibilities' and 'parental rights'. To that end, section 1 defines 'parental responsibilities'; this includes two general responsibilities, namely 'to safeguard and promote the child's health, development and welfare'[23] and 'to provide, in a manner appropriate to the stage of development of the child – (i) direction; (ii) guidance, to the child'.[24] As well as this, the section sets out two more specific responsibilities: 'if the child is not living with the parent, to maintain personal relations and direct contact with the child on a regular basis',[25] and 'to act as the child's legal representative'.[26] Relatedly, section 2 defines 'parental rights' as existing to 'enable [the parent] to fulfil his [or her] parental responsibilities'.[27] It is apparent from this statutory definition that in Scots law 'parental rights' are understood as subordinate to 'parental responsibilities'. Indeed, when first describing the approach that was ultimately enacted in the 1995 Act, the Scottish Law Commission observed that 'it would enable the law to make it clear that parental rights were not absolute or unqualified, but were conferred in order to enable parents to meet their responsibilities'.[28] On this basis, the definition clearly mirrors that of 'parental responsibilities' with the legislation providing two general rights, namely 'to have the child living with him or otherwise to regulate the child's residence',[29] and 'to control, direct or guide, in a manner appropriate to the stage of development of the child, the child's upbringing'.[30] As well as this, the section repeats the two specific responsibilities of maintaining contact[31] and acting as the child's legal representative[32] as specific parental rights. It is through a combination of the parental responsibility 'to safeguard and promote the child's health, development and welfare'[33] and this right to act as the child's legal representative

[22] s 3(1) Children Act 1989.
[23] s 1(1) (a).
[24] s 1(1) (b).
[25] s 1(1) (c).
[26] s 1(1) (d).
[27] s 2(1).
[28] Scottish Law Commission, 'Report on Family Law', [2.1] at 3.
[29] s 2(1)(a).
[30] s 2(1)(b). In this context, see I Goold, C Auckland and J Herring, 'Medical-Decision Making on Behalf of Children in English and Welsh Law: A Child-Centred Best Interests Approach' in this book, considering the different statutory framework, for England and Wales regarding 'parental responsibilities' in the Children Act 1989.
[31] s 2(1)(c).
[32] s 2(1)(d).
[33] s 1(1)(a).

that the parent derives their right to consent[34] to medical treatment on their child's behalf.[35]

However, despite this different approach taken to defining parental responsibilities and parental rights by the relevant legislation in Scots law and English law, the impact of these definitions on substantive outcomes across judicial decisions concerning the upbringing of children is less clear.

II. The Procedural Framework

As well as these differences in statutory definition, there are also differences between the jurisdictions in relation to the procedural regimes through which such disputes would come before the relevant courts. The most fundamental difference relates to the absence in Scots law of the concepts of 'wardship'[36] and the 'inherent jurisdiction',[37] which are central to the approach of the English courts to these issues. In England and Wales applications to withdraw life-sustaining medical treatment are made to this inherent jurisdiction of the High Court.[38] In such applications, as McFarlane LJ's judgment in *Gard* states:

> As the authorities to which I have already made reference underline again and again, the sole principle is that the best interests of the child must prevail and that must apply even to cases where parents, for the best of motives, hold on to some alternative view.[39]

The absence of authority in Scotland necessarily results in conditional statements regarding the procedural route through which such a case would come to court,[40] but it is suggested that two alternative options are possible. Firstly, under the 1995 Act, as Joe Thomson observes, 'it is open to any person with an interest in the welfare of a child to apply under s 11(3)(a)(ii) for a specific parental

[34] s 15(5)(b) defines the right 'to act as the child's legal representative' as including 'acting in, or giving consent to, any transaction where the child is incapable of so acting or consenting on his own behalf'.

[35] See eg Thomson (n 12) 276, and Wilkinson and Norrie (n 7) 232.

[36] See Practice Direction 12D of the Family Procedure Rules.

[37] R George, 'The Inherent Jurisdiction and Child Protection' (2015) 37 *Journal of Social Welfare and Family Law* 250 observed that '[t]he scope of the inherent jurisdiction of the High Court is, theoretically, limitless except where Parliament has expressly intervened to restrict the court's power'.

[38] Practice Direction 12D of the FPR, at [1.2], sets out the 'most common' orders made under the inherent jurisdiction in relation to 'the child's protection' which includes 'orders relating to medical treatment'.

[39] *In re Gard (A Child) (Child on Life Support: Withdrawal of Treatment)* [2017] EWCA Civ 410; [2018] 4 WLR 5 (McFarlane LJ) 21.

[40] The statement of Lord Clyde in *Law Hospital NHS Trust v Lord Advocate* 1996 SLT 848 (863) that 'I have no doubt that by one route or the other the Court of Session has the power to grant the necessary authorisation in the present case' illustrates the flexibility that may be available to the court given the absence of previously decided cases.

responsibility or right'.[41] Notably, the example given in this textbook of how this provision may be used is that of 'a doctor seeking the right to consent to medical treatment on behalf of a child whose parents are refusing to consent'.[42] Such a situation could be dealt with through an application for a 'specific issue order',[43] which would grant the doctor such parental responsibilities and rights as required to allow them to consent to the medical treatment on the child's behalf.[44] As mentioned above, the court, when considering any order under section 11, 'shall regard the welfare of the child concerned as its paramount consideration',[45] therefore such orders are determined by the 'best interests' of the child.[46] However, the absence of any judicial consideration results in there being no clarity or guidance as to how the Scottish courts would define and determine how those 'best interests' would be served in the context of withdrawal of life-sustaining treatment from a child. As Goold, Auckland and Herring observe, elsewhere in this volume, regarding the position in England and Wales: 'At the heart of the challenge to the best interests approach are questions about the legitimate bounds of state involvement in citizen's private lives.'[47] Self-evidently, these same questions can be raised in the context of Scotland.

Secondly, if for whatever reason a section 11 order was not considered to be available, Wilkinson and Norrie suggest that an alternative procedural route exists through the Court of Session's *parens patriae* jurisdiction,[48] observing that:

> [T]he control of parental power is based on the *nobile officium* of the Court of Session which acts as *parens patriae* as does the High Court in England in its wardship jurisdiction, and is, in principle, no less extensive. It would therefore be open to the Court of Session in exercising of its *parens patriae* jurisdiction to make orders authorising or prohibiting medical treatment.[49]

This observation is supported by the decision of the Inner House of the Court of Session in *Law Hospital NHS Trust v Lord Advocate*,[50] a case involving the

[41] Thomson (n 12) 266.

[42] ibid.

[43] s 11(2)(e) Children (Scotland) Act 1995. This procedural approach is described by Wilkinson and Norrie (n 7) 240.

[44] In terms of s 11 Children (Scotland) Act 1995, there is no apparent conceptual distinction between the situation described by Thomson and that of a doctor seeking the parental responsibilities and rights to withdraw medical treatment where a parent is refusing to consent to said withdrawal.

[45] s 11(7)(a) Children (Scotland) Act 1995. This provision reflects the language of s 1(1) Children Act 1989.

[46] Therefore, such an application would be treated no differently to any other made under the provisions of s 11.

[47] Goold et al (n 30). In that chapter, the authors consider the arguments in favour of the 'significant harm' threshold; this argument clearly recurs throughout many of the jurisdictions featured in this book. See further eg Boone (n 11).

[48] See eg J Seymour, '*Parens Patriae* and Wardship Powers: Their Nature and Origins' (1994) 14 *OJLS* 159 for consideration of the historical relationship between the *parens patriae* and the wardship jurisdiction in English law.

[49] Wilkinson and Norrie (n 7) 239.

[50] *Law Hospital NHS Trust v Lord Advocate* 1996 SLT 848.

withdrawal of life-sustaining treatment from an adult in a 'persistent vegetative state'. In his judgment, Lord President Hope (as he then was) stated that: 'The measures which led to the abolition of the *parens patriae* jurisdiction in England and Wales plainly do not extend to Scotland.'[51] This meant that the approach of seeking declaratory relief from the court to authorise withdrawal of treatment[52] was not necessary under Scots law. Instead, the court stated that the *parens patriae* jurisdiction allowed for decisions to be taken by the court in relation to adults who lacked capacity[53] and that, 'authorisation in the exercise of that jurisdiction will have the same effect in law as if consent had been given by the patient'.[54] The court stated that such decisions should be taken on the basis of the 'patient's best interests'.[55] Moreover, his lordship explicitly affirmed the above passage from Wilkinson and Norrie,[56] noting that '[t]heir observation … may be taken to be an accurate statement so far as jurisdiction over minors is concerned'.[57] Therefore, it would appear from this remark that the *parens patriae* jurisdiction of the Court of Session provides an alternative procedure through which an order for the withdrawal of life-sustaining treatment from a child in a minimally conscious state[58] could be granted.[59] However, similarly to a section 11 order, there is no judicial authority for how the 'best interests' would be interpreted when the 'patient' in question was a child. Indeed, Graeme Laurie has commented that: '[I]t would seem that there are few limits to the discretion of a court exercising the *parens patriae* jurisdiction, the main proviso being that it does so in an appropriately beneficial manner.'[60]

[51] ibid, per Lord President Hope, 856.

[52] As set out in *Airedale NHS Trust v Bland* [1993] AC 789 in relation to English law.

[53] G Laurie, '*Parens Patriae* Jurisdiction in the Medico-Legal Context: The Vagaries of Judicial Activism' (1999) 3 *Edinburgh Law Review* 95(97) argues that '[u]nfortunately, the narrowness of this judgment and the absence of detailed historical precedents leave a number of questions about the nature and scope of this jurisdiction in Scotland'. See further H Lardy, 'Euthanasia and Euphemism: *Law Hospital NHS Trust v Lord Advocate*' (1997) 1 *Edinburgh Law Review* 227.

[54] *Law Hospital NHS Trust v Lord Advocate* 1996 SLT 848, per Lord President Hope, 858.

[55] ibid (Hope LP) 859 and (Cullen L) 864.

[56] The judgment referred to the substantively similar passage from the first edition of that text.

[57] *Law Hospital NHS Trust v Lord Advocate* 1996 SLT 848, per Lord President Hope, 857. His Lordship went on to further clarify that this was 'subject to the point that in my opinion the origin of the tutory jurisdiction lies in the power of the Sovereign as *parens patriae* rather than in the residual power of the court in the exercise of the *nobile officium*'. Detailed discussion of the nature of the relationship between the *parens patriae* jurisdiction and the *nobile officium* of the Court of Session is outside the scope of this chapter. See further S Thomson, *The Nobile Officium: The Extraordinary Equitable Jurisdiction of the Supreme Courts of Scotland* (Edinburgh, Avizandum Publishing, 2015), and the Inner House judgment in *Cumbria County Council v X* [2016] CSIH 92; 2017 SC 451.

[58] The contemporary scope of the *parens patriae* jurisdiction in relation to children is unclear, but Lord Hope's obiter dicta in *Law Hospital NHS Trust* appears to suggest that this jurisdiction would be available as an alternative means (in situations where a s 11 order was not considered to be available) of authorising medical treatment for any child who lacked capacity.

[59] However, Elliston (n 14) 12 argues that '[i]n Scotland, this jurisdiction was revived specifically in relation to the medical treatment of incompetent adults and its scope for such use in respect of children is uncertain in modern times'.

[60] Laurie (n 53) 105.

Consequently, regardless of which of these procedural approaches was adopted (and indeed of the differences between these approaches and that of English law) the 'best interests' test remains paramount within judicial decision-making. While there are clear differences between the jurisdictions regarding both the statutory definition of 'parental responsibilities' and 'parental rights', as well as the process through which such an application would come before the court, the ultimate basis on which the decision would be made is the same test – that of the 'best interests of the child'. The next part will set out why, given the absence of any Scottish judicial consideration of that test in this factual context, it is highly likely that the relevant English authorities would be followed.

III. The Scots Law Approach to 'Best Interests' in this Context

As mentioned above, there is no direct judicial authority considering these issues in Scots law, but the commonly held view amongst academic writers is that the Scottish courts would follow the approach of the English authorities to determining best interests in such cases.[61] It is suggested that this view is correct and that this would be true regardless of which of the two procedural approaches were adopted by the Scottish courts. Firstly, if the issue was considered in terms of a 'specific issue order', under section 11 of the 1995 Act, the court would engage in an analysis of the 'welfare of the child' in the same way as it would for any other order under that provision.[62] Given the absence of any previous Scottish decisions, as a matter of precedent any relevant English authority would be considered highly persuasive. Moreover, as a matter of practice, it is rare for the courts of the two jurisdictions to disagree on the substantive content[63] of the 'welfare test'.[64] Secondly, if the court utilised the *parens patriae* jurisdiction, the decision in *Law Hospital* is instructive in showing the significance that is likely to be granted to the relevant English authorities. In his judgment, Lord President Hope notes the lack of Scottish authorities on the exercise of the *parens patriae* jurisdiction and refers approvingly to the English authorities on 'best interests' under the inherent

[61] See eg Thomson (n 12) 276, Wilkinson and Norrie (n 7) 235 and Elliston (n 14) 146.

[62] s 11(7)(a).

[63] Although the procedural approach is different, most obviously through the lack of a Scottish equivalent of the statutory 'checklist', s 1 (3) Children Act 1989.

[64] For an example of an apparent difference of interpretation related to the rejection in Scotland of the so-called '*Payne* discipline' in relocation cases, see *M v M* [2011] CSIH 65; 2012 SLT 428. However, more recent English cases appear to have limited the application of this 'discipline'; see eg *Re F (International Relocation Cases)* [2015] EWCA Civ 882; [2017] 1 FLR 979 and *K v K (Relocation: Shared Care Arrangement)* [2011] EWCA Civ 793; [2012] 2 FLR 880.

jurisdiction,[65] before stating: 'I think that we can accept the same test as appropriate for the jurisdiction which this court is entitled to exercise.'[66] The reasoning of the judgment prompted Graeme Laurie to observe that: '[T]he endorsement of *Bland* may suggest that the Scottish concept of "best interests" will be close to the English precedents.'[67] While there have not been any subsequent cases considering this issue in the context of the medical treatment of children, it is difficult to see why a similar approach of following the test set out in the English authorities would not be taken.

Therefore, as a consequence of the absence of Scottish cases considering the content of these tests, it is difficult to identify any specific normative basis that would underpin the interpretation of 'best interests' in this context, beyond that which is apparent from the English authorities. This raises three points on which to conclude. Firstly, from a normative perspective, it is somewhat unsatisfactory that there has been no judicial consideration in Scots law[68] of the underlying values that should inform decisions about the balance between parental autonomy, medical expertise, children's rights and the 'best interests' of the child when there is a dispute about the withdrawal of life-sustaining medical treatment. Secondly, however, the lack of reported cases may suggest that these disputes between parents and medical professionals are not occurring with the same regularity as in England and Wales,[69] although it is difficult to ascertain a clear reason for this divergence. Finally, therefore, the ultimate note is one of uncertainty; it has been suggested above that it is likely that Scots law would follow the approach of the English authorities, but until a such dispute comes before a Scottish court, this remains a suggestion, not an authoritative statement of the law.

[65] See eg *Re B (A Minor) (Wardship: Sterilisation)* [1988] 1 AC 199, *Re F (Mental Patient: Sterilisation)* [1990] 2 AC 1, *Airedale NHS Trust v Bland* [1993] AC 789 and *Frenchay Healthcare NHS Trust v S* [1994] 1 WLR 601.

[66] *Law Hospital NHS Trust v Lord Advocate* 1996 SLT 848 (Hope LP) 858.

[67] Laurie (n 53) 105.

[68] As mentioned above, this is by no means a jurisdiction-specific problem; see eg Leviner (n 8) and Boone (n 11).

[69] As well as other jurisdictions where there have been reported cases on similar issues.

5

Parental Decisions on their Children's Medical Treatment in Switzerland

ANDREA BÜCHLER

I. Introduction*

When adults make decisions about medical procedures being performed on their own bodies, they are exercising their right to self-determination. Under Swiss law, children have the right to self-determination once they are competent. Until this time, they are reliant on the consent of their parents as their legal representatives.

Both parents' rights and children's rights have high priority in the Swiss legal system. On the one hand, parents are primarily responsible for protecting their child's interests and welfare. This principle implicitly results from the Federal Constitution of the Swiss Confederation (Bundesverfassung der Schweizerischen Eidgenossenschaft, BV) of 18 April 1999, namely from the right to personal freedom and the right to have a family (Articles 10(2), 14 BV), the right to privacy in one's family life (Article 13(1) BV) as well as the child's need for protection and encouragement of its development (Article 11(1) BV). On the other hand, Switzerland has ratified numerous multilateral conventions that oblige it as a state to provide children with special protection. Of note is the UN Convention on the Rights of the Child (CRC) of 20 November 1989 and in the field of medicine, the Convention for the Protection of Human Rights and Dignity of the Human Being with regard to the application of Biology and Medicine: Convention on Human Rights and Biomedicine of 4 April 1997.

These two legal positions – those of parents with their right to determine how they raise their children and those of children, who are dependent on third parties for the protection of their interests – may actually conflict with each other. Where does the decision-making power of the parents end? This problem is particularly evident in the medical context, since the health of the child is a legally protected right and doctors are involved as expert third parties. As the much-discussed cases of Charlie Gard and Alfie Evans have shown, the views of parents and doctors on

* I thank my research assistant Jasmin Häcker-Winkenbach (MA Law) for her invaluable support.

the treatment of a child may diverge. In the following, an explanation is presented of how a conflict situation such as this can be resolved under Swiss law.

First, the legal status of minors and the legal basis for parental responsibility are discussed. The focus then moves to the decision-making power of parents in medical matters. The principles that guide parents in making medical decisions for their children and the limits of their decision-making power are explored. In particular, the question arises as to the role that cultural and religious aspects play in this and to what extent they should be taken into account. There is little by way of case-law in this respect. Using the example of neonatology, it is shown that applying the principles in practice sometimes proves difficult. Finally, the situation in which the opinions of parents and doctors about the medical treatment of a child are in conflict is discussed. The aim here is to show what means the law provides to resolve this conflict.

II. Decision-Making Ability and Competence of the Child

According to Article 296(2) of the Swiss Civil Code (Schweizerisches Zivilgesetzbuch, ZGB) of 10 December 1907, children, ie persons under the age of 18, are under their parents' responsibility. It is therefore primarily the responsibility of the parents to guide the care and upbringing of their child. Accordingly, they enjoy broad discretion in the exercise of parental authority. However, in doing so they must orientate themselves around the welfare of their child. They make the necessary decisions for the child, whereby, according to Article 301(1) ZGB, the child's own capacity to act remains reserved. This means that parents have to take into account the discretion that the law grants to minor, yet competent children in some areas.[1]

In addition, parental authority includes the power to decide on the child's place of residence (Article 301a ZGB), their upbringing and education (Article 302 ZGB) and the legal representation of the child vis-a-vis third parties (Articles 304–06 ZGB). Furthermore, parents are entrusted with the child's religious upbringing (Article 303 ZGB) and the management of the minor's property (Articles 318–23 ZGB). The child is under joint parental responsibility of their father and mother irrespective of whether both are married to each other or not (Article 296(2) ZGB). Divorce has no influence on parental responsibility. Parental responsibility can, however, be assigned to one parent alone if this is necessary to safeguard the child's best interests.

[1] eg competent children may accept advantages that are free of charge or carry out minor everyday transactions without the consent of their legal representative (Art 19(2) ZGB); once a child is sixteen years of age he or she is free to decide his or her own religious denomination (Art 303(3) ZGB); competent children manage and enjoy the benefits and fruits of their own labour (Art 323(1) ZGB).

In principle, according to the ZGB, children cannot participate independently in legal transactions due to their age. As a rule, parents therefore represent their child in all areas. Any interference in the physical integrity of a child – including medical intervention – is an infringement of a legally protected personality right (Article 28 ZGB) and thus requires justification. As such, in the medical field, the consent of the competent person or their representative is a primary consideration. Under the concept of informed consent, consent is given following a comprehensive explanation of the medical intervention being considered, thus eliminating any unlawfulness. However, the right to decide on medical treatment is a strictly personal right. Competent minors, ie minors with the capacity of judgement, are capable of action in this regard (Article 305(1) in conjunction with Article 19c ZGB). Therefore, they exercise these rights independently and without the consent of their legal representative, unless otherwise provided by law. Official intervention by the authorities is then also excluded.

Capacity of judgement denotes the capacity to act rationally. In the medical context, this firstly presupposes that a person is able to understand their medical condition, the treatment options and the implications of these, and the consequences of a treatment decision, and weigh up the advantages and disadvantages of the various treatment options. Second, they also require the ability to form an appropriate intention and act upon this.[2] Competence is not something that is gained when a certain age is reached; it is temporally and objectively relative.[3] This means that the question of whether the child can act rationally in this regard at the particular time must always be judged by the attending physician in relation to the specific medical issues at stake.[4] Either the child is competent or not. If the child is judged to be competent, the comprehensive explanation of the medical treatment is addressed solely to the child and he or she can and must decide on the execution of a medical intervention. If the child refuses therapy, the consent of the parent to the procedure cannot replace the child's missing consent.[5] In this situation, there is no room for a parental decision or intervention by the authorities. If a dentist detects tooth decay in a child, in order to assess whether the child is competent to give their consent he or she must assess whether the child is able to understand the diagnosis, have an idea of the treatment required and its purpose, and whether the child can see the consequences in the case of non-treatment, make up his or her mind and act accordingly. The child does not need to understand all the medical details of the condition and the treatment. It is sufficient he or she can understand

[2] See ruling of the Swiss Federal Court (BGE) 144 III 264, 271, E. 6.1.1; 134 II 235, 239 E. 4.3.2; 117 II 231, 232, E. 2a.

[3] See BGE 134 II 235, 240, E. 4.3.2.

[4] To determine the capacity of judgement, see Swiss Academy of the Medical Sciences (ed), *Medical-Ethical Guidelines on Assessment of Capacity in Medical Practice* (Bern, 2019) 12 et seq.

[5] See BGE 134 II 235, 239, E. 4.2, 240, E. 4.3.2 regarding an osteopathic treatment of a 13-year-old girl who resisted the therapy, but the osteopath performed the treatment nonetheless at the behest of the girl's mother.

both of these in general terms and evaluate the treatment options. In addition, the child must be able to make a decision based on their assessment.

If the child lacks the capacity for rational action, ie the child is incompetent, he or she cannot effectively consent to a medical procedure. The child's consent is legally irrelevant and the treatment is unlawful. The decision to carry out the procedure lies with persons who have custody of the child. However, this does not apply to every procedure: a distinction is made between absolute, strictly personal rights and so-called relative, strictly personal rights. With respect to absolute, strictly personal rights, there is no parental power of representation[6] and such rights cannot be exercised at all as long as the child is incompetent. However, assignment to these categories is not an easy task. It is subject to social change and is ultimately carried out by focusing on results. The distinction between absolute and relative, strictly personal rights is based on whether an intervention serves the health interests of a child.

A. Absolute, Strictly Personal Rights

Absolute, strictly personal rights are so closely linked to the personality of the holder as to make representative authority absolutely inadmissible.[7] In the medical field, only a few decisions are of an absolute personal nature. However, assignments to this category are not clear-cut in many cases. The right to consent falls into the category of absolute, strictly personal rights in treatments that are not medically indicated and thus do not directly serve the health interests of the incompetent minor. Examples include cosmetic procedures that are neither medically nor psychosocially indicated and with which only aesthetic purposes are pursued. The classification of sex-reassignment surgery in intersex children is controversial, however. In Switzerland it has long been common practice to have children with disorders of sex development undergo sex reassignment surgery shortly after birth or in infancy. Based on new insights into the physical pain and the psychological consequences of gender misassignment, it is now believed that it is better to wait until the child can decide their own gender identity and whether they wish for surgery. Thus, the right to consent to sex reassignment surgery is increasingly regarded as an absolute personal right.[8] In concrete terms, this means that the

[6] See generally A Büchler and T Gächter, *Medical Law in Switzerland*, 2nd edn (Bern, Stämpfli Publishers, 2016) 382 et seq; see BGE 116 II 385, 387, E. 4; 117 II 6, 7, E. 1b.

[7] Other absolute, strictly personal rights are, for example, marriage, acknowledgement of paternity or drawing up a will.

[8] See BP Piller, *Kindesschutz in der Medizin, Elterliche und Staatliche Bestimmungsrechte bei der Medizinischen Behandlung des Kindes* (Zürich, Schulthess, 2016) 6.75 et seq; M Werlen, 'Rechtlicher Schutz für Kinder mit bei Geburt Uneindeutigem Geschlecht' in M Groenberg and K Zehnder (eds), *"Intersex". Geschlechtsanpassung zum Wohl des Kindes? Erfahrungen und Analysen* (Freiburg, Academic Press, 2008) fn 127; see also A Büchler and M Cottier, 'Intersexualität, Transsexualität und das Recht – Geschlechtsfreiheit und Körperliche Integrität als Eckpfeiler einer Neuen Konzeption' in N Degele and N Penkwitt (eds), *Queering Gender – Queering Society* (Freiburg i.Br., Freiburger Frauenstudien, 2005) 128.

parents cannot consent to a child's sex reassignment surgery and thus it cannot be performed. This is justified with reference to the best interests of the child; in particular the child's right to an open future. The child should be able to decide for themselves on such serious, irreversible and non-urgent surgery once they are competent.[9]

Parental competence in religiously motivated interventions on the body of their child, eg the circumcision of male infants, is equally controversial. Some authors argue that consent to such a non-medically indicated intervention with irreversible consequences must be an absolute, strictly personal right and that it cannot be granted by the parents as representatives of the child.[10] Others justify the admissibility of circumcision of male infants by the parents' rights to bring up their child in line with their religion. A cantonal court followed the latter view, denying the existence of an absolute, strictly personal right of the child. However, the child's interests have to be taken into account.[11] This point will be returned to in the following.

Ultimately, the assignment of legal positions to absolute personal rights is not clear-cut and is subject to changes. Overall, the trend is that non-medically indicated and non-urgent treatments, as well as irreversible and not absolutely necessary interventions, are counted as absolute, strictly personal rights. They must be delayed until the child can decide for themselves about the intervention.[12]

B. Relative, Strictly Personal Rights

Representative authority is admissible in the case of relative, strictly personal rights. The right to consent to medically indicated therapeutic treatment belongs to this category.[13] Consequently, parents can and must consent to medically required treatments that should not be delayed, and for curative, diagnostic or preventive purposes. They directly serve the health interests of the child. If a ten-year-old child complains of pelvic pain, the parents may consent to removal of the inflamed appendix if this has been diagnosed.

With regard to the Charlie Gard case the question arises of whether parents are also entitled or even obliged to consent to experimental treatment.[14] Experimental

[9] See A Büchler and C Schlatter, 'Der (zu) Frühe Start ins Leben' (2016) 1 *Die Praxis des Familienrechts* 35, 42; with further references in C Schlatter, *Lebenserhaltung in der Neonatologie, Entscheidungsbefugnis, Entscheidungsfindung, Entscheidungsverantwortung* (Basel, Helbig Lichterhahn, 2014) 119, fn 560.

[10] See ibid, with further references in T Trost, *Das Elterliche Erziehungsrecht und die Persönlichkeitsrechte des Kindes, Eine Untersuchung am Beispiel von Cognitive Enhancement* (Bern, Stämpfli, 2017) 54.

[11] See judgment of the Cantonal Court of Grisons, 8 October 2013, ZK1 13 42.

[12] See generally M Michel, *Rechte von Kindern in Medizinischen Heilbehandlungen* (Basel, Helbing Lichterhahn, 2009) 144.

[13] See BGE 114 Ia 350, 362, E. 7.b.bb.

[14] The participation of the child in a clinical trial is not part of the consideration.

treatment is understood as a treatment aiming at the improvement of the child's health although it is not (yet) part of a medical standard. Such treatment may be medically indicated when there is either no standard therapy or the standard therapy has not shown any effect. Furthermore, the efficacy and tolerability of the experimental treatment must appear scientifically plausible.[15] Only if these criteria are met may the parents agree to experimental treatment of their child. However, given the unknown risks and uncertain success of the therapy, there can be no obligation to do so.

What is less clear is parental power of representation for procedures that are not medically indicated, but which nevertheless impact on the child's health interests. Correction to straighten teeth or corrective surgery for protruding ears lies in the grey area between aesthetic and medically indicated procedures. Both interventions can negatively influence the child's well-being as well as their psychological and social development due to external societal ideas that may have an impact on the child. If protruding ears are surgically corrected when the child is at kindergarten or school age because the child has been teased by other children, the intervention, while not medically necessary, supports the child's self-confidence. Consequently, it is in the child's health interests and must be viewed as a relative, strictly personal right. But how is the case to be judged if the surgery is to be carried out at the request of the parents in infancy, but the child has not had any negative experiences with respect to their protruding ears, due to their age, and may never do so in the future? In this case, there is an interplay between social norms about outward appearances and the parents' authority to decide on the future development of the child. Both play a part in the assessment of the child's interests and there must be careful examination of whether the intervention benefits the child's welfare.

III. Guidelines and Limits of Parental Decision-Making Power for Incompetent Minors

A. Child's Welfare, State Duty to Protect and the Limits of Parental Action

Although parents have the power of representation in the medical affairs of their children who are incompetent minors, they are still not completely free in their decision-making. Article 296(1) ZGB obliges the parents to prioritise the child's welfare. The child's welfare is thus the guideline and, at the same time, sets the limits for parental action. The welfare of the child is not defined by law, but is instead an open concept. The Federal Supreme Court states that child welfare

[15] See Michel (n 12) 141.

means the age-appropriate development of the child from a mental, psychological, physical and social point of view.[16] The best possible solutions for the child should be found in each individual case, taking into account all of the specific circumstances. The emotional and psychological needs of the child should also be included in the assessment. Both cultural and religious affiliation fall under psychological needs; these aspects also directly shape the identity and the living environment of the child.

Swiss child law assumes that parents are better able than anyone else to judge what is in the child's best interests and what measures are required for this. Accordingly, parents have the authority to determine their child's welfare. However, their authority is more limited in medical matters than in other areas. According to the Federal Supreme Court, the decision as to whether a certain treatment is in the best interests of the child must be based on objective criteria.[17] The general principle is that a clinically indicated medical intervention performed in accordance with the rules of medical science is in line with the best interests of the child. From this it follows that the parents can only, and in fact must, give consent to interventions for the purpose of therapeutic treatment. Therapeutic treatment is characterised as being based on a medical indication, performed in accordance with a standardised, scientifically proven procedure and pursuing a therapeutic purpose.

Since a medical indication is the starting point for the assessment of the child's best interests, the medical diagnosis and the medical recommendations are of great importance. The latter are based on examinations in line with medical standards and are expressed in terms of the chances of a successful outcome. However, medical views on the indication for and the appropriate type of treatment may diverge. Often there is no 'right' and 'wrong', so evaluation of the objective best interests of the child must be carried out cautiously. The more uncertain the medical diagnosis and prognosis and the greater the treatment options, the more room must be given to parents' values. Finally, there is a risk that the assessor is guided by their own values instead of those of the parents.

Even if the child's best interests – understood in an objective sense, ie primarily based on medical indications – is the guiding principle with regard to medical matters, the welfare of the child should not be judged in a way that is detached from the child's social and cultural environment. Although subjective views of parents should be left out when assessing the best interests of the child, the postulate that psychological factors and the individual living environment of the child should also be included in the assessment make these aspects relevant once again. After all, parents pass on certain values and social rules to their child. They shape the child's environment and decide on their lifestyle. The child's own experiences of their illness, and their social environment, eg if there will be a long separation

[16] BGE 129 III 250, 255, E. 3.4.2.
[17] See BGE 114 Ia 350, 363, E. 7b.bb; see generally BGE 135 V 134, 137, E. 3.1.

from their caregiver due to the stay in hospital, should also be considered. The literature also advocates including the future prospects of the child in the evaluation of his or her best interests.[18] Overall, the decision made should best serve the welfare of the child as a whole, taking into account the circumstances of the individual case.[19]

B. Personality of the Child

While exercising parental responsibility, the parents owe respect to the personality of the child. The child should not be regarded as an object of medical treatment; instead, their dignity as a person should be respected. The legal doctrine asserts the right of the incompetent child to be heard,[20] the right to have a say[21] and the right to veto.[22] Participation rights[23] arise from the international conventions ratified by Switzerland, eg Article 12 CRC. Also, according to Article 301(2) ZGB, the parents shall, wherever feasible, take due account of the child's opinion. With regard to medical procedures incompetent minors should be involved in the decision-making process, as appropriate for the child's age.

C. Newborn and Extremely Premature Children

In medical matters, the example of extremely premature babies illustrates the difficulty of describing the child's welfare objectively. Progress in the field of neonatology is the reason why extremely premature infants have ever greater chances of survival. With regard to these children, the Swiss Society of Neonatology has published recommendations on perinatal care at the limit of viability between 22 and 26 completed weeks of gestation.[24] According to these recommendations, parents can neither insist on inappropriate treatment nor reject a presumably

[18] See generally A Büchler and M Michel, *Medizin – Mensch – Recht, Eine Einführung in das Medizinrecht der Schweiz* (Zürich, Schulthess, 2014) 106.

[19] See BGE 135 V 134, 137, E. 3.1.

[20] See M Werlen, *Persönlichkeitsschutz des Kindes, Höchstpersönliche Rechte und Grenzen Elterlicher Sorge im Rahmen Medizinischer Praxis, Das Beispiel von Varianten der Geschlechtsentwicklung und DSD* (Bern, Stämpfli, 2014) 1074–75.

[21] See Michel (n 12) 196 et seq; see F Sprecher, 'Patientenrechte Urteilsunfähiger' (2011) 2 Die *Praxis des Familienrechts* 270, 282.

[22] See Michel (n 12) 157–58; see Sprecher (n 21) 281.

[23] Right to be heard before court (eg in the divorce proceedings of the parents) and in administrative proceedings which affect the child (eg disciplinary action in school), and, if the child has not been granted the right, he or she has the right of appeal; right to be heard in all matters concerning the child according to his or her age and maturity (eg change of school, surgery).

[24] Swiss Society of Neonatology, 'Perinatal Care at the Limit of Viability Between 22 and 26 Completed Weeks of Gestation in Switzerland', 2011 Revision of the Swiss Recommendations [2011] *Swiss Medical Weekly* 141:w13280, https://smw.ch/article/doi/smw.2011.13280. The recommendations are not legally binding because they are not referenced by state law.

promising treatment for the newborn. For births before the 24th week, therefore, only palliative measures should be taken, while from the 26th week intensive care measures should be implemented. There is a grey area in between in which each case must be evaluated individually. However, the prognosis regarding the survival of the premature baby or their future health is very uncertain, because the development of a premature baby is very difficult to predict, due to lack of experience and because it is always very individual. In addition, physical disabilities or conditions caused by preterm birth cannot be estimated with any certainty. This uncertainty meets the requirement for an approach that is in the child's objective interest. A clear answer to the question of what is in the best interests of the child is often not possible. In this area, the wishes and cultural values of the parents with respect to the decision about the treatment are given increased weight. The recommendations provide for there being a shared decision-making process. In view of its far-reaching consequences as well as its acceptance, the decision is taken together in a dialogue between the parents and the doctors treating the child.

The recommendations of the Swiss Society of Neonatology are currently being revised. In the future, not only the gestational age, but also other factors influencing the prognosis, such as gender, fetal weight and the induction of pulmonary maturation, will be taken into account. Moreover, there will be greater emphasis on the involvement of parents in the decision-making for the premature baby, their involvement no longer strictly limited to the narrow period of the 25th week of pregnancy.

IV. Dissent between Parents and Doctors

The legal difficulty and the ethical dilemma of a conflict situation between parents and doctors are both illustrated in a case that took place at the Zurich Children's Hospital. A child was born with a severe heart defect. The child's parents refused to allow multiple surgeries that would, according to medical opinion, provide the child with a good quality of life and almost normal mental but limited physical development.[25] The parents argued that they did not want the child to undergo surgery or suffer from complications and that they did not see themselves in a position to cope with the additional burden of caring for a child with a disability. From the point of view of the treatment team, however, the treatment should not have been withheld from the child. After several rounds of ethical discussions between the parents, doctors, social workers and ethicists, the decision of the parents was finally accepted. This case provides an example of the fact that many conflicts can be resolved within the hospital setting. The hospitals in Switzerland have interdisciplinary child protection groups that promote cooperation between doctors

[25] See *Kinderschutzgruppe und Opferberatungsstelle des Kinderspitals Zürich* (Jahresbericht, 2010) 5–6.

and parents in cases of disagreement. If this is not successful, the doctors are entitled, but not obliged, to report the danger to the child protection authority under Article 314c(2) ZGB (see Article 314d(1) ZGB). If child protection proceedings are begun, the authority clarifies the case ex officio (Article 314(1) in conjunction with Article 446(1) and (3) ZGB). Due to the small number of court decisions in this area, it can be assumed that, in practice, many conflicts can be resolved within the hospital with the parents, or that any interventions undertaken by the authorities are rarely challenged before the courts. In contrast, the child protection authority, in principle, has no power to provide an opinion if the parents request treatment for their child but the doctor refuses this on the grounds that it is unreasonable or medically inappropriate. The parents are only entitled to careful and appropriate treatment in accordance with the standards of medical science. If the doctor treating the child refuses to provide the treatment desired by the parents because he or she does not consider it reasonable from a medical point of view, the parents may demand treatment from another doctor or contest the assessment of the hospital through legal proceedings.

A. The Child Protection Authority's Assessment Process

i. Significant Risk to the Child's Welfare

The decision of parents to refuse treatment for their child can be overruled on the grounds of serious endangerment to the child's health. The existence of a serious risk to the child's welfare (Article 307(1) ZGB) is a requirement for intervention by the child protection authority in the conflict between the parents and the doctor providing treatment for the child. The margin of discretion pertaining to the best interests of the child is of note here. Cultural and religious values can come into play in very different ways. Restraint is called for in state intervention. The dividing line between socially undesirable, but not legally relevant, behaviour of the parents and a serious risk to the child is certainly difficult to draw. Whether a child is endangered cannot be determined in the abstract but requires a case-by-case assessment. An intervention by the child protection authority is legitimate if, taking into account all of the circumstances, there is a serious possibility that the child's mental, physical or moral welfare are adversely affected.

In a case of a three-year old with cancer ruled on by the Cantonal Court of St Gallen,[26] the doctors turned to the child protection authority because the parents twice refused a chemotherapy that was indicated for their son. According to the doctors, the refusal qualified as endangerment of the child's welfare and they asked the authority to take measures. However, the child protection authority did not

[26] See judgment of the Cantonal Court of St Gallen 8 July 2011, FO.2011.16-K2 (2011) 4 *Die Praxis des Familienrechts* 1036.

intervene. In order to overturn this decision, the doctors went to court and again argued that the boy would die within a few weeks if he did not receive treatment. Serious endangerment to the child's health was confirmed by the court when the parents discontinued the first round of chemotherapy for their child despite the probability of cure being over 90 per cent. Regarding the second chemotherapy, which was the subject of the procedure, the chance of survival was still 50 per cent. The court finally stated that the life of the child and its 50 per cent chance of survival should carry more weight than the right of the parents to decide on their child's medical care. Unfortunately, the boy died during the proceedings.

The question also arises as to whether non-medically indicated interventions on the child's body per se represent a risk to the child's welfare. The Cantonal Court of Grisons was asked to rule in this regard in connection with the religiously motivated circumcision of a four-year-old boy.[27] The court ruled that the child's welfare was not seriously endangered, provided that the intervention was carried out under anaesthetic by a medical professional in line with the recognised principles of medical science. In addition, the wound usually heals without any problems and the risk of complications is low. Nonetheless, the interests should be weighed on a case-by-case basis for any procedure that is not medically indicated. In this case, the interests of the custodial mother with regard to the religious education of her son and his integration into the religious community were weighed against the best interests of the child. The religious awareness of the child and the right to an open future were taken into account as part of the child's best interests. Since the parents belonged to different religious communities, the child would, according to the court, later inevitably be confronted with the question of his own religious affiliation. For this reason, the child should not be immutably affected by a particular religion as a result of the parent's decision before reaching the age of religious majority (16 years).

If the parents want to continue their child's medical treatment in another place – as in the case of Charlie Gard – they can do this. However, if the doctors treating the child consider that this poses a significant risk to the child's welfare, they can involve the child protection authority.

ii. Proportionality

The principle of proportionality, which also represents a constitutional principle as per Article 5(2) BV, is very important in terms of child protection. The subsidiarity of child protection measures and the principle of complementarity substantiate the principle of proportionality. Accordingly, a child protection measure may only be ordered if the child's best interests are threatened and the parents are unwilling or unable to remedy the situation. In addition, the measure

[27] See judgment of the Cantonal Court of Grisons 8 October 2013, ZK1 13 42.

must be complementary to parental or family deficits and only compensate for these. A child protection measure is also only permissible if it is adequate to eliminate or mitigate the endangerment of the child's welfare in a specific individual case. The least restrictive measure with the greatest probability of success is always the one that should be chosen. Finally, the child protection authority must examine proportionality in the strict sense: on the one hand, the interests and legally protected rights concerned, on the other hand, the purpose of the intervention and its aim. Intervention may only take place if the interests for the protection of the child prevail; it must also correspond to the degree of risk to the child's welfare, after the intended benefits and possible disadvantages have been reasonably weighed against each other.

There are highly protected legal positions around parents making medical decisions for their children as incompetent minors. The exercise of parental custody is weighed against the welfare of the child. There is general agreement in both the legal doctrine and the case-law that the interests of the child must take precedence over the parents' interests, however. The starting point for the assessment of the child's welfare is – as has already been shown – a medical indication. If, due to there being several treatment alternatives or an uncertain medical prognosis, there is a margin of discretion as to how the parents define the welfare of their child, and their subjective views are nevertheless limited. For example, the religious beliefs of the parents may not endanger the welfare of the child. Parental refusal for religious reasons to give the child a necessary blood transfusion is contrary to the objective welfare of the child. In a life-threatening situation for the child, the doctor may therefore perform the blood transfusion. If the parents refuse to treat their child in an emergency, as an exception the doctor is entitled to carry out the necessary therapy against their will and in the interests of the child. If there is still enough time to act, the doctor must, however, contact the child protection authority. Moreover, on the side of the child's interests, their entire life situation – especially their social environment, health situation and mental state – is to be examined. The influence of the treatment on the child's future must also be considered. However, the younger the child is, the more all of their life circumstances will be influenced by parental ideas, and the more difficult consideration of all aspects can be.

If a risk to the child's welfare is identified in the refusal to provide medical treatment for the child or in the method of treatment chosen by the parents, there are four types of child protection measures available. They are differentiated by the severity of the intervention in parental custody. The law provides for a sequence of steps depending on the degree of risk. The least restrictive measure is the issue of warnings which are of a more recommendatory nature – to remind parents of their duties – or more binding instructions (Article 307(3) ZGB). In the medical field, they can be applied if there is disagreement between parents who have custody of a child or if a life-saving operation is refused. In the case mentioned above of the three-year-old with cancer, the doctors treating the child requested instructions to the parents to entrust the child to the children's hospital and to allow the chemotherapy.[28]

A more severe measure is the establishment of a deputyship pursuant to Article 308 ZGB. The deputy is assigned a well-defined scope of activity in relation to children and given concurrent power of representation. This is conceivable, for example, in the case of agreement to an operation. However, if it is clear from the outset that the parents are uncooperative in a medical matter concerning their child and thwart the intentions of the deputy, parental responsibility may be restricted accordingly and parental power of representation in this area can also be completely withdrawn.[29] As a result, the parents no longer have the right to consent to medical treatment. The decision-making power is thus solely with the deputy. Nevertheless, the deputy is dependent on the participation of the parents, as the child is in their care and they have health-related information about their child. However, there is also the possibility of temporary withdrawal of the right to decide on the child's place of residence under Article 310(1) ZGB for the medical treatment of the child, usually in combination with the withdrawal of the right of representation in medical matters. This may be considered if the parents do not agree with a long stay in hospital even though medical treatment is urgently required for their child. *Ultima ratio* is the transfer of parental custody to one parent or the withdrawal of parental responsibility of both parents (Article 311 ZGB).

V. Conclusions

The ultimate guideline in the exercise of parental custody is the welfare of the child. In the medical affairs of their children as incompetent minors, the discretionary power of parents is less extensive than in other areas of childcare, as it concerns an elementary interest and legal right of their child – their health and physical integrity. Although parental rights in medical matters must be based on the objective welfare of the child, the assessment of whether and which treatment best suits the interests of the child is always made on a case-by-case basis. The concept that a medically indicated treatment is always in the best interests of the child is only a starting point. The entire life situation of the child is to be examined in order to make the decision. Due to the parental autonomy in organising the child's education, cultural and religious aspects in particular are included in the assessment

[28] See judgment of the Cantonal Court of St Gallen 8 July 2011, FO.2011.16-K2, E. 8 (2011) 4 *Die Praxis des Familienrechts* 1036, 1039–40.

[29] Example of withdrawal of decision-making power in medical matters: judgment of the Cantonal Court of Zurich 15 March 2012, LY110046-O/U, E. 7.3 concerning the treatment of a mentally ill and drug-addicted teenager.

of the overall situation of the child. In the existing court decisions on parental authority in medical matters, these aspects are barely addressed, however. Even in legal debate, they are given little consideration. However, it can be assumed that it is precisely the views that arise from cultural and religious affiliation and the resulting conflicts between doctors and parents that play a key role in practice. How these are ultimately resolved cannot be determined in general terms. Setting up hospital-based child protection groups that can be activated in such situations, with the possibility of involving representatives of a particular religion, for example, would seem to be a feasible conflict resolution tool in everyday clinical practice.

If this route proves to be unsuccessful or if a decision is needed urgently, the medical practitioners would then send a risk report to the child protection authority. If a considerable risk to the child's welfare is present, the state must exercise its duty to protect the child. The legal framework for planning possible child protection measures leaves room to ensure a child-friendly response to a conflict between the parents and the doctors treating their child in each individual case.

6

Medical Decision-Making on Behalf of Minors: The Hong Kong Context

DAISY CHEUNG

I. Introduction

As a former colony of the United Kingdom that has since been reunified with China, Hong Kong provides a unique vantage point into the way a common-law system has been supplemented by the sociocultural factors that are often said to play a role in Chinese societies. This is particularly so in the context of medical decision-making on behalf of minors, where there is a clear legal position as affirmed by case-law and yet a host of sociocultural considerations exist that may affect the outcome of the case before there is any question of judicial involvement.

This chapter proceeds as follows. Section II provides a brief introduction to the current legal position in Hong Kong, which largely follows that of the wardship jurisdiction in the United Kingdom. Despite a largely similar legal tradition, however, there appears to be a paucity of such cases, which may in part be attributable to sociocultural factors that play a role prior to judicial intervention. Section III explores such factors, looking at what they may be and how they may have an influence on medical decision-making in Hong Kong. The issue of whether the law should be amended to reflect these factors is also considered. Section IV provides a brief conclusion.

II. The Legal Position in Hong Kong

As a common-law jurisdiction that inherited much of its legal system from the United Kingdom, Hong Kong also inherited the wardship jurisdiction, which has been codified as section 26 of the High Court Ordinance (Cap 4) (HCO) since the handover in 1997. In general, parents are given extensive rights and authority in relation to their child's care, including the right to consent to medical treatment on behalf of the child.[1] Such rights and authority, however, remain subject

[1] A Liu, *Family Law for the Hong Kong SAR* (Hong Kong, Hong Kong University Press, 1999) 217.

to the principle that the welfare of the child must be the first and paramount consideration.[2] Thus, where the parents make a medical decision on behalf of their child that does not appear to be in line with the child's interests, an application may be made to court to intervene with the decision.[3]

Having said that, there are very few examples of such decisions, with most of these cases dating prior to the handover in 1997. These cases demonstrate that the test applied by the courts to determine how a dispute should be resolved is the best interests test. In *Director of Social Welfare v Tam & Chan*,[4] an application was made to court for surgery to be performed on an infant with spina bifida. At first instance, the judge refused leave on the basis that it would not be in the child's best interests, because the child's life was likely to be full of misery and suffering even if the operation were successful.[5] At appeal, there was further evidence showing that the child would probably be able to attend school if the surgery were carried out. Even if not, however, the child was not at immediate risk of death, although his condition would become more serious. The Court of Appeal held that the surgery should be carried out on the basis that the child's condition would deteriorate and his life would be much more difficult otherwise.[6] In coming to this decision, the court emphasised that the child's interests were what the court was concerned with, and not the interests of the parents.[7] Thus, even though evidence showed that the family situation was not very suitable for raising a child such as this one, the court had a duty to disagree with the parents and order that the surgery be performed.[8,9]

The court similarly overrode the parents' refusal of medical treatment for their child in *Director of Social Welfare v Lam Kwok Wah & Another*.[10] In this case,

[2] ibid 216. See further Guardianship of Minors Ordinance (Cap 13) s 3.

[3] This type of case is the focus of this section, ie cases where parents refuse consent to treatment for their children and the courts intervene by ordering the treatment. There are no reported cases in Hong Kong where the parents wish for their child to undergo treatment and are refused by the doctors or the courts. It can only be a matter of speculation as to why this is the case, but the general reluctance of the Chinese to engage in legal proceedings is likely to be a significant factor (for a detailed discussion of this phenomenon, see BC Goh, *Law Without Lawyers, Justice Without Courts: On Traditional Chinese Mediation* (Hampshire, Ashgate, 2002) 24–41).

[4] *Director of Social Welfare v Tam & Chan* [1987] HKLR 66 (CA).

[5] This understanding of best interests is similar to that of other jurisdictions as well. See eg section II of I Goold, C Auckland and J Herring, 'Medical Decision-Making on Behalf of Children in England and Welsh Law: A Child-Centred Best Interests Approach', in this book.

[6] ibid [67I], [68A]–[68B].

[7] ibid [67I]. See also [68C]–[68D] where the best interests of the child are considered.

[8] ibid [68A]–[68B].

[9] For a discussion of other jurisdictions where the child's interest similarly trumps parental views, see part IV of I Boone, 'Parental Rights, Best Interests and Significant Harm: Medical Decision-Making on Behalf of Children in Belgium'; part IV of A Büchler, 'Parental Decisions on their Children's Medical Treatment'; section III 'Parental Decisions with Respect to their Children' in L Francis, J Botkin and D Diekema, 'Decision-making on Behalf of Children in the Research and Clinical Context: A United States Perspective'; and section I of Goold et al (n 5), all in this book. See also R Gilbar, 'Withholding and Withdrawal of Life-Prolonging Treatment from Young Children in Israel' in this book for a discussion of how the dominant sanctity of life principle plays a role in best interest determinations.

[10] *Director of Social Welfare v Lam Kwok Wah & Another* [1988] 1 HKLR 206.

an eight-year-old child suffered head injuries in a traffic accident, and a surgical procedure with very small risks was unanimously recommended by the doctors to protect the child from accidental injury. The parents refused consent for the procedure on the basis of religious objections and a general lack of faith in Western medicine. In its decision, the court made it clear that the paramount consideration in such cases was the interests of the child.[11] Since (i) the evidence demonstrated that the benefits of the proposed procedure vastly outweighed any of the risks and (ii) the parents had failed to put forward valid objections to the procedure,[12] the court ordered that the procedure be performed.[13]

A third case, *Re C (A minor) (Wardship: Medical Treatment)*,[14] involved a situation where the parents had carefully considered reasons to refuse consent. In this case, a severely disabled baby required surgery without which she would have died. Unlike the previous two cases above, the procedure had not been performed in Hong Kong before and there was only a 50/50 chance of success. If the procedure was successful, however, the baby would likely be able to live a relatively normal life. Both parents were unwilling to give consent for the procedure. The father, after consultation with members of the extended family, preferred to allow the baby to die from natural causes than risk surgery given the possibility of complications and further suffering afterwards.[15] The mother was concerned that if the procedure were not completely successful, the baby would be left severely disabled.[16] While the court acknowledged that it was a 'very serious matter to overrule the wishes of caring parents who have carefully weighed up all the factors before refusing to consent to an operation',[17] it reaffirmed that the test was the best interests of the child.[18] Given that there was a real chance the baby may survive and enjoy a normal life, it was clear that it was in the best interests of the baby to undergo the procedure.[19]

All of the three cases above date from before the handover in 1997. There appears to be only one case of relevance, *C v S*,[20] since the handover. This decision, which was recently handed down, was one in a long line of decisions between the parties, who are the father and mother of a child. It was an appeal of an earlier decision (the 'June decision'),[21] in which the issue was whether the child, who

[11] ibid [207H].

[12] Apart from the fact that the father did not consider the procedure to be desirable from a Buddhist perspective (without further elaboration), and his general lack of faith in Western medicine, there was no further evidence as to the reasons behind the refusal. See further ibid [207D], [207G].

[13] ibid [207I]–[207J].

[14] *Re C (A minor) (Wardship: Medical Treatment)* [1994] HKLR 60.

[15] ibid 62, lines 1–4.

[16] ibid 62, lines 9–10.

[17] ibid 63, lines 11–12.

[18] ibid 62, lines 18–22; 63, line 13.

[19] ibid 63, lines 25–27.

[20] *C v S* [2018] HKCFI 2106.

[21] *C v S* [2018] HKCFI 1381.

had begun exhibiting psychiatric symptoms in November 2017, should receive psychiatric treatment at the Yaumatei Child and Adolescent Mental Health Service (the 'YMT Service'). At the time, although not as part of an explicit discussion of the wardship jurisdiction, the court held that the parents' attitudes were not in the best interests of the child, and that it would be in the child's best interests to receive treatment at the YMT Service along with the private psychiatrist she was already seeing.[22]

At the appeal, the father challenged the June decision on several grounds, one of which included the fact that the court had erroneously ordered treatment at both the YMT Service and the private psychiatrist when neither party had suggested this.[23] In response to this, the court clarified that in exercising the wardship jurisdiction, it is not bound by the submissions of the parties, and can make any order or determine any issue having regard to 'the best interests of the ward as the first and paramount consideration'.[24]

The above cases thus make it clear that in relation to disputes about medical decision-making on behalf of minors, the courts are to decide on the basis of what they would regard as being in the best interests of the child, even if this is contrary to the view of the parents. Although the threshold for judicial intervention is not explicitly discussed, the cases demonstrate that the best interests test is also likely to be the relevant threshold. That is, the courts can intervene when the parents' decision cannot be said to be in the best interests of the child.[25]

It is not clear why there are so few cases of this nature after the 1997 handover. One of the reasons may be that, post-decolonisation, the sociocultural factors that play a role in medical decision-making in Chinese societies have become more prominent in Hong Kong. The following section will examine this in closer detail, exploring in particular how Chinese cultural values may be informing decisions, as well as the extent to which the law should reflect such values, if at all.[26]

[22] ibid [25]–[26]. Each parent had exhibited behaviours that the judge considered not to be in the best interests of the child. For example, the judge was of the view that the father had criticised the professionalism of the child's private psychiatrist for no good reason, while the mother had been unreasonably inflexible in her attempts to secure an appointment with the YMT Service. In holding that the parents' attitudes were not in the best interests of the child, the judge further commented that the child was clearly disturbed by 'being the focus of prolonged parental disputes and being trapped in between for years' [25].

[23] *C v S* (n 20) [6].

[24] ibid [16].

[25] While *Director of Social Welfare v Tam & Chan* (n 4), *Re C (a minor)* (n 14), and to a lesser degree *Director of Social Welfare v Lam Kwok Wah & Another* (n 10) may be said to be cases in which the parents' choice may have caused a risk of significant harm to the child, the facts of *C v S* (n 20) – where the issue concerns what type of psychiatric treatment the child should receive – suggest that significant harm is not necessary for judicial intervention.

[26] See section IV.C of D Chunyan, 'Medical Decision-Making on Behalf of Children in China: A Multi-dimensional Analysis of Parental Authoritarianism' in this book for a discussion of how Chinese cultural values may also inform medical decision-making on behalf of children in mainland China.

III. Sociocultural Factors Prior to Judicial Intervention

While Confucianism does not currently have a place in official state ideology, whether in Hong Kong or other East Asian jurisdictions such as China or Taiwan, it has been argued that Confucianism still retains a role in guiding behaviour in Chinese societies.[27] In the context of medical decision-making, commentators have drawn extensively upon Confucian bioethics to explain the cultural differences observed between what can loosely be referred to as the West and the East.[28] The crux of the cultural difference appears to lie in the unit of decision-making. Whereas the liberal individualist tradition of the West calls for the competent adult patient to be the decision-maker as an exercise of her autonomy,[29] the unit for decision-making in Chinese culture is said to be the family.[30] As Fan and Li argue, the family as an entity cannot be reduced to its members; families are autonomous entities that are themselves the source of legitimating authority.[31] Because the family is the autonomous unit, medical decisions are to be made by the family as a whole, with the emphasis being on 'harmonious interdependence'.[32] This analysis is similarly applicable to the context of medical decision-making on behalf of minors. With the interests of young and vulnerable children at stake in such cases, however, the question becomes what the attitude of the physician responsible for the patient is likely to be when the family makes a decision not to follow the physician's advice.

What is the physician's role in Confucian ethics? Should a physician act contrary to the family's decision if the physician disagrees with it? In their discussion of the

[27] See eg TS Cheung et al, 'How Confucian are Contemporary Chinese? Construction of an Ideal Type and its Application to Three Chinese Communities' (2006) 5 *European Journal of East Asian Studies* 157.

[28] See eg R Fan, 'Confucian Familism and its Bioethical Implications' in SC Lee (ed), *The Family, Medical-Decision Making, and Biotechnology: Critical Reflections on Asia Moral Perspectives* (Dordrecht, Springer, 2007); R Fan and B Li, 'Truth-Telling in Medicine: The Confucian View' (2004) 29 *Journal of Medicine and Philosophy* 179; E Hui, 'Parental Refusal of Life-Saving Treatments for Adolescents: Chinese Familism in Medical Decision-Making Revisited' (2008) 22 *Bioethics* 286; and C Tse and J Tao, 'Strategic Ambiguities in the Process of Consent: Role of the Family in Decisions to Forgo Life-Sustaining Treatment for Incompetent Elderly Patients' (2004) 29 *Journal of Medicine and Philosophy* 207.

[29] This is, of course, a simplification of the different theories of autonomy that have been proposed, including relational theories of autonomy that place less of an emphasis on the individual (see eg C Mackenzie and N Stoljar, *Relational Autonomy: Feminist Perspectives on Autonomy, Agency, and the Social Self* (New York, Oxford University Press, 2000)).

[30] This communitarian emphasis can also be seen in other jurisdictions. See eg section II of S Ujewe, 'Making Decisions for Children in Healthcare and Medical Research: African Communal Responsibility or Individual Rights?'; section III.C of A Moyo, 'Parental Responsibility and Medical Decision-Making in Southern Africa: A Comparative Analysis of South Africa and Botswana'; and section IV.C of Chunyan (n 26), all in this book. In contrast, see section VI in P Leviner, 'Who Has the Final Word? On Trust and Legal Uncertainty Within the Swedish Health Care System' in this book for an example of a jurisdiction where the family is not considered the most important social unit.

[31] Fan and Li (n 28) 188.

[32] Tse and Tao (n 28) 212.

acceptability of disclosing information to the patient's family prior to the patient herself, Fan and Li present a description of the Confucian physician, arguing that following the family decision would in fact be consistent with this role.[33] Fan and Li suggest that the end goal of a Confucian physician's medical practice is as a means of leading a Confucian way of life, as opposed to merely treating diseases as a skilled technician. Given the key role of the family in decision-making for family members, the Confucian physician's cooperation with the family is naturally derivative.[34] There is some question as to whether this depiction of Confucian physicians is still relevant in contemporary Chinese societies. At a more basic level, however, physicians in Chinese societies may be less willing to contradict family decisions because this can be seen as disruptive of family harmony and integrity. As Tse and Tao suggest, harmony has always had an integral role in Chinese tradition, and thus one of the main concerns for Chinese bioethics is how the patient's autonomy might be upheld while maintaining family unity and integrity at the same time.[35]

How have the above considerations manifested themselves in Hong Kong society? I turn now to look at empirical studies that have been conducted and what their results might indicate. In the context of medical decision-making generally, Chan conducted a study of informed consent in Hong Kong where he interviewed physicians, patients and family members at a public hospital in Hong Kong.[36] He argues, based on his results, that there appears to be a 'robustly family-oriented practice' where the physician first informs the family regarding the diagnosis and then asks the family to inform the patient, sometimes together with the physician.[37] He contends, however, that the authority of the family is not absolute – the physician is to be the judge of whether the patient would accept disclosure to the family,[38] and thus this 'familist' approach is to be considered a moderate one.[39] Even so, Chan suggests that the findings show that the preferred arrangement in Hong Kong is for the patient and the family to make a decision as one unit.[40] This is consistent with the above discussion regarding the family being seen as the autonomous unit of decision-making in Chinese societies. It should also be noted, however, that there are some concerns with Chan's study, the largest of which is perhaps in relation to its scale, which only involved interviews with eleven physicians, three patients and four family members with no justification of the sampling

[33] Fan and Li (n 28) 184.
[34] ibid.
[35] Tse and Tao (n 28) 217–18.
[36] HM Chan, 'Informed Consent Hong Kong Style: An Instance of Moderate Familism' (2004) 29 *Journal of Medicine and Philosophy* 195.
[37] ibid 197–98.
[38] The paternalism demonstrated by this statement is not explored in Chan's study, and is beyond the scope of this discussion. There is also no indication in Chan's data as to how the physician would make such a judgement (eg the factors she would consider).
[39] Chan (n 36) 198.
[40] ibid 200.

method. Even amongst these interviewees there was often no clear consensus, making it questionable as to whether firm conclusions can be drawn from the data.

Hui's work looks specifically at medical decision-making on behalf of minors. He reports on two case studies in which parents of two adolescents refused life-saving treatment on their behalf.[41] In the first case, the father of a 17-year-old with osteogenic sarcoma wanted him to seek traditional Chinese medicine treatment in China instead of undergoing chemotherapy and leg amputation as recommended by the doctors. Although the patient expressed a preference to stay for the recommended treatments when interviewed alone, he was unwilling to contradict his father's decision. The father took the patient to China for treatment and returned to the hospital three weeks later, when both the size of the tumour and the patient's pain had increased. Two months after the recommended surgery, the patient's cancer metastasised to the lung, and subsequently recurred after surgical removal of the tumour.[42]

In the second case, the father of a 15-year-old with a primitive neuroectodermal tumour refused the recommended chemotherapy and limb amputation on his behalf and proposed taking him to see a medical practitioner in Taiwan. The patient, when interviewed alone, did not indicate any treatment preference but expressed that it was important to maintain family harmony, which would be achieved by following his father's wishes. The father took the patient to Taiwan and returned to the hospital four months later, at which time the tumour was no longer operable. After radiotherapy and chemotherapy, however, the tumour responded surprisingly well and the doctors again recommended immediate amputation. The father refused on the patient's behalf yet again, however, and the tumour eventually grew into a large fungating mass which ruptured and bled, causing the patient's tragic death.[43]

It is difficult to understand why the fathers in these two cases were so adamantly opposed to the treatment recommended by the doctors. In his paper, Hui suggests that the fathers' poor decision-making likely stemmed from three beliefs: (i) the mistaken belief that amputees would be 'doomed to life-long unemployment, societal rejection and misery', something to which they did not want to subject their sons; (ii) the belief that amputation is contrary to the Confucian doctrine of filial piety and the notion that the body is a gift from one's parents, one that should not be mutilated; and (iii) the belief that natural remedies are better than 'artificial' remedies.[44] Although these are all possible reasons, we cannot be sure of their motivations without speaking to the parties, and larger conclusions about Chinese parents cannot be drawn without more empirical data being collected. It does appear, however, that the presence of traditional Chinese medicine provides

[41] Hui (n 28).
[42] ibid 288.
[43] ibid 288–89.
[44] ibid 289.

Chinese parents with an often false sense that the more permanent forms of Western medical intervention (such as limb amputation) are not the only option, and should only be pursued as a last resort.

What of the doctors, and why did they not apply for judicial intervention? In his analysis of the doctors in these two case studies, Hui suggests that Confucian ideology may have contributed to the doctors' hesitation to challenge the fathers' decisions given that the doctors were also from the same cultural background.[45] While Hui does not elaborate further on how this might have been the case, it is consistent with the above discussion regarding the physician's role. That is, given the family's key role in medical decision-making and the cardinal importance of maintaining family harmony and integrity, physicians are generally less willing to challenge decisions made by the family. Of course, the second case study is much more extreme than the first, and it remains very difficult to see why the doctors did not seek a court order to intervene.[46,47]

The above discussion demonstrates how various Confucian values may have an effect on medical decision-making in Hong Kong, and in particular on whether medical decisions that are made on behalf of minors are brought before a court for judicial intervention where they do not seem to be in the child's best interests. The question then becomes whether the law in Hong Kong should be amended to be in line with such values.

There are at least two arguments against this. The first is that the empirical data collected in Hong Kong thus far do not appear to consistently demonstrate the prevalence and influence of a clearly identifiable set of values or sociocultural factors. Although Chan's study on informed consent provides some evidence of the importance of the family in medical decision-making, the scale of the study is simply too small and the results too inconsistent for firm conclusions to be safely drawn.

Even if the effect of a clear set of sociocultural factors can be identified, there remains the second issue, which is arguably the more important one. As has been argued by proponents of common morality theory, cultural and religious traditions may be used to justify actions that are oppressive or discriminatory.[48]

[45] Hui (n 28) 290.

[46] There is also some question as to whether the decisions in this case could be properly described as family choices, as they appear to have been made by the father alone (with the wife and child reluctant to express their own opinion). This is consistent, however, with the roles of the family in Confucian thought, where the father/husband is generally seen as occupying a higher status in the family hierarchy.

[47] It appears that, although for other reasons, there is a similar lack of deferral to the courts in some other jurisdictions; see eg section VI in Leviner (n 30). A Brown, '"Parental Rights", "Best Interests" and the Withdrawal of Life-Sustaining Medical Treatment of Children in Scotland: A Lack of Authority' in this book notes that there is an absence of relevant case-law in Scotland, but it is unclear whether this is due to the lack of deferral of such cases to the courts. In contrast, there has been considerable judicial attention in similar cases in the UK, as discussed in section II of Goold et al (n 5).

[48] See eg TL Beauchamp, 'Common Morality, Human Rights, and Multiculturalism in Japanese and American Bioethics' (2015) 3 *Journal of Practical Ethics* 18, 31. See also critics of culturally sensitive bioethics such as T Bracanovic, 'Against Culturally Sensitive Bioethics' (2013) 16 *Medicine, Health Care and Philosophy* 647.

The concern here is that Confucian values and ideology may be used to justify the continuing existence of unjust social arrangements, where patients such as women and children who are in subordinate positions in the family hierarchy are taught to believe that submission is the only morally acceptable choice.[49] There is also the concern that there is insufficient protection from abuse in dysfunctional families. This concern is particularly acute in the context of medical decision-making on behalf of minors. Even where the families are well intentioned, they may not make decisions that are in the best interests of their children, as Hui's two case studies demonstrate. Judicial intervention remains an important safeguard in such situations – the healthcare team needs to be able to step in and apply to the court to protect the children of such families.

IV. Conclusion

We have seen in this chapter that the legal position regarding medical decision-making on behalf of minors in Hong Kong largely follows the wardship jurisdiction inherited from the United Kingdom, where the court determines how disputes should be resolved on the basis of the child's best interests. The relative lack of such cases, however, and the fact that the majority of them took place prior to Hong Kong's reunification with China, suggest that there may be other factors at play. Commentators have argued that Confucian ethics and values are helpful in explicating the cultural differences in medical decision-making in Chinese societies. Although the empirical data from Hong Kong appears to be initially supportive of this explanation, such data are sparse, and much more work needs to be done to substantiate the validity of such claims. Even where such claims can be validated, I have argued that the law in Hong Kong should not be made to be aligned with such values. A Confucian model which allows the family to have the decision-making power in relation to the members of the family cannot adequately protect the interests of family members in more vulnerable positions, and in particular, children. Judicial intervention should be preserved to ensure that the best interests of children are protected even where they are not born into well-functioning families, or where the family's well-intentioned decisions cannot be said to be in the best interests of the child.

[49] Hui (n 28) 292.

7

Medical Decision-Making on Behalf of Children in China: A Multidimensional Analysis of Parental Authoritarianism

DING CHUNYAN

I. Introduction

According to the sixth national population census conducted in 2010, in China, the number of children aged 0–14 years was 222,459,737, accounting for 16.60 per cent of the total population, and the overall number of children (ie including those up to 18 years) was close to 400 million.[1] Do Chinese children have the right to patient autonomy? Given the developing autonomy of children associated with their age and maturity, to what extent should they participate in medical decision-making? How should disagreements between minor patients, their guardians and medical practitioners be solved? How should their parents or guardians as legal representatives make proxy medical decisions when children are unable to decide for themselves? What are the proper roles of the state (the judiciary in particular) in protecting children in cases involving medical decision-making on behalf of children? Had cases similar to those of Charlie Gard or Alfie Evans occurred in China, would courts intervene in parental decisions? And if so, how? Despite the importance of these questions, they have not attracted extensive attention and discussion among scholars and the public in China.

Under Chinese law, as children lack full legal capacity to make medical decisions, it is their guardians (in most cases parents) as legal representatives who make a proxy decision on their behalf. Article 35 of the General Provisions of

[1] The State Council, *Tabulation on the 2010 Population Census of the People's Republic of China* (2011) www.stats.gov.cn/tjsj/pcsj/rkpc/6rp/indexch.htm.

Civil Law 2017 (GPCL)[2] for the first time explicitly required guardians to exercise their responsibilities of guardianship in accordance with the child's best interests. It also requires the child's will to be respected in the light of the child's age and intelligence when making a proxy decision. However, in reality, the parents retain authoritarian power and there has been no case of judicial intervention even when the parental medical decision appears prejudicial to the child.

This chapter reports a multidimensional analysis of the gap between the law and the practice of medical decision-making on behalf of children in China. A number of factors combine to contribute to parental authoritarianism, including the medical care insurance system, the sociolegal responsibility for protecting child welfare, utilitarian familism, the strained patient–doctor relationship, and the civil procedure law. China ratified the United Nations Convention on the Rights of the Child in 1991 and promulgated the Minors Protection Law 1991 (MPL) in the same year,[3] and the government is consequently required to undertake all appropriate measures for the implementation and protection of the rights of the child. This chapter therefore argues that the Chinese government (through the judiciary in particular) should meet its responsibilities and serve as a safety valve to protect children when medical decisions are made on their behalf.

II. Statutory Restrictions on Medical Decision-Making on Behalf of Children

There is no specific law governing medical decision-making on behalf of children in China. Instead, the relevant provisions are scattered across two laws: the GPCL and the MPL. First, Articles 13 and 14 of the GPCL declare that natural persons are equal in terms of their 'capacity for civil rights',[4] which begins at birth and ceases at death. As the rights to personal freedom, dignity and bodily integrity are explicitly recognised by Articles 109 and 110 of the GPCL, minors are equally entitled to the right to bodily integrity and the right to patient autonomy under Chinese law.

Second, minors who are under the age of eighteen are divided into three categories in terms of their 'capacity for civil acts'.[5] A minor reaching the age of sixteen and primarily relying on his or her own labour income to live is deemed a person

[2] General Provisions of Civil Law (民法总则), promulgated by the National People's Congress 15 March 2017, effective 1 October 2017.

[3] Law on the Protection of Minors (未成年人保护法), promulgated by the Standing Committee of the National People's Congress 4 September 1991, effective 1 January 1992, amended 2006 and 2012.

[4] 'Mingshi quanli nengli' (民事权利能力). The term 'capacity for civil rights' refers to legal capacity to have civil rights and obligations in civil law.

[5] 'Minshi xingwei nengli' (民事行为能力). The term 'capacity for civil acts' is interchangeable with 'capacity for juristic acts'. It refers to legal capacity to perform civil/juristic acts that aim at establishing, altering, terminating or otherwise affecting a legal right (concluding a contract, making a will, disposing of an alienable right, etc).

with full capacity for civil acts.[6] A minor under the age of eight is a person without capacity for civil acts, who should be represented by his or her legal representative in performing civil acts.[7] Apart from these two categories, a minor reaching the age of eight is a person with limited capacity for civil acts, who should either be represented by his or her legal representative in performing civil acts or perform civil acts with the consent or ratification of the latter. However, a minor with limited capacity for civil acts may independently perform civil acts that purely provide benefit or fit his or her age and intelligence.[8]

Making a medical decision is seen as a civil act that is intended to and is capable of having a legal effect. Therefore, a decision-maker must have legal capacity to make a medical decision. Under the three-category framework concerning minors' capacity for civil acts: (1) minors with full capacity for civil acts can make their own medical decisions; (2) minors without capacity for civil acts must rely on their legal representative to make proxy medical decisions on their behalf; and (3) minors with limited capacity for civil acts may make a medical decision for themselves provided that the medical treatment concerned purely benefits them or that their age and intelligence enable them to make such a medical decision. Otherwise, they have to additionally seek their legal representative's consent or ratification, or their legal representative should simply make proxy medical decisions on their behalf. This approach is similar to the equivalent in Belgian law (see Boone, Chapter 3 in this volume) where children considered able to make a reasonable judgment of their interests are allowed to exercise patient autonomy themselves (although Chinese law stipulates a minimum age of eight years for this purpose, while Belgian law does not set a minimum age).

Third, when making proxy medical decisions for a child without full capacity for civil acts, guardians must meet two requirements according to Article 35(1) and (2) of the GPCL: (1) the guardian should perform the duty of guardianship (including making proxy decisions) in the best interests of the child; and (2) the guardian should respect the child's true will when making proxy decisions in the light of the child's age and intelligence. Article 14 of the MPL echoes the second requirement by providing that parents or other guardians of minors, in making decisions concerning the rights and interests of the minors, must inform them of the decisions and consider their opinions in the light of their age and intellectual development. In other words, children who lack capacity to make a medical decision retain the right to know and the right to participate in proxy decision-making so long as they are able to have and express their own views on the concerned matter. This requirement is similar to the equivalent under Belgian law (see Boone, Chapter 3 in this volume) and Swedish law (see Leviner, Chapter 14 in this volume), where children are allowed to be involved in their

[6] Art 18 GPCL.
[7] Art 20 GPCL.
[8] Art 19 GPCL.

parents' or guardians' proxy medical decision-making in accordance with their age and maturity. In other words, despite lacking capacity to exercise patient autonomy themselves, their evolving capacities and their views are recognised in law. Such a requirement, however, is absent under English law.

It is noteworthy that Article 35(3) of the GPCL requires the guardian of an adult without full capacity for civil acts to safeguard and assist the adult ward in performing civil acts that fit with his or her intelligence and mental health condition; the guardian should not interfere with any affairs that the adult ward is capable of handling independently. However, Article 35(2) of the GPCL does not impose similar requirements on the guardian of the minor ward even though the minor ward is in the same legal position as the adult ward. The subtle difference implies strong paternalism toward minors with limited capacity for civil acts.

III. Parental Authoritarianism in Medical Decision-Making for Children

Despite these statutory restrictions, in reality the guardians of minors have an absolute authority to make medical decisions for children, and this results from multiple factors.[9] In China, parental authoritarianism is threefold. First, the guardian's proxy decisions dominate the practice of medical care of minor patients. The Ministry of Health has stipulated in a number of enactments that the guardian's informed consent is needed for performing medical treatments on minors without full capacity for civil acts, such as Article 10 of the Basic Norms on Making Medical Records 2010[10] and Article 21 of the Norms on the Quality Management of Clinical Trials of Medical Devices 2016.[11] Therefore, hospitals and medical practitioners always seek the written informed consent of the guardian before performing a surgery, medical examination or treatment of a minor, regardless of to which category of capacity for civil acts the minor belongs. Indeed, few medical practitioners understand that minor patients reaching the age of eight may have capacity to make medical decisions which fit their age and intelligence, let alone think to invite minor patients to make their own medical decisions. Belgian law (see Boone, Chapter 3 in this volume) provides that some children may independently exercise their patient autonomy if they have ability to exercise reasonable

[9] A multi-dimensional analysis of parental authoritarianism in China is given in section IV of this chapter. Parents also have substantial authority in Thailand (see Tengaumnuay, Chapter 23 in this volume), however there cultural factors primarily explain the primacy given to parents.

[10] Basic Standards on Making Medical Records (病历书写基本规范), promulgated by the Ministry of Health 22 January 2010, effective 1 March 2010.

[11] Norms on the Quality Management of Clinical Trials of Medical Devices (医疗器械临床试验质量管理规范), jointly produced by the National Health and Family Planning Commission (whose predecessor was the Ministry of Health) and the State Food and Drug Administration, 1 March 2016, effective 1 June 2016.

judgement of their interests, and it is the treating doctors who assess *in concreto* whether they have such ability. Although Chinese law has a similar provision, it fails to specify who has authority to assess the capacity of children to make medical decisions. In reality no medical professionals or otherwise are available to conduct such an assessment for child patients, which makes the provision merely rhetorical.

Second, the best interests of the child principle laid down in Article 35(1) of the GPCL has hardly restricted how guardians make proxy medical decisions for children. Hospitals and medical practitioners always follow the guardian's proxy medical decision even when the guardian's refusal to allow treatment proposed by the treating doctor appears prejudicial to the child.[12] For instance, it was reported that a new-born baby girl who suffered from an imperforate anus received medical treatment in a hospital for thirteen days until her father decided to discontinue medical care and let her die in a palliative care centre. The baby's mother had been prevented from knowing about the baby's health condition as well as the father's proxy medical decision in the name of 'therapeutic privilege'.[13] In another case reported by the media, the father of a new-born baby girl suffering from congenital esophageal atresia refused to give proxy consent to an operation proposed by the doctor and the baby eventually died without medical care.[14] Although the children in both cases were curable and the treating doctors deeply regretted the guardians' proxy decisions not to save them, the hospitals chose to respect and follow their decisions. These two cases were both concerned with the guardian's refusal of treatment on behalf of children. If the guardian requests a life-prolonging treatment to be performed on the child patient, as in the case of Alfie Evans, hospitals and medical practitioners in China will likely provide it as long as the guardian is able to afford the medical expenses for the treatment.[15] The deference of Chinese medical professionals to parents or guardians in terms of medical decision-making on behalf of children presents a sharp contrast to the situation in England, where medical professionals act as gatekeepers to ensure the parents' proxy medical

[12] The sociolegal reasons for Chinese doctors' deference to parents will be explained in section IV of this chapter.

[13] 'The Father Discontinued Treatments of a Baby Girl with Imperforated Anus' (肛闭女婴父亲放弃治疗) *Guangzhou Daily* (5 February 2010) gongyi.ifeng.com/news/detail_2010_02/05/443433_0.shtml.

[14] 'The Newborn Baby Has Serious Disease, the Parents Decide to Discontinue Treatments' (新生儿身患重病 父母要放弃治疗) *Today's Morning Post* (17 October 2009) news.sina.com.cn/c/2009-10-17/052416451799s.shtml.

[15] Although no case like that of Alfie Evans has been reported in China, there was a relevant criminal case where a patient's husband was convicted of murder for switching off his brain-dead wife's ventilation system in an intensive care unit. The legal grounds of the conviction were that a brain-dead patient was not dead under Chinese law (see 'The High Court Tried the Appeal Case Involving the Husband Killing the Wife by Switching Off the Ventilation System in Shenzhen' (省高院二审深圳拔管杀妻案) *Nanfang Daily* (15 March 2012) epaper.southcn.com/nfdaily/html/2012-03/15/content_7066664.htm). To avoid the risk of legal liability, doctors in China normally are unwilling to terminate a life-sustaining system without the consent of the patient's family, especially when the family agrees to bear medical expenses.

decision is in the best interests of the child and any disagreement between parents and medical professionals about medical care of a child will be presented to and solved by the English courts (see Goold, Auckland and Herring, Chapter 11 in this volume). Other jurisdictions (eg Sweden and Spain: see Leviner, Chapter 14 and Navarro-Michel, Chapter 19 in this volume) also demonstrate strong deference to medical professionals although it may vary from jurisdiction from jurisdiction whether medical professionals can seek judicial intervention in the parent's proxy medical decisions.

Third, the Chinese courts have never intervened in a guardian's medical decision for a child in judicial practice.[16] For instance, the above case of the baby girl with an imperforate anus was widely reported in China and aroused heated public debate. A non-governmental organisation acting in the interests of minors and a number of warm-hearted citizens independently contacted the baby's father after learning about his decision not to treat her. Although they tried to persuade him to change his mind, sought the medical advice of famous paediatricians in Beijing, and helped arrange surgery and treatments for the baby, no one thought about seeking judicial intervention throughout the event.

The lack of judicial intervention in the guardian's medical decisions made on behalf of children distinguishes China from most of the jurisdictions discussed in this book. Moreover, unlike Israel (see Gilbar, Chapter 10 in this volume) where the medical institutional ethics committee has authority to decide disagreements between parents and treating doctors concerning medical care for a terminally ill child, Chinese law does not grant ethics committees authority to scrutinise the guardian's proxy medical decisions. Nor does Chinese law give the public authority responsible for child welfare authority to intervene (as Sweden and Norway do: see Leviner, Chapter 14 and Sovig, Chapter 21 in this volume). As a result, Chinese guardians have the final say on medical decisions on behalf of their children. Given the lack of the relevant judicial decisions, it is difficult to speculate how Chinese courts would interpret and decide 'the best interests of the child' had the cases of Charlie Gard or Alfie Evans occurred in China.

IV. Multidimensional Analysis of Parental Authoritarianism in China

Economic, cultural, social and legal factors combine to cause parental authoritarianism in medical decision-making on behalf of children in China and the gap between the law and the practice in this regard. Specifically, there are five factors to be discussed in this part: the medical care insurance system, the

[16] At the time of writing no case of this kind can be found in the Supreme People's Court's official online database, China Adjudication Decisions Online (中国裁判文书网) wenshu.court.gov.cn.

sociolegal responsibility for protecting child welfare, utilitarian familism, the strained patient–doctor relationship, and the civil procedure law.

A. Medical Care Insurance for Children

In China, local governments are responsible for providing medical care insurance to their residents. There are three major medical care insurance systems in which residents are able to participate: the urban employees' basic medical insurance system, the urban residents' basic medical insurance system and the new rural cooperative medical system.[17] However, all three medical care insurance systems are aimed at adult residents; children are not considered or covered by them in most parts of the country.[18] Although urban and rural children in some developed cities (eg Beijing, Shanghai and Shenzhen) may voluntarily join the urban residents' basic medical insurance system and the new rural cooperative medical system, few cities provide outpatient coverage for children, and inpatient coverage for children is limited to a few listed diseases[19] and subject to various caps.[20] These restrictions, as a disincentive to parents, greatly discourage them from subscribing their children to the medical care insurance system.[21] Moreover, a social relief system is generally lacking for children in need of financial assistance in China.[22]

As a consequence, families with children have to self-insure for medical care for the children. Because parents have to bear medical costs for their children, it is up to parents to decide whether treatment for their children is affordable. In other words, the payer decides, and the parents' burden of self-insurance for medical care costs for children is an economic justification for parental authoritarianism in proxy medical decision-making. With medical costs increasing,[23] financial concerns have inevitably become an important consideration for guardians making proxy medical decisions on behalf of children although they might refuse to admit it. One source revealed that there are about 800,000 newborns with disabilities in China annually;[24] among them, the guardians of 300,000

[17] C Ding, *Medical Negligence Law in Transitional China* (Cambridge, Intersentia, 2012) 18.

[18] M Wang, 'Study on the Medical Care Insurance of Minors in China' (中国未成年人医疗保障问题研究) (master's thesis 2013) available at CNKI, 13.

[19] For instance, inpatient coverage for children is limited to five diseases in Beijing and to eleven diseases in Zhuhai. Child cerebral palsy is not covered in either of these cases. See Wang (n 18) 15.

[20] H Li, 'Turning to State Responsibility: Improvement and Upgrade of the Child Welfare System in China' (国家责任回归：我国儿童福利的制度优化与升级) (2018) 23 *Labor Security World* (劳动保障世界) 16, 17.

[21] J Wang, Y Wang and J Xu, 'Problems of Medical Care Insurance of Minors in China and Study on Countermeasures' (我国未成年人医疗保障的问题及对策研究) (2018) 20 *Labor Security World* (劳动保障世界) 29, 29.

[22] ibid.

[23] Ding (n 17) 33–37.

[24] The rate of disabled newborns has increased by 70.9% in China from 1996 to 2010. See *China's 2011 Report on the Development of Health Care Services for Women and Children* (中国妇幼卫生事业发展报告2011) www.gov.cn/gzdt/att/att/site1/20110921/001e3741a4740fe3bdab01.pdf.

disabled newborns choose to refuse medical treatment due to unbearable financial burdens.[25]

B. Sociolegal Responsibility for Protecting Child Welfare

In China, it is widely accepted that parents or guardians have the primary obligations and responsibilities for child welfare.[26] The state child welfare system primarily cares for orphans, and homeless and abandoned children who live in social welfare institutions.[27] 'Left-behind children',[28] a label for children whose parents work as immigrant workers in urban areas and leave their children in their rural homes, receive insufficient care and protection. Although the state has recently given more attention to children harmed by their guardians through domestic violence, sexual abuse, maltreatment and abandonment cases, etc,[29] it has not assumed the responsibility to protect children with regard to other affairs, such as medical decision-making on behalf of children. Moreover, guardians are required to bear full legal responsibility for the acts of children. For example, the guardian must assume strict liability for any harm caused by a tort committed by the child although the guardian's liability may be mitigated at the discretion of the court if the duty of guardianship is fulfilled, as provided by Article 32 of the Tort Liability Law 2009.[30]

The full obligations and responsibilities of parents or guardians to protect children generate two related implications. First, guardians have full authority of guardianship, including educating, controlling, supervising and making various proxy decisions on behalf of children. Chinese parents often see their children as property that they own,[31] and this view is even shared by judges in adjudication. For example, Chinese courts have often split up twins or siblings when deciding

[25] Wang (n 18) 13.

[26] L Gao and G Wan, 'China's Child Welfare System: Involvement, Status Quo and Proposed Reform' (中国儿童福利制度:时代演进、现实框架和改革路径) (2016) 36 *Hebei Academic Journal* (河北学刊) 182, 186; P Wu, 'State Responsibility to Safeguard Child's Right to Welfare' (儿童福利权国家义务论) (2015) 30(5) *Legal Forum* (法学论坛) 32, 36.

[27] Wu (n 26) 37.

[28] 'Liushou ertong' (留守儿童).

[29] See Opinions of the Supreme People's Court, the Supreme People's Procuratorate, the Ministry of Public Security, and the Ministry of Civil Affairs on Legally Handling Several Issues on Guardian's Infringement of the Rights and Interests of Minors 2014 (最高人民法院、最高人民检察院、公安部、民政部关于依法处理监护人侵害未成年人权益行为若干问题的意见) ('Opinions on Guardian's Infringement') promulgated 18 December 2014, effective 1 January 2015.

[30] Tort Liability Law (侵权责任法), promulgated by the Standing Committee of the National People's Congress 26 December 2009, effective 1 July 2010.

[31] J Ma and Z Li, 'Spouse and Parent–Child: Comparative Study of Cultural-Family Ethics between Chinese and Western Society' (夫妻与亲子:中西方文化家庭伦理观比较研究) (2017) 10 *Journal of Shenyang Industrial University (Social Science Edition)* (沈阳工业大学学报(社会科学版)) 278, 280.

child custody issues in divorce cases on the ground that parents have an equal right to child custody and should also bear an equal burden of child maintenance costs.[32] As shown in a report on judicial decisions of child custody disputes, siblings were separated in 67 per cent of cases involving multiple children, and twins were separated in 72 per cent of cases involving twins.[33] Although courts decide the child custody issue based on the mantra of the best interests of the child,[34] they are in effect more concerned with the interests of the parents. The reason why courts often split up siblings (in particular twins) to let each parent equally enjoy the right to child custody is because the courts implicitly deem children to be property that their parents co-own, which coincides with the view of full authority of guardianship over the child.

The second implication is that non-guardian parties (such as the state and the society) need to give the greatest respect and free rein to the guardian's exercise of their authority of guardianship and their proxy decision-making on behalf of children, whether for refusing or requesting treatment (as long as the guardian can afford medical expenses for their children). Although Article 35(1) of the GPCL has recently added the best interests of the child principle to regulate guardians in performing their duty of guardianship, the common culture-based understanding regarding the guardian's primary responsibility and full authority for protecting child welfare cannot be changed easily. Taking persons with mental disability as an example, Article 44 of the Mental Health Law 2013[35] provides that the guardian is entitled to request the hospital to release the mentally disabled patient who has been hospitalised because he harmed himself or had the potential to harm himself, even though the hospital is of the view that it is inappropriate to release him. The rationale for the rule is that a guardian has full authority over a patient without full capacity for civil acts and can make a proxy medical decision on his behalf that the hospital must respect. Despite it concerning proxy medical decisions on behalf of persons with mental disability, such a legal policy also applies to children without full capacity for civil acts.

[32] R Zhang, 'Study of Judicial Decisions on Right to Child Custody in Divorces Cases Involving Domestic Violence' (家暴致离婚案件子女抚养权归属审判研究) (2017) 1 *Journal of Study on Women* (妇女研究论丛) 46, 50.

[33] 'Report on the Analysis of Child Custody Disputes' (关于子女抚养权归属纠纷的分析报告) *Sohu.com* (25 July 2017) www.sohu.com/a/159792286_535672.

[34] eg in the case *Li v Huang* ((2018)豫16民终2073号) an intermediate court in Henan Province held that twin girls would be placed separately in the custody of their mother and father by considering the children's interests as well as the financial abilities and conditions of each parent to support the child in custody. Similar child custody cases where twins are split include, eg *Wu v Zhang* ((2017)赣02民终639号), *Yuan v Zhao* ((2017)甘11民终506号), and *Wang v Yang* ((2016)冀08民终2208号). In *Wang v Yang*, the trial court held that it made the decision by considering both the twins' interests and equal treatment of each parent.

[35] Mental Health Law (精神卫生法), promulgated by the Standing Committee of the National People's Congress 26 December 2012, effective 1 May 2013.

C. Utilitarian Familism

Parents' proxy medical decisions on behalf of children in China are often made based on familism or 'family-paternalism'.[36] In making such decisions, parents not only consider the interests of the child but also those of the family as a whole, including the financial burden on the family, the interests of other children in the family, the impact on the career of adult family members, the implications for family life, etc. When interests conflict, there is a strong possibility that the family's collective interests will prevail over the child's interests,[37] especially when the parents make a decision by taking a utilitarian approach of weighing up interests to maximise the family's utility. Although China has ancient utilitarian traditions,[38] utilitarianism has in fact been emphasised in China only since the market-oriented economic reform that started in the late 1970s. It was understood at that time that economic reform could not be initiated without the state making a strategic change in ideological positioning to embrace utilitarianism; this institutionally and socioeconomically infiltrated and assimilated various personal preferences into a new sole, dominant public rationale and preference, namely 'concentration on economic construction'.[39] After a four-decade-long period of economic reform, utilitarianism has received widespread acceptance among the public and has become an influential factor in the decision-making of Chinese people.[40]

By way of contrast, it is noteworthy that Irish courts (see Bracken and Lombard, Chapter 15 in this volume) apply the constitutional presumption that the welfare of the child will be met by the marital family when dealing with disagreements between parents and medical professionals over medical care for a child. Despite that, Irish courts retain the authority to overrule the parent's decisions in exceptional cases where the safety or welfare of any of their children is likely to be prejudicially affected. By contrast, the Chinese family is not subject to judicial intervention and therefore enjoys almost absolute decision-making rights about the welfare of their children. The Chinese familism approach shares similarity with the African practice (see Ujewe, Chapter 25 in this volume) where the child's interests are situated in a family setting and the interests of other family members are justifiably taken into account because of an appreciation of shared responsibility among family members. In Hong Kong (see Cheung, Chapter 6 in this volume) people also give great weight to family harmony and integrity

[36] Ruiping Fan (ed) *Family-Oriented Informed Consent: East Asia and American Perspectives* (Cham, Springer, 2015) 16.

[37] H Chen and H Li, 'On the Familism Mode of Informed Consent' (论知情同意的家庭主义模式) (2013) 5 *Moral and Civilization* (道德与文明) 103, 105.

[38] J Yan, 'Utilitarianism in Chinese Thought' (PhD thesis, University of Toronto 1995) 26.

[39] S Huang, *The Evolution of Regional Uneven Development in Jiangsu Province Under China's Growth-Oriented State Ideology* (Cambridge, Cambridge Scholars Publishing, 2016) 53.

[40] X Liu and Y Chen, 'Information Ethics: A Cross-Cultural Study of Ethical Decision-Making Between US and Chinese Business Students' (2012) 3 *International Journal of Business and Social Science* 51, 58.

and medical decisions are often made collectively by the patient and the family members; however, the familism approach is less influential in Hong Kong than in Mainland China. Although one Hong Kong case shows that the treating doctor chose not to seek a court order to invite judicial intervention when the parents' proxy medical decision would harm the interests of the child, more reported cases have evidenced otherwise.

Against the backdrop of utilitarian familism in Chinese family law, it is common for parents making medical decisions on behalf of children to include a popular utilitarian consideration: eugenics.[41] The public's wide acceptance of the notion of eugenics resulted from the state's iron-fist one-child policy, which was introduced in 1979 in order to curb the country's growing population.[42] Under this birth control policy, Han Chinese couples (the ethnic majority) were allowed to have only one child. To support this one-child policy, the government instilled the notion of eugenics into public consciousness and encouraged couples to apply the notion to family planning in order to have a healthy single child.[43] For example, the Maternal and Infant Health Care Law 1994[44] was called 'China's eugenics law' because, in Articles 9 and 10, it mandates postponement of marriage, marriage under the condition of long-term contraception or sterilization, and termination of pregnancy, as the case may be, where prospective parents are diagnosed with a risk of having a fetus with serious disease or deformity; doctors are also required to make the relevant recommendation to facilitate such requirements. Although the state loosened its birth-control policy and replaced the one-child policy with a two-child policy in October 2015, the government maintains a policy of eugenics. More importantly, the notion of eugenics is now rooted in the public's mind (including that of medical professionals) after having been effectively propagandised and implemented for about four decades. Therefore, parents are inclined to avoid seeking treatment for children who are seriously ill or have long-term health conditions when making proxy medical decisions, which helps explain why there have been few cases in China where parents request treatment on behalf of seriously ill children such as Charlie Gard and Alfie Evans.

D. Strained Doctor–Patient Relationship

The healthcare reform initiated in China in the mid-1980s has two features that have seriously eroded public trust in medical institutions and worsened the

[41] This is a unique feature of Chinese practice concerning medical decision-making on behalf of children.

[42] X Yuan, 'The Evolution of China's Birth Control Policy and the Balanced Development of Population' (我国生育政策演进与人口均衡发展) (2016) 38 *Population Journal* (人口学刊) 5, 6.

[43] The government's popular slogan for implementing the one-child policy was 'late marriage, late childbirth, less childbirth, quality childbirth' (晚婚、晚育、少生、优生).

[44] Maternal and Infant Health Care Law (母婴保健法) made by the Standing Committee of the National People's Congress, 27 October 1994, effective 1 July 1995.

doctor–patient relationship. The first one is profit-oriented management of medical institutions.[45] As one of its reform measures, central government decentralised medical care subsidy to local governments. However, local governments prioritised economic development over other goals including healthcare provision. On the one hand, they retreated from direct management of public hospitals, and on the other, they significantly reduced the subsidies year after year.[46] Therefore, public hospitals, despite holding themselves up as 'public welfare entities', have been run in a profit-oriented fashion and have competed for financial gain in the healthcare market. As the official data show, 89.70 per cent of public hospital revenue came from medical care provision in 2010, and the figure decreased slightly to 88.40 per cent in 2016.[47] Moreover, 59.67 per cent of outpatient medical expenses and 47.19 per cent of inpatient medical expenses were for drugs and medical procedures in 2010, and the figures decreased to 55.21 per cent and 39.87 per cent, respectively, in 2016.[48] To maximise profits, hospitals often provide patients with unnecessary medical care, such as performing expensive high-tech procedures and prescribing lucrative medicines. Some hospitals reject patients who cannot afford medical expenses even in emergency situations.[49]

The second feature is the moral decay of medical professionals. Due to the atmosphere of profit maximisation and low service fees paid to doctors, it is common for doctors to request or receive a 'red-packet'[50] containing a substantial amount of cash from patients or their families in advance of treatment and in addition to standard medical fees and charges.[51] Moreover, both those in charge of purchasing drugs for hospital pharmacies and doctors take kickbacks from pharmaceutical companies (through their agents) after making such companies a successful bidder in a tender or prescribing to unwitting patients lucrative medications manufactured by those companies.[52] As a survey conducted by China Youth Daily in 2005 reported, 81.2 per cent of the respondents saw public hospitals as for-profit entities, and 75.5 per cent of them thought that medical professionals had suffered moral decay as a result of the healthcare reform.[53]

[45] In China, public medical institutions accounted for 55.17% of the total medical institutions in 2016; however, of 1,602 medical institutions with 800 or more beds, 95.97% were public hospitals (see National Health and Family Planning Commission, *China Health Care and Family Planning Yearbook 2017* (Peking Union Medical College Press, 2017)) 10, 15.

[46] The Chinese government's subsidies accounted for 25.06% of total healthcare expenditure in 1990, down to 15.47% in 2000, before gradually rising to 30.01% in 2016 (ibid 94).

[47] ibid 103.

[48] ibid.

[49] Ding (n 17) 22.

[50] 'Hongbao' (红包).

[51] Ding (n 17) 24; see also 'Online Disclosure of a Doctor Receiving Red-Packet in the Ward; A Video Taken that Recorded the Whole Process' (网曝医生病房内收红包　还被人拍下交接视频画面) *Wangyi News* (16 January 2018) news.163.com/18/0116/07/D88M9DBG0001875P.html.

[52] Ding (n 17) 25; see also 'GlaxoSmithKline Fined $490m by China for Bribery' *BBC News* (19 September 2014) www.bbc.com/news/business-29274822.

[53] S Yu, 'Ninety Per cent of the Public Unsatisfied with the Changes Resulting from the Health Care System Reform in Recent Ten Years' (九成公众不满意近10年来医疗体制方面的变化) *People.com* (22 August 2005) finance.people.com.cn/GB/1045/3633842.html.

Moreover, the doctor–patient relationship has been further strained by increased conflicts between them in medical dispute resolution. Since 2000, numerous disgruntled patient victims or their families have committed acts of nuisance and violence in the allegedly liable hospitals in order to get swifter or higher compensation, a phenomenon popularly called 'hospital chaos making'.[54] Some hospital medical staff have even been killed by violent patients or their families.[55] Although the state has made great efforts to control 'hospital chaos making' and deploy mediation to more efficiently resolve medical disputes,[56] it is difficult to mend such a strained doctor–patient relationship.

Therefore, when parents make medical decisions on behalf of children, doctors are normally hesitant to disagree given the lack of mutual trust between them, thus leaving critical and grave medical decisions solely to the parents of minor patients. By contrast, although doctors in Thailand (see Tengaumnuay, Chapter 23 in this volume) also passively follow the parent's proxy medical decision and play a limited role in protecting the interests of child patients, such practice primarily rests on cultural roots. However, in China, the deference of medical professionals to the parent has been associated with the long-standing strained doctor–patient relationship. By the same token, it is difficult for Chinese medical professionals to engage in harmonious communication with the child's family members to solve their disagreement over medical care for the child (as happens with the healing *indaba* process adopted in Africa). Specifically, when parents request an affordable treatment for their children, doctors are inclined to follow this decision in order to avoid the legal risk of medical negligence liability for adverse consequences resulting from a refusal of treatment. When parents refuse a proposed treatment on behalf of a child, doctors are also concerned about the suspicion of excessive medical care from the patient's side as well as the risk of legal liability if they insist on a view opposite to that of the parents. To protect both personal and institutional interests, doctors prefer to show absolute deference to the parents' proxy medical decision even if it appears prejudicial to the minor patient.

E. Civil Procedure Law

If a doctor or other relevant party disagrees with and wants to challenge the parents' proxy medical decisions on the ground of the best interests of the child principle, the current Chinese civil procedure law fails to establish supporting procedural rules to facilitate such special proceedings. As provided by Article 119 of the Civil Procedure Law 1991 (CPL),[57] successfully instituting a civil case in court requires

[54] 'Yinao' (医闹).

[55] C Ding, 'A Dose to Cure "Medical Chaos": Medical Mediation in China' (2015) 10 *Journal of Comparative Law* 158, 158.

[56] ibid 159–60.

[57] Civil Procedure Law (民事诉讼法) made by the National People's Congress 9 April 1991, effective the same day, amended 2007, 2012 and 2017.

the identity of the plaintiff, the identity of the defendant, specific claims along with facts, proper cause of action and reasons, and the jurisdiction of the court, which only fits those actions involving adversarial parties. Although the CPL provides a number of special procedures that do not involve adversarial parties,[58] a proper procedure is lacking that enables either doctors or other relevant parties to file an action to challenge the parents' medical decision on behalf of children under China's civil procedure law. Moreover, the Provisions on Causes of Action in Civil Cases 2011[59] does not provide a proper cause of action that can fit this type of special proceedings either. This appears similar to the case of Scotland (see Brown, Chapter 4 in this volume), where also lack the legal concepts of 'wardship' or 'inherent jurisdiction' that are regarded as justification for judicial intervention in parents' medical decisions on behalf of the child. However, Scottish law has two alternative procedures to facilitate judicial intervention, while Chinese civil procedural law has no alternative procedures at all.

Article 36 of the GPCL provides that courts, upon the request of a relevant party, have the power to disqualify the guardian, arrange necessary provisional guardianship measures, and designate another guardian in accordance with the law and the best interests of the ward principle in three situations, the third of which is a catch-all provision covering 'other serious infringements of the lawful rights and interests of the ward'. However, the statutory definition of 'infringement of the rights and interests of minors' does not cover parents making proxy medical decisions that are not in the best interests of their child.[60] To date, there has been no case of judicial intervention in proxy medical decisions on behalf of children in China.

V. Conclusion

This paper presents a multidimensional analysis of parental authoritarianism prevalent in the practice of medical decision-making on behalf of children in China. It further reveals that the government has been guilty of laches in protecting and safeguarding the rights and interests of children that may be infringed by the proxy decision-making of their guardians, including in the case of proxy medical decisions. Regrettably, medical professionals restrain themselves from overseeing how parents make proxy medical decisions on behalf of children in a utilitarian familism approach. Chinese courts have been voiceless in this regard and have never performed judicial scrutiny of proxy medical decisions of guardians on behalf of children.

[58] C 15 of CPL.

[59] Provisions on Causes of Action in Civil Cases (民事案件案由规定) made by the Supreme People's Court 4 January 2011, effective 18 February 2011.

[60] Art 1 of Opinions on Guardian's Infringement.

Compared to other jurisdictions, Chinese law presents a unique (though unsatisfactory) solution to deal with the issue of medical decision-making on behalf of children due to its sociolegal circumstances. The critical factor which distinguishes China from other jurisdictions is that parents self-insure for medical care costs for their children. Because the Chinese government does not finance medical care for children, and guardians have full financial and sociolegal responsibilities for their children, guardians have full authority to make proxy decisions. Making medical decisions on behalf of children falls within the realm of parental authoritarianism and many parents decide not to treat or continue treating children based on utilitarian familism concerns. Had cases similar in facts to those of Charlie Gard or Alfie Evans happened in China, requests by parents for life-sustaining treatment on behalf of their children would likely be respected and followed by doctors, provided the parents could afford the medical expenses for the treatment. Chinese courts would not intervene in a parents' decision to sustain or extend a child's life because of the parental authoritarianism that is widely recognised and accepted by society.

As provided by Article 19 of the United Nations Convention on the Rights of the Child, which China ratified in 1991 and which is echoed in the MPL, governments should ensure that children are properly cared for and protected from violence, abuse, neglect, negligent treatment, maltreatment or exploitation by their parents, guardians, or anyone else looking after them. Governments should also provide appropriate protective measures, effective procedures and other appropriate forms, including judicial involvement, to fulfil the obligations of protection from child maltreatment described above. The proxy medical decision-making by parents or guardians that is not in the best interests of the child is governed by this provision. Therefore, the Chinese government (especially through the judiciary) should establish an appropriate procedure to facilitate judicial scrutiny, in order to create a safety valve to protect children in the practice of medical decision-making on their behalf. In the long term, the government should assume more responsibilities for providing medical care to children, offer a wide range of child welfare services, and take measures to improve the doctor–patient relationship.

8

Parental Rights in Mexican Law

MARIANA DOBERNIG GAGO

I. Introduction

Mexico was conquered by Spain in 1510; when the fight for independence was over in 1810 and Mexico was established, the country's colonial past provided the precedents for the law system of the new nation. The origins of Mexican law come from Roman law *ius civile*, enabling each state of the republic to legislate on civil matters. In 2017, the Mexican Supreme Court ruled on a difficult case related to an underage person who needed medical treatment. The case took place in Chihuahua and involved an indigenous family from an ethnic group called known as '*rarámuri* from the *Tarahumara*'.[1] This chapter will discuss parental rights and obligations in Mexico by analysing this case.

In Mexico, parents have parental rights over their children,[2] incorporated through civil rights derived from filiation. The purpose of this law is to protect

[1] The Tarahumara are an Indian tribe who live in the northern parts of Mexico (Chihuahua State). The name Tarahumara means 'where the night is the day of the moon'; 'raramuri' (uto-aztec) is a description given to the tribespeople and means 'the light-footed one'. To be raramuri you must have time and care for each other, and love people more than goods. www.raramuridesign.com/raramuri-tarahumara.html.

[2] In Mexican law the legal status of a child under the age of eighteen is that of a minor (Arts 646, 647 Federal Civil Code) who lacks legal capacity to make medical decisions for themselves. Parents are duty bound to act in the best interests of their children (Arts 23, 24, 450 Federal Civil Code) and a child's parents are their presumptive legal guardians (Art 412 Federal Civil Code). This principle also applies in, for example, Belgium: as I Boone, 'Parental Rights, Best Interests and Significant Harm: Medical Decision-Making on Behalf of Children in Belgium' in this book explains, under Belgian civil law anyone under the age of eighteen is a minor (Art 388 Civil Code) and the general rule is that minors are legally incompetent and must be represented by their parents or a legal guardian. As long as the child is a minor, the child's parents hold rights and responsibilities (Art 372 Civil Code) which they should exercise in the best interests of the child (Art 374 §1 Civil Code). Parental responsibilities in Belgium include the right to make decisions concerning the child's health and medical treatment. Although incompetence of minors is the general principle, Belgian law recognises, following the UN Convention on the Rights of the Child, that minors have evolving capacities and are entitled to participation and autonomy according to the level of their capacity.

children's welfare,[3] including but not limited to education, health and the obligation to represent them both inside and outside court.[4] If there is a dispute between the parents and the minor, the state can appoint a guardian to represent the minor.

In 2017, a controversial case occurred regarding the suspension of the parental rights of a Jehovah's Witness couple, Luisa and Manuel, who had two children. Carmen, born in 2006 and Clara, born in 2011. On 19 April 2017, when Clara began presenting signs of chickenpox, her mother took her to the doctor. She was told that Clara probably had acute lymphoblastic leukaemia, making it urgent to transfer her to the children's hospital for cancer treatment in Chihuahua. That same day the girl was admitted to intermediate therapy and given antiviral treatments, antibiotics and products derived from blood.

The haematologist informed Luisa and Manuel how serious Clara's condition was; she considered that blood transfusion was the ideal treatment. Despite this, the parents wanted to find a different solution since their religion did not permit blood transfusions. The social worker from the children's hospital came to the view that the minor should be placed under the care of the 'District Attorney for the Auxiliary Protection of Children and Adolescents of the Judicial District of Morelos, Chihuahua'[5] due to the seriousness of Clara's condition, and the need to carry out blood transfusions despite her parents' opposition.

The District Attorney interviewed the parents and again they refused treatment. The Prosecutor initiated an administrative procedure to protect Clara, which grants the state guardianship[6] of the minor to protect her rights, based on the diagnosis of a possible acute lymphoblastic leukemia; the immediate need, according to specialists, for Clara to receive blood transfusions to save her life; and the parents' refusal to allow their daughter to receive medical treatment.

The District Attorney authorised an operation to remove bone marrow samples to confirm the diagnosis. This confirmed that Clara had acute lymphoblastic

[3] A Büchler, 'Parental Decisions on their Children's Medical Treatment', in this book observes that in Swiss Law 'Both parents' rights and children's rights have high priority in the Swiss legal system. On the one hand, parents are primarily responsible for protecting their child's interests and welfare. This principle implicitly results from the Federal Constitution of the Swiss Confederation, BV of 18 April 1999, namely from the right to personal freedom and the right to have a family (Art 10 para 2, 14 BV), the right to privacy in one's family life (Art 13 para 1 BV) as well as the child's need for protection and encouragement of its development (Art 11 para 1 BV). On the other hand, Switzerland has ratified numerous multilateral conventions that oblige it as a state to provide children with special protection. Of note is the UN Convention on the Rights of the Child of 20 November 1989.' (Mexico also ratified the CRC on 25 January 1991 and issued a General Law for boys, girls and adolescents (Ley General de los Niños, Niñas y Adolescents) on 4 December 2014.

[4] F de la Mata Pizaña et al, *Derecho Familiar y sus Reformas Más Recientes y a la Legislación del Distrito Federal* (México, Porrúa, 2012) 3339.

[5] Subprocuraduría de Protección Auxiliar de Niñas, Niños y Adolescentes del Distrito Judicial Morelos, Chihuahua.

[6] Art 498 of the Federal Civil Code in Mexico states that if a judge does not make an opportune appointment of guardianship, then the state is responsible for any damage suffered by the minor as a result.

leukaemia and led to the District Attorney authorising initiation of chemotherapy. The Supreme Court withdrew the custody rights of her parents due to their refusal to allow their daughter to receive medical treatment.[7]

II. Indirect Habeas Corpus[8] 1049/2017[9]

A. The Trial

Luisa and Manuel filed an indirect habeas corpus suit against the District Attorney's decision to take over the guardianship of their daughter and initiate medical procedures that were against their religious beliefs.[10] They argued that they had not received adequate information in order to make an informed decision nor were they offered alternative treatments. They stated that the District Attorney unfairly removed their right to make decisions about Clara, arguing that they were good parents who had always taken care of the child and were being discriminated against. This meant, in their statement, that their right to equality had been violated due to their ethnic and religious background. The Eighth District Court of the State of Chihuahua accepted the indirect habeas corpus suit and suspended the District Attorney's guardianship of the minor.

During the trial, a psychological evaluation of the parents was made, which concluded that both were suitable to take care of their daughter. The parents appointed a legal representative to take responsibility for the child's interests. This attorney indicated that the District Attorney had indeed exceeded her authority.

[7] L Francis, J Botkin and D Diekema, 'Decision-Making on Behalf of Children in the Research and Clinical Context: A United States Perspective' in this book note that in the US legal system: 'In general, the approach of US states to medical decision-making on behalf of children is ultimately rooted in the legal and ethical concept of informed consent and has been for over a hundred years. The general rule that a person must give permission (or have permission given on their behalf) prior to the performance of a medical examination, diagnostic testing or treatment has ethical roots in the principle of respect for autonomy. The legal grounding of informed consent, on the other hand, rests in the concepts of battery and medical malpractice. From a legal perspective, a healthcare provider cannot touch a child without the permission of the parents or legal guardian without the authorisation of the state. The only exception to this general rule is when emergency action is necessary for the child's welfare and no parent or legal guardian is readily available to provide permission.' In this Mexican case the Supreme Court had the authority to give permission the parents did not give, acting in accordance with the best interests of the child.

[8] Amparo Indirecto: a process to review acts of authority including laws, statutes and resolutions.

[9] Juicio de Amparo Indirecto Juzgado Octavo de Distrito en el Estado de Chihuahua, June 30 2017.

[10] M Navarro-Michel, 'Young Children and Healthcare Decisions in Spain: Who Decides?' in this book details how in Spanish law the court has a duty to protect the child's best interests and may override parental wishes in order to protect the child's paramount interests. To assist that process the Spanish Attorney General (Ministro Fiscal) has issued guidelines on the substantive and procedural treatment of parent–doctor conflicts about blood transfusions and other medical interventions on minors in the event of serious risk. Presently there are no similar guidelines in Mexico to assist the courts in resolving cases of this kind.

In urgent cases, according to the Regulations of the General Health Law on the Provision of Medical Care Services,[11] it is not necessary to have the consent of the parents. Her request for temporary guardianship had caused the parents to feel discriminated against because of their culture and religion. The court decided to entrust the protection of Clara to the mother, arguing that the circumstances were insufficient to consider that Clara's parents had been negligent in the care of their child and they were never presented with any alternative treatment. It also declared that the District Attorney had initiated the guardianship proceedings illegally.

The District Attorney requested suspension of the decision, on the basis of the seriousness of Clara's health. However, the judge granted the suspension definitely, making the parents the ones to make all the decisions regarding their child, and requested the hospital be kept informed about the child's condition. At that time, the mother was updated about Clara's prognosis, which was a 90 per cent survival rate if a treatment regime involving chemotherapy and blood transfusion was followed. The doctor emphasized that the use of blood components was vital, and superior to the use of any alternative treatments.

B. Court of Appeals

An appeal was filed to review the judgment, which was dismissed by the Civil Court of Appeals.[12] It was agreed that there was no jurisdiction to revise the indirect habeas corpus, because the conflict involved religious freedom and the right of parents to make medical decisions regarding their daughter's health. The court referred the matter to the Mexican Supreme Court, whose president declared jurisdiction to hear an appeal about the review. The Supreme Court[13] regarded the analysis of this matter challenging, given the future of a minor was at stake.

The discussion focused on whether it was constitutional for the state to assume authority to make decisions affecting the health of a minor in place of the parents. The Mexican Constitution acknowledges that parents have the right to make free decisions about their children in matters of health and religious education. The Supreme Court considered that, in the first place, the parents are the ones who are legally entitled to authorise any medical procedure on their minor children and the Constitution protects the right to the life and health of minors as a preponderant constitutional interest. Nonetheless, there is a limit to the former when parents put the latter rights at risk; at this point the state and courts can intervene wherever the health of a child is in any way threatened.

[11] Art 81 of the Regulation of the General Health Law on the Provision of Medical Care Services, we understand that the duty to inform, as well as the requirement of consent, cede only in those situations in which 'urgency does not allow delays before the possibility of causing irreversible injuries or there is danger of death'.

[12] Segundo Tribunal Colegiado en Materia Civil y de Trabajo de Decimoséptimo Circuito.

[13] Amparo en Revisión 1049/2017, Quejosa: [Luisa] y otra. Recurrentes: Parte Quejosa y Autoridades Responsables.

Therefore, parents can refuse to allow their daughter to be given blood transfusions in the exercise of their religious freedom as long as the Supreme Court considers that an alternative treatment to blood transfusion can be used, provided this is feasible and has similar efficacy. The final judgment was that the District Attorney's intervention to temporarily remove the parental rights was correct, given that the preponderant constitutional interest was the right to life of the minor.

III. Legal Rights

A. Parental Rights

In this case, the Supreme Court[14] posed the question of whether parents have the right to intervene in decisions regarding custody of their children in order to consider if it is justified to remove parental custody temporarily in order to carry out a medical procedure against the wishes of the parents. Section 4 of the Mexican Constitution grants protection to the family and religious freedom on account of the importance of a social nucleus because the family provides identity to the person and facilitates their social integration. In light of this, the Mexican Supreme Court has ruled that section 16 prohibits arbitrary interference with the family.[15] On the other hand, the American Convention on Human Rights, also signed by Mexico, in section 12 (and subsection 12.4) and 17 grants protection of religious freedom and of the family. Section 11.2 of the Inter-American Court of Human Rights[16] recognises the right of every person to receive protection against arbitrary or abusive interference in the life of the family, also stating that freedom of religion allows each person to determine their own beliefs and act according to them.[17]

Similarly, the International Covenant on Economic, Social and Cultural Rights (section 10), the International Covenant on Civil and Political Rights

[14] As well as the Mexican Supreme Court, courts in many other countries have dealt with the question of whether parents will always know what is in the best interests of their child. C MacIntosh, 'Decisionally Incapable Children and Medical Treatment Choices in Canada', in this book, points out that, according to the jurisprudence of the Supreme Court of Canada, parental rights have presumptive primacy; this is due to the assumption that parents will know, and will act to advance, the best interests of their children.

[15] Amparo Directo en Revisión 3859/2014. Amparo en Revisión 208/2016.

[16] Inter-American Court of Human Rights *Atala Riffo and Daughters v Chile*, Judgment of 24 February 2012 (Merits, Reparations and Costs); *'Las Dos Erres' Massacre v Guatemala*, Judgment of 24 November 2009 (Preliminary Objection, Merits, Reparations and Costs).

[17] Inter-American Court of Human Rights *'The Last Temptation of Christ' (Olmedo-Bustos et al) v Chile*, Judgment of 5 February 2001 (Merits, Reparations and Costs). This case dealt with the annulling of a prior decision on cinematographic censorship. The Court's decision led to constitutional reform in Chile and to the establishment of an important hemispheric standard in this area.

(sections 23 and 18), the UN Convention on the Rights of the Child (section 8) and the Universal Declaration of Human Rights (section 12) all declare protections for the family and children, including in regards to their religious freedom.

The Mexican Supreme Court[18] has also previously ruled on this aspect, pointing out that every person is free to profess any religion they want. This right is linked to the autonomy of each person to freely decide their own spiritual life.[19] The state must remain neutral and respectful of the various religious beliefs professed by its citizens as stated by the European Court of Human Rights, and therefore must promote tolerance.[20] However, like any other right, religious freedom is not absolute since it is limited by the Constitution. The Supreme Court then established that parents cannot for religious reasons oppose a medical treatment necessary to safeguard the life of their minor child.

B. Minor's Rights in Medical Decision-Making

When children are under age and do not have the capacity to make their own decisions about their health, the parents have the right and obligation to make such decisions on their behalf, always looking out for the best interests of the child; this has its basis in family law[21] The right of the parents is not permanent because parental authority is temporary, lasting until the time that minors acquire greater autonomy and the ability to make their own decisions. The Convention on the Rights of the Child states in section 5 and 12 that minors have rights and are individuals capable of making decisions about their own lives and health. This decision-making ability increases with age and as the child's autonomy increases, the parents' ability to make decisions on their behalf decreases.[22]

The Supreme Court considers that it is fundamental to be able to analyse a minor's capacity to make decisions for themselves, so judges must take this into

[18] Amparo en Revisión 1595/2006.

[19] Tesis 1ª. LX/2007 de Rubro: Libertad Religiosa, sus Diferentes Facetas, Febrero 2007, Tesis 1ª. LX/2007 de Rubro: Libertad Religiosa y Libertad de Culto, sus Diferencias, Febrero 2007.

[20] *Begheluri and others v Georgia* App no 28490/02 (ECtHR, 7 October 2014). In that case the Court said: '[F]reedom of thought, conscience and religion is one of the foundations of a democratic society within the meaning of the Convention. This freedom is, in its religious dimension, one of the most vital elements that go to make up the identity of believers and their conception of life, but it is also a precious asset for atheists, agnostics, sceptics and the unconcerned. The pluralism indissociable from a democratic society, which has been dearly won over the centuries, depends on it. That freedom entails, *inter alia*, freedom to hold or not to hold religious beliefs and to practice or not to practice a religion. … The Court has frequently emphasised the State's role as the neutral and impartial organiser of the exercise of various religions, faiths and beliefs, and has stated that this role is conducive to public order, religious harmony and tolerance in a democratic society.'

[21] In the same direction: *MARK and RK v UK* App no 45901/05 and App no 40146/06 (ECtHR, 23 March 2010), and *Gard and others v UK* App no 39793/17 (ECtHR, 3 July 2017).

[22] Amparo Directo30/2008, Resuelto por la Primera Sala el 1 de Marzo de 2009, Amparo Directo en Revisión 354/2014, Resuelto por la Primera Sala el 9 de Abril de 2014.

consideration when making their decisions. Therefore, the Court considers that, as long as the child is of reasonable age, they may make their own decisions about treatments or medical interventions.

C. Legal Custody

In the event that during initial investigations it is determined that the interests of the minor are at risk, the state can take over guardianship in consideration of the best interests of the minor. However, parents should not be excluded from the medical process. If they are exercising their religious freedom, they should be informed as to why an alternative treatment cannot be used. The government's guardianship is limited to medical decisions concerning the recovery of the child's health and should not in any way displace the other rights that parents have in their family nucleus.[23]

IV. Conclusion

With this ruling the Mexican Supreme Court has established a precedent that the best interests of the child is the fundamental rule that should prevail in any legal issue in which the rights of minors are involved. This cannot be established in a general or universal way,[24] given that family relationships are complex, and therefore the judge must weigh the particular situation of each child and decide according to their best interests. In this sense, the fundamental right is the right to life and health of the child. This is what must be regarded as 'best interests'. Despite religion or any other parental freedom, the right to the protection of life is a higher right from which all other rights derive.

The right to private and family life is framed as a guarantee against the state and against third parties so that they cannot unjustifiably intervene in decisions

[23] Best Interest of the Child: Mexican Constitution Art 4 and Civil Code Art 416 Ter, www.diputados.gob.mx/LeyesBiblio/htm/1.htm, www.aldf.gob.mx/archivo-c9dc6843e50163a0d2628615e069b140.pdf.

[24] Francis et al (n 8) establish that in the US legal system '[a] parent who refuses to follow a medical recommendation is effectively withholding consent. In that case, the healthcare provider is faced with a situation where acting contrary to the parents' wishes would constitute a battery, or "unconsented touching". With few exceptions, these situations require state authorisation before the healthcare provider can act. The 'best interest standard' has become the prevailing ethical and legal standard used in US states to determine when state interference is justified. The best interests standard directs the healthcare provider or state actor to determine which among the routes offered maximises the net benefit and choose the option that optimises the welfare of the child. It is commonly used by clinicians, ethics consultants and ethics committees to determine when to challenge a parent's decision to refuse medical intervention on behalf of a child.' Mexico has a National Commission of Bioethics (Comisión Nacional de Bioética) that could help courts establish ethical and legal guidelines regarding these kinds of cases.

that fall within the private family sphere, since it is considered that parents are adequate persons to make decisions on behalf of their children, based on the fact that parents should always be expected to act in the best interests of their child. The Mexican jurisprudence has established that the right of parents to make decisions about their children's medical procedures is limited by the need to protect the health and life of the child. Parents have autonomy, in respect for their private and family life, but this is constrained if they place their child's health at risk. In this case, the Constitution provides that the state can intervene to serve the best interests of the child, such as to protect their health and life. Courts must therefore hold that parents' rights do not confer authority over the life and death of their children, and parents do not have the right to affect the health of their children on the basis of their beliefs or customs.

9

Decision-Making on Behalf of Children in the Research and Clinical Context: A United States Perspective

LESLIE FRANCIS, JEFF BOTKIN AND DOUGLAS DIEKEMA

How would United States (US) law and ethics address the case of Charlie Gard, an infant with irreversible neurological damage due to MDDS, whose treating physicians believed that further intervention would not be in his best interest and would be futile in reversing the course of his condition, but whose parents sought to try untested therapies in the hope of prolonging his life or achieving some improvement in his condition? The answers are complex, given the US constitutional protections for individual liberty and the free exercise of religion, the federal system of interconnected state and federal powers, ethical support for autonomy and the rights of parents to make decisions for their children, and ethical objections to disability discrimination and failures to protect the right to life.

I. US Legal Framework

The US federal system creates a delicate balance between the roles of the federal government and the states. The federal constitution and statutes enacted under constitutional grants of authority to the US Congress are supreme over state laws. But the federal government is a government of enumerated powers, and the power to provide for the public welfare began and remains largely for the states. Among these traditional state powers are tort law, public health law and regulation of the healthcare professions.

The US federal constitution sets out a minimum floor of basic rights that must be recognised by all states. Most importantly, these rights include the First Amendment rights to free exercise of religion and freedom of expression and the Fifth and Fourteenth Amendment rights not to be deprived of liberty without due process of law. 'Due process' requires states to have particularly strong justifications – compelling state interests, with any interferences narrowly tailored to furthering these interests – to deprive persons of fundamental liberties. Among these fundamental liberties are the rights of parents to raise their children as they see fit[1] and, arguably, the rights of competent adults to decline medical care or to provide in advance for the treatment they would not want to receive if they were to become incompetent.[2] Among compelling state interests are protecting children from abuse, including medical neglect, protecting life and protecting the integrity of the medical profession.

Under its enumerated powers to regulate interstate commerce and to tax and spend to provide for the general welfare, Congress has enacted a number of statutes that would be relevant to a case such as that of Charlie Gard. Under the commerce power, Congress regulates the approval and marketing of drugs.[3] Approval by the Food and Drug Administration (FDA) is needed for introduction into interstate commerce of drugs[4] such as the nucleotide precursors thymidine and deoxycytidine in the clinical trial at Columbia University[5] of potential interest to Gard's parents. Clinical trials used in applications for approval of new drugs must meet FDA standards for protection of human subjects in research.[6] As described further below, however, federal law now also allows several pathways permitting access to experimental drugs.

In addition, under its power to spend for the general welfare, Congress may set conditions on the acceptance of federal funds. Especially relevant to the Gard case are the 'Baby Doe' regulations adopted under the Child Abuse Prevention Act (CPTA) which require states accepting federal child abuse prevention funds to have policies in place to ensure that newborns with disabilities are not denied medically indicated treatment.[7] The CPTA defines treatment as not medically indicated only if the infant is chronically and irreversibly comatose; the treatment would only prolong dying, not be effective in addressing all of the infant's life-threatening conditions or otherwise be futile for the infant's survival; or the treatment would be virtually futile for the infant's survival and under the circumstances would be inhumane.[8] This version of the Baby Doe requirement emphasises the preservation of life and was supported by advocates of the right to life. It replaced an earlier version that prohibited disability discrimination in newborn care but that had been invalidated by the Supreme Court as not within the authority granted by Congress in the Rehabilitation Act.[9] The Court's controversial reasoning in this

[1] *Pierce v Society of Sisters*, 268 US 510 (1925).

[2] *Cruzan v Director, Missouri Department of Health*, 497 UW 261 (1990).

[3] Food, Drug, and Cosmetic Act, 21 USC §§ 321–99i.

[4] 21 USC § 355(a).

[5] *Treatment of TK2 Deficiency with Thymidine and Deoxycytidine* (2018) clinicaltrials.gov/ct2/show/NCT03639701.

[6] 21 CFR §§ 50.1 et seq.

[7] 42 USC § 5106a (b)(2)(C).

[8] 42 USC § 5106g (a)(5).

[9] *Bowen v American Hospital Association*, 476 US 610 (1986). For the significance of the difference between the two approaches – right to life and anti-discrimination – see A Silvers and LP Francis, 'Playing God With Baby Doe: Quality of Life, Sanctity of Life and Unpredictable Life – Standards at Start of Life' (2009) 25(4) *Georgia State Law Review* 1061.

decision was that hospitals acceding to parental wishes were not discriminating on the basis of disability but only honouring the traditional rights of parents to consent to treatment on behalf of their children.[10] Evidence suggests that current medical practice may continue to recognise greater scope for parental choices than would be permitted under a strict reading of the Baby Doe regulations, although controversies continue about abortion and aggressive treatment of extremely premature infants.[11]

Also potentially relevant to the treatment of a severely ill infant such as Charlie Gard is the requirement of the Emergency Medical Treatment and Active Labor Act (EMTALA) for facilities operating an emergency room and receiving federal funding to provide patients with appropriate screening examinations and stabilising treatment.[12] Under this statute, severely disabled infants residing outside of the hospital might be entitled to screening examinations and emergency treatment at most emergency departments throughout the United States. This statute does not require treatment beyond stabilisation, however.

Federal laws may pre-empt state laws under the supremacy clause of the US Constitution. Whether state laws are pre-empted depends on the provisions of the federal statute; some statutes explicitly pre-empt an entire field of law, some impliedly pre-empt contradictory state laws, and some explicitly permit states to enact their own laws provided that they at least meet the federal standards. The FDA Act's regulation of the entry of drugs into interstate commerce pre-empts state laws to the contrary; states may not engage in their own drug approval processes in contradiction to the federal, for example by imposing stronger standards for marketing than those imposed by the FDA.[13] The scope of this pre-emption remains legally unsettled, however, and state initiatives with respect to importation of unapproved drugs, drug labelling and access to drugs have placed increasing pressure on the scope of federal pre-emption in this area.[14] The federal right-to-try (RTT) law permitting access to unapproved drugs is quite new and it is unclear whether it will be held to pre-empt the variety of RTT laws enacted by the vast majority of states. Federal laws such as the CPTA and EMTALA, and laws governing the protection of human subjects in research, however, set a federal minimum floor but permit states to impose more stringent requirements.

[10] For the 'strong but rebuttable' presumption that 'parents are the appropriate decisionmakers for their children', the plurality opinion of Justice Stevens cited the 1983 report of the President's Commission for the Study of Ethical Problems in Medicine and Biomedical and Behavioral Research: *Deciding to Forego Life-Sustaining Treatment: A Report on the Ethical, Medical, and Legal Issues in Treatment Decisions*, 478 US 627, no 13.

[11] eg JC Partridge, MD Sendowski, EA Drey and AM Martinez, 'Resuscitation of Likely Nonviable Newborns: Would Neonatology Practices in California Change if the Born-Alive Intants Protection Act Were Enforced?' (2009) 123 *Pediatrics* 1088; SA Sayeed, 'Baby Doe Redux? The Department of Health and Human Services and the Born-Alive Infants Protection Act of 2002: A Cautionary Note on Normative Neonatal Practice' (2005) 116 *Pediatrics* e576; LM Kopelman, TG Irons and AE Kopelman, 'Neonatologists Judge the Baby Doe Regulations' (1988) 318 *New England Journal of Medicine* 677.

[12] *Matter of Baby K*, 16 F3d 590 (4th Cir 1994).

[13] eg *Merck Sharp & Dohme Corp v Albrecht*, SCt, 2019 WL 2166393 (20 May 2019).

[14] See eg P Zettler, 'Pharmaceutical Federalism' (2017) 92 *Indiana Law Journal* 845.

Beyond this set of federal provisions, parents will encounter a variety of state laws depending on the location in which they seek treatment. Parents may even wish to move to another state depending on the laws of that particular jurisdiction, but here, too, the law is unsettled. On the one hand, the US Constitution had been long held to protect the right to travel.[15] On the other hand, states might be permitted to prevent parents from taking their children across state lines to seek to withhold or withdraw medical care in ways that the state might consider medical neglect.[16] (Parenthetically, whether states that criminalise abortion may also criminalise efforts by their citizens to travel to other states for abortions is an issue that is sure to re-emerge[17] if the Supreme Court overrules or severely limits *Roe v Wade*[18] in the coming years.) In the following sections, we consider, first, access to experimental treatment in the United States; and, second, the rights of parents with respect to decisions about their children within this complex framework.

II. Access to Experimental Interventions in the US System

As explained above, in the United States a set of interwoven federal and state ethical and regulatory considerations could be applicable in cases such as that of Charlie Gard. Within this framework, potential avenues for access to experimental therapies include 'off-label' treatments, use within an experimental protocol, compassionate use and a 'right to try' opportunity.

A. Off-Label Use

In the United States, as outlined above, the FDA is responsible for approving medical drugs and devices based on evidence of safety and efficacy. In conducting research with an experimental drug or device and applying for FDA approval, applicants are required to articulate the indicated use or uses of a drug or device. Indicated uses will include such elements as the health condition targeted and the relevant demographic group, primarily whether the drug or device is to be used by adults and/or children. However, an aspect of the FDA regulations is that once approved for an indication or set of indications, physicians can legally use the drug

[15] *Crandall v Nevada*, 73 US (6 Wall) 35 (1867); *Shapiro v Thompson*, 394 US 618 (1969).

[16] Compare the recent UK decision in *Raqeeb and Barts NHS Foundation Trust*, no CO/2767/2019, applying the best interests of the child standard in concluding that parents might seek to take their child to Italy for further treatment.

[17] For an earlier discussion of this issue, see CS Bradford, 'What Happens if Roe Is Overruled? Extraterritorial Regulation of Abortion by the States' [1993] *Arizona Law Review* 35, 87.

[18] 410 US 113 (1973).

or device 'off-label', meaning for indications not formally evaluated or approved by the FDA. Thus, drugs approved for adult use are commonly used in the healthcare of children, particularly when there are no approved drugs for paediatric use in a particular clinical context.

In a case such as Charlie Gard's, if there were an FDA-approved drug for any indication, a physician could try the drug off-label in the child without running afoul of FDA regulations. This approach would also not run afoul of the regulations for protecting human subjects in the United States. The definition of research in these regulations is: 'a systematic investigation, including research development, testing and evaluation, designed to develop or contribute to generalizable knowledge'.[19] This definition excludes what is commonly referred to as 'innovative treatments'. An innovative treatment is one selected by a treating physician with hope that it may benefit a particular patient. Of course, such treatments may or may not be a good idea, but the regulatory system affords this flexibility to physicians with the informed consent of patients or parents in this context. The borderline between innovative therapy and human subject research is not always distinct, but once a provider undertakes a series of treatments with a protocol in hand and data collection, an institutional review board (IRB) is likely to determine that the activity constitutes research.

B. Access through Research

The second avenue for access to experimental drugs is through a research protocol. All federally funded research and all research intended for submission for FDA approval of a drug or device must conform to the federal regulations protecting human subjects in research and must be approved by an IRB. For research with children to be approved, it must fall into one of four categories of approvable research.

First, research involving no more than minimal risk is approvable. Minimal risk is pegged to the risks and burdens of everyday life for healthy individuals.[20] In general, any use of an experimental drug such as those considered in the Gard case will be considered greater than minimal risk and thus not approvable under this category.

Second, research that is greater than minimal risk but with a prospect of direct benefit to the child is approvable if the potential benefit justifies the risk and the risk–benefit ratio is at least as favourable as the ratio for available alternatives.[21] This is the category under which most drug and device research is conducted with children; it permits a substantial degree of risk as long as there is the potential for

[19] 45 CFR § 46.102(l).
[20] 45 CFR § 46.404.
[21] 45 CFR § 46.405.

commensurate benefits. Whether a child such as Charlie Gard could be provided access to an experimental drug under this 'prospect of direct benefit' category is not necessarily straightforward, however. In approving a protocol for a condition such as MDDS, the investigators are likely to describe the patient population that they believe will potentially benefit from the experimental treatment. For many neurodegenerative diseases, there is a high priority on identifying and treating individuals early because, typically, once there has been significant brain or neuronal damage, the injury is irreversible. Including a profoundly neurologically impaired child in a research protocol may not be appropriate if there is no longer a prospect of benefit. How 'benefit' is defined in this context might be a subject of discussion between investigators, the manufacturer and the IRB. If a treatment marginally prolongs the life of a permanently comatose child, the parents might consider that beneficial, although this type of benefit might not be what the manufacturer or investigators are hoping to demonstrate in the research.

In the Charlie Gard case, there was a general consensus by the experts that the nucleoside treatment protocol did not offer the prospect of meaningful neurologic improvement. Under the US regulations, access to the experimental protocol would likely depend on the spectrum of severity described in the inclusion/exclusion criteria. A child such as Charlie Gard would not be enrolled if an exclusion criterion was pre-existing neurologic impairment of a profound degree. If the enrolment criteria were broader such as, say, all children with MDDS, then enrolment would not be precluded but would depend on the consent of the parents and the willingness of the investigators to include such a child. The point here is that enrolment might not be precluded by the approved protocol, but it may not be consistent with the spirit of a 'prospect of direct benefit' or meaningful from a research perspective. Patients do not have a right to access research protocols; access is a determination of the research team, perhaps along with the IRB.

The third category of approvable research is a rather complex provision aimed at allowing valuable research with no direct benefit to the children participating. Criteria for approval in this category include no prospect of direct benefit, a minor increase over minimal risk and the prospect of valuable information about children with a condition under study.[22] This category might be relevant to some types of research with children such as Charlie Gard such as, say, research involving tissue biopsies or imaging studies, which involve a minor increase over minimal risk. But such research would not address the desire of parents for clinical improvement through research.

Finally, a fourth category of approvable research with children includes research that is not otherwise approvable under the regulations but is considered ethically appropriate by an expert committee and the Secretary of Health

[22] 45 CFR § 46.406.

and Human Services.[23] This is a relatively cumbersome and rarely used provision that is unlikely to be applicable to the type of research in cases such as that of Charlie Gard.

C. FDA Expanded Access

A third avenue for potential access to experimental drugs lies under the provisions for expanded access in the FDA regulations.[24] There are several types of access under the FDA's Expanded Access Program (EAP) but the one relevant to this discussion involves individual use. This set of regulations permits individuals with a serious condition to obtain access outside of a formal research protocol to a drug that has not been FDA approved. In this context, a physician and the family would request access to an experimental drug. The process requires the physician to determine that the treatment does not pose a greater risk than the disease, the drug manufacturer must agree to the use, and the FDA must determine that there are no acceptable alternatives to the use, the risk–benefit assessment is favourable, and that access will not interfere with clinical trials.[25] The process also requires that an IRB or the IRB chair or designee attest that the conditions for expanded access have been met. In cases such as Charlie Gard's, access through this route might be deemed appropriate at an earlier stage in his disease course. Once he was profoundly impaired, it seems unlikely that the various stakeholders would approve this approach, particularly if there were limited or no data on the safety or efficacy of the experimental drug. If a drug or other biological had shown some promise with MDDS and there was a meaningful prospect of benefit for the child, including some information on risks, then the expanded access route might be feasible and appropriate.

D. Right-to-Try Laws

The fourth potential route to access to an experimental drug in the United States is under the new RTT law passed by Congress in 2018.[26] This law is designed to provide access to drugs not approved by the FDA for patients with terminal conditions who do not have other treatment options and are not able to participate in a clinical trial.[27] This approach invites a patient or guardian, along with a treating

[23] 45 CFR § 46.407.

[24] 21 CFR § 312.310.

[25] JJ Darrow, A Sarpatwari, J Avorn and AS Kesselheim, 'Practical, Legal, and Ethical Issues in Expanded Access to Investigational Drugs' (2015) 372 *New England Journal of Medicine* 279.

[26] 21 USC § 360bbb-0(a).

[27] B Roxland and EA Hurley, 'Taking a Closer Look at the New Federal "Right to Try" Law' (21 August 2018) blog.primr.org/right-to-try-law.

physician, to request the manufacturer to provide access to an experimental drug that has gone through Phase 1 clinical trials. The manufacturer need not provide the drug but is given certain protections from liability if it does. The main difference between the RTT law and the EAP is that the FTT essentially removes the FDA from the approval process, potentially streamlining access for critically ill patients and giving full recognition to patient autonomy. However, commentators note that the FDA has approved approximately 99 per cent of EAP applications over the years, and therefore it remains to be determined whether the FTT law will improve access and efficiency.[28] Concerns have also been voiced that RTT laws may open the door for patients to access unsafe drugs and for pharmaceutical companies to sell investigational drugs through the statute's provision, allowing them to recover the direct costs of the drugs.[29] In a case such as Charlie Gard's, the decision to allow treatment would be contingent on the assessment of the manufacturer of the drug, the treating physician, and the family regarding the adequacy of existing data and perceptions of benefit and risk. Again, it is likely that such an approach would be more feasible and appropriate earlier in the disease progression and assuming alternative approaches were not available.

Also of note regarding the legal complexity of the situation in the United States, the federal RTT law was enacted after many states had adopted their own RTT laws. At present, some forty states have these laws. Their provisions vary, however, and an additional open legal question is whether the federal RTT law will pre-empt these state laws.[30]

In sum, US law has laid out at least four ways in which parents might legally be able to obtain access to experimental therapy for their children: 'off-label' treatments, use within an experimental protocol, compassionate use and the RTT. Whether such treatment would actually be available as a practical matter is unclear, however. Moreover, any pursuit of these options would need to comply with state laws applicable in the jurisdiction in which they occur, as described in the next section.

III. Parental Decisions with Respect to their Children

In the United States, laws about many aspects of medical care and the rights of parents with respect to their children are primarily matters of state law.

[28] A Bateman-House and CT Robertson, 'The Federal Right to Try Act of 2017 – A Wrong Turn for Access to Investigational Drugs and the Path Forward' (2018) 178 *Journal of American Medical Association* 321.

[29] eg K Folkers, C Chapman and B Redman, 'Federal Right to Try: Where Is It Going?' (2018) 49 *Hastings Center Report* 26.

[30] RB Termini, 'The Latest "Federal Movement" in the Food and Drug Law Arena: The Federal Right-to-Try or Rather Right-to-Know and thus Request Investigational Therapies for Individuals with a Life-Threatening Disease or Condition' (2018) 16 *Indiana Health Law Review* 101; Zettler (n 14).

States define death,[31] determine standards for withdrawing or withholding care, establish standards for informed consent and define medical neglect. Only when federal constitutional rights are implicated or explicit federal statutory provisions apply will federal law come into play.

In general, the approach of US states to medical decision-making on behalf of children is ultimately rooted in the legal and ethical concept of informed consent and has been for over a hundred years. The general rule that a person must give permission (or have permission given on their behalf) prior to the performance of a medical examination, diagnostic testing or treatment has ethical roots in the principle of respect for autonomy. The legal grounding of informed consent, on the other hand, rests in the concepts of battery and medical malpractice. From a legal perspective, a healthcare provider cannot touch a child without the permission of the parents or legal guardian without the authorisation of the state. The only exception to this general rule is when emergency action is necessary for the child's welfare and no parent or legal guardian is readily available to provide permission.

When dealing with children and adolescents, the concept of informed consent is complicated by the fact that the child possesses either limited or absent capacity for informed medical decision-making. Under US state laws, minors are generally viewed as incompetent to provide a legally binding consent within the healthcare realm, and parents or guardians are generally authorised to make healthcare decisions on their behalf; some states recognise mature minor doctrines, however, on which minors may under some circumstances act on their own behalf.

US law (and most ethical analysis) begins with the assumption that parents are the persons best suited and most inclined to act in the best interests of their children, and that in most cases they will act accordingly. There are several good reasons for granting decision-making authority to parents. These include the presumption that because most parents care about their children, they will usually be better situated than others to understand the unique needs of their children and make decisions that ultimately benefit their children. Parents are also usually better situated than others outside of the family to weigh the competing interests of family members in making a final decision. Finally, allowing parents to make decisions on behalf of their children recognises the family unit as crucial to

[31] Controversy is growing in the US regarding the constitutionality of state law definitions of death based on the Uniform Determination of Death Act criteria of either irreversible cessation of circulatory and respiratory functions or irreversible cessation of all functions of the entire brain, including the brain stem. Uniform Law Commission, Uniform Determination of Death Act § 1 (1980) www.uniformlaws.org/HigherLogic/System/DownloadDocumentFile.ashx?DocumentFileKey=341343fa-1efe-706c-043a-9290fdcfd909&forceDialog=0. See eg *Fonseca v Smith*, 2017 WL 4237865 (ED Cal 2017); M Martindale, 'Federal Court May Decide if Teen Stays on Life Support' *Detroit News* (8 November 2019) www.detroitnews.com/story/news/local/oakland-county/2019/11/08/federal-court-may-decide-if-teen-stays-life-support/2533140001; T Pope, 'Brain Death Rejected: Expanding Legal Duties to Accommodate Religious Objections' in HF Lynch, IG Cohen and E Sepper (eds), *Law, Religion, and Health in the United States* (New York, Cambridge University Press, 2017) ch 20.

a healthy society, and granting some degree of family autonomy and freedom from outside intrusion allows family relationships to flourish.[32]

In most situations, parents are granted significant discretion to make decisions on behalf of their children, and the state generally respects parental decisions except when they place a child's health, well-being or life in jeopardy. Parental authority is not absolute, however, and when a parent or guardian fails to adequately guard the interests of a child, the state may intervene. The doctrine of *parens patriae* allows the state to act as 'surrogate parent' when necessary to protect the life and health of those who cannot take care of themselves, including children. This doctrine is not inconsistent with the fundamental federal constitutional liberty right of parents to make decisions about their children. According to the US Supreme Court in *Prince v Massachusetts*:

> [N]either rights of religion nor rights of parenthood are beyond limitation. Acting to guard the general interest in youth's well being, the state as parens patriae may restrict the parent's control by requiring school attendance, regulating or prohibiting the child's labor, and in many other ways.[33]

Child abuse and neglect laws exist in all fifty states to allow state action in cases where a parent refuses to provide important medical care to a child. In those cases, the state can authorise medical care under a claim of medical neglect.

It is important to recognise that two kinds of situations exist in which a medical professional or state agent might seek to limit the ability of a parent to make a medical decision on behalf of a child. The first includes those situations in which a parent refuses to follow a medical recommendation and the refusal is considered to be medical neglect. The second encompasses those situations in which a parent requests or demands something from the medical professional. This distinction is an important one, since both the legal and ethical issues differ from one to the other.

A. Parental Refusals to Provide Consent

A parent who refuses to follow a medical recommendation is effectively withholding consent. In that case, the healthcare provider is faced with a situation where acting contrary to the parents' wishes would constitute a battery, or 'unconsented touching'. With few exceptions, these situations require state authorisation before the healthcare provider can act. The 'best interests standard' has become the prevailing ethical and legal standard used in US states to determine when state interference is justified. The best interest standard directs the healthcare provider

[32] J Goldstein, 'Medical Care for the Child at Risk: On State Supervision of Parental Autonomy' in W Gaylin and R Macklin (eds), *Who Speaks for the Child: The Problems of Proxy Consent* (New York, Plenum Press, 1982) 158–62.

[33] *Prince v Massachusetts*, 321 US 158 (1944).

or state actor to determine which among the routes offered maximises the net benefit and choose the option that optimises the welfare of the child. It is commonly used by clinicians, ethics consultants and ethics committees to determine when to challenge a parent's decision to refuse medical intervention on behalf of a child.

However, in recent years, several scholars have suggested alternative standards for deciding when invoking state power to override a parental decision to refuse consent is justified. Lainie Friedman Ross has suggested a model of constrained parental autonomy that allows parents, as surrogate decision-makers, to balance the 'best interest' of the minor patient with his or her understanding of the family's best interests as long as the child's basic needs, medical and otherwise, are met.[34] A parent's authority under this model is constrained by the basic welfare of the child. Similarly, Douglas Diekema has proposed the harm principle as the most appropriate interference principle for minor patients. The intent of the harm principle is not to identify a single course of action that is in the minor's best interest, but to identify a lower threshold beyond which parental refusals of consent should be challenged. This harm principle identifies a threshold below which parental decisions will not be tolerated and outside intervention is indicated to protect the child: when the decision made by the parents significantly increases the likelihood of serious harm to the child as compared to alternative available options (those recommended by medical providers) that have been rejected by the parents.[35] The American Academy of Pediatrics also seems to use something like this harm principle when it recommends that infants, children and adolescents, regardless of parental religious beliefs, receive effective medical treatment when such treatment is likely to prevent substantial harm, serious disability or death.[36]

States take a variety of approaches to the understanding of medical neglect, moreover. Many states provide some kinds of religious exemptions to their medical neglect statutes. To illustrate, Utah takes one of the broadest approaches to parental rights of refusal. Under Utah law, medical 'neglect' means 'action or inaction causing: … (iii) failure or refusal of a parent, guardian, or custodian to provide proper or necessary subsistence or medical care, or any other care necessary for the child's health, safety, morals, or well-being'. However, 'neglect' does *not* include:

> (i) a parent or guardian legitimately practicing religious beliefs and who, for that reason, does not provide specified medical treatment for a child … [or] (ii) a health

[34] LF Ross, *Children, Families, and Health Care Decision-Making* (New York, Oxford University Press, 1998).

[35] DS Diekema, 'Parental Refusals of Medical Treatment: The Harm Principle as Threshold for State Intervention' (2004) 25 *Theoretical Medicine and Bioethics* 243; DS Diekema, 'Revisiting the Best Interest Standard: Uses and Misuses' (2011) 22 *Journal of Clinical Ethics* 128.

[36] American Academy of Pediatrics, Committee on Bioethics, 'Religious Objections to Medical Care' (1997) 99 *Pediatrics* 279. The chapter in this book by Goold, Auckland and Herring suggests that such a harm principle approach may be under consideration in England and Wales. The chapter by Lathrop Gomez indicates that in Chile parental decisions that place their children at risk of serious harm require referral. The chapter by Navarro-Michel indicates that Spain adopts a harm threshold for parental decisions.

> care decision made for a child by the child's parent or guardian, unless the state or other party to a proceeding shows, by clear and convincing evidence, that the health care decision is not reasonable and informed.[37]

Under statutes such as this one, states must have very strong reasons for overcoming parental decisions that are made on the basis of religion or parental beliefs about what would be medically best for their child.

B. Parental Requests for Medical Interventions

Parental requests for interventions against the recommendation of a medical provider represent a situation distinct from parental refusals of treatment recommended by a healthcare provider. The federal constitutional protection against deprivation of liberty without due process of law is a right to non-interference, not a right to actually receive care or to receive funding needed for care.[38]

Ethically, the healthcare provider's primary responsibility in such circumstances is demarcated by the best interests standard. Professional integrity does not require providers to breach a duty to serve the patient's interests by giving in to a parental request for something the provider believes would either fail to provide benefit to a child or increase the risk of harm to the child without a corresponding benefit. For example, it is generally accepted that a surgeon can choose not to operate on a child if they believe that to do so would result in greater harm than benefit. Similarly, healthcare providers are encouraged to refuse antibiotics for children who they believe, on the basis of their clinical judgement, to have a viral illness. These cases are supported by a desire to honour professional integrity and the physician's duty to wield their craft in a way they believe to benefit the patient. Standards of professional licensure also permit revocation of providers' licences for treatments that are considered gross negligence, such as a transfer of an excessive number of embryos in the effort to achieve a pregnancy.[39]

The primary legal constraint in the context of parental requests for treatment would be the possibility of a tort action if the parents can demonstrate that the provider failed to provide an appropriate standard of care that resulted in harm to the child. In this situation, state tort law of battery also is not the issue, since the provider is not placed in a situation where to act would represent an unconsented touching. Rather, these are situations in which a parent desires an option that the provider believes would conflict with acceptable medical practice. Most state tort law cases in which a parent requests a particular treatment that a provider is reluctant to provide do not represent requests for standard accepted proven medical

[37] Utah Code Ann §78A-6-105 (36)(a) (2019).

[38] eg *Harris v McRae*, 448 US 97 (1980).

[39] A Dobuzinskis, '"Octomom" Doctor Loses California Medical License' *Reuters* (1 June 2011) www.reuters.com/article/us-octomom/octomom-doctor-loses-california-medical-license-idUSTRE7507TL20110601.

therapies. Rather, they often represent experimental or theoretical management or diagnostic options. This was the situation in the case of Charlie Gard, and it is unlikely that parents would be successful in tort litigation claiming that the provider had failed to meet the standard of care.

The situation in which a parent requests an intervention on behalf of a patient is more easily resolved than situations in which a treatment modality has been started but has failed to achieve what the medical provider believes to be an adequate (beneficial) therapeutic response. For the past thirty years, the concept of 'futility' has been offered as one justification for refusing to continue an intervention that a parent or patient wishes to be continued. In 1986, Brett and McCullough suggested that 'physicians are under no obligation to render useless "care," regardless of its safety, just because a patient requests it'.[40] Shortly thereafter, the term futility came into use to describe those situations in which a physician bore no obligation to offer an intervention on the basis of failure to benefit the patient. Schneiderman, Jecker and Jonsen, early scholars advocating for a concept of futility, defined futile situations as those in which a physician could conclude (on the basis of experience, professional consensus or data) that a therapy had proven useless in the last 100 similar cases or when its use would 'merely preserve permanent unconsciousness' or 'fail to end a patient's total dependence on intensive medical care'.[41] Over time, the concept proved increasingly controversial on the grounds that prognostic ability could rarely achieve a level of certainty to determine an intervention truly futile in an individual case and that ultimately what was determined to be "useless" represented a value judgement and the concept of futility favoured the medical provider's determination.[42]

Finding a balance between accommodating the reasonable wishes of a family and utilising medical interventions in a way that is beneficial to the patient and society (by not wasting resources when they can cannot accomplish a reasonable goal) has been the challenge. It has been pointed out that the problem with most notions of futility is that clinical situations are rarely defined by a situation in which the intervention in question is truly futile (ie will not achieve a physiological goal). Rather, most 'futility' cases are situations in which healthcare professionals believe they are causing excessive harm to the child or utilising resources in a way that is wasteful.[43] As a result, over time, greater attention has been paid to creating a fair process for determining when an ongoing intervention could be stopped.[44]

[40] AS Brett and LB McCullough, 'When Patients Request Specific Interventions: Defining the Limits of the Physician's Obligation' (1986) 315 *New England Journal of Medicine* 1347.

[41] LJ Schneiderman, NS Jecker and AR Jonsen, 'Medical Futility: Its Meaning and Ethical Implications' (1990) 112 *Annals of Internal Medicine* 949.

[42] E Bengualid, 'The Futility of Futility: An Analysis of the Charlie Gard Case Within the Framework of US Law' (2018) 40 *Cordozo Law Review* 463.

[43] M Nair-Collins, 'Laying Futility to Rest' (2015) 40 *Journal of Medicine and Philosophy* 554; RD Truog, AS Brett and J Frader, 'The Problem with Futility' (1992) 326 *New England Journal of Medicine* 1560.

[44] PR Helft, M Siegler and J Lantos, 'The Rise and Fall of the Futility Movement' (2000) 343 *New England Journal of Medicine* 293.

Most recently, the Society of Critical Care Medicine, the American Thoracic Society, the American Association of Critical-Care Nurses, the American College of Chest Physicians and the European Society of Intensive Care Medicine published a joint policy statement on 'Responding to Requests for Potentially Inappropriate Treatments in Intensive Care Units'.[45] This multi-organisation policy statement distinguishes between futile and potentially inappropriate treatments, defining 'futile' interventions as 'those that simply cannot accomplish the intended physiologic goal', and 'potentially inappropriate treatments' as those that 'have at least some chance of accomplishing the effect sought by the patient, but clinicians believe that competing ethical considerations justify not providing them'. The Society for Critical Care Medicine has further defined 'potentially inappropriate treatments' to include those where

> there is no reasonable expectation that the patient will improve sufficiently to survive outside the acute care setting, or when there is no reasonable expectation that the patient's neurologic function will improve sufficiently to allow the patient to perceive the benefits of treatment.[46]

The multi-organisation policy statement defines three scenarios. In the rare situation in which the requested intervention is truly futile in that it cannot accomplish the intended physiological goal, the statement asserts that clinicians should not provide those interventions and should carefully explain their rationale to families. In situations where a family has requested a treatment that is legally proscribed in that it is prohibited by law or widely accepted public policies such as those governing organ allocation, or legally discretionary in that specific laws or judicial precedent give physicians permission to refuse to offer them, physicians may unilaterally refuse those interventions after explaining the rationale to the family and consulting any experts necessary to ensure that they are applying and interpreting the law appropriately. Finally, in situations where interventions are 'potentially inappropriate', a seven-step process should be followed, when time allows, to ensure an equitable and transparent approach to all patients and families. This approach includes enlisting expert consultation to assist in the dispute resolution process, giving notice of the process to the surrogate decision-makers, obtaining a second medical opinion, obtaining review by an interdisciplinary hospital committee (ethics committee), offering surrogates the opportunity to transfer the patient to an alternate institution, informing surrogates of the opportunity to pursue extramural appeal, and implementing the decision of the resolution process. In situations where time pressures do not allow for all seven steps *and* the 'clinicians have a high

[45] GT Bosslet, TM Pope, GD Rubenfeld et al, 'An Official ATS/AACN/ACCP/ESICM/SCCM Policy Statement: Responding to Requests for Potentially Inappropriate Treatments in Intensive Care Units' (2015) 191 *American Journal of Respiratory and Critical Care Medicine* 1318.

[46] AA Kon, EK Shepard, NO Sederstrom et al, 'Defining Futile and Potentially Inappropriate Interventions: A Policy Statement from the Society of Critical Care Medicine Ethics Committee' (2016) 44 *Critical Care Medicine* 1769.

degree of certainty that the requested treatment is outside accepted practice, they should refuse to provide the requested treatment and endeavor to achieve as much procedural oversight as the clinical situation allows'.[47]

With respect to futility, state laws also differ.[48] Of particular note, Texas has enacted a statute that permits healthcare facilities to refuse to provide requested treatment judged to be futile, if certain conditions are met. The refusal must be reviewed by an ethics committee and the person requesting the care must be given notice and an opportunity to attend the committee meeting and be given a written explanation of the committee's decision. If the provider or the person requesting the treatment does not agree with the decision, the reasonable efforts to arrange a transfer must be made and appropriate life-sustaining treatment must be provided during these efforts.[49] Thus in Texas, providers could refuse treatment in a case such as that of Charlie Gard, but would need to make reasonable efforts to facilitate transfer to a facility willing to offer the care.

In sum, both ethical discussions and legal provisions in the United States may grant considerable scope to parental decisions. At the outside, state law will constrain parental neglect and abuse and federal law may intervene to require emergency stabilisation and aggressive treatment of premature infants in at least some cases. Legal recognition of parental rights, however, extends primarily to rights to refuse care, not to rights to obtain it.

IV. Conclusion

Thus US law and ethics do not provide a univocal answer to the case of an infant such as Charlie Gard. US law sets outside constraints in the protection of constitutional liberties and state law prohibitions of grossly negligent care. Within these constraints, however, patients in the United States might have a variety of routes to seek out experimental therapies. Some jurisdictions may give parents quite wide scope in the decisions they make, while others may place greater limits in the interests of protecting children against what is viewed as medical neglect. The willingness of providers to offer the therapy, of pharmaceutical companies to provide experimental drugs, or the ability to receive payment for the care, however, are entirely separate matters, and there would be no guarantees that parents would be successful in their efforts to obtain the care they seek for their child.

[47] Bosslet et al (n 45).

[48] Other examples include a Virginia statute requiring hospitals equipped to provide life-sustaining treatment to develop policies governing the appropriateness of proposed care, including documentation and rights of review, Code of Virginia §32.1-127 (21), and an Idaho statute prohibiting withdrawal of life-sustaining treatment over the objection of a surrogate, Idaho Code § 39-4514 (3).

[49] Texas Health and Safety Code § 166.046. For a criticism of the statute for failing to provide due process, see R Thompson, 'Searching for Fairness: Examining the Texas Advance Directives Act in Light of the Clear and Convincing Evidence Standard' (2019) 56 *Houston Law Review* 667.

10

Withholding and Withdrawal of Life-Prolonging Treatment from Young Children in Israel

ROY GILBAR

I. Introduction

Deciding whether to prolong the life of a seriously ill child is a complex issue, one that is addressed by Israeli law. However, there are no reported cases in Israel like that of Charlie Gard. The cases that have so far reached Israeli courts dealt with parents' requests to withhold or withdraw treatment. In ruling on these requests, the Israeli courts have addressed the issue of parental autonomy as well as the relationship between clinicians, patients who are minors and their parents. This chapter describes the Israeli position and provides legal analysis and critique.

As in English law, the test of the child's best interests governs Israeli law. As will be elaborated below, both the legislator and the courts determine that parents must make decisions which promote the child's best interests. Furthermore, when the courts are asked to intervene, they have the ultimate authority to make a decision that they believe promotes the child's best interests. This test essentially reflects a utilitarian mechanism that promotes the child's overall welfare and in which the personal interests and wishes of the parents take second place. Moreover, the bioethical principle of sanctity of life is highly influential in Israeli law and has led the courts to accept requests (usually from clinicians) to provide life-prolonging treatment when the parents express their opposition.

The structure of the chapter is as follows. First, I will discuss the relevant legislation and following that the relevant case-law. This will be followed by an analysis of the legal position and its implications. My central critique is that the dominance of the principle of sanctity of life leads the courts to support clinicians' requests and overly intervene in parents' decisions.

II. Legislation

Israeli law is based on the principle that Israel is both a democratic and a Jewish state. Thus, religion (ie Judaism) and religious views and values influence the legislation, and its interpretation by the courts. In medical law, sanctity of life, which is a prominent principle in Judaism, and autonomy, an important principle in democracy, influence both legislation and case-law in Israel. Clearly, in the context of life-prolonging treatment of seriously ill children, there is a tension between these two principles in Israeli law.

The Legal Capacity and Guardianship Act 1962 ('the Act') regulates, inter alia, the legal status of parents with respect to their children.[1] The Act states that the child's parents are his/her natural guardians, which means that they have the right and duty to consider the child's needs, make decisions on his/her behalf and promote his/her welfare, including – according to the courts – his/her health.[2] The Act requires parents to act as 'devoted parents' under all circumstances.[3] In our context, this is unhelpful in a situation where the only treatment available for a sick child prolongs his/her life artificially.[4] In practice, the treating clinicians and the parents usually concur on whether or not to withhold treatment and in that case there is no party that approaches the courts. The court is asked to intervene only when there is disagreement between the clinicians and the parents.

In determining the mechanism of judicial intervention, section 68 of the Act states that the Attorney General or any other relevant party (such as the parents or the treating clinicians) can approach the court with a request for measures to protect the child's welfare and interests. Section 68(b) focuses on health issues, stating that the court can issue relevant orders if it is convinced, according to professional medical opinion, that the requested measures are required to protect the child's physical or mental health. The Act states that the court must consider the patient's wishes, the significance of treatment, its necessity and frequency, the possible harm to the patient's way of life, and the chance of improving the patient's quality of life. The court can appoint an attorney who will represent the child in court, particularly if she/he refuses the proposed treatment or if she/he is in disagreement with her/his legal guardians (ie the parents). In these proceedings, the court can approach the patient's family in order to ascertain their views.

A close reading of the Act reveals that the legislator has provided clinicians with a significant role in the court's decision regarding life-prolonging treatment. However, according to the Act, judges must consider non-medical considerations

[1] The Legal Capacity and Guardianship Act 1962, Sefer Hukim 380 (17 August 1962) 120.

[2] ibid, s 17.

[3] ibid.

[4] The Act also states that the decision should be agreed on by both parents. This led the Israeli Supreme Court in Civil Appeal 506/88 *Yael Shefer v Ziv Hospital in Zefat*, PD 48 (1) 87 (1993) to reject the request of a mother not to prolong the life of her daughter who had Tay–Sachs disease. The child's father did not join the mother in her petition to the court.

as well, such as the patient's way of life, as in our context. Arguably, since the patient in these circumstances is a young child, his/her 'way of life' is determined by his/her parents. If we agree that an individual determines his/her way of life according to his/her wishes, views, interests and moral values, then the Act implicitly includes the parents' perspective and moral values in the judge's decision regarding life-prolonging treatments. Furthermore, and as already stated, judges must consider the chances that the proposed medical treatment will improve the patient's quality of life. This requires judges to determine what the quality of life of the particular patient is and how it can be improved. An obvious and overly discussed question thus arises as to whether prolonging the life of a child who suffers from an incurable disease improves his/her quality of life.[5] I will deal with this below when analysing the case-law.

Another important piece of legislation in this context is the Dying Patient Act 2005 ('the 2005 Act').[6] This Act regulates the provision of medical treatment to dying patients. It is based on two often conflicting principles: patient autonomy and sanctity of life. The 2005 Act defines a dying patient as one who, according to professional medical assessment, is suffering from a terminal illness and has six months or less to live. The 2005 Act adds that a patient is in the final stage of an illness when she/he has two weeks or less to live regardless of the medical treatment administered.[7]

Those who are defined as dying patients or in the final stage of life are subject to the Act's provisions. They – or their legal guardians if they do not have legal capacity – are to be informed that they are defined as dying patients or as a patient in the final stage of an illness. The explicit requests regarding life-prolonging treatment of patients who have legal capacity are to be respected by their clinicians. However, when patients are not legally competent to express their wishes and did not provide any directives in advance, the 2005 Act establishes several mechanisms to assist the treating clinicians in making the decision of whether to provide life-prolonging treatment.

As for young children, section 24 of the 2005 Act states that the parents can represent their child in matters concerning the provision and withholding/withdrawal of life-prolonging treatment. In other words, parents can decide whether or not their sick child will receive a life-prolonging treatment. Section 28 states that if there is disagreement between the parents and the treating clinicians the matter will be brought before the institution's ethics committee which has the authority to make decisions in these matters. The function of the institutional ethics committees is to avoid going to court on these matters and to facilitate quick decision-making that is not subject to rigid legal procedures. An ethics

[5] This issue raises the bioethical principles of non-maleficence and beneficence. See eg R Gilbar and N Karako-Eyal, 'Making Decisions on Artificial Ventilation at the End of Life: Does Law Affect Medical Practice?' (2017) 24 *Elder Law Journal* 293.

[6] The Dying Patient Act of 2005, Sefer Hukim 2039 (15 December 2005) 58.

[7] ibid, s 8.

committee is composed of doctors, nurses, a bioethicist, a lawyer, a social worker/psychologist and a clergyman (according to the patient's religion).[8] In our context, the committee is authorised to deal with conflicts between clinicians and parents and between the parents themselves. Section 28 states that when the institutional ethics committee deals with a disagreement concerning the treatment of minors it must give priority to the child's best interests. Significantly, the 2005 Act permits the institutional ethics committee not to prolong the child's life if it is convinced that it is not in his/her best interests.[9]

In sum, the relevant legislation divides patients who are minors into two groups. The Dying Patient Act 2005 addresses children who are terminally ill and have six months or less to live. The parents, as the child's legal guardians, can request that the clinicians provide or withhold life-prolonging treatment. If there is a disagreement, the case will be brought before the institutional ethics committee which is authorised to make a decision in these matters, including a decision to withhold treatment.

The Legal Capacity and Guardianship Act 1962 addresses seriously ill children who are not dying but suffer from incurable conditions. When there is a disagreement between parents and clinicians, the matter is brought before the Family Court. In both acts, the child's best interests test is the applicable legal rule. However, the Act is more detailed and specifies the criteria to be considered and applied by the courts. While the Dying Patient Act 2005 focuses on the child's best interests exclusively, the Legal Capacity and Guardianship Act 1962 Act adds that the patient's quality of life and way of life must be considered. Focusing on the legal status of parents, both acts state that their voice must be heard in decisions about life-prolonging treatments, but that they do not have the final word. This leaves room for judicial intervention, which is discussed next.

II. Case-Law

A. Best Interests Test

When a case concerning a child is brought to the courts, the judges have, according to Israeli law, the ultimate authority to make the decision. The Israeli Supreme Court has established the child's best interests as the main test for making decisions about his/her welfare.[10] The essence of this test is a cost–benefit evaluation. The courts weigh the benefits of the proposed medical treatment vis-a-vis the harm (eg pain and suffering) it might inflict. The court will be convinced that

[8] ibid s 45.

[9] There are no published data on the cases brought before institutional ethics committees.

[10] Civil Appeal 2266/93 *John Does v John Doe*, PD 49(1) 221 (1995); cf *Yael Shefer v Ziv Hospital* (n 4); Civil Appeal 5587/97 *A-G v John Doe (a minor)*, PD 51(4) 830 (1998).

the proposed medical treatment promotes the child's best interests if the benefits outweigh the harm.[11]

The Israeli Supreme Court has stated that this utilitarian-based test is 'flexible, broad and unspecific' and is applied 'according to the relevant evidence and judicial discretion'.[12] The judges acknowledged that the best interests test helps them to determine whether a proposed treatment should be administered, particularly when it concerns life-prolonging treatment. In any event, the Israeli Supreme Court acknowledges that the existing legal mechanism requires judges to identify the child's relevant interests and rights and make decisions which take into consideration society's values with respect to life-prolonging treatments.[13]

In the specific context of prolonging the life of a young child who suffers from an incurable condition, the courts consider the following principles: the right to life, the sanctity of life, prevention of pain and suffering, and the quality of life of a dying patient, which includes not only prevention of physical harm and bodily pain and suffering but also mental and emotional anguish. The courts also consider respect for the dignity of the patient as an individual, including protection of privacy.[14]

Interestingly, an analysis of court decisions reveals that among these principles, sanctity of life (or the legal right to life)[15] is given preference over prevention of pain and suffering.[16] It should be noted that so far the courts dealt only with children whose medical conditions were serious and incurable. These children were not defined as dying patients under the 2005 Act.

For example, in the most important such case in Israeli law, that of Ben Ikar, there was a dispute between the parents of an infant and the clinicians. The child was born with cerebral palsy and suffered from advanced kidney failure. When his renal condition deteriorated and his life was at risk, the clinicians wished to provide treatment that could prolong his life. The parents objected, knowing full well that without it their son would probably die within a short period of time. In accepting the clinicians' view, the Supreme Court held that the proposed treatment would enable the child to live for a number of years despite his kidney failure. The fact that the child suffered from cerebral palsy was not, according to the court, relevant to the decision whether to provide the proposed treatment. The Court stated that:

> [W]hen we consider a child who suffers from serious disabilities, his life with these disabilities is the life he enjoys. As far as Ben is concerned, another type of life is not, and

[11] Civil Appeal 1354/92 *A-G v Jane Doe*, PD 48(1) 711, 725 (1994).

[12] cf *A-G v John Doe* (n 10) (Orr J), [20].

[13] cf *John Does v John Doe* (n 10) 250.

[14] cf *A-G v John Doe (a minor)* (n 10) (Orr J), [22]–[25].

[15] The right to life is secured under ss 2 and 4 of Basic Law: Human Dignity and Liberty (1992). Israel does not have a written constitution and Basic Laws are parliamentary acts that are considered to be part of an unwritten constitution. Any piece of legislation must be interpreted in light of the Basic Laws.

[16] In bioethics terminology, sanctity of life is preferred over principles of non-maleficence. See T Beauchamp and J Childress, *Principles of Biomedical Ethics*, 7th edn (Oxford, Oxford University Press, 2013).

> has never been, an option. Such a life deserves the same legal protection in the same way as the life of a child who was normal at birth and experienced normal development.[17]

This led the Supreme Court to clarify that in light of the dominance of the principle of sanctity of life, making judicial decisions not to provide life-prolonging treatment due to the child's pain and suffering would be rare.[18] Making such a decision requires evidence that the prognosis is so grim that there is no point in providing life-prolonging treatment. It was stated in the case of Ben Ikar that 'the principle of sanctity of life requires us to obtain a full picture of the child's medical state before making a decision about withholding life-prolonging treatment'.[19]

At first glance, this is convincing. The patient is not dying and treatment can prolong life by months or years. Nevertheless, we need to take a closer look at the actual attitude of the courts. Although the Supreme Court discussed the prevention of pain and suffering at length, it explicitly dismissed them as relevant factors: 'Taking into considerations a patient's quality of life, as society sees it, might risk the life of those who suffer from serious physical or mental disabilities.'[20]

This position relies on the following argument: there are situations in which the patient cannot communicate with others, such that she/he is unable to express that his/her pain is intolerable and that she/he prefers to end his/her life. Therefore, we need to protect his/her life. In this context, the Supreme Court sees itself as a moral guide and as such gives preference to sanctity of life over the interests of patients not to live a life full of pain and misery. In the case of Ben Ikar, the Court was explicit:

> Assessments of quality of life in the case of a child are to a large extent subjective … there is a real risk that such a subjective assessment of the quality of life of weak patients will be exploited and lead to serious, perhaps irreversible, harm to the basic principle of sanctity of life.[21]

Accordingly, the extent to which the life of the child is intolerable is not particularly relevant and is not assigned much weight when making decisions about providing life-prolonging treatment to children who suffer from an incurable condition. In this context, one might wonder if there is a point at which the courts would be prepared to decide not to prolong life due to intolerable pain and suffering. The Court's decision in Ben Ikar indicates that if the child is not defined as a dying patient according to the 2005 Act, then there is only a slim chance that his/her life

[17] cf *A-G v John Doe (a minor)* (n 10) (Orr J), [23].

[18] In contrast, in England, the Charlie Gard case demonstrates that where the child experiences substantial pain and suffering, it is unlikely that parents will be offered treatment if it serves only to prolong life in a heavily disabled condition. See I Goold, C Auckland and J Herring, 'Medical Decision-Making on Behalf of Children in England and Welsh Law: A Child-Centred Best Interests Approach', in this book.

[19] See *A-G v John Doe (a minor)* (n 10), [28].

[20] ibid [23a] and [23b].

[21] ibid.

would not be prolonged.[22] Notably, the clinicians in Ben Ikar were of the view that the proposed treatment would provide the child with the same quality of life as he had previously with an insignificant reduction in life expectancy.[23] Their professional view convinced the judges who did not consider the futility of the situation to be a decisive factor.[24]

B. Parental Autonomy and Judicial Intervention

As described above, when there is a disagreement between clinicians and parents, the courts (or the institutional ethics committee when a patient who is a minor is dying) have the final say.[25] The main question is the extent of the court's intervention in the autonomy of the parents to make decisions on their child's behalf. There are those who argue that the courts (or the institutional ethics committees) should have substantial authority to intervene, up to the point of nullifying the parents' decision. This is based on the parents' emotional involvement which prevents them from reaching an objective and reasonable decision. Furthermore, it is argued that the interests of the child and those of the parents are not necessarily identical, particularly in our context.[26] This position is based on the view that such decisions should be rational. It is also based on an approach that perceives the individual patient as a separate entity from his/her significant others.

In what follows, an opposing argument will be made, according to which the intervention of the courts in the discretion of parents should be minimal in this context, particularly when it is agreed that the parents are devoted parents.

[22] In 2014, a one-year-old child who suffered from congenital muscular dystrophy with a life expectancy of 10–15 years swallowed a piece of food which reached her lungs. As a result, she was temporarily connected to a ventilator. The clinicians wanted to perform a procedure to make ventilation permanent. Her parents objected. They asked the court to let their daughter breathe without medical assistance, having been told that she would die as a result. Applying the decision in *Ben Ikar*, the Family Court dismissed the parents' request, allowing the clinicians to provide treatment. Case (Family Court Jerusalem) 24638-02-14 *Shaare Zedek Medical Center v A*. A was not defined as a dying patient under the 2005 Act (n 6).

[23] Despite the clinicians' view Ben Ikar died in 1999, two years after the court hearing and following fourteen failed attempts to provide the treatment the court authorised.

[24] A similar case came recently before the courts in the UK. In the case of *Raqeeb v Barts NHS Foundation Trust* [2019] EWHC 2531 (Admin) and [2019] EWHC 2530 (Fam) the medical evidence was that with a tracheotomy and continued ventilation the child may live 10–20 years, but without it she would die. Interpreting the Israeli Dying Patient Act 2005, if this case was brought before the Israeli courts Tafida Raqeeb would not be defined as a dying patient because the 2005 Act states that a dying patient is a patient who will die within six months regardless of the medical treatment given to them. For a discussion about the Raqeeb case, see Goold et al (n 19).

[25] cf *John Does v John Doe* (n 10) 235. The courts have the authority to make decisions under the Dying Patient Act when, for various practical reasons, it is not possible to convene the institutional ethics committee.

[26] Y Green, 'Who Has the Responsibility for Making Decisions About Provision or Withholding of Treatment to a Premature Infant?' (2007) 36 *Medicine and Law* 43 (in Hebrew).

Thus, if the parents believe that ending the pain and suffering of their young and seriously ill child fulfils his/her best interests (with the consequence his/her life will not be prolonged artificially), then their position should be respected by the court subject to the provisions to be discussed below. This view is based on values of care, commitment, responsibility, and justice as fairness and will be developed in what follows.[27]

In the case of Ben Ikar, Justice Orr addressed the issue of parental autonomy. He stated that in addition to the natural bond that exists between parents and their child, it is justifiable that parents should have the authority to make decisions on the child's behalf. The following reasons were given: (1) the parents are intimately familiar with the various aspects of the issue and therefore are the best equipped to make the correct decision; (2) the issue has implications for the delicate and complicated parent–child relationship; (3) there is no consensus in public opinion on whether life-prolonging treatment should be forced on a patient, and therefore courts should tread cautiously when intervening in the parents' decision; and (4) the parents are the ones who will have to deal with the consequences of the decision of whether to provide life-prolonging treatment and therefore they should have the sole decision-making power. Consequently, Justice Orr stated that a judicial decision to intervene in the parents' decision in this context should be based on a special and exceptional cause, and the clinicians who apply to the courts for judicial intervention in the parents' decision must explain how this is to be justified.[28]

Despite the courts' position that care should adopted when intervening in cases of life-prolonging treatment, they nevertheless intervened, based on a utilitarian cost–benefit mechanism. They came to the conclusion that since the proposed treatment would improve the life of the child (by prolonging it) and since there is a low risk that the proposed treatment would cause physical harm to the child, it is justified to intervene in the decision of parents not to provide such treatment to their child. This was essentially the Supreme Court's decision in Ben Ikar.[29]

In contrast, the position advocated here holds that the four considerations stated by Justice Orr should lead the courts to intervene in parents' decisions whether or not the child is terminal or suffering from an incurable condition, such that the proposed treatment will be futile only in exceptional cases. The extent of judicial intervention should be minimal, provided the following criteria are satisfied: (1) the parents present a united front, namely they both concur with the decision; (2) the parents are viewed as being devoted parents, namely they are acting in what they view to be the best interests of the child; (3) the level of pain and suffering being experienced by the child is substantial and his/her quality

[27] R Gilbar, 'Between Unconditional Acceptance and Responsibility: Should Family Ethics Limit the Scope of Reproductive Autonomy?' (2009) 21 *Child & Family Law Quarterly* 309.

[28] cf *A-G v John Doe (a minor)* (n 10) (Orr J), [26].

[29] ibid; see also *Shaare Zedek Medical Center v A* (n 22) and *Yael Shefer v Ziv Hospital* (n 4).

of life is low; and (4) the proposed treatment is futile and prolongs life with no improvement in the child's welfare. According to this view, the role of the courts is to determine whether these four criteria are met, and, if they are, then there is no justification for judicial intervention even when the outcome of the parents' decisions is the child's death.

It might be argued that this view grants excessive authority to parents. Several responses to this claim are possible. First, making a decision not to prolong their child's life goes against the parents' natural instinct. They desire – more than anything – that their child should live. Therefore, a decision by them not to prolong their child's life will be the result of a long and well thought-out process of deliberation. Their emotional involvement should not exclude them from having the final say; on the contrary, their strong emotional bond with the child justifies their right to make a decision free from external interventions.

Second, familial relationships are based on intimacy: love, care, responsibility, mutual commitment and solidarity.[30] The intimacy between parents and children creates a sense of responsibility and mutual commitment. Parents and their children share common interests and goals and strive to achieve them. According to Jonathan Herring, children live in the context of relationships. Therefore, it is not possible to decouple the interests of a child from those of its parents. Indeed, their interests are so intertwined that it is artificial to consider the welfare of the child as distinct from those of the parents.[31]

Given that parents and their children have common interests, decision-making authority should lie with the parents, especially when the child – due to his/her young age – cannot express his/her view. An approach that perceives the child as detached from his/her parents highlights a possible divergence of interests. Such a confrontational approach justifies a substantial level of judicial intervention and will compromise the right of parents to make decisions on behalf of their young children. Ultimately, it will lead to decisions with which the parents will be unable to comply. In contrast, according to an approach that highlights the positive aspects of the parent–child relationship and the values they share, parents will not only be granted more autonomy but they will be better able to face the most difficult decision in their lives.

Third, close and intimate relationships should be based not only on care and commitment but also on fairness and equality.[32] This is particularly important in our context because within the tripartite clinician–patient–parent relationship the patient (ie the young child) is unable to express his/her view. The parents carry the main burden of taking care of the young child, and the clinicians are the most influential party in determining the type treatment provided to the patient.

[30] HL Nelson and JL Nelson, *The Patient in the Family* (London, Routledge, 1995).
[31] J Herring, *Caring and the Law* (Oxford, Hart Publishing, 2013); see also HL Nelson and JL Nelson, 'The Romance of the Family' (2008) 38 *Hastings Center Report* 19.
[32] SO Moller, *Justice, Gender and the Family* (New York, Basic Books, 1991).

Creating relationships that are based on fairness means allowing the parties to voice their views and providing equal weight to medical and non-medical considerations in decision-making. According to John Hardwig, the person most affected by a decision should have the final word.[33] In the context of end-of-life decision-making, the differential impact of a particular decision on the three relevant parties (clinicians, the patient and parents/family members) may lead to the conclusion that the position of the parents should be given preference. Furthermore, when a young child cannot express his/her view, the decision can be made by either the clinicians, the parents or the judges. Since the decision is neither purely medical nor purely legal, no party should have exclusive authority. Nonetheless, it is the parents who are most affected by the decision. Therefore, fairness dictates that parents should have the final word in decisions about whether to provide life-prolonging treatment. According to this view, courts should only intervene when one (or more) of the above conditions is not met.[34] As demonstrated above, this is not the approach adopted by the courts and they have intervened substantially in parents' decisions.

IV. Conclusion

Israeli law adopts a conservative approach to decisions about whether to provide life-prolonging treatment to young children. It promotes sanctity of life as the dominant consideration, particularly when the child is not terminally ill but suffers from an incurable condition. This violates the right of a child to avoid a life full of pain and suffering when the proposed treatment is futile and prolongs life artificially. Only when the child is terminal does the law provide a mechanism to respect requests by the parents to withhold treatment, although there is no obligation on the courts or institutional ethics committees to accept these requests.

Furthermore, the level of judicial intervention in parents' decisions is substantial. It is based on a narrow utilitarian mechanism coupled with an individualistic approach that distinguishes between the interests of the child and those of his/her parents. An alternative approach – which has so far not been adopted by the courts – is to perceive the close parent–child relationship as empowering and as promoting the child's shared interests with significant others.

Undoubtedly, many view it as morally imperative to prolong the life of young children even when their medical condition is terminal. However, it has been argued here that Israeli law should adopt an alternative approach. More autonomy

[33] J Hardwig, 'What About the Family?' in J Hardwig (ed), *Is There a Duty to Die? And Other Essays in Medical Ethics* (London, Routledge, 2000).

[34] Interestingly, similar arguments have been deployed in the UK and the US to justify changing the law to a harm threshold. See Goold et al (n 19) for the UK view and L Francis, J Botkin and D Diekema, 'Decision-Making on Behalf of Children in the Research and Clinical Context: A United States Perspective' for the US view, both in this book.

should be provided to parents in the decision of whether or not to provide life-prolonging treatment, based on the nature of the relationship between parents and their child and the impact of the decision on the parents. The relationship between parent and child may be problematic, in which case there is more room for judicial intervention. However, when the parents are devoted to their children, judicial intervention is required and justified only when one parent disagrees with the other or the parents are not fully meeting their obligations to the child.[35] The default position should be to respect the parents' decision even when it is opposed by clinicians.

Finally, in light of the prominence of sanctity of life as a value in Israeli society, the chances that cases like that of Charlie Gard would reach the courts are slim. Interestingly, so far there has been no case where parents approached the courts with a request for life-prolonging treatment for their child in light of the clinicians' refusal. The cases that reached the courts so far concerned either clinicians' requests to provide life-prolonging treatment in light of parents' refusal, or requests submitted jointly by the child's clinicians and parents (when the child was too young to express a view). Nonetheless, the discussion of parental autonomy and judicial intervention in Israeli law may shed light on the debate in English law and elsewhere.

[35] cf *John Does v John Doe* (n 10) [8].

11

Medical Decision-Making on Behalf of Children in English and Welsh Law: A Child-Centred Best Interests Approach

IMOGEN GOOLD, CRESSIDA AUCKLAND AND JONATHAN HERRING

I. Introduction

The question of how disagreements between parents and medical professionals over the care of very ill children should be resolved has been considered numerous times in recent years by the English courts.[1] In each recent case, including those of Charlie Gard, Alfie Evans and Tafida Raqeeb,[2] the courts have confirmed the orthodox approach, namely that in cases of dispute, it is open to the court to decide whether to authorise a hospital's proposed withdrawal of or use of medical treatment based on what is in the child's best interests. This has long been the approach in the English courts, although over time they have developed a nuanced, considered approach to this question. These recent cases in particular offer insights into the delicate balancing undertaken when determining questions of best interests. In this chapter, we outline the background to this orthodox position and explain how it applies in the current law. We also explain the recent challenges to this position, which were raised in *Great Ormond St Hospital v Yates and Gard* (*Gard*),[3] where opponents of the current law argue for a shift to some form of 'risk of significant

[1] *Great Ormond Street Hospital v Yates and Gard* [2017] EWHC 972 (Fam) (*Gard*); *Great Ormond Street Hospital for Children NHS Foundation Trust v Yates Court of Appeal (Civil Division)* [2017] EWCA Civ 410 (*Gard 2*); *Alder Hey Children's NHS Foundation Trust v Mr Thomas Evans, Ms Kate James, Alfie Evans (A Child by his Guardian CAFCASS Legal)* [2018] EWHC 308 (Fam) (*Evans*), [2018] 2 FLR 1223; *Kings College Hospital NHS Foundation Trust v Ms Thomas, Haastrup and Haastrup* [2018] EWHC 127 (Fam), [2018] 2 FLR 1028 (*Haastrup*); *Raqeeb v Barts NHS Foundation Trust* [2019] EWHC 2531 (Admin) and [2019] EWHC 2530 (Fam).

[2] ibid.

[3] *Gard* (n 1).

harm' threshold to be passed before courts can override the wishes of parents. We briefly outline the cases for and against such a change to the law.

II. The Current Position Confirmed: The Best Interests Approach

Cases normally come to court when a disagreement arises between parents and a hospital over what treatment should be provided to a child, and either the hospital seeks an order authorising a proposed course of action (eg withdrawal of treatment) or the parents seek authorisation for an alternative medical treatment. The court's power is, however, importantly limited by the fact it cannot order a hospital or medical professionals to provide treatment it does not want to offer: it can only authorise doctors to provide (or not provide) the treatment.

In court the dispute is often framed as a clash between what doctors think is best for the child and what the parents regard as best promoting their child's interests. Until recently, the law appeared to be very much settled on when the courts could override parental wishes in treatment decisions about children. It is a core tenet of child law in England and Wales[4] that the child's welfare takes precedence above other concerns, including parental 'rights', and as Rachel Taylor writes

> the law regards the upbringing of children not as a matter of exclusive parental rights, to be defended unless forfeited, but as a collaborative responsibility in which parents take the leading role.[5]

Consequently, the court has the authority to take a decision in such matters at the point where the child's welfare is engaged, and when it makes such a decision, it does so by balancing various factors to determine what is in the child's best interests. In *Wyatt v Portsmouth Hospital NHS Trust*,[6] the Court of Appeal explained:

> The judge must decide what is in the child's best interests. In making that decision, the welfare of the child is paramount, and the judge must look at the question from the assumed point of view of the patient (*Re J*). There is a strong presumption in favour of a course of action which will prolong life, but that presumption is not irrebuttable (*Re J*). The term 'best interests' encompasses medical, emotional, and all other welfare issues (*Re A*). The court must conduct a balancing exercise in which all the relevant factors are weighed (*Re J*) and a helpful way of undertaking this exercise is to draw up a balance sheet (*Re A*).[7]

[4] Scottish Law has fundamentally different principles.

[5] R Taylor, 'Parental Decisions and Court Jurisdiction: Best Interests or Significant Harm?' in I Goold, J Herring and C Auckland (eds), *Parental Rights, Best Interests and Significant Harms: Medical Decision-Making on Behalf of Children Post-Great Ormond Street Hospital v Yates* (Oxford, Hart Publishing, 2019).

[6] *Wyatt v Portsmouth Hospital NHS Trust* [2005] EWCA 1181.

[7] ibid [87].

The court's approach is the same whether the issue is the withdrawal or the withholding of treatment: as in many other jurisdictions, including Belgium, Spain and Hong Kong, the question is whether the treatment is in the patient's best interests. Lady Hale in *Aintree University Hospital NHS Trust v James*[8] made clear[9] that

> the focus is on whether it is in the patient's best interests to give the treatment rather than whether it is in his best interests to withhold or withdraw it. If the treatment is not in his best interests, the court will not be able to give its consent on his behalf and it will follow that it will be lawful to withhold or withdraw it. Indeed, it will follow that it will not be lawful to give it.

The authority the court has to make decisions on behalf of children has a fairly long history, and can be traced to the feudal notion of *parens patriae*, under which 'the monarch as the ultimate superior' has 'jurisdiction over the very "person" of those who inhabited the land'. As Graeme Laurie explains, 'the monarch was *parens patriae* – parent of the country', which afforded the monarch 'the right and duty to care for those not able to care for themselves'.[10] It is a doctrine that is about both the power and the responsibility of the monarch towards citizens, especially the vulnerable. By the mid-nineteenth century, it was made clear in *Re Flynn* that the court had the power to protect children from their parents' decisions where this was 'essential to their safety or to their welfare, in some very serious and important respect'.[11] This position was developed and consolidated during the twentieth century, with Lord Justice Waite clarifying in *Re T* that the court has the authority to intervene whenever the child's best interests will otherwise not be promoted. He confirmed that this position rests on the court's authority to protect the child's welfare.[12]

This does not mean, however, that parents have no authority under English law. The courts have been very clear that parents retain power to make decisions for their children in relation to general issues of upbringing, and even in respect of medical care. For example, Lord Scarman said in *Gillick v West Norfolk and Wisbech Area Health Authority* that:

> It is abundantly plain that the law recognises that there is a right and a duty of parents to determine whether or not to seek medical advice in respect of their child, and, having received advice, to give or withhold consent to medical treatment.[13]

[8] *Aintree University Hospital NHS Trust v James* [2013] UKSC 67, [22].

[9] The case concerned an adult without capacity, but on this point the approach applies whenever the court is making a best interests assessment in relation to a person without capacity.

[10] GT Laurie, 'Parens Patriae Jurisdiction in the Medico-Legal Context: The Vagaries of Judicial Activism' (1999) 3 *Edinburgh Law Review* 95, 95.

[11] *In re Flynn* (1848) 2 De G & Sm 457, 474.

[12] *Re T (A Minor) (Wardship: Medical Treatment)* [1997] 1 WLR 242.

[13] *Gillick v West Norfolk and Wisbech Area Health Authority* [1986] AC 112, 184 (Scarman LJ) (*Gillick*).

The balance between parental responsibility and the role of the state was summed up by Lady Hale in *Williamson* thus:

> Children have the right to be properly cared for and brought up so that they can fulfil their potential and play their part in society. Their parents have both the primary responsibility and the primary right to do this. The state steps in to regulate the exercise of that responsibility in the interests of children and society as a whole. But 'the child is not the child of the state' and it is important in a free society that parents should be allowed a large measure of autonomy in the way in which they discharge their parental responsibilities.[14]

This view accords with the point made by Ward LJ in *Re A* that this authority 'exist[s] for the performance of their duties and responsibilities to the child' and hence 'must be exercised in the best interests of the child'. In this sense, parental authority is more limited than it is in some of the other countries considered in this book, such as Thailand or China. Once an issue over children is brought to the court, 'overriding control is vested in the court',[15] but parents do have the ability to make decisions on behalf of their child so long as they do so in line with their responsibilities. Baroness Hale, drawing on the United Nations Convention on the Rights of the Child has explained that 'the state's role is to assist the parents in carrying out their responsibilities', but added that the state is also required to 'take appropriate measures to protect the child from all forms of abuse or neglect'.[16] This delicate balance between respecting parental decisions over children and protecting children from harm plays out differently in respect of different issues. The court will be reluctant to rule that a parent's religious upbringing is harming a child, absent clear evidence,[17] but seems much more willing to determine that a decision in relation to medical treatment is a faulty assessment of welfare. No doubt this is in part because the courts will accept the authority of the medical profession in claiming expertise on children's medical welfare, whereas no one has similar standing in relation to religious issues.[18]

III. Two Challenges to Orthodoxy

This long-standing approach was recently subjected to challenge and scrutiny in the context of medical treatment in the *Gard*, *Evans* and *Raqeeb* cases, in two ways. First, what was the extent of the courts' power, and specifically did it extend to preventing a child being taken abroad for alternative treatment if the courts

[14] *R (on the application of Williamson and others) v Secretary of State for Education and Employment and others* [2005] UKHL 15; [2005] 2 All ER 1, [72]; further discussed below.
[15] *Re A (Children)* [2001] 1 Fam 147 (CA); [2001] 2 WLR 480, 178 (Ward LJ).
[16] *The Christian Institute v the Lord Advocate* [2016] UKSC 51, [72].
[17] eg *Re N (A Child: Religion: Jehovah's Witnesses)* [2011] EWHC B26 (Fam).
[18] J Herring, 'Medical Decisions about Children' in J Eekelaar (ed), *Family Law in Britain and American in the New Century* (Leiden, Brill, 2017).

considered this was not in the child's best interests? Second, whether the threshold for judicial intervention in some cases should be higher than the engagement of welfare and best interests, and instead be raised to prevent intervention unless the parents' decision poses a risk of significant harm to the child.

Both challenges arose first in *Gard*, which provided an opportunity to argue for a change to the law because the facts were so unusual. Charlie Gard suffered from mitochondrial DNA depletion syndrome, a progressive condition that had left him unable to move his arms and legs or to breathe unaided. The syndrome also affected his heart, liver and kidneys, had caused him to become deaf and he suffered regular epileptic fits. Following a series of particularly severe fits, he was also severely brain-damaged. The condition was incurable and would inevitably result in his death. His parents wanted to take him to the United States to receive experimental nucleoside therapy, as they felt it might improve his condition. Charlie was being treated at Great Ormond Street Hospital (GOSH), which had initially been happy to try the therapy, but after the severe damage to his brain, took the view that any treatment was now effectively futile. GOSH applied to the court to confirm that would not be in Charlie's best interests to undergo nucleoside therapy and that it could lawfully withdraw life-sustaining treatment. GOSH's application requested that the court make a determination on, amongst other things, whether it was 'lawful, and in Charlie's best interests, for his treating clinicians to provide him with palliative care only' and whether it was 'lawful, and in Charlie's best interests, not to undergo nucleoside therapy provided always that the measures and treatments adopted are the most compatible with maintaining Charlie's dignity'.

The unusual aspect was that although his treating team wanted to stop treatment and support, an alternative treating team in the United States *was* willing to provide experimental treatment to Charlie. Here, then, the dispute was not solely between parents and doctors, but whether parents could change treating teams and, specifically, remove Charlie from the hospital where he was receiving treatment and move him to another country. This case did not present the kind of impasse that generally gives the courts a basis on which to intervene, as parents cannot demand that an unwilling doctor treat their child. It was really a choice between treatments, rather than the kind of intractable dispute courts are usually asked to resolve. Since under English law, doctors cannot be *compelled* to treat,[19] courts are usually just being asked to decide whether it is lawful for them to withdraw treatment (ie confirm that to do so would not be a failure of their care responsibilities). Normally, a decision in favour of the doctors would prevent parents from being able to access the treatment, but in *Gard* the parents were not trying to force GOSH to treat Charlie, they were merely asking for him to be allowed to be transferred to a different hospital in the United States.

[19] Jo Bridgeman has rightly demonstrated that many of these cases can be seen as instances of professional conscience: J Bridgeman, 'Parental Responsibility, Professional Conscience and the Protection of the Court?' in Goold et al (eds) (n 5).

The questions of the limits of parental decision-making authority and the court's jurisdiction were squarely at issue.

The cases of Alfie Evans, Isaiah Haastrup and Tafida Raqeeb that followed took similar form, as all involved applications by the treating hospital for life-sustaining treatment to be withdrawn from a seriously ill child, and some included requests to remove the child to another country for treatment. Each contributed to the highly charged debate over the past few years about whether the courts were right to intervene and take a decision about each child's care, but it was *Gard* in which a direct attempt to alter the orthodox position was made. In all but *Raqeeb*, the court overrode the wishes of the parents and held that the children could not be moved and that continuing with life-sustaining treatment was not in the child's best interests. Only in *Raqeeb* did the court allow the child to be moved to another country (Italy) to allow life-sustaining treatment to continue. The key reason was that, as she was suffering no harm (as she was at best minimally conscious and in no pain), her sanctity of life prevailed and her parents could, in line with their religious beliefs, take her to where she would continue to be kept alive until she died naturally.[20]

The request by the hospital in *Gard* suggests that they were sufficiently concerned about the impact of the experimental treatment on Charlie's welfare that they felt it necessary to seek a determination that to give it would not have been in Charlie's best interests. They were effectively hence also wanting to be sure that they were not required in any sense to *facilitate* Charlie receiving a treatment they felt was not in his best interests. But in asking for this determination, they opened up the question of whether the court could step into a situation and prevent parents from taking up an offer of treatment from a medical professional. This is another aspect of how the case tested the boundaries of the orthodox position, as the court had to clarify the extent of its own jurisdiction to intervene, including whether this extended to preventing Charlie from being moved to another country. *Evans* and *Raqeeb* were even more specifically about this aspect of the courts' power.

A. Extent of the Courts' Authority

Usually, under English law, parents' decisions about *choice* of medical team or hospital are not policed, and they are free to choose between those options available to them. Such choices could, as was the conclusion in *Gard*, mean that a child receives a treatment that is not in his or her best interests. But for the most part, there is the implicit assumption that medical professionals offer treatments that are in a child's interests and if they treat in a way that falls below the *Bolam* standard, they will be negligent.[21] However, the question here was not about the

[20] *Raqeeb v Barts NHS Foundation Trust* [2019] EWHC 2531 (Admin) and [2019] EWHC 2530 (Fam).

[21] *Bolam v Friern Hospital Management Committee* [1957] 1 WLR 583.

treatment itself, but the parents' liberty to choose it amongst the range of options before them.

The Court of Appeal in *Gard* not only held that it had the power to determine whether a treatment that GOSH did not want to (and could not be compelled to) administer was (or was not) in Charlie's best interests, but further implied that it would prevent his parents moving Charlie to obtain the treatment if necessary. In doing so, the court effectively held that it had the power to prevent his parents from making this choice of treatment, that in making a best interests determination this extended to preventing parents from opting for a treatment offered by a responsible medical professional. This is unusual, as the court's authority is more traditionally used merely *to declare* that what the doctors want to do is lawful, not to go further and declare that parents *cannot* accept what is offered. Had the court in *Gard* declared that the option offered by the American doctor was outside the bounds of responsible medical practice (ie outside *Bolam*) the matter would have been different, but it did not. The court arrived at this conclusion via the orthodox best interests threshold. Hence, the current English position is effectively that the court can make a determination on parental *choice* of treatment.

On whether Charlie could be taken out of the country for treatment, the matter did not strictly arise, as GOSH had been given guidance that it need not keep Charlie alive so that he could be moved. McFarlane LJ indicated, however, that he would have been prepared to prevent his being moved:

> If necessary, and one hopes it that the situation will not arise, such an order would be backed up by an injunction in due course; but, if so, it would be an injunction made by the court.[22]

In *Evans*, moving Alfie was much more explicitly dealt with – his parents wanted to take him to Italy for treatment or at least ongoing life support. Mr Justice Hayden was clear in holding that he was refusing the parents' application to 'permit the child's immediate removal to Italy',[23] and the Court of Appeal upheld this decision. In particular, the Court of Appeal rejected the argument that this breached EU free movement law. In the view of McFarlane LJ:

> There can be no derogation from the mandatory requirement to apply the gold standard, namely the best interests of the young person concerned. … To submit, as Mr Coppel does, that in some manner that legally entrenched principle should be eroded or adapted where it is possible to contemplate moving the child for treatment elsewhere is one to my mind which can have no merit at all.[24]

Clearly, both courts considered that if further treatment was not in the child's best interests, then they had the authority to prevent the child being moved to another facility where a different set of doctors would be prepared to continue treatment.

[22] *Yates & Anor v Great Ormond Street Hospital for Children NHS Foundation Trust & Anor* [2017] EWCA Civ 410, [2017] WLR(D) 391, [117].
[23] *Evans* (n 1) [8].
[24] ibid [32].

In the European context, the free movement point is important. It was argued in *Evans* that Alfie had the right to go elsewhere in the EU for treatment, and that to detain him in the UK breached this. The Court of Appeal disagreed, albeit that their treatment of this issue was only cursory. Similar arguments were raised in *Raqeeb*,[25] which concerned whether a young child who was in a minimally conscious state could be moved to Italy, where a hospital was offering to provide ongoing life-sustaining treatment. Counsel for the parents argued that not only had the hospital acted unlawfully in preventing the child from leaving for Italy without considering the impact of this decision on her rights under EU law, but that had the hospital done so, it would have found the interference with her rights to free movement and to receive services in other EU Member States to be unjustifiably interfered with. The High Court rejected this argument. Although it did accept that the hospital had acted unlawfully in failing to take account of the impact of its decision on Tafida's EU rights, MacDonald J nonetheless held that *had* the hospital followed the correct process and considered Tafida's EU law rights, the court would nevertheless have reached the same decision, as such an interference could be justified on public policy grounds and so would not have been contrary to EU law.[26]

In general, what this means is that the English courts consider that the welfare of the child and the protection of his or her best interests affords them the authority to prevent that child being removed to another country, and that this does not constitute an infringement of the child's rights under EU law. Therefore, the English law's limits on parental decisions go beyond merely the court having the power to choose between parent and doctor, and instead prevent parents from accessing the treatment offered by other doctors, in England and abroad. It is interesting to note that in the United States, Francis et al observe that despite the constitutional protection of the right to travel between states, states similarly 'might be permitted to prevent parents from taking their children across state lines to seek to withhold or withdraw medical care in ways that the state might consider medical neglect', though this is a somewhat higher bar than merely where it would not be in the child's best interests to travel.[27]

B. The Threshold for Intervention

The second challenge, posed specifically in *Gard*, was that the threshold for intervention by the courts should be raised. Under the orthodox position, the court can intervene merely if the child's welfare is engaged. In *Gard*, it was argued that if

[25] *Raqeeb v Barts NHS Foundation Trust & Anors* [2019] EWHC 2531 (Admin).

[26] ibid [146].

[27] L Francis, J Botkin and D Diekema, 'Decision-Making on Behalf of Children in the Research and Clinical Context: A United States Perspective', in this book.

judges can decide upon *any* matter relating to a child's welfare and intervene wherever they disagree with the parents' assessment of the child's best interests, this would be an exceptionally large intrusion by the state into the private decisions of parents. Counsel for Charlie Gard's parents put it before the Supreme Court as follows:

> [I]f the State can, without the highest of justification, intrude into so private an area of human life as a joint parental decision made about one's child's upbringing, the scope for protection against state interference afforded by our most basic constitutional values, as well as by Article 8 ECHR, is considerably eroded.[28]

The proposed alternative was that the threshold should be such that parents are the final arbiter in decisions about the medical treatment of a child unless there is a risk that their decision will result in significant harm to the child, similar to that applied in varying forms across Chile,[29] Switzerland,[30] Singapore,[31] and, in practice, in some US states.[32] This argument was unsuccessful in *Gard* and to date the courts have not expressed any intention to make such a reform.

IV. Evaluating the Challenge to Best Interests

At the heart of the challenge to the best interests approach are questions about the legitimate bounds of state involvement in citizens' private lives. The response to the cases that prompted calls for change suggests that, for many people in English society, decisions about very ill children are considered private or the purview of parents alone.[33] For example, many thousands of people protested the hospital's position on Charlie and Alfie's treatment, and a comment from an article about the case of Charlie Gard gives a sense of the tenor of some of the protestors' views:

> No matter how skilled the doctors, this was NOT their decision to make, they should have recommended a course of action, of course, but NEVER ever should have they felt they had the right to impose their wishes over those of the parents.[34]

[28] *In the matter of Charlie Gard* (n 17).

[29] F Lathrop Gomez, 'Decisions About Their Body: Children's Rights and Parental Responsibility in Chile', in this book.

[30] A Buechler, 'Parental Decisions on their Children's Medical Treatment', in this book.

[31] CWL Ho and S Kaur, 'Parental Rights, Best Interests and Significant Harms: Singapore and Malaysia perspectives on Medical Decision-Making on Behalf of Children', in this book.

[32] Francis et al (n 27).

[33] See eg: 'Charlie Gard's Parents Refused Permission to Spend His Last Night at Home Before His Life Support Machine Is Switched Off on Friday' *The Telegraph* (27 June 2017) www.telegraph.co.uk/news/2017/06/29/charlie-gards-parents-refused-permission-spend-last-night-home/. Chris Gard, Charlie's father, has himself argued that 'our parental rights have been stripped away' by the court decisions. See M Robinson et al, 'Devastated Parents of Charlie Gard Spend their Last Night with their Baby and Blast "Heartless" Doctors for Refusing to Let Them Take Him Home to Die Before They Turn Off His Life Support Later Today' *Daily Mail* (30 June 2017) www.dailymail.co.uk/news/article-4653894/Outpouring-grief-worldwide-Baby-Charlie-Gard.html.

[34] 'Charlie Gard's Parents Refused …' ibid.

Both Charlie and Alfie's parents have, with the support of some MPs, begun to lobby for changes to the law. Their aim is, as Steven Woolfe MEP put it, '[to] restore the rights of parents in such decisions'.[35] If successful, the law would be changed such that the court would be permitted to intervene only where the parents' decision exposes their child to a risk of significant harm.[36] These efforts have so far been unsuccessful, but as of October 2018, the Parliamentary Under-Secretary of State for the Department of Health and Social Security had agreed to work on possible future steps.[37] The challenge made both in *Gard* and by proponents for reform of the law rests on the view that parents ought to have the final say over a child's medical care, except to the point where a parent's decision puts the child at risk of significant harm. By reframing the situation so that parents are prima facie final arbiters of what will happen, this position reflects a desire to push back against state involvement and protect the privacy and authority of parental decisions. Similar debates over whether to move to a significant harm threshold have also taken place in the United States.[38]

There are a number of reasons to support a change in English law. One is that parents ought to be given greater authority as decision-makers on behalf of their children. There are good reasons for treating parents as prima facie decision-makers for their children. Parents may be best placed to know what is in their child's interests because they know the child best.[39] Parents are also almost always motivated by love for their child, and so will be making a decision very much focused on what the child needs or what is good for the child. In doing so, they are also well positioned to consider the child's interests in the broadest possible sense, not purely the medical interests. It is also good to give parents latitude in decision-making generally, because supporting parents as far as possible to be decision-makers is likely to support the familial connections that may be vital to their well-being. As Douglas Diekema argues, the family unit is a vital support for children, and this unit is fostered by giving parents autonomy and hence 'sufficient space and freedom from intrusion from others' to flourish.[40] This recognition of the centrality of the family unit is certainly reflected in the legal position of other jurisdictions, including Thailand, Peru and China. Notably, as John Lombard and Lydia Bracken explain, the family is, according to the Irish constitution, 'the natural primary and fundamental unit group of Society', and accordingly a presumption exists in Ireland that the best interests of the child will be met by the marital family.[41]

[35] 'MEP Launching Campaign for 'Alfie's Law' to Give Parents More Say' *ITV News* (26 April 2018) www.itv.com/news/granada/2018-04-26/mep-launching-campaign-for-alfies-law-to-give-parents-more-say/.

[36] The Charlie Gard Foundation, 'Charlie's Law' https://www.thecharliegardfoundation.org/charlies-law/.

[37] HL Deb 15 October 2018, vol 793, col 387.

[38] Francis et al (n 27).

[39] D Diekema, 'Parental Refusals of Medical Treatment: The Harm Principle as Threshold for State Intervention' (2004) 25 *Philosophy of Medical Research and Practice* 243, 244.

[40] ibid.

[41] J Lombard and L Bracken, 'Medical Decision-Making on Behalf of Children in Ireland', in this book.

Those wanting a change in the law clearly feel that the current position does not do enough to foster this kind of respect and freedom. But it can be readily argued that the law as it stands already sufficiently accounts for parental views. As we have seen, the courts routinely emphasise the respect they have for parental decision-making freedom. Taylor also points out that, although the law seems to allow the courts to override parents very easily, this is not the case in practice. The courts regularly express respect for the importance of taking account of parents' views, and give parents a wide margin of discretion, as demonstrated by the recent case of *Raqeeb*, where the court acceded to the parents' requests to take their child abroad for further treatment that accorded with their Muslim beliefs, notwithstanding the evidence that her current medical condition is 'substantially irreversible' and so would not be improved or ameliorated to any great extent.[42] The courts do not lightly intervene, and there are mechanisms for them to resist vexatious requests to override parents. An application for court intervention can only be made where the applicant can demonstrate a genuine interest in the child, regardless of whether the applicant is an individual or a state institution such as an NHS Trust. This allows the courts, Taylor argues, to 'filter out vexatious or unwarranted applications' but provides 'no substantial hurdle to the applicant with genuine welfare concerns'.[43]

In addition, it is true in the English medical system that doctors tend to defer to parents as far as possible, and generally attempt to balance parental autonomy, parental needs and the best interests of the child when deciding how to treat.[44] While medical professionals in England are not as deferential as in some countries discussed (in Thailand and China contributors described a reluctance to challenge parental decisions *even* where they may be harmful),[45] as Dominic Wilkinson points out, doctors generally do not pursue court intervention until they have real concerns that the child will be harmed if the parents' wishes are acceded to.[46] He comments:

> Paediatricians and general practitioners spend a good deal of time counselling parents and encouraging them to make health care decisions for their children that are likely to promote the child's interests. However, if parents make suboptimal decisions, professionals will usually only seek to override parents if what parents have decided poses a real risk of harming the child.[47]

Giles Birchley's empirical research on clinical practice supports this view, demonstrating that clinicians defer to parents to a great extent, but resist at the point

[42] *Raqeeb* (n 25).

[43] Taylor (n 16).

[44] Birchley (n 6).

[45] T Tengaumnuay, 'Parental Authoritarianism and Medical Decision-Making in Thailand: The Need to Limit Parental Authority'; and D Chunyan, 'Medical Decision-Making on Behalf of Children in China: A Multidimensional Analysis of Parental Authoritarianism', both in this book.

[46] Wilkinson (n 7).

[47] ibid.

where the child may be harmed.[48] Practice in the English healthcare system, therefore, affords parents considerable authority, and courts are called upon usually only in situations of intractable disagreement.

Some also argue that a change to a harm threshold would actually be counterproductive. It could be the case that moving to a harm threshold would entail shifting away from an approach that emphasises deciding what is *best for* a child, towards one that explicitly requires the court to demonstrate that it has authority because a parental decision will place that child at risk of harm. Birchley suggests that if judges must evaluate the impact of a parent's decision and then determine whether that decision is likely to harm the child, this could have damaging 'pejorative connotations'.[49] At present, the court's intervention tends to be framed as a mediation in a conflict between parents and medical practitioners, where the court takes the authoritative view on what is best for the child. A shift to a harm threshold would change the character of this approach, rendering it one in which the court must determine whether the quality of the parents' decision means they can be overridden. For parents who are making decisions they think will protect a loved child, deeming them to be choosing a course of action that will harm might be particularly difficult for them to deal with. This concern is aptly summed by Katie Gollop and Sarah Pope, barristers who are often involved in these cases, as follows:

> It's bad enough to have a court finding that what you wanted for your child was not in your child's best interests. It's worse to have a court finding that you have caused your child significant harm.[50]

For those already critical of its adversarial system, this may exacerbate concerns that the approach of England and Wales inappropriately sets people against each other to determine who 'wins'. Certainly this approach can be contrasted with that across some African countries. Moyo notes, for example, that in both South Africa and Botswana attempts are made to 'limit conflict at all costs',[51] and achieve consensus and harmony, thus avoiding this entrenched position.

Given the approach currently taken, we might also think that changing to a harm threshold would not make much difference in practice, beyond employing more overtly judgemental statements about parents' decisions. For, as we have seen, doctors rarely make applications for court interventions unless they think the child will be harmed. The current system arguably de facto operates on a harm threshold basis but avoids the negative associations it would bring to state this openly.

[48] G Birchely, 'The Harm Threshold: A View from the Clinic', in Goold et al (eds) (n 5).

[49] ibid.

[50] Gollop and Pope (n 41).

[51] A Moyo, 'Parental Responsibility and Medical Decision-Making in Southern Africa: A Comparative Analysis of South Africa and Botswana', in this book.

This assumes that it is better to obscure what is really happening. However, the fact that this is the practice already, but the law does not reflect actual practice, might also be a good reason to consider change. There may be situations in which it helps for parents to be given a clear message as to why their decision is being overridden. It might be fairer and in some ways more open and transparent and allow parents to understand their position and enable both parties to have a clear, open, honest debate about why someone other than a parent may decide about their child's treatment in matters as important as whether or not to continue life-sustaining treatment.

Perhaps the strongest reason in favour of moving to a harm threshold is to allow for tolerance of difference of views. England is a multicultural, democratic and largely libertarian society. Ensuring diversity in children's upbringing is essential if that is to continue. As Baroness Hale has noted

> Individual differences are the product of the interplay between the individual person and his upbringing and environment. Different upbringings produce different people. The first thing that a totalitarian regime tries to do is to get at the children, to distance them from the subversive, varied influences of their families, and indoctrinate them in their rulers' view of the world. Within limits, families must be left to bring up their children in their own way.[52]

There are many hard decisions about a child's care that need to be made, and some of these are on questions where there is space for reasonable disagreement. These will very often be questions of *value*, about what is important in life, about what makes a life go well. In the medical context, a good example is the question of whether length or quality of life is more important. Such a question is often one that challenges the courts in cases of this kind. The courts find these difficult precisely because they test our commitment to respect for plurality of values, pitting our commitment to respect for belief against the communal responsibility for the vulnerable in our society. The recent *Raqeeb* case was an example of such a challenge, one in which the court balanced the parents' religious views about sanctity of life against other factors, including whether Tafida would be harmed by being kept on life-sustaining treatment. The court's decision essentially rested on its finding that she would not be harmed, and *therefore* her parents' wishes were followed. Effectively, if not overtly, the approach taken was actually one based on harm and, in doing so, allowed the courts to protect the vulnerable child at the heart of the situation, while having a sound basis on which to allow space for the parents' views when they differed from those of the treating team.[53] That said, the court arrived at this conclusion via a best interests balancing exercised, so the lack of a harm threshold was not an obstacle to the outcome.

[52] *The Christian Institute v the Lord Advocate* [2016] UKSC 51, [73].
[53] See also the arguments for and against moving to a harm threshold: Francis et al (n 27).

V. Conclusion

The English position on decisions about a child's medical care is strongly centred around the child's welfare, and considers this the paramount consideration. Parental views are taken account of, and decisions are generally left to parents, but the court retains the authority to step in where parents might be thought not to be acting in the child's best interests. In doing so, the English approach attempts to balance respect for private and family life with protection of those who are most vulnerable. Over the past thirty years, a substantial body of case-law has built up that offers guidance on how factors are to be balanced, and how the court must consider all sides of a situation. As such, the legal position in England is relatively nuanced and developed, but there remains ongoing debate about whether steps towards reform should be taken.

12

Parental Rights, Best Interests and Significant Harms: Singapore and Malaysia Perspectives on Medical Decision-Making on Behalf of Children

CALVIN WL HO AND SHARON KAUR

I. Introduction

A series of high-profile cases in the UK concerning the withholding and/or withdrawal of medical (and in one case, experimental) interventions for infants recently occurred in close succession, with the decisions in *Gard*,[1] *Evans*[2] and *Haastrup*[3] being the most prominent. These legal tussles have not escaped public attention in Singapore or Malaysia. In the main English-language newspaper in Singapore, for instance, a journalist observed that Singapore has yet to have a test case of desperate parents fighting healthcare professionals in court to prolong treatment for their children, even though the legal requirements are broadly similar in both countries.[4]

As in many other jurisdictions, Singaporean and Malaysian parents (and guardians) are legally required to make decisions in the best interests of children under their care. Healthcare professionals are also under legal and professional obligations to act in the best interests of children who are their patients. When parents (or guardians) and healthcare professionals disagree, English law is clear

[1] *Great Ormond Street Hospital v Yates and Gard* [2017] EWHC 972 (Fam), [2017] 4 WLUK 260.

[2] *Alder Hey Children's NHS Foundation Trust v Mr Thomas Evans, Ms Kate James, Alfie Evans (A Child by his Guardian CAFCASS Legal)* [2018] EWHC 308 (Fam), [2018] 2 FLR 1223.

[3] *Kings College Hospital NHS Foundation Trust v Ms Thomas, Mr Haastrup and Isaiah Haastrup* [2018] EWHC 127 (Fam), [2018] 2 FLR 1028.

[4] J Tai, 'Singapore Yet to See UK-Style Test Case' *Straits Times* (3 June 2018) www.straitstimes.com/singapore/health/singapore-yet-to-see-uk-style-test-case.

that doctors cannot be forced to treat nor can paediatric patients (through their parents or guardians) compel treatments.[5] Although there is no explicit legal or judicial pronouncement, the position that is (particularly in Singapore) endorsed in professional regulations is effectively similar to that in English law. If an agreement cannot ultimately be reached between parents (or guardians) and healthcare professionals, the dispute may be taken to court, as in the UK. In this respect, the courts in Singapore and in Malaysia – like the courts in the UK – will have ultimate say over a child's medical treatment where parents (or guardians) and healthcare professionals cannot agree.

The absence of case-law in Singapore or Malaysia creates an opportunity to examine possible differences in the legal construction and application of best interests and other principles or requirements. In the sections that follow, we consider the following questions in the context of Singapore and Malaysia: (1) What is the appropriate threshold for judicial intervention and its normative basis? (2) What values and considerations do and should inform judicial decisions? Additionally, we broadly consider the extent that judicial responses to these questions are likely to be influenced by social (inclusive of cultural and religious) forces and public perception.

II. Threshold for Judicial Intervention and its Normative Basis

A. Singapore

The Children and Young Persons Act (CYPA) defines a child in section 2 as a person who is below the age of fourteen years.[6] Operative statutory principles are set out in section 3A as follows:

> (a) the parents or guardian of a child or young person are primarily responsible for the care and welfare of the child or young person and they should discharge their responsibilities to promote the welfare of the child or young person; and (b) in all matters relating to the administration or application of this Act, the welfare and best interests of the child or young person shall be the first and paramount consideration.

The term 'best interests' is not explicitly defined, but there is some guidance as to what 'welfare' encompasses. In Part II of the statutes, the subtitle 'Welfare' encapsulates provisions on the care and protection of a child and young person against ill-treatment and various forms of exploitation. Section 4 in particular enumerates

[5] *R (Burke)* [2005] EWCA Civ 1003, [2006] QB 273.

[6] Cap 38 of Singapore, Rev Ed 2001, sso.agc.gov.sg/Act/CYPA1993.

a number of 'harms' that empower the state to intervene in aid of a child or young person in need of care or protection. Notably, these 'harms' include abandonment, neglect, inability to provide care and protection, and ill-treatment by parents or guardians. Ill-treatment is elaborated in section 5(2) as subjecting the child or young person to physical or sexual abuse; or wilfully or unreasonably causing, through any act or omission, the child or young person any unnecessary physical pain, suffering or injury, any emotional injury or any injury to health or development. The failure to provide medical aid by the parents or guardian may be deemed as neglect under section 5(3) of the CYPA.

On its face, the state may appear to have significant discretionary latitude in constraining parental rights, although case-law in Singapore has been consistent that state intervention – particularly where the courts are concerned – should be an avenue of last resort. In *UNB v Child Protector*,[7] an issue was raised as to whether the state should intervene when serious disagreement between parents arises over the parenting of children. The appellant in this case sought to enforce access to her children who were in the care of their father. On an occasion when the children were scheduled to have their overnight access with their mother, they refused to leave their father's car. As the children were displaying post-traumatic stress symptoms, they were admitted into a hospital and were referred to the Child Protection Service (CPS). An interim order for care and protection was obtained from the Youth Court and subsequently endorsed by the District Court. While there were previous allegations of ill-treatment by the mother, they had not been substantiated and no further action was taken in respect of them. The mother appealed against these decisions, which was allowed by the appellate court on the basis that the orders made by the lower courts were not in the children's welfare and best interests. It was concerned that state intervention risked entrenching the status quo at that time of parental conflict. Under these circumstances, the father would be even less likely to cooperate with the mother, and the children's negative perception of the mother might be reinforced, thereby also severely undermining any prospect of restoring the children's relationship with their mother. Of especial relevance to the discussion in this chapter is the court's indication that the state might not intervene just because the child might be suffering from some emotional injury. Rather, the state should only intervene as a last resort. In determining if the court should intervene under the CYPA, it must be considered whether the nature of the risk and the extent of the emotional injury in question justified judicial intervention.[8]

The threshold for judicial intervention in Singapore appears close to that proposed by Auckland and Goold in their analysis of the decisions in *Gard*, *Evans* and *Haastrup*, which is that judicial intervention should be warranted

[7] *UNB v Child Protector* [2018] SGHCF 10 (Debbie Ong J).
[8] ibid [24] and [37].

(on the basis of best interests) when the risk of harm is serious and significant.[9] As they explain:

> Once relations break down or an intractable disagreement arises, as it did in Gard and Evans, whatever words one uses, the point at which there is any thought of judicial intervention is the point at which there is already a view by the treating team that the parents' wishes pose a serious risk of significant harm to the child … doctors often acquiesce to parental requests if they are non-harming and even suboptimal, but they resist (and request judicial support) when there is a risk of harm.[10]

Although a high bar has been set as the threshold for judicial intervention under Singapore law when compared with English law, it is not generally seen as prohibitive or inaccessible. In the public domain, the prospect of judicial intervention has been discussed in the local press from time to time.[11] As a matter of professional practice, having recourse to the courts is explicitly indicated as a means of dispute resolution. A professional guidance document details the decision-making process in the case of vulnerable infants in the following manner.[12] First, comprehensive and objective assessment of an infant patient's medical diagnosis and prognosis must be made, and should be agreed upon by at least two specialists. Parents are recognised as playing a central role in decision-making, and must be provided with sufficient information, including about the treatment options. The guidance makes clear that decision-making should be collaborative, and all members of the multidisciplinary team should have the opportunity to share their insights on values and preferences of the parents, which they may have become aware of while caring for the infant. Consensus in decision-making should be reached through facilitated discussions between the healthcare team and the family. The guidance also notes that differences in opinion may arise in multiple ways, including from within the treating team, within the family, and between the family and the team caring for the patient. The treating team is encouraged to consider seeking a second opinion from in-house clinicians not involved in the care of the patient or external to the neonatal unit concerned. A referral to the hospital ethics committee or involvement of dedicated staff trained in conflict resolution may be made. Where necessary, legal advice may also be sought when differences cannot be resolved in spite of intensive dialogue between the treating team and the family.

Due to the limited availability of relevant case-law in Singapore, professional guidance such as that considered above draw on legal norms in English law that

[9] C Auckland and I Goold 'Parental Rights, Best Interests and Significant Harms: Who Should Have the Final Say Over a Child's Medical Care?' (2019) 78 *Cambridge Law Journal* 287.

[10] ibid 321–22.

[11] M Pang, 'Parents Resisting Urgent Medical Care for Seriously Ill Kids May Face Court Order' *Straits Times* (11 July 2012) ifonlysingaporeans.blogspot.com/2012/07/when-childs-health-is-at-stake.html.

[12] Duke-NUS Medical School and Lience Centre for Palliative Care, *LPLC Guidance on Supportive and Comfort Care in Vulnerable Babies* (2018) 15–17, www.duke-nus.edu.sg/docs/librariesprovider12/neonatal-guidance/guidance-on-supportive-and-comfort-care-in-vulnerable-babies-2018.pdf?sfvrsn=85c94b1d_2.

are likely to be applied by the Singaporean courts. For instance, the framework for practice published by the Royal College of Paediatrics and Child Health has been influential on healthcare practitioners and bioethicists in Singapore.[13] Hence, there is general recognition that: the principle of the sanctity of life is not absolute, and that the right to life is not the same as the right to be kept alive; there is no obligation to give treatment that is futile or burdensome; when individuals ask for treatment that the healthcare professional does not consider to be clinically appropriate for the patient second opinions should be arranged and/or care transferred to another healthcare professional where possible; and life-sustaining treatment can lawfully be withheld for a patient who lacks capacity in circumstances where commencing or continuing such treatment is deemed not to be in their best interests.[14] These legal principles and considerations are implicit in practice guidelines in specific specialties, such as neonatal intensive care, and also embedded in the ethical code and guidelines of healthcare professionals, which have regulatory force in Singapore.[15] A crucial point to be made for the purposes of this chapter is that the requirement of 'best interests' remains the anchoring normative reference (as a matter of law and ethics) for all considerations and practices, as well as for all stakeholders concerned. We shall consider below what 'best interests' could mean, and the other values and considerations that are entailed.

B. Malaysia

The development of Malaysian law is influenced by religious[16] views and values, particularly that of the Islamic faith. Although Malaysia is not an Islamic state,[17] Article 3(1) of the Federal Constitution states that: 'Islam is the religion of the Federation; but other religions may be practised in peace and harmony in any part of the Federation.' A number of provisions in the Penal Code reflect conservative

[13] V Larcher, F Craig, K Bhogal, D Wilkinson and J Brierley on behalf of the Royal College of Paediatrics and Child Health, 'Making Decisions to Limit Treatment in Life-Limiting and Life-Threatening Conditions in Children: A Framework for Practice' (2015) 100 *Archives of Disease in Childhood* S1.

[14] ibid s 19.

[15] Singapore Medical Council, *Ethical Code and Ethical Guidelines* (2016) www.healthprofessionals.gov.sg/docs/librariesprovider2/default-document-library/2016-smc-ethical-code-and-ethical-guidelines---(13sep16).pdf; Singapore Nursing Board, *Code for Nurses and Midwifes* (2018) www.healthprofessionals.gov.sg/docs/librariesprovider4/publications/code-for-nurses-and-midwives-april-2018.pdf.

[16] This is similar to the Israeli position; see R Gilbar, 'Withholding and Withdrawal of Life-Prolonging Treatment from Young Children in Israel', in this book.

[17] While there is some debate as to whether Malaysia is an Islamic state, the Federal Constitution does not specifically recognise Islamic law as being the law of the land. Although the legal system and the courts are primarily secular in nature, there is a separate – although restricted – syariah legal system. The system might best be described as a hybrid legal system. See SS Faruqi, 'The Malaysian Constitution, the Islamic State and Hudud Laws' (2005) *Islam in Southeast Asia: Political, Social and Strategic Challenges for the 21st Century* 256.

religious positions. For example, homosexual acts are criminalised.[18] Abortions are only permitted in cases where there is a risk to the physical or mental health of the mother,[19] and attempted suicide is a crime.[20]

In relation to laws pertaining to welfare of children, the Guardianship of Infants Act 1961 (Revised 1988) ('the Guardianship Act') stipulates in section 3 that: '[T]he guardian of the person of an infant shall have the custody of the infant, and shall be responsible for his support, health and education.' Courts have wide powers under the Guardianship Act to restrict parental access; appoint, restrict or amend the powers of guardians; or make any order in relation to the care or guardianship of an infant. In exercising the powers conferred by the Guardianship Act, the court is required to 'have regard primarily to the welfare of the infant and shall, where the infant has a parent or parents, consider the wishes of such parent or both of them, as the case may be'.[21] There is no further guidance in the legislation as to how the court should determine the welfare of the infant or balance the wishes of a parent against other considerations. Typically, the court has flexed its powers under the Guardianship Act in custody dispute cases. It is difficult to draw any direct lessons from such cases as they are concerned with conflict within the family, whereas *Gard*, *Evans* and *Haastrup* involve disputes between parents and third parties (healthcare providers). However, it is possible to make a number of general observations. First, in cases involving custody disputes and parental access, judges are generally loath to deny parental access unless there are serious welfare concerns.[22] Second, where parental access is denied or restricted, the courts have done so based on the potential for serious harm such as concerns about the medical condition of a child[23] or mistreatment.[24] Therefore, this would indicate that the bar for judicial intervention in the parent–child relationship is fairly high.

The Child Act 2001 may also provide a route for judicial intervention in situations involving conflicts between parents and healthcare providers. This Act was enacted to ensure compliance with Malaysia's obligations under the United Nations Convention on the Rights of the Child (CRC). The Act provides for the protection and care of children as well as imposing legal obligations on parents and family members for the care of their children. Section 17 of the Child Act provides for a number of situations where a child is considered in need of care and protection. Section 17(a)[25] might apply to a situation where parents are insisting that their

[18] ss 377A & 377B Penal Code (Act 547).
[19] s 312 Penal Code (Act 547).
[20] s 309 Penal Code (Act 547).
[21] Guardianship of Infants Act 1961, s 11.
[22] *Melissa Marie Albert v Malcolm Fernandex and another* Appeal [2018] 1LNS 1693.
[23] *Thanalecthimy Batamallai v Vijaya Kumar Kassinathn* [2018] 8 CLJ 61.
[24] *Hoong Wai Kit v Teh Toong Joo*; Boonsri Kanjanawadee [2017] 1 NS 467.
[25] s 17(a) states: 'The child has been or there is substantial risk that the child will be physically injured or emotionally injured or sexually abused by his parent or guardian or a member of his extended family.'

child receive treatment, which the healthcare provider believes is detrimental to the child, whereas section 17(f)[26] would apply in a situation where parents are refusing treatment. Once a child is so designated, the state would have very broad powers to take the child into custody and care for the child. Chapter 2 (sections 18–30) provides for the temporary custody and medical examination and treatment of children in need of care and protection. Healthcare providers regularly rely on the Child Act to provide medical care for abandoned children and prevent parents from refusing necessary conventional treatments for their children.

The fact that the courts have never been asked to intervene in a situation where parents and healthcare providers disagree about a child's treatment options is instructive. Malaysian parents may be reluctant to challenge decisions made by healthcare providers. There is some evidence that parents in most instances defer to recommendations of doctors. A 1999 study on withdrawal and limitation of life-support in paediatric intensive care at the University of Malaya Medical Centre found that families often requested paediatricians to do what was best for their children.[27] A more recent multinational study on resuscitation decisions for extremely preterm infants reported that 72 per cent of Malaysian respondents felt that physicians should make the final decision.[28]

In the past, judges have used both the welfare principle as well as best interests interchangeably as a basis for their decisions. Significantly, as observed above,[29] both these principles may mean very different things and some clarity and consistency in this regard would be very welcome. In a number of recent cases,[30] judges have also acknowledged and drawn from principles of the CRC, particularly Articles 3 and 9, which state that the best interests of the child shall be the consideration for the matters provided therein.

III. Values and Considerations that Inform Judicial Decisions

In the Malaysian context there appears to be a growing acceptance and adoption of the CRC. In recent cases, judges have acknowledged as well as drawn from the CRC. As a state party to the CRC, Malaysia is legally bound by all its provisions

[26] s 17(f) states: 'The child needs to be examined, investigated or treated – (i) for the purpose of restoring or preserving his health; and (ii) his parent or guardian neglects or refuses to have him so examined, investigated or treated.'

[27] AYT Goh, LCS Lum, PWK Chan, F Bakar and BO Chong, 'Withdrawal and Limitation of Life Support in Paediatric Intensive Care' (1999) 80 *Archives of Disease in Childhood* 424.

[28] AM Martinez et al, 'Physician Counselling Practices and Decision-Making for Extremely Preterm Infants in the Pacific Rim' (2005) 41(4) *Journal of Paediatrics and Child Health* 209.

[29] Notably the difference between the welfare and best interests principles in the CYPA in Singapore.

[30] *Indira Gandhi a/p Mutho v Pengarah Jabatan Agama Islam Perak & Ors and other appeals* [2018] 1 MLJ 545; *Lai Meng v Toh Chew Lian* [2012] 8 MLJ 180.

save for Articles 2, 7, 14, 28(1)(a) and 37. In recent cases involving questions of the interpretation of local statutes and policies, and the right of a child to know and be cared for by his or her parents under the CRC, judges have chosen to apply the best interests of the child as a primary consideration (Article 3 CRC) and reject traditional methods of interpretation. In *CAS v MPPL & Anor*,[31] the Court of Appeal noted that:

> [T]he 'supposed' policy reasoning behind s 112 of the Evidence Act in not wanting to illegitimise children ought no longer to be the sole judicial philosophy in light of modern day global advancements in science and international human rights law.

In the case of *Heng Choon Lee & Anor v Wong Choon Ho*,[32] the High Court insisted that despite its reservation, Malaysia 'cannot continue to have policies and laws that run contrary to the intent, purpose and object of the CRC, including the reserved Article 7'.

Singapore acceded to the CRC in October 1995,[33] and the CYPA represents Singapore's commitment to protect and promote the best interests of children in a manner that is consistent with the Convention's principles.[34] As one of four core principles of the CRC, Article 3 requires that the child's best interests must be a primary consideration in all decisions affecting her or him. At least on its face, there are two important differences between the wording of the section 3A of the CYPA and Article 3 of the CRC: (1) CYPA makes reference to best interests as being the 'first and paramount' consideration, whereas CRC states that the 'best interests of the child shall be a primary consideration';[35] and (2) welfare is being used in the former whereas well-being is used in the latter. We consider each of these differences in turn.

The term 'best interests' is not defined in either the CYPA or the CRC. Although the precise meaning of 'best interests' remains elusive, the United Nations Committee on the Rights of the Child ('the CRC Committee') preferred to retain the use of an open-texture term which it considers to have the advantage of flexibility to apply to a great variety of circumstances, contexts and sociocultural factors that are applicable to children.[36] As the CRC Committee explains:

> Determining what is in the best interests of the child should start with an assessment of the specific circumstances that make the child unique. This implies that some elements

[31] *CAS v MPPL & Anor* [2019] CLJ 454.

[32] *Heng Choon Lee & Anor v Wong Choon Ho* [2019] 1 LNS 115.

[33] United Nations General Assembly, Convention on the Rights of the Child (20 November 1989) United Nations Treaty Series vol 1577, 3, www.ohchr.org/en/professionalinterest/pages/crc.aspx.

[34] United Nations Committee on the Rights of the Child, *Consideration of Reports Submitted by States Parties Under Article 44 of the Convention: Singapore*, CRC/C/SGP/4-5 (3 November 2017) www.msf.gov.sg/media-room/Pages/Singapores-fourth-and-fifth-periodic-report-to-the-United-Nations-Committee-on-the-rights-of-the-child.aspx.

[35] ibid, Art 3(1).

[36] United Nations Committee on the Rights of the Child, *General Comment No 14 (2013) on the Right of the Child to Have His or Her Best Interests Taken as a Primary Consideration* (Art 3(1)) CRC/C/GC/14 (29 May 2013) www2.ohchr.org/English/bodies/crc/docs/GC/CRC_C_GC_14_ENG.pdf.

will be used and others will not, and also influences how they will be weighted against each other.[37]

On this basis, it recommends that best interests assessment should include a non-exhaustive and non-hierarchical list of elements.[38] These elements have been set out as follows: the child's view; the child's identity (which the CRC explains as including the child's ethnic, religious, cultural and linguistic background, as well as her or his personality and national origin); preservation of the family environment and maintaining relations; care, protection and safety of the child; situation of vulnerability; the child's right to health; and the child's right to education.[39] As to the provision on best interests being the primary consideration, the CRC Committee explains that the child's best interests may not be considered on the same level as all other considerations.[40] There may be other situations where other interests and rights (such as those of other children, the public or the parents) may come into conflict with those of the child. Resolution of the conflict may require some of these other rights to be given greater weight over those of the child, provided that the final outcome is one that is best for the child. In Singapore, the requirement in the CYPA for best interests to be the 'first and paramount' consideration seems to put the emphasis differently from what the CRC Committee has in mind. Arguably, the CYPA requires the interests of a child to be considered individually and prioritised over and above those of others whose rights may come into conflict with those of the child. There may not ultimately be a substantive difference in terms of parental rights, as parents will still need to show that their preferred course of action, in a context such as that in *Gard*, produces the best outcome for the infant.

Another ambiguous term introduced in Article 3(2) of the CRC is 'well-being', which is not used in the 1959 Declaration of the Rights of the Child and, where Singapore is concerned, has 'welfare' as its corollary in the CYPA. While both terms lack the cachet of 'best interests', they are in relatively common usage in international organisations and in national constitutions and legislation. The use of 'well-being' in close proximity to 'best interests' in the CRC suggests that both terms must mean something different from each other. In this regard, the CRC Committee appears to suggest that, rather than being a criterion for decision-making, well-being denotes an outcome to be achieved, and a measurable outcome. This is consistent with its explanation that children's well-being is intended to be broad, and includes their basic material, physical, educational and emotional needs, as well as the need for affection and safety.[41]

Significantly, in thinking about how judges in Malaysia might determine the best interests of a child in cases such as *Gard* and *Evans*, it is instructive to consider

[37] ibid 12, [49].
[38] ibid 12, [50].
[39] ibid 13–17, [52]–[79].
[40] ibid 10, [36]–[40].
[41] ibid 16, [71].

Gray's assertion (see Chapter 26 below) that the best interests of a child is culture bound. The values that are likely to influence Malaysian judicial decisions would be in keeping with Islamic values, which would place a high value on the sanctity of life. This would be similar to other jurisdictions which are heavily influenced by religious values such as Argentina, Peru and Israel.[42]

From an academic standpoint, child welfare may be broadly understood as putting the focus on child protection and safety, whereas child well-being puts emphasis on development and empowerment.[43] The notion of 'well-being' in particular has been linked to indicators developed by organisations such as UNICEF and OECD to support evaluation and comparison.[44] Others consider differences between well-being and welfare to be more a matter of normative framing, regarding the terms as synonymous depending on contextual requirements.[45] As a practical matter and in a Singaporean context, child welfare is used interchangeably with child well-being, as a published communication by the Director of Social Welfare of the Ministry of Social and Family Development issued to social services practitioners illustrates.[46] In a recent decision on child custody, the Supreme Court of Singapore did not find the need to distinguish between 'best interests' and 'welfare', but it did recognise that both requirements necessitated the consideration of non-exhaustive factors that were set out by an expert body in relation to the contended issue.[47]

As a matter of ethical and professional obligation, medical decision-making in relation to an infant should be undertaken collaboratively between parents (or guardians) and healthcare professionals. There is nothing new in this requirement; a guideline issued by the Ministry of Health in Singapore more than a decade ago provides that opportunities 'shall be provided for parental participation in the NICU [neonatal intensive care unit] in the care of their infant, as the infant's condition permits. Hospital visiting policies shall reflect the principle of reducing parent/infant separation.'[48] However, it also clearly states that the ultimate

[42] See PS Bavio, 'Who Decides the Best Interests of the Child in the End-of-Life Process? A Look at the Peruvian and Argentinian Reality' and Gilbar (n 16), both in this book.

[43] A Ben-Arieh, 'From Child Welfare to Children Well-Being: The Child Indicators Perspective' in SB Kamerman, S Phipps and A Ben-Arieh (eds) *From Child Welfare to Child Well-Being* (Springer, Dordrecht, 2010); AS Jones, T LaLibertie and KN Piescher, 'Defining and Strengthening Child Well-Being in Child Protection' (2015) 54 *Children and Youth Services Review* 57.

[44] OECD, *Doing Better for Children* (1 September 2009) www.oecd-ilibrary.org/social-issues-migration-health/doing-better-for-children_9789264059344-en; LH Lippman, KA Moore and H McIntosh 'Positive Indicators of Child Well-Being: A Conceptual Framework, Measures and Methodological Issues', UNICEF (October 2009) www.unicef-irc.org/publications/580-positive-indicators-of-child-well-being-a-conceptual-framework-measures-and-methodological.html.

[45] D Taylor, 'Wellbeing and Welfare: A Psychosocial Analysis of Being Well and Doing Well Enough' (2011) 40 *Journal of Social Policy* 777–794.

[46] BL Ang, 'Working with Partners for Child Welfare', Office of the Director of Social Welfare, Ministry of Social and Family Development (21 March 2016) www.msf.gov.sg/odsw/social-insights/Pages/2016-Working-with-Partners-for-Child-Welfare.aspx.

[47] *TSF v TSE* [2018] SGCA 49, [9].

[48] Ministry of Health, *Guidelines for Hospitals with Neonatal Intensive Care Service: Regulation 4 of the Private Hospitals and Medical Clinics Regulations* [Cap 248, Rg 1] Sep 2001: Guideline 13.

responsibility for the admission and care of each neonate in the NICU lies with the attending doctor(s).[49] This position has been rearticulated more recently in an article published by a leading neonatologist in Singapore, in which healthcare professionals are reminded that 'the parents' rights should always be respected for they bear the moral and legal responsibilities for their children'.[50] However, healthcare professionals should not be forced to under-treat or over-treat an infant based on their best medical judgement. Beliefs and preconceptions that parents and doctors hold may not be consistent with the best interests of the infant, and conflicts have been noted to arise from a number of sources including language barriers, internal disagreement about treatment options, and inappropriate time to inform about withdrawal of care.[51]

An infant is clearly unable to articulate what is in her or his best interests, whereas the determination of well-being or welfare may be challenging as the preferences and values of the parents or guardians may not be readily ascertained. Some scholars, such as Giles Birchley,[52] have argued for the need for a clear threshold by relying on considerations such as genetic propriety and non-personhood of children as justifications for their parents to make decisions that may involve subjecting their children to some harm. Harm is intrinsic to best interests evaluation, and involves other considerations including notions of dignity.[53] Our discussion above, based on the views of the CRC Committee and on the experiences in Singapore and Malaysia, suggests that it may not be constructive or even sensible to specify a rigid threshold, whether in the form of specific definitions (of 'harms', for instance) or through a specific set of considerations. As Elaine Sutherland observes:[54]

> [I]ndividualised decision-making requires the nuanced application of a range of flexible criteria. That process will always be more difficult than simply employing a bright line rule but, if the price for ensuring tailor-made solutions, suited to the circumstances of the individual child, is a degree of unpredictability, then it is a price worth paying.

Whether in Singapore or in Malaysia, collaborative relationship may imply no absolute threshold beyond what is clearly harmful to the infant (in that there is no reasonable expectation of benefit). In bioethics, this approach to reduce the separation of parents from their sick infant has been referred to as family-centred

[49] ibid, Guideline 4.

[50] TAP Nguyen and LY Ho, 'Review on Neonatal End-of-Life Decision-Making: Medical Authority or Parental Autonomy?' (2013) 22 *Proceedings of Singapore Healthcare* 140, 144.

[51] ibid 145.

[52] G Birchley, 'Charlie Gard and the Weight of Parental Rights to Seek Experimental Treatment' (2018) 44 *Journal of Medical Ethics* 448.

[53] Auckland and Goold (n 9) 322.

[54] E Sutherland, 'Article 3 of the United Nations Convention on the Rights of the Child: The Challenges of Vagueness and Priorities' in E Sutherland and LB Macfarlane (eds) *Implementing Article 3 of the United Nations Convention on the Rights of the Child: Best Interests, Welfare and Well-being* (Cambridge, Cambridge University Press, 2016) 21–50, 49.

(or family-focused) care.[55] Such an approach to care reflects an understanding that sick children are accompanied and supported by parents (or guardians). Caring for children must be holistic in necessarily attending to the needs of their parents (or guardians) as the former's wellbeing cannot be extricated from the relationship with their carers. The application of the best interests standard or considerations of welfare or well-being tends to require a number of factors to be considered, including the infant's apparent experience of the illness or condition; whether the patient appears to be suffering physically or psychologically; the benefits and burdens of each of the treatment options; and the infant's ability to tolerate the treatment.[56] The benefits and burdens in turn depend on the infant's particular interests and also on the experiential and/or developmental consequences of different treatment options. A best interests standard does not require the continuation of efforts to sustain life if it does not confer any physiological benefits and fails to address directly the underlying psychological needs.

IV. Social Forces and Public Perception

Determination of 'best interests' or 'welfare' is not purely confined to considerations of best medical or clinical interests, but includes other cultural, religious, emotional and social factors. The courts are not bound to the clinical assessment of what is in the patient's best interests and will reach their own conclusions on the basis of careful consideration of the evidence before them, ensuring that the best interests and welfare of the child are of paramount consideration. Similar to the courts in the United Kingdom,[57] the courts in Malaysia and Singapore will weigh up the overall advantages and disadvantages of any proposed intervention, and undertake a balancing exercise to determine what the child's best interests are.[58] High-profile cases tend to draw public interest, and where Singapore is concerned, the Chief Justice Mr Sundaresh Menon has indicated that judicial decisions cannot be dictated or determined purely based on what a majority of the population desires.[59] While the judiciary should be aware of public sentiments, its decisions

[55] N Berlinger, B Jennings and SM Wolf, *The Hastings Center Guidelines for Decisions on Life-Sustaining Treatment and Care Near the End of Life: Revised and Expanded Second Edition* (Oxford and New York, Oxford University Press, 2013) 73.

[56] ibid.

[57] See I Goold, C Auckland and J Herring, 'Medical Decision-Making on Behalf of Children in England and Welsh Law: A Child-Centred Best Interests Approach'; and A Brown, '"Parental Rights", "Best Interests" and the Withdrawal of Life-Sustaining Medical Treatment of Children in Scotland: A Lack of Authority', both in this book.

[58] See eg (in Singapore) *BNS v BNT* [2015] 3 SLR 973; *UFZ v UFY* [2018] SGHCF 8.

[59] CC Neo, 'Judicial Decisions Cannot Be Influenced by Public Opinion: Chief Justice' *Today* (21 August 2013) www.todayonline.com/singapore/judicial-decisions-cannot-be-influenced-public-opinion-chief-justice.

must be justified in the public interest and consistent with social values. This point was reiterated more recently by Minister of Home Affairs Mr K Shanmugam.[60]

Malaysia, like Singapore, is a multicultural and multifaith society. Broadly speaking, there are three main ethnic and four main religious groups, namely the Malay, Chinese and Indian ethnic groups; and the Muslim, Buddhist, Hindu and Christian communities. Islam is recognised as the religion of the Federation[61] and the legal system is often referred to as being a hybrid system, being made up of both secular and syariah[62] laws. In general, there is little tension or overlap between the legal systems. However, in a number of situations, the courts have had to navigate a difficult path between the two systems, a task made all the more difficult by social and religious forces. For example, the question of whether after a divorce, a parent can unilaterally convert the children of the marriage into another religion (typically Islam). This thorny issue bedevilled the legal system for decades, until a recent decision by the Federal Court (the highest court in Malaysia).[63] One of the main reasons why the situation remained unresolved was that the secular civil courts were unwilling to claim jurisdiction over what they viewed as a syariah matter even though this left the non-Muslim spouse without recourse to courts of law. Similarly, in 2018, the Federal Court[64] appeared to retreat from directly challenging syariah law when three transgender women were arrested in the state of Negeri Sembilian for cross-dressing. In 2014, the Court of Appeal had overturned an earlier High Court decision and ruled that the syariah law[65] banning cross-dressing was unconstitutional as it violated a number of constitutionally protected fundamental liberties. However, the Federal Court overturned the decision of the Court of Appeal on a purely procedural ground relating to the granting of permission to appear before the court. It would thus appear that in matters which touch on issues relating to religious sensitivities (Islam in particular), the civil courts are unlikely to challenge any position taken by the religious authorities. It would therefore seem likely that conservative religious positions such as sanctity-of-life arguments would be afforded great weight by the courts.

Gollop and Pope argue that the role of a judge should not be simply seen as deciding on a treatment dispute, but to explain why the parents' view or that of the hospital best fits with what is right for the child in a manner that also addresses

[60] RN Charles, 'Public Should Avoid Putting Pressure on Judges in Sentencing: Shanmugam on Annie Ee's case' *Straits Times* (20 December 2017) www.straitstimes.com/singapore/courts-crime/sentence-defendant-gets-must-not-depend-on-how-public-react-during-the-case.

[61] Art 3, Federal Constitution of Malaysia.

[62] 'Syariah' is the Malay spelling of 'sharia', which is a religious law based on the precepts of Islam.

[63] *Indira Gandhi Mutho v Pengarah Jabatan Agama Islam Perak & Ors and other Appeals* [2018] 3 CLJ 145.

[64] *State Government of Negeri Sembilan & Ors v Muhammad Juzaili Bin Mohd Khamis & Ors* [2015] 6 MLJ 736.

[65] s 66 of the Negri Sembilan Shariah Criminal Enactment 1992.

public concerns.[66] Hospital ethics committees, particularly in Singapore, have performed this role, albeit in an institutional setting, and have helped to provide guidance on what actions are ethically justified in the patient's best interests. To some extent, a hospital ethics committee functions like an independent ethics committee as proposed by Wilkinson and Savulescu in the UK context,[67] and 'independence' in the context of Singapore and Malaysia tends to means clinicians and lay-persons who are not involved in the care of the patient concerned. There are limitations to such an approach relative to a formal legal process,[68] but its strengths have also been well noted.[69] Where the *Gard* decision is concerned, Bridgeman argues that the focus should perhaps have been on whether the infant's parents were able to establish that the experimental therapy was a viable alternative therapeutic option.[70] In such instances, caring for the patient may be indistinguishable from child protection, and stigmatisation (of parents or of healthcare professionals) could well go either way. The concern that introducing a significant harm threshold will create problems that include obstruction of consensus building between parents and healthcare providers is not apparent within the Singaporean context.[71] As far as the authors are aware, no parent has considered it necessary to persist with a formal legal challenge, lodge a complaint with the medical council or seek public support in social media. In Singapore, and to a more limited degree in Malaysia, a combination of such ethics committees and complementary arrangements, including the active facilitation of obtaining a second opinion and a mediation mechanism, appear to have been effective in preventing a disagreement from escalating into a full-scale legal battle. However, more could certainly

[66] K Gollop and S Pope, 'Charlie Gard, Alfie Evans and R (A Child): Why a Medical Treatment Significant Harm Test Would Hinder Not Help' *Transparency Project* (28 May 2018) www.transparencyproject.org.uk/charlie-gard-alfie-evans-and-r-a-child-why-a-medical-treatment-significant-harm-test-would-hinder-not-help.

[67] D Wilkinson and J Savulescu, 'Hard Lessons: Learning from the Charlie Gard Case' (2018) 44 *Journal of Medical Ethics* 438.

[68] E Close, L Willmott and BP White, 'Charlie Gard: In Defence of the Law' (2018) 44 *Journal of Medical Ethics* 476.

[69] R Huxtable, 'Clinics, Courtroom or (Specialist) Committee: In the Best Interests of the Critically Ill Child?' (2018) 44 *Journal of Medical Ethics* 471.

[70] J Bridgeman, 'A Threshold of Significant Harm (f)or a Viable Alternative Therapeutic Option?' (2018) 44 *Journal of Medical Ethics* 466.

[71] Vicki Xafis's 'Zone of Parental Discretion' (ZPD) framework (although developed in the context of paediatric decision-making in Australia) better explains clinical practice in Singapore and Malaysia. In this framework, clinicians have a professional and moral duty to strive for the very best clinical decisions for their patients, especially in cases where parents have opted for what clinicians consider to be a less-than-optimal treatment choice. However, the framework also brings to the fore the value of respecting parental autonomy. The practical result is that clinicians are under an obligation to make clear all the facts that support their recommendations. While clinicians ultimately decide on the treatment option, their obligation to explain why one option is supported over another is strongly emphasised. See V Xafis, 'Overruling Parental Decisions in Paediatric Medicine: A Comparison of Diekema's Harm Threshold Framework and the Zone of Parental Discretion Framework' (2017) 12 *Clinical Ethics* 143, 148.

be done to clearly set out considerations that help to identify relevant values and interests for the purposes of decision-making and communication in difficult cases.[72] There are already some initiatives to this effect outside of Singapore and Malaysia,[73] although not yet adapted to our local and institutional needs.

V. Conclusion

The *Gard* decision makes abundantly clear that the proposed experimental treatment offers no realistic chance of helping the child, while also having a real prospect of harming him. In that situation, healthcare professionals have a fundamental ethical obligation to safeguard the interests of the child. Questions of dignity concern not merely the right of parents to decide, but should also account for the rights and interests of others, along with higher-order moral and social values. If a similar case were to be argued before the courts in Singapore or Malaysia, the outcome would not be different from the one in the UK. However, Malaysia and Singapore may differ from the UK in their sociocultural emphasis on family-centred care, and are in this respect culturally similar to Hong Kong, mainland China and Thailand.[74] Healthcare providers are generally respectful of parental autonomy in deciding for their children, and of familial integrity, which court intervention will disrupt. On exceptional occasions when healthcare providers do threaten to take legal action due to real concerns that their paediatric patient will suffer serious harm, our experience has been that parents have tended to relent on their decision.

As we have attempted to show above, the threshold for judicial intervention is a high one. While the prospect of a serious and significant harm is relevant to the determination of this threshold being reached, the therapeutic relationship between the parents (or guardians) and the healthcare profession must have reached the point of irreconcilable differences. The normative basis for judicial intervention must remain firmly grounded in 'best interests' and 'welfare'. As we

[72] G Birchley, 'Harm Is All You Need? Best Interests and Disputes About Parental Decision-Making' (2016) 42 *Journal of Medical Ethics* 111; RJ McDougall, 'Indeterminacy and the Normative Basis of the Harm Threshold for Overriding Parental Decisions: A Response to Birchley' (2016) 42 *Journal of Medical Ethics* 119.

[73] Nuffield Council on Bioethics, 'Disagreements in the Care of Critically Ill Children' (2019) nuffieldbioethics.org/wp-content/uploads/Disagreements-in-the-care-of-critically-ill-children.pdf; D Wilkinson and J Savulescu, *Ethics, Conflict and Medical Treatment of Children: From Disagreement to Dissensus* (London, Elsevier, 2019).

[74] D Cheung, 'Medical Decision-Making on Behalf of Minors: The Hong Kong Context'; D Chunyan, 'Medical Decision-Making on Behalf of Children in China: A Multidimensional Analysis of Parental Authoritarianism'; T Tengaumnuay, 'Parental Authoritarianism and Medical Decision-Making in Thailand: The Need to Limit Parental Authority', all in this book.

have argued, any threshold that applies cannot be an absolute one. Making a best interests determination must be done collaboratively with parents and will require contributions from a multidisciplinary team of suitably qualified professionals. Where disagreement arises, transparent and objective processes, along with child-friendly procedural safeguards, should be in place to enable the involvement of other parties (such as members of the hospital ethics committee and mediators). These may also be means by which broader and legitimate social and/or public concerns can be included.

13

Decisions about their Body: Children's Rights and Parental Responsibility in Chile

FABIOLA LATHROP GÓMEZ

I. Introduction

The exercise of autonomy requires certain personal skills, including a minimum capacity for reflection and connection with one's own feelings, as well as several essential conditions such as having alternatives to choose from and a certain degree of freedom from interference from third parties. Notwithstanding any inadequacies in these capacities or conditions, we attribute normatively a basic autonomy to adults in recognition of their equal moral and political status.[1] But what happens in the case of children and adolescents? The United Nations Convention on the Rights of the Child views them as subjects of rights endowed with personality and progressive autonomy. This conception challenges classic regulations on the expression of the will of underage children in health and family contexts, as well as those referring to relations between parents and children. The models of substitution of will and parental authority have been only gradually replaced by more democratic ones in Latin America.

In Chile, the law, dogmatics and precedent on decision-making on health matters by underage children and possible collisions with the exercise of parental responsibility are inadequate. Moreover, existing regulations are unsystematic and, in many cases, contradictory.[2] Some limited analysis has emerged in the context of judicial proceedings when such issues arise, such as the regulation of emergency

[1] *cf* V Undurraga Valdés, 'Anticoncepción de Emergencia: Autonomía de las Adolescentes y Derechos de sus Padres' (2007) 3 *Anuario de Derechos Humanos, Centro de Derechos Humanos de la Universidad de Chile* 165.

[2] *cf* D Parra Sepúlveda, 'El Consentimiento Informado de Niños, Niñas y Adolescentes en el Ámbito Sanitario' in C Domínguez Hidalgo (comp), *Estudios de Derecho de Familia III* (Santiago de Chile, Thomson Reuters, 2018) 337–39.

contraception or applying laws with a strong value content, but, overall, the situation is particularly lacking when it comes to very young children. Furthermore, precedent does little to provide further analysis in resolving conflicts of this type. As a result, this chapter will address a number of cases and their interpretation by the most informed authorities.

II. Patient Rights and Responsibilities in Chile

Article 17 of Law 20,584 on 'Regulations on the rights and responsibilities of people in the context of actions related to their health care', of 24 April 2012, addresses situations involving serious harm to health or risk of death, as well as the refusal to receive treatment or limit medical efforts. In both cases, the law assigns an important role to ethics committees.

Originally, this legislation included specific regulations for children and adolescents under the age of 18. The Presidential Message that accompanied the original text submitted to Congress for consideration noted that international law recognised children as rights-holders and alluded to respect for their psychological development, cognitive competencies and personal situation.[3] Although such regulations are absent from the final text, the general belief is that one of the principles underpinning this law is respect for underage children.[4]

Existing legislation fully reflects the status of underage minors when referring to questions about competency in decision-making. It is important to note that while minors are not necessarily, nor automatically, deemed incompetent, in our context, in which their autonomy is undervalued, a legal professional could easily claim incompetence. Something similar would probably occur in situations of babies with severe brain damage, such as the cases that inspired this book (*Great Ormond Street Hospital v Yates* [2017] and *Alder Hey Children's NHS Foundation Trust v Evans and James* [2018] EWHC 308 (Fam)).

Furthermore, the legislation is based on the premise that children's representatives are empowered to provide consent in their stead. If the decision of the person whose competency is called into question – or that of his/her representative – puts the patient at risk of serious harm to health or risk of death, which would be prudentially avoidable by following the recommended treatments, the opinion of the establishment's ethics committee shall be sought. The same procedure is to be followed if treatment or medical effort are refused by the individual or his/her representatives. Article 17, subsection 2, second part establishes that if the opinion

[3] Chilean Library of Congress, 'Historia de la Ley 20.584', www.bcn.cl/historiadelaley/fileadmin/file_ley/4579/HLD_4579_37a6259cc0c1dae299a7866489dff0bd.pdf, 5. During discussions a note was made that the Bill failed to 'sufficiently safeguard the rights of parents as regards their children … and that debilitates the family', 37.

[4] A Leiva López, 'La Regulación de la Eutanasia, Según la Ley N° 20.584 Sobre Derechos del Paciente' (2013) XLI *Revista de Derecho de la Pontificia Universidad Católica de Valparaíso* 528.

sought involves the care of minors, the committee must take into account the best interests of the child. This is the sole reference to this principle in the law. So, if the parents' decision puts the child at risk of serious harm, the doctors must refer to an ethics committee, which will determine what course of action is in the child's best interests.

The committee's decision can be appealed to the Court of Appeals for review and consideration. Furthermore, if the treating medical professional disagrees with the decision expressed by the person or his representative, he/she may declare his/her wish not to continue as the person responsible for the treatment, provided that said provider ensures that the responsibility will be taken on by another health professional.

This law solely limits the possibility of ordering involuntary treatments. Thus, if the representative does not agree to carry out the treatment recommended by the committee following the request for review posed by the physician, assuming that the committee has no power to compel such treatment, the only other option provided in the law is to allow the doctor or the committee (the law says 'either') to appeal to the Court of Appeals on behalf of the patient in an effort to secure a court order to proceed with the recommended treatment.[5] But, as in England and Wales, in Chile doctors cannot force them to; the courts can only authorise doctors to provide (or not provide) the treatment.[6]

Some observers have noted that in these cases the committee becomes a mediator for problems that have more to do with mistrust within the family than clinical ethics. While the committee can – and should – give its advice, turning to it should be the exception, not the rule.[7] These situations should primarily be resolved in the context of the doctor–patient relationship extended in these cases to include the patient's relatives.[8] While I agree with this approach for the most part, I disagree in that I believe that the decision is individual and, except when strictly necessary, the people closest to the child (who may not necessarily be family members) should not meddle in it.

[5] J Wilenmann Von Bernath, 'Lesión Punible e Intervención Terapéutica en un Incapaz de Consentir en el Derecho Chileno' (2017) 44 *Revista Chilena de Derecho* 229.

[6] In I Goold, C Auckland and J Herring, 'Medical Decision-Making on Behalf of Children in England and Welsh Law: A Child-Centred Best Interests Approach', in this book. Although there is no law expressly established by this prohibition, the Chilean Code of Medical Ethics establishes that the doctor from whom treatments are requested that go against his/her conscience or his/her clinical conviction may refuse to intervene. In these circumstances, he/she will ensure that another colleague continues to assist the patient, unless it causes serious and immediate damage to health of the patient (Art 20).

[7] In B Gray's chapter ('The Relevance of Cultural Competence to Resolving Disputes in Relation to Medical Decisions for Children') in this book, it is said that a clinician giving a second opinion could either see the role as reanalysing what is in the child's best interests, or they could instead function as a mediator, understanding what had undermined trust and relationships and facilitating the finding of a compromise. Similarly the role of clinical ethics support services vary as to how they approach their task.

[8] F Javier León, 'Información y Consentimiento Informado de Menores de Edad en Chile' (2012) 83 *Revista chilena de pediatría* 114.

Additionally, observers note that ethics committees appear to have powers of review even though it is not clear who the primary decision-making authority is. In addition, regarding the reference to the best interests of the child, although appropriate, it appears to be a particularly indeterminate principle. While establishing a decision by the representative or proxy that specifically allows for the treating physician to challenge such a decision, the regulation of medical challenge and third-party review is clearly contradictory: the challenge is filed with an advisory body lacking enforcement powers with its sole recourse against the recommendations emanating therefrom being the Court of Appeals. An ethics committee, rather than formulating a recommendation, has alternative decision-making powers, ie the power to review the patient's decision – or the parent's decision – and the one submitted by the physician.[9]

III. Latin American Context

In Chile, the opinion and decision of parents are not in general contested by anyone – not society, not government agencies – since it is presumed that the parents know the life history and needs of their child best (except in cases of neglect or serious violation of the child's rights). In the medical field, however, discrepancies may occur more frequently, since it is the doctors who are, in principle, in the best position to determine the most appropriate treatment for the child, insofar as they are trained to make decisions about a patient's health on the basis of scientific criteria. The role of the parents would be to confirm or authorise, through their consent, the decision taken by medical professionals.

However, if the parents and doctors disagree, the law seems to give priority, in principle, to the decision of the parents, unless this puts the child at serious risk. Indeed, as noted above, according to the law, if the decision puts the child at risk of serious harm, the doctors must refer to an ethics committee which will determine what course of action is in the child's best interests. The committee will reason on the basis of the best interests of the child, and not on the basis of parental authority or medical judgement.

In the case of very young children, this situation becomes more complex as they do not have sufficient autonomy to express their own opinions or to give informed consent for the treatment in question. The information that parents can provide about their child, and especially their willingness to care for that child and to provide the best context for successful treatment, are essential to determine the child's chances of improvement. One could say that the physician is best

[9] Wilenmann Von Bernath (n 5) 218. The power of challenge to which this author alludes refers to the fact that it is not the physician who has the capacity/competence/power to decide which medical interventions are carried out on a patient. In the case of children, they have the power because they are the patient; the primary decision falls to the parents.

placed to decide based on the child's clinical needs, but what about the child's best interests overall?

Chilean jurisprudence does not yet reflect cases involving very young children. That said, on 14 May 2009, the Court of Appeals of Valdivia ruled on an unprecedented case having to do with an 11-year-old boy who refused chemotherapy that offered a 40 per cent survival rate.[10] The mother supported her son's decision. The Court noted that:

> [T]he coercive action of the State can be well justified when the refusal of medical treatment of a minor meets the following test: the disease or condition is assuredly curable or holds a high statistical likelihood of cure; and, that does not cause physical or psychological deterioration of the patient in such a fashion that would compromise his essential dignity as a person, or that intolerably affects his quality of life. *If these circumstances occur with respect to a minor and his parents refuse treatment, that refusal shall not be deemed reasonable, in which case it shall fall to the State to intervene to safeguard the life of the child.* The aforesaid notwithstanding, in all other cases absent these conditions, the State must retreat and allow *the family*, with sufficient information provided in the context of the doctor–patient relationship, to make the decision that best suits its *belief system, previous experiences, values, perception of what life is worth living, and understanding of what is best for them to exercise their right 'to live life'*.[11]

In Argentina, the parents of young children always decide for them, in their capacity as legal representatives. But the limit of the parents' decision is the best interests of the child; the state can intervene if that interest is contradicted. Courts in Argentina have heard some cases involving very young children.[12] In 2006, faced with an action brought by the parents of a newborn with trisomy 18 seeking to avoid artificially prolonging his life, the court found that:

> [T]he assessment by third parties in truly extreme situations entails an undue invasion of the sphere of privacy of the persons directly involved – in the case of co-patients – whose decision has been taken in the sphere of conscience and in accordance with reasoned convictions.[13]

[10] Rol 103-2009 FAM.

[11] ibid, Considerando 15 (emphasis added).

[12] Under Art 26 of the Argentine Civil Code, minors exercise their rights through their representatives. However, if they are of sufficient age and maturity, they are recognised as being able to exercise their rights themselves in acts permitted by law. In the case of adolescents between the ages of sixteen and eighteen, the person is considered an adult in matters pertaining to their healthcare. In addition, it is presumed that between the ages of thirteen and sixteen they are able to decide on non-invasive treatments; for invasive treatments that jeopardise their health or pose a serious risk to their life or physical integrity, consent must be given by the parents. (In cases where the parents disagree, medical experts must decide in the best interests of the child, taking into account the consequences for the child's life if the treatment is or is not performed.) It has been noted that, with regard to children under these ages, there is a degree of legal ambiguity due to provisions in the Argentine Constitution and international human rights treaties. (See G Gabriel Carranza and C Elizabeth Zalazar, 'La Autonomía de la Persona Menor de Edad en la Toma de Decisiones Sobre su Propio Cuerpo: Cuerpos Normativos en Argentina' (2019) 36 *Revista de Derecho Privado* 51.

[13] MdCM y NAA Juzgado en lo Correccional N° 4 de Mar del Plata, 27 December 2006.

Although in this case there is no dissent between doctors and parents, the ruling is interesting because it highlights the role of parents in these complex situations. On the other hand, in another case involving the vaccination of very young children, the court ruled that parental refusal should not stand because of the rights of third parties would be compromised, as would the best interests of society overall.[14] Similarly, in a case involving a child under eleven years of age who had suffered from an untreatable chronic neurometabolic condition since the age of three, the court found that the treating physicians should provide palliative care, provide for the child's physical and spiritual comfort, alleviate his suffering and facilitate the quality of his remaining life, but ordered that he not be admitted for invasive treatments. In this regard, the ruling upheld the parent's wishes.[15]

In Colombia, the Constitutional Court has stated that, as a general rule, the parents or legal representatives of children and adolescents must provide authorisation for any medical procedure or treatment. This is known as 'substitute consent'. However, this consent does not represent an absolute power because parents are not in fact able to make all medical decisions on behalf of their children. With regard to the capacity of children and adolescents to make decisions about medical procedures,[16] the Court has ruled that the application of the concept of parental 'substitute consent' varies depending on the age of the child and their intellectual wherewithal. Therefore, such consent will be carry more weight when children are young than when they are closer to the age of majority, for example.[17] The Constitutional Court set important criteria in a 1999 ruling on an eight-year-old child's gender identity case and that test has been reiterated in subsequent decisions.[18] In that case, the Court concluded that since there was no obvious risk that the right to life of the child would be compromised if the sex-reassignment operation was not carried out, the mother could not authorise the surgery and hormonal treatments for her daughter.

The Court found that:

> [T]he importance of family privacy in the development of pluralism has an impact on the ability of judges to exclude parents from making certain medical decisions on behalf of their children. … [I]n the medical field there is also a certain pluralism, since there is no single way of dealing with ailments, so the displacement of parents by state authorities in healthcare decisions about their children should, in principle, be avoided.

Indeed, invoking the principle the Court calls *in dubio pro familia*, the ruling suggests that although the need and urgency of the treatment, its impact and risks,

[14] FS de BÑ y RNS de B Superior Tribunal de Justicia de la Provincia de Jujuy, 12 July 2016.

[15] Juzgado de Familia, Niños y Adolescencia N° 2, Neuquén, 20 March 2016.

[16] T-474-96. Art 14 of Act 23 (1981) provides that: 'A doctor shall not operate on minors, unconscious persons or mentally incompetent persons without the prior authorisation of their parents, guardians or close relatives, unless the urgency of the case requires immediate intervention.'

[17] T-1021-03.

[18] T-551-99, T-692-99, T-1021-03.

and the age and maturity of the child must be taken into account, there is also an element of closure involved that the Court describes as follows:

> If the judge has lingering doubts about the proper decision, such questions must be resolved in favor of the respect for the privacy of the household and, therefore, displacements of parents by state authorities must be minimized.

It should be noted that Colombia is the only Latin American country that regulates child euthanasia. Resolution 825 of 2018, in compliance with a 2017 ruling of the Constitutional Court,[19] regulated the procedure to make the right to die with dignity effective for minors, including conditions for access to the euthanasia. The law recognises the right of children between the ages of six and twelve years with terminal illness or condition to opt for this procedure provided that: (i) they have achieved an exceptional level of neurocognitive and psychological development that allows them to make a free, voluntary, informed and unequivocal decision in the medical field; (ii) their understanding of death reaches the level expected for a child over the age of twelve.[20] In the case of children six years of age or older who have already given their consent in keeping with the law and are unable to repeat it, the substitute consent of the parents shall be admitted.[21]

This regulation is germane because when referring to pediatric palliative care, it states that if the child or adolescent lacks the capacity to make medical decisions, the individual who exercises parental authority or is otherwise responsible for care may refuse treatment and request that the principles of therapeutic proportionality and rationality be observed. They may also deny the application of treatments and clinical interventions that are futile or disproportionate given the patient's condition or that may result in dysthanasia or therapeutic obstinacy. The law also authorises such individuals to refuse paediatric palliative care.[22]

IV. Spotlight on the Children

The treatment afforded to the representative's consent is complex because it depends on politically and ideologically controversial decisions: parental responsibility and the limits that the state may establish for its exercise. In ascertaining the conditions under which adults may intervene on behalf of children, at least two conflicting values are in play: the extent of parental rights vis-a-vis state agency, and the decision-making autonomy granted to minors vis-a-vis their parents.[23]

[19] T-544-17.

[20] Art 3. This resolution suggests that, from the age of twelve, the concept of death 'is linked to the capacity for abstraction from which the understanding is achieved that everyone, including one's self, is going to die, sooner or later. In spite of this, death itself is perceived as very distant; there is a critical period of acceptance and fear of what may happen before [death]' (Art 2, [2],[3],[4]).

[21] Art 11.

[22] Art 6.

[23] Wilenmann Von Bernath (n 5) 224.

In the area of healthcare decisions, it has traditionally been understood that the legal representative is tasked with providing consent on behalf the minor. This tradition is now being replaced thanks to practices that redefine both the relationships between doctors and patients and between family members. In some Latin American countries, including Chile, the wishes of the patient are now included as a core tenet in the practice of medicine. In contrast with that, however, the Roman law model of *patria potestas* has not yet disappeared. The delayed enactment of an array of international instruments due to prolonged dictatorships, among other factors, has hampered the transition towards societies that are more democratic and respectful of the rights of the child across the region. As a result, with rare exceptions – such as we have seen in Argentina[24] – the statutes fail to address the issue of legal representation of the child when his or her most fundamental rights are affected.

To what extent and in what way does a child consent to an intervention or treatment? What role do their parents, legal representatives or caregivers play in this? What role do healthcare professionals play, especially when the patient him/herself refuses consent, is too young to consent, or in cases of a difference of opinion between parents and children? Finally, what role does the state play in these controversies and how does it ensure respect for the rights of the child without disproportionately limiting the rights and responsibilities of parents? All of these questions remain unanswered in Chilean law.

In bioethics,[25] the distinction between beneficence and non-maleficence has been shown to solve many adult issues, but in the case of children it poses a bigger challenge. Very young children do not have their own system of values, nor can they therefore define their own beneficence. On the other hand, the state cannot intervene directly in the determination of a child's value system, pushing him or her towards a type of life or determining the child's idea of good (beneficence). In fact, it can only address the child's non-maleficence. The question then arises as to how to determine the content of beneficence. The issue is one of the so-called 'decisions of substitution'. According to the classic model, substitution decisions were always made by projecting on the legally unfit person what the family, the doctor, the judge or society as a whole considered to be to the benefit of this individual. Today, this is not possible, since society cannot and should not determine the benefit to an individual but, rather, only protect him or her from harm. Some laws provide that such decisions are, in principle, the responsibility of the family. The reason for this is probably that the family is, at its root, a charitable institution. The role of the state is to ensure that parents do not overstep their limits and – under the pretext of promoting the best interests of their children – are not acting to their children's detriment, that is to say, maleficently. The doctor, moreover,

[24] See n 12.
[25] D Gracia, Y Jarabo, N Martín and J Ríos, 'Toma de Decisiones en el Paciente Menor de Edad' (2001) 117 *Medicina Clínica* 183.

should not be the one to define a child's beneficence. Despite deeply rooted traditions granting such power, that approach today must be deemed incorrect.

Therefore, those representatives who have the primary power must act and decide according to the best interests of the child or the adolescent, independent of their own beliefs. What happens if that fails to occur? A well-designed system should regulate the measures professionals can take, such as requesting the intervention of an ethics committee, or alternatively that of a judge. This is especially important for cases of subrogation of the will of very young children: the professional should be particularly attentive to the position of the representatives if it is contrary to the child's best interests.[26]

[26] Factors to consider include: whether the illness or health of the patient will improve with the medical treatment; whether the illness or health will improve without the treatment; whether the benefit the person can expect from the treatment is worth the risks of the treatment; and whether a less restrictive or less invasive treatment could provide the same benefit as the proposed treatment. See S Fernández 'Responsabilidad parental y autonomía progresiva de niñas, niños y adolescentes' in S Fernández (dir), *Tratado de Derechos de Niños, Niñas y adolescentes* Tomo I (Abeledo Perrot Buenos Aires, 2015) 685.

14

Who has the Final Word? On Trust and Legal Uncertainty within the Swedish Healthcare System

PERNILLA LEVINER*

As already mentioned in the introduction, this anthology focuses on the legal issues raised by the English best interests cases of Charlie Gard and Alfie Evans. Overall, these cases raise issues as to the right to decide regarding the treatment of very young, severely ill or seriously injured children where there is disagreement between the treating physician and the parents as to what care measures are appropriate and necessary. Swedish healthcare providers are also inevitably faced with such complicated cases. The world-wide attention the Charlie Gard case attracted created headlines in the Swedish media such as 'Who decides what is a dignified death?'[1] The focus of this chapter is on how similar cases are handled in Sweden, who has the final authority and how is this regulated?

The simple answer to these questions is that we really do not know much more than the little anecdotal information that healthcare providers relate. No similar cases have been tried in a Swedish court and, as will become clear in this chapter, it is also unlikely that such cases would be brought to court due to the lack of such mechanisms in the Swedish legal system. There are no legal regulations specifically governing the right to decide with respect to children in the healthcare system or similar, as found in England, giving the healthcare provider the opportunity to petition a court for authority to decide such issues. The legal question falls back instead on the regulations setting out the authority and discretion of guardians (parents), children's right to health, access to healthcare services, healthcare responsibility as well as society's obligation to intervene to protect children at risk of harm.

* I thank my colleagues Anna-Sara Lind and Moa Kindström Dahlin of Uppsala University and Kavot Zillén of Stockholm University for valuable comments on earlier drafts on this chapter.

[1] 'Vem bestämmer hur en värdig död ser ut?' *Svenska dagbladet* (22 July 2017) www.svd.se/vem-bestammer-hur-en-vardig-dod-ser-ut.

The overall purpose of this chapter is to analyse the lack of legal certainty regarding the right to decide as allocated in terms of the care of seriously ill or seriously injured children under Swedish law. The starting point for the analysis is how children's rights and best interests can be guaranteed as far as possible. The analysis deals with how the right to decide on questions related to the healthcare of children is regulated, the absence of specific regulations, what decisions *can* be taken and by whom, but above all, to underscore the legal gaps and uncertainties and discuss their underlying reasons. These questions are naturally tied to the constitution of the Swedish welfare system – including the healthcare and social services sectors, the overall view and legal tradition when it comes to rights, and other more comprehensive legal-cultural aspects. A discussion is provided in the last section as to possible solutions regarding the right to decide when it comes to healthcare for severely ill children in the Swedish context. This includes reflections as to the roles of the courts and lawyers, and the risks the different legal alternatives entail.

I. Sweden and its Healthcare Regulation Generally

Before analysing the specific issues that are the focus of this chapter, some information about Sweden and its healthcare system and regulation generally is necessary. Sweden is the largest of the five Nordic countries with a population of approximately ten million inhabitants, a population that is generally healthy with a high life expectancy. Sweden is a member of the Council of Europe and has ratified the Convention for the Protection of Human Rights and Fundamental Freedoms (ECHR) and the 1996 Revised European Social Charter, both of which are important in defining the content of the right to health in Sweden. Sweden has also been a Member State of the European Union since 1995, and although EU law does not guarantee a right to healthcare, under certain circumstances it protects the rights of patients to access to healthcare in other Member States, and it should be noted that under the Charter of Fundamental Rights of the European Union there is a right of access to preventive healthcare and the right to benefit from medical treatment under the conditions established by national laws and practices.

Although facing significant challenges today in practice, the Swedish public healthcare sector is founded on the principle of providing good healthcare to everyone on equal conditions. The majority of the healthcare provided is financed through taxation, and the healthcare system is a core part of the universal residence-based welfare system. For children up to eighteen years old, healthcare is free, whereas adults have access to healthcare for a fee, generally considered very low with a fixed maximum per year.[2] The responsibility for healthcare is shared

[2] AS Lind, 'The Right to Health in Sweden' in CM Flood and A Gross (eds), *The Right to Health at the Public/Private Divide: A Global Comparative Study* (Cambridge, Cambridge University Press, 2014); M Hartlev, 'The Raison D'être of Nordic Health Law' in E Rynning and M Hartlev (eds), *Nordic Health Law in a European Context – Welfare State Perspectives on Patients' Rights and Biomedicine* (Malmö, Liber, 2012).

between the state, counties and municipalities. Central state agencies in the healthcare field are the National Board of Health and Welfare (Socialstyrelsen), the Medical Responsibility Board (Hälso- och sjukvårdens ansvarsnämnd) and the Health and Social Care Inspectorate (Inspektionen för vård och omsorg).[3]

Healthcare is mainly governed by the Health and Medical Care Act (2017:30), legislation drafted as a goal-oriented framework law that prescribes the goals of healthcare as good health and care on equal terms for the entire population. This act is supplemented by, among others, the Patient Safety Act (2010:659) and the Patient Act (2014:821). The law in general regulates the responsibility for healthcare but provides only limited rights for patients. Importantly, there are very limited possibilities for patients to appeal decisions as to care received or lack thereof. Thus, the right to healthcare is not justiciable in Sweden, and accordingly, there is little litigation in this area. Healthcare is therefore not 'governed' by the courts but 'only' by supervisory authorities on a more general level. However, health and medical care personnel are liable under criminal law if they commit criminal acts within the framework of their professional practice. These cases are tried in court, but are still very rare.[4]

II. The Requirements of Consensus and Consent in Swedish Healthcare

Fundamental to Swedish healthcare is the premise that it should be based on respect for the patient's self-determination and integrity. Apart from following overall statements in the Instrument of Government (1974:152), one of four constitutional acts in Sweden, as well as the ECHR, this is regulated in section 5:1 of the Health and Medical Care Act. In addition, section 4:1 of the Patient Act also emphasises that the patient's self-determination and integrity must be respected. This requirement entails that healthcare interventions cannot be imposed on individuals other than in an emergency where consent cannot be

[3] The National Board of Health and Welfare is responsible for enacting national guidelines in relation to public and private care providers and developing healthcare through standards-setting procedures. The Medical Responsibility Board is responsible for overseeing the licensing and regulation of health and medical care staff and the Health and Social Care Inspectorate, and has the responsibility of supervising the realisation of health and medical care. The public healthcare sector is also supervised by the Parliamentary Ombudsmen (Justitieombudsmannen).

[4] Lind (n 2) and L Wahlberg, 'Skäligt Straffansvar för Misstag Inom Medicinsk Vård och Behandling?' [2019] *Nordisk Socialrättslig Tidskrift*. However, after a reform in 2010 when the Patient Safety Act came into force, the possibility was discussed that healthcare professionals might be reported and prosecuted at a higher degree than before. This was mentioned as a risk in the preparatory works to this reform – Prop 2009/10:210 Patientsäkerhet och Tillsyn, 96. See also report from the Health and Social Care Inspectorate, Inspektionen för vård och omsorg, Årsredovisning 2017, which indicates that this authority is increasingly reporting healthcare professionals to the police.

obtained, eg if a patient is unconscious and in need of lifesaving care, see section 4:2 and 4:4 of the Patient Act.[5] The Patient Safety Act further clarifies, inter alia, that healthcare staff should carry out their work in accordance with science and well-tested experience, and that the care as far as possible should be designed and implemented in consultation with the patient. Finally, section 8:1 of the Patient Act also ensures patients have access to second opinions for reassessment of their diagnoses, as well as of their treatment options, in accordance with science and well-tested experience (*vetenskap och beprövad erfarenhet*) if the patients' medical conditions pose a serious health threat to their quality of life.[6]

In conclusion, consent is a premise for providing somatic care and there is no legal guardian-like legal institution that covers healthcare for individuals who lack decision-making abilities. Psychiatric care can, under certain circumstances, be imposed on an individual,[7] but what applies when a patient has limited or no decision-making ability when it comes to somatic care is not clear. Nor is it clear what should occur when the healthcare provider and the patient (or the patient's guardian when the question concerns a young child lacking the ability to exercise his/her own self-determination) do not agree.[8] The legal regulations concerning the rights of children and guardians to decide is described below, followed by an examination of the powers of society through the municipal social welfare committees to intervene in situations where the guardians act (or not) in a way that might seriously injure children.

III. Children's Rights and the Discretion of Guardians

Children have the right to healthcare in the same manner as adults. The legal regulations governing healthcare and patients' rights – eg the Health and Medical Care Act and the Patient Act (see above) – naturally also apply to children. A child's right to healthcare is also regulated generally in Article 24 of the UN Convention on the Rights of the Child (CRC). The CRC is applied within Swedish law as it

[5] That somatic care in emergency situations can be given with 'an emergency situation' as a defence against liability is a consequence of the general provision in section 24:4 in the Criminal Code. As for consent in the Swedish healthcare law, see generally E Rynning, *Samtycke till Medicinsk vård och Behandling – En Rättsvetenskaplig Studie* (Uppsala, Iustus, 1994) 44.

[6] For further analysis of the closer meaning and problems connected to the term 'vetenskap och beprövad erfarenhet', see J Garland, 'Testing the Bounds of Lawful Medicine in Sweden: Vetenskap och beprövad erfarenhet as a Legally Enforceable Standard of Care' [2019] *Nordisk Socialrättslig Tidskrift* 79.

[7] See § 3 of the Act on Psychiatric Emergency Care (1991:1128) and MD Dahlin, *Psykiatrirätt: Intressen, rättigheter och principer* (Stockholm, Jure Förlag AB, 2014).

[8] Wahlberg (n 4); Y Litins'ka, *Assessing Capacity to Decide on Medical Treatment: On Human Rights and the Use of Medical Knowledge in the Laws of England, Russia and Sweden* (Department of Law, Uppsala University, 2018).

was ratified by Sweden in 1990. In January 2020, the CRC was incorporated and consequently became Swedish law.[9]

There are certain specific provisions in the national healthcare legislation concerning children. Section 1:8 of the Patient Act states that the best interests of the child must be taken into account when healthcare is provided to children. This can be compared with certain other jurisdictions described and analysed in this book (notably England and Wales, Scotland and Belgium),[10] in which legislation prescribes that healthcare must be provided in the best interests of the child, rather than merely taking these interests into account as in the Swedish legislation. The best interests concept in the Swedish Patient Act is moreover not defined in any more detail under Swedish law, except that both the objective and subjective best interests of the child are to be investigated and taken into account. Section 4:3 of the Patient Act states that a child's views as to current care or treatment should be clarified as far as possible and be assessed in relation to the child's age and maturity. Of particular importance here is the requirement for health and medical care facilities (as well as schools and other institutions dealing with children and families) to notify municipal social welfare committees if there is any concern that a child is not faring well, as regulated in section 5:8 of the Health and Medical Services Act.[11] The majority of child protection cases (see more below) are initiated based on such notifications and the threshold for the duty to report is low. Even unverified information raising concerns around children is to be reported.[12] Considering the absence of decision-making powers for healthcare providers in relation to the care of a child, this duty to report is significant. It is only the social welfare committees, in accordance with their responsibility under social law legislation (described in more detail below), who can intervene to protect children against the will of guardians.

The realisation of a child's rights is primarily the responsibility of parents in their role as legal guardians. According to section 6:2 of the Parental Code (1949:381), parents have a responsibility for their child's personal circumstances and to ensure that their child's needs are met, which includes necessary health and medical care. In order to be able to assert this responsibility, parents have the right and obligation, according to section 6:11 of that same act, to decide on issues relating to their child's personal affairs (eg healthcare activities), taking into account the child's views and wishes successively in line with the child's increasing age and

[9] Prop 2017/18:186 Inkorporering av FN:s Konvention om Barnets Rättigheter. However, the importance of incorporation is unclear – for a discussion on this, see P Leviner, 'Barnkonventionen som Svensk lag – en Diskussion om Utmaningar och Möjligheter för att Förverkliga Barns Rättigheter' (2018) 2 *Förvaltningsrättslig Tidskrift* 287.

[10] I Goold, C Auckland and J Herring, 'Medical Decision-Making on Behalf of Children in England and Welsh Law: A Child-Centred Best Interests Approach'; A Brown, '"Parental Rights", "Best Interests" and the Withdrawal of Life-Sustaining Medical Treatment of Children in Scotland: A Lack of Authority'; I Boone, 'Parental Rights, Best Interests and Significant Harm: Medical Decision-Making on Behalf of Children in Belgium', all in this book.

[11] This section refers to s 14:1 of the Social Services Act (2001:453).

[12] See for more information P Leviner, 'Child Protection Under Swedish Law – Legal Duality and Uncertainty' (2013) 17 *European Journal of Social Work* 206.

development. The issue in focus here is the influence parents have as to which care efforts should be provided when it comes to a child who lacks self-determination. This issue is taken to its limits in cases concerning a gravely ill child, where parents may wish to attempt a treatment that the physician considers not to be in accordance with the child's best interests, such as the use of a drug that can have significant side effects or an uncertain outcome, or where the parents do not want the child to be given a certain type of treatment that the healthcare provider deems necessary and in accordance with the child's best interests.[13]

There is no specific regulation of the right to decide as to the provision of healthcare for a seriously sick or injured child who cannot express wishes, or does not have the ability themselves to consent to or refuse treatment and care. Assessment then falls back on the regulations in the Parental Code. In accordance with the above-mentioned provision in section 6:11, the main rule is that the child's guardians decide as to the care the child should or should not receive. It is thus the parents – in any case as long as the child is so young that they cannot express their own will – who represent the child and have the mandate to seek care, and also can accept or reject any healthcare offered.[14] Parents thus have far-reaching authority even though section 6:13a of the Parental Code clearly states that certain types of treatment, though not somatic care, under certain conditions and with the approval of the social welfare committee, can be provided with the consent of only *one* parent. Despite this, it must be concluded that parental rights are strong. But are they so strong that they can trump the assessment of healthcare providers in questions concerning the type of healthcare a child needs?

Unlike some other countries described in this book, eg England and Wales,[15] healthcare providers in Sweden cannot petition courts to make decisions on issues relating to the somatic care of children (or adults). This indicates that it is the parents who have the final word. But this is still not entirely self-evident. As described below in more detail, society – through the municipal social welfare committees – has special and ultimate responsibility for children and young persons, and has the power to intervene in situations where parents act (or not) in a way that risks seriously injuring children. The question raised is whether this legal mechanism is sufficient and appropriate to protect the rights of children in such difficult situations as are the focus of this book.

[13] With respect to the right to decide for older children to be provided with psychiatric care, see MK Dahlin, 'I Gränslandet Mellan Social Omsorg och Hälso- och Sjukvård' in P Leviner and T Lundström (eds), *Tvångsvård av Barn och Unga: Rättigheter, Utmaningar och Gränszoner* (Wolters Kluwer, 2017); MK Dahlin, 'Att Tvinga ett Barn – Om Barns Rättigheter i Hälso- och Sjukvården och Behovet av en Tydligare Tvångsvårdslagstiftning' (2016) 2 *Förvaltningsrättslig Tidskrift* 245. See also J Garland, *On Science, Law, and Medicine: The Case of Gender-"Normalizing" Interventions on Children Diagnosed as Different in Sex Development* (Uppsala, Uppsala University Press, 2016), comparing medical law in Sweden and the US dealing with medical interventions on children diagnosed as different in their sex development.

[14] See E Rynning, 'Barnens Rätt i Vården – Juridiska Aspekter' in M Söderbäck (ed), *Barn och Ungas Rätt i Vården* (Stockholm, Allmänna Barnhusets Skriftserie, 2010).

[15] Goold et al (n 10).

IV. The Municipal Social Welfare Committee's Ultimate Responsibility for Children – An Inadequate 'Solution'

The responsibility for society to intervene to protect a child where there is a risk that the child will be seriously harmed, which generally follows from Article 19 of the CRC, is governed in Swedish law under the Social Services Act (2001:453) and by the Act (1990:52) on the care of young persons (LVU). In Swedish law, the municipalities,[16] through their social welfare committees and social services administration, have been given the ultimate responsibility for supporting and protecting children and young persons. Section 5:1 of the Social Services Act states that this responsibility includes an obligation to investigate whether different types of actions are needed and grants the authority to place children outside the home if the child's best interests demand this. When the situation of a child or young person is very serious, the social services can make an exception to the primary rule that interventions should be made on a voluntary basis, and intervene against the will of the guardians (and the child) in order to provide necessary support and protection. Such coercive measures may be necessary due to deficiencies in the guardian's caring capacity, as well as in the home environment, and/or because of destructive behaviour by the child or young person. While the child is in care, the social services have the right to make decisions about questions relating to health-care interventions.

The focus here, of course, is the parent's caring ability, or otherwise expressed, deficiencies in care. In order for a social welfare committee to be able to make a decision on petitioning for non-voluntary interventions, parental abuse, neglect or other deficiencies in care must pose a significant risk to the child's health or development. The legislative preparatory works (relied on heavily in the Swedish legal system) for the LVU emphasize that the risk must be serious and significant. Concrete circumstances indicating a risk of harm must therefore exist.[17] In order to intervene with the support of the LVU, a social welfare committee needs also to be able to show that voluntary efforts are not sufficient or possible. This can be seen as an expression of the strong consensus paradigm in Swedish law.[18] Only a social welfare committee has the authority to decide to petition for intervention with the support of the LVU, and a committee also has the power to intervene acutely for

[16] There are 290 municipalities in Sweden.

[17] Prop 1989/90:28 Vård i visa fall av barn och ungdomar, p 63 and 107. This threshold seems to be the same as the law in England and Wales, under s 31 of the Children Act 1989, regarding when the local authorities can take children into care. See Goold et al (n 10).

[18] P Leviner, 'Samtyckeskonstruktionen i LVU – En Analys av Gränsdragningen Mellan Frivillighet och Tvång, Grundantaganden om Människans Autonomi Samt Barns Begränsade Självbestämmanderätt' in Leviner and Lundström (eds) (n 13).

immediate care (by emergency orders). Both such acute interventions and petitions for care are decided by an administrative court under the LVU.

A central question here is if compulsory LVU interventions are possible in situations where parents and healthcare providers do not agree as to what care is in the child's best interests? As stated above, healthcare providers do not have the opportunity to petition for the authority to decide on the medical care initiatives that are to be carried out or withheld. In addition, a social welfare committee cannot petition for LVU interventions only for the purpose of being granted authority to decide on medical care without the committee showing that the parents' attitude to healthcare for their child demonstrates deficiencies in care that entail an overall significant risk for the child. This is not a situation that is explicitly addressed under the law or its legislative preparatory works and no similar cases have been tested in the Swedish administrative courts, at least not at the highest levels. The LVU and its requirements simply do not address this type of care deficiency, but rather other types of harm in the home such as abuse, neglect, exploitation, etc.

As mentioned above, a social welfare committee can place children under 'immediate care', but when assessing the legality of such acute actions, it must be shown that it is likely that there is a need for continued care with the support of the law; in other words, that there are serious deficiencies in care that require the child to be placed outside the home on a longer-term basis. To take a child into involuntary custody 'simply' to provide short-term medical care that the guardians oppose is therefore questionable. In situations such as those addressed in this book, ie severely ill children whose guardians advocate a care other than that which the healthcare provider considers to be adequate, and which often can be assumed to be longer term in nature, the question is whether this can be considered a deficiency in care serious enough to be governed by the LVU.

In summary, the LVU is not adapted to be applied in situations such as those that are the focus here. It is doubtful whether a social welfare committee would prevail in an argument that the conditions for intervention with the support of the LVU are fulfilled in a case involving a longer period. As far as is known, no case has been tried in Sweden where the guardians want to give their child medical care that differs from that recommended by healthcare providers. Neither is it known how these issues are actually resolved in those concrete situations that must undoubtedly have arisen even in Swedish healthcare.[19]

[19] There are guidelines in some regions in Sweden for how to handle difficult situations such as those here dealing with, for example, blood transfusions for children of Jehovah's Witnesses, eg from the Region Östergötland, see vardgivarwebb.regionostergotland.se/Startsida/PM-medicinska-o-vardadm/PM-dokument/Barn--och-Kvinnocentrum/Barn--och-ungdomsklinikerna-i-Ostergotland/Lansovergripande-Medicinska-PM/Jehovas-vittnen.

V. The Trust and Consensus Paradigm as an Explanation for the Regulatory Gap

The focus here has been on who actually has the right to decide when it comes to the provision of healthcare for severely ill or seriously injured young children. Issues raised include whether parents can and should decide with respect to their child's life and death, even in opposition to the healthcare provider's assessment, whether lawyers and courts should determine who should decide or whether it is a purely medical issue that the physician in the role of expert should be able to decide. A central issue, at least when it comes to older children, is also when a child should decide. And a further complication is how a judge should assess the will of very young children, including expressions of will that may not be verbal. And ultimately: what really is in the best interests of a child? These questions arise in different ways in all societies and legal systems. However, as seen in this book, different systems have different legal solutions, or at least attempts, to solve the problematic issues that arise.[20] At times – as in the Swedish system – there is no legal solution, which perhaps is because there has been resistance to seeing these types of issues as legal in the first place. The issue has simply been left to the healthcare system to resolve.

Why is this the case, and is this 'solution' appropriate? The simple explanation to why is plausibly that it depends on how we in Sweden traditionally view rights in the healthcare sector where the responsibility has been placed on the healthcare providers rather than on creating legally enforceable rights for individual patients.[21] This in turn can be explained by the fact that Sweden, at least historically, has been a society in which residents have a high degree of trust both in each other and in public institutions.[22] Historians Henrik Berggren and Lars Trädgårdh have coined the term 'Swedish state individualism', which describes the unusually strong role of the individual in Sweden.[23] In contrast to many other countries – see, for example, the chapters in this book describing the situations

[20] For further discussion, see K Zillén, J Garland and S Slokenberga, *The Rights of Children in Biomedicine: Challenges Posed by Scientific Advances and Uncertainties* (Strasbourg, Council of Europe, 2017) in which potential areas of heightened concern for the rights of children that may be unfavourably affected by scientific advances and uncertainties in biomedicine are identified, analysed and discussed. The report provides illustrations of the diversity of problems generated by biomedical developments, including the expanded use of certain biomedical procedures, emerging technologies and innovative therapies. It also addresses the uncertain risks to children through the continuation of longstanding biomedical practices that lack sufficient scientific support.

[21] Lind (n 2).

[22] H Berggren and L Trägårdh, *Är Svensken Människa? – Gemenskap och Oberoende i det Moderna Sverige* 2nd edn (Stockholm, Nordstedts, 2015); E Ortiz-Ospina and M Roser, 'Trust' (2016) ourworldindata.org/trust.

[23] Berggren and Trägårdh (n 22).

in China and Hong Kong[24] – in Sweden the family is not considered the most important social unit. Instead, the individual holds a clear and independent relationship with the state and authorities, and this relationship is built on mutual trust. The degree of confidence may be particularly strong for doctors who traditionally have been respected as a profession, and there has been a strong feeling that 'doctor knows best'. This in itself may seem to be 'conflict-solving', but possibly with a patronising undertone that transforms this into 'conflict-burying'. In addition, in line with the Swedish state individualism and the described mutual trust between individuals and public institutions, a 'consensus paradigm' exists, whereby authorities also have confidence that parents, with government support (parental courses, etc), should be able to make the best decisions for their children. This generally means that a need for a legal conflict resolution model has not been identified, but rather the approach (if any) has been that different views with respect to healthcare and other efforts by authorities should be resolved in consultation and with consensus.

The legal regulations, as noted above, clearly give expression to this spirit of consensus. This emphasis on consensus, however, may be hiding the fact that healthcare providers can have too much power, and that the rights of parents can be too strong. It may be that parents are deferring to healthcare providers, or alternatively, that decisions about treatment are made 'in consensus' without doctors presenting other justifiable options for parents to consider. If justifiable treatment options are not presented to parents, ie doctors misuse their knowledge and power advantage, consent to treatment cannot be considered informed, which of course is a problem in itself. Conversely, it may also be the case that healthcare providers defer to the will of parents without necessarily having the best interests of the child at stake. The consensus paradigm consequently can conceal coercion that should possibly be tested legally, or a child's right to care in accordance with science and well-tested experience may take second place in situations where parents claim that their child should receive other treatment.[25]

We do not know very much about how such cases in Sweden really arise and how questions about the provision of healthcare are resolved from a legal perspective. These issues are relegated to the general regulations concerning healthcare responsibilities, the authority of parents, children's rights and society's duty to intervene to protect children who are at risk of being harmed. No regulations specifically address disagreement and the right to decide with respect to severely ill young children in healthcare. It is implausible that similar situations do not arise in Sweden, even if perhaps these are not as polarised as the English cases, but as stated, to date there are no known court cases or agency decisions concerning these issues.

[24] D Cheung, 'Medical Decision-Making on Behalf of Minors: The Hong Kong Context'; and D Chunyan, 'Medical Decision-Making on Behalf of Children in China: A Multidimensional Analysis of Parental Authoritarianism', both in this book.

[25] For this development, see Leviner (n 18) and P Leviner, *Rättsliga Dilemman i Socialtjänstens Barnskyddsarbete* (Stockholm, Jure Förlag AB, 2011).

VI. Who should have the Final Word?

Do we need clarifications and opportunities for judicial review in Sweden? Who ought to have the final word and authority – parents, doctors or lawyers through the courts? Or should the opportunities for social welfare committees to intervene be expanded to cover more clearly situations such as those discussed here?

A possible model would be to appoint a specific legal representative for the child when there is disagreement, and enable this representative to make decisions about care instead of the parents.[26] But this model would bring with it questions about what competence and mandate such a representative should have. And what about the rights of children? When children themselves are considered to have the capacity for decision-making – which can be more frequent and earlier than adults often envision – there is in my opinion no doubt that their wishes should be respected to a very high degree.[27] But when it comes to very young children who cannot express their will in a way that ought to be considered, who should then decide?

Under the Swedish legal system today there is both the undesirable risk of concealed coercion by healthcare providers, where parents are simply persuaded or 'highly motivated' to defer to the doctors as to what treatment is most appropriate and reasonable in a difficult situation. This could often give rise to such a restriction on the rights of parents and children to private and family life that it should require judicial review. It might also be that the 'Swedish way' to solve, and sometimes conceal conflicts, is challenged in a society which is now more pluralistic and 'multicultural' and in which trust in authorities – traditionally very strong in Sweden – cannot be taken for granted. In parallel with these strong arguments for introducing some kind of judicial review in Sweden, it can be questioned whether different views on what medical care should be given to an individual is a legal issue that should be solved by lawyers; or rather a question of different views on the treatment of a very sick child entailing a crisis situation for the family. Even if a court is given the mandate to make decisions about these matters, this basically becomes a question of assessing medical expertise and reviewing the evidence about the different options. The question of who should decide in such a situation is difficult and definitely has philosophical and ethical dimensions. Hard legal questions and problems seldom have simple solutions.

Both the fact that medical treatment is getting more advanced, leading to healthcare being able to save more lives, etc, and because society is changing in a way that challenges the Swedish consensus paradigm, it seems probable that more complex legal and practical questions will arise within the healthcare sector. An alternative to the currently unregulated situation in Sweden – which may be

[26] SOU 2015:80 Stöd och Hjälp till Vuxna Vidställningstaganden till Vård, Omsorg och Forskning.

[27] See the Children Autonomy Principle suggested by Aoife Daly, see A Daly, *Children, Autonomy and the Courts – Beyond the Right to be Heard*, vol III (Leiden, Martinus Nijhoff, 2018).

concealing or burying conflicts – could be to clarify the routines regarding second opinions and codes of conduct in healthcare, as well as creating opportunities to refer questions to a legal council consisting of doctors, lawyers and those well versed in ethics. Another option may be to extend and better define opportunities for social welfare committees to intervene in place of parents and decide on specific issues of medical care without the need to place a child in care. There is a need for more research in the Swedish context – both legal, including soft law such as code of conducts, and empirical, looking at how situations such as those present in the Charlie Gard case are resolved in Sweden? There are no doubts that a clarification of the rights of children in such situations, as well as how the child's wishes should be handled and assessed, is necessary.

15

Medical Decision-Making on Behalf of Children in Ireland

LYDIA BRACKEN AND JOHN LOMBARD

I. Introduction

The medical treatment and care provided by neonatology and paediatrics has advanced to the point where viability can be extended further than ever before, and there is a greater capacity to prolong the life of the child. Although advances in medical technology are to be welcomed, they also raise questions surrounding the appropriateness of medical intervention and can lead parents to falsely believe that actual or potential advances in treatment will secure an improved outcome. It follows that decision-making in this context remains clinically, legally and ethically challenging. Yet, there is scant legal authority to address these issues in Ireland. Only a handful of relevant cases have reached the Irish courts and there is a paucity of pertinent professional guidelines. Moreover, the codes of conduct that are in place tend to address end-of-life decisions from the perspective of an adult patient, thereby failing to reflect the unique position of the infant. Ireland's constitutional framework is also a defining feature in parental decision-making and, in many ways, serves to buttress the adult-centred provision of care. Although Article 42A of the Irish Constitution specifically recognises the rights of children, this Article must be read alongside Articles 41 and 42. The latter Articles recognise the special position of the family and give parents robust decision-making powers vis-a-vis their children. Irish legislation and professional standards are constrained by the constitutional framework, and the judiciary must always remain cognisant of parental rights in the cases that come before the Irish courts.

This chapter explores decision-making on behalf of children in Ireland over the course of three substantive sections. The first section examines the influence of the Irish Constitution and draws out the threshold for state intervention in parental decision-making. The second section considers the cases of *SR (A ward of court)*[1] and *An Irish Hospital v RF*.[2] These cases demonstrate the application of the

[1] *SR (a Minor and a Ward of Court): An Irish Hospital v RH and J McG* [2012] 1 IR 305.
[2] *An Irish Hospital v RF* [2015] 2 IR 377.

best interests assessment and highlight the influence of substituted judgment. The third section outlines the professional guidelines and codes of conduct that shape healthcare decision-making in the jurisdiction.

II. Background: Birth Rate and Decision-Making

In 2018, there were a total of 61,016 births in Ireland, 1,037 fewer births compared with 2017. There are 300 neonatal cots across the country, comprising 193 special-care cots, 52 high-dependency cots and 55 intensive-care cots.[3] There are over 11,000 neonatal admissions in Ireland each year. Each one of these admissions requires the making of healthcare decisions, interaction between parents/guardians and healthcare professionals, and the balancing of a variety of considerations.

In a report of the National Clinical Programme for Paediatrics and Neonatology it was noted that there are two categories of end-of-life decisions in neonatology. The first decision is about the initiation of resuscitative care at birth. The second decision is whether care is to be withdrawn after a period of intensive care. In neonatal intensive-care units, 62 per cent of deaths were due to withdrawal of care, 20 per cent to withholding treatment, and 18 per cent occurred while the infant was receiving full neonatal intensive care.[4] It should be noted that these figures are illustrative of neonatology alone and do not capture the broader ambit of decision-making for older children. In any case, this level of decision-making underlines the importance of the legal framework in this area.

III. The Irish Constitution: The Role of Parents

The Irish Constitution is the highest-ranking domestic source of law in Ireland. As a result, the validity of all other sources of law depend on compliance with the Constitution. It is necessary, therefore, to examine the constitutional legal framework as it relates to children and to the family to fully understand the nuances of parental decision-making and the limits of state intervention in this jurisdiction.

Article 42A of the Irish Constitution requires the State to recognise and affirm 'the natural and imprescriptible rights of all children' and 'as far as practicable, by its laws protect and vindicate those rights'. This Article was signed into law on 28 April 2015 and provides for express constitutional protection of the rights of the child for the first time in Ireland. Prior to the introduction of Article 42A, children's rights were largely subsumed into the rights of the family as a result of Articles 41 and 42 of the Irish Constitution. Indeed, notwithstanding the existence

[3] National Clinical Programme for Paediatrics and Neonatology, 'Model of Care for Neonatal Services in Ireland' (Health Service Executive, 2015) 14.

[4] ibid 21.

of Article 42A, the latter Articles continue to dictate the legal framework in many areas of law, including medical decision-making. The Irish courts have long recognised that, pursuant to these Articles, parents have primary responsibility for their children and that the best interests of the child will be met within the marital family, unless the case is an exceptional one that meets the high threshold for State intervention. Therefore, although Article 42A recognises the independent rights of the child, the child's rights continue to be interpreted within the existing constitutional framework.[5]

Articles 41 and 42 of the Irish Constitution protect the rights of the family. Article 41.1.1° recognises the family as 'the natural primary and fundamental unit group of Society, and as a moral institution possessing inalienable and imprescriptible rights, antecedent and superior to all positive law', while Article 41.1.2° guarantees 'to protect the Family in its constitution and authority, as the necessary basis of social order and as indispensable to the welfare of the Nation and the State'.[6] The 'Family' referred to in Article 41 is that which is based on marriage. Article 42 is entitled 'Education'. It is concerned will all aspects of a child's education by his or her parents, not merely his or her academic schooling. This is clear from Article 42.1, which provides that:

> The State acknowledges that the primary and natural educator of the child is the Family and guarantees to respect the inalienable right and duty of parents to provide, according to their means, for the religious and moral, intellectual, physical and social education of their children.

Articles 41 and 42 provide strong protections for the family and the Irish courts have found that the effect of the Articles is to create a presumption that the best interests of the child will be met by the marital family. Thus, decisions made by married parents about their children must be respected unless the threshold for state intervention is met, that is where the parents fail in their duty towards the child 'to such extent that the safety or welfare of any of their children is likely to be prejudicially affected'.[7]

The presumption that the welfare of the child will be met by the marital family was applied in a medical context in *North Western Health Board v HW*.[8] In this case, married parents had refused to give their consent to allow a PKU heel-prick test to be administered to their child.[9] This test checks for a range of inheritable conditions, and is administered by a blood test via a needle prick to the baby's heel. Following the parents' refusal, the Health Board applied for an order to take the child temporarily into State care so that the procedure could be performed.

[5] For a general overview of the constitutional framework as it relates to children, see L Bracken, *Child Law in Ireland* (Dublin, Clarus Press, 2018) 33–43.

[6] Bunreacht na hÉireann, Arts 41.1.1° and 41.1.2°.

[7] Bunreacht na hÉireann, Art 42A.2.1°.

[8] *North Western Health Board v HW* [2001] 3 IR 622.

[9] The phenylketonuria (PKU) test is used to check for a range of inherited conditions and is usually carried out 3–5 days after birth when a small blood sample is taken via a needle prick to the baby's heel.

This request was denied by the Supreme Court on the basis that the case did not meet the threshold to displace the presumption in favour of the marital family. The Court noted that the Constitution accords a primacy to the parents and that the courts could not interfere with their decision unless the case was an 'exceptional' one so as to displace the presumption in accordance with the now-deleted Article 42.5 of the Constitution.[10]

Article 42A.2.1° has now altered the standard for State intervention in family life. The presumption in favour of the marital family still applies but may now be displaced in 'exceptional cases' where the parents have failed in their duty towards the child 'to such extent that the safety or welfare of any of their children is likely to be prejudicially affected'. Previously, the State could only intervene 'where the parents for physical or moral reasons fail[ed] in their duty towards their children'.[11] The full impact of the amended threshold has yet to be seen but it seems unlikely that the new standard will lead to a dramatic change in the judicial approach to parental decision-making. Under Article 42A.2.1°, the case must still be 'exceptional' to displace the presumption. Hence, it has been noted that

> cases such as *North Western Health Board v HW* would probably have the same outcome because a refusal to consent to a PKU test arguably does not amount to an 'exceptional' case nor one that is 'likely' to prejudicially affect the child's welfare.[12]

The discussion above demonstrates that married parents can refuse medical treatment for their children in all but the most exceptional of cases. This means that where there is a dispute between the medical profession and the parents as to the treatment of the child, the medical profession will often have little choice but to bow to the parent's decision or to seek judicial intervention. In line with the constitutional framework, court orders are only sought in the most serious of cases, where there is a dispute as to the best course of action for the child. When the cases reach the courts, the judiciary is also constrained by the constitutional framework. Case-law such as *North Western Health Board v HW* demonstrates that the presumption as to the welfare of the child is the primary consideration for Irish courts in cases concerning the marital family, which in turn impedes individualised consideration of the child's best interests and independent rights.[13] This situation stands in marked contrast to the English and Scottish approaches, where, as discussed in this book by Goold, Herring and Auckland and Brown respectively, the courts are much less deferential to parental decisions in their application of the best interests test.

By contrast, the constitutional presumption in Ireland as to the welfare of the child does not apply where the parents are unmarried; it only arises in cases

[10] Art 42.5 was deleted upon insertion of Art 42A into the Constitution. The threshold for state intervention is now set out in Art 42A.2.1°.

[11] Bunreacht na hÉireann, Art 42.5 (now repealed).

[12] Bracken (n 5) 40–41.

[13] ibid 40.

concerning the marital family. Thus, it has been argued that the best interests of the child can be *better* protected by the Irish courts where the parents are unmarried as the primary consideration for the court must be the child's best interests, not the marital status of the parents.[14] In this situation, the application of the best interests principle is very similar to that in other jurisdictions, such as England and Wales. Although there is a paucity of jurisprudence on this point in the medical context, the dicta of McGuinness J in *N v Health Service Executive*, a case concerning adoption, are illustrative:

> Once the marriage took place the applicants became a constitutional family with all the concomitant rights and presumptions. … The central issue to be considered by the court underwent a metamorphosis; *it was no longer the best interests of the child* but the lawfulness or otherwise of the second and third respondents' custody of her.[15]

In this case, unmarried parents placed their child for adoption. They later married and sought to have the child returned to them. As the quote above demonstrates, by the time this application came to court, the constitutional presumption as to welfare applied, meaning that the child's best interests and individual rights could not be afforded the same weight that they had received in earlier proceedings.

Regardless of whether the parents are married or unmarried, medical professionals will require court authorisation if they are to treat a young child in the absence of parental consent, outside of an emergency situation. In deciding whether to seek judicial intervention, Irish medical professionals are guided by professional standards and guidelines but, as discussed in later sections, there is a lack of detail concerning the appropriate response where the parents disagree with the approach suggested by the medical professionals.

IV. 'Exceptional' Cases

As outlined above, the Irish Constitution gives parents the power to refuse medical treatment for their children, unless the case is deemed 'exceptional'.[16] In such cases, the Irish courts may authorise the medical treatment of children against the wishes of parents. The most common scenario is that involving parents who are Jehovah's Witnesses and who refuse consent to life-saving treatment for their children where this will involve a blood transfusion.[17] For example, in the case of *Baby Janice*,[18] the High Court directed that a five-month-old baby girl receive

[14] ibid; Geoffrey Shannon, *Child Law*, 2nd edn (Dublin, Thomson Reuters, 2010) 14.

[15] *N v Health Service Executive* [2006] 4 IR 374, 497 (emphasis added).

[16] Bunreacht na hÉireann, Art 42A.2.1°.

[17] M Carolan, 'Court Orders Life-Saving Transfusion' *Irish Times* (Dublin, 12 January 2011); 'HSE Asks Court for Ruling on Blood Transfusion for Babies' *Irish Examiner* (Cork, 24 April 2008); D McDonald and R Managh, 'Jehovah's Witness Forced to Have Life-Saving Transfusion' *Irish Independent* (Dublin, 22 September 2006).

[18] *Baby Janice* (unreported, High Court, 5 August 2004).

life-saving open-heart surgery despite parental objections. The child's mother had initially signed consent for the unqualified use of blood and blood products but, following intervention from her Jehovah's Witness community, had withdrawn that consent. An urgent application was brought before the High Court where Finnegan J ordered that Janice be made a ward of court and authorised the hospital to provide medical treatment as it deemed appropriate. Therefore, although the Constitution gives parents the right to raise their children by reference to their own religious and philosophical views, that right is not absolute. The courts will override the decisions of the parents where the child's life, general welfare and other vital interests are at stake.

Where the child has been made a ward of court, the Court has *parens patriae* jurisdiction to decide all matters relating to the ward and the Supreme Court has confirmed that the exercise of such jurisdiction 'does not, in any way, amount to a failure to protect the family in its constitution and authority'.[19] In determining the treatment, if any, to be provided, the best interests of the child will be the paramount consideration for the court. The Court will also take into account the views of the family and carers but the ultimate decision rests with the Court. The nature of this assessment was considered in cases such as *SR (A ward of court)* and *An Irish Hospital v RF*.

V. Application of the 'Best Interests' Assessment

In *SR*, the hospital authorities sought a declaration that would permit the non-resuscitation of a six-year-old boy, who was a ward of court, were he to experience an acute deterioration requiring invasive treatment.[20] The ward was just under two years old when he suffered a near drowning incident which resulted in cardiac arrest and extensive, irreversible brain damage. Kearns P outlined the condition of the child, who had developed 'severe spastic quadriplegic cerebral palsy involving all four limbs'.[21] The child was blind, incontinent and had no method of communication, although he was able to cry out at times. Kearns P noted that the child appeared to feel pain and had demonstrated periods of irritability. It was suggested that such irritability was probably due to muscle spasm pain. There was no prospect of recovery and his condition continued to deteriorate due to recurrent respiratory tract infections and chronic lung disease. These developments meant it was necessary to consider the question of resuscitation.[22]

[19] *A Ward of Court (withholding medical treatment) (No. 2)* [1996] 2 IR 79, 117.

[20] *SR (a Minor and a Ward of Court): An Irish Hospital v RH and J McG* [2012] 1 IR 305, 307.

[21] ibid 305.

[22] ibid 308. As Kearns P stated: 'In the event of a severe deterioration in his condition a decision must be made whether to resuscitate him and to decide whether it is in his best interests to be intubated and placed on invasive ventilation in circumstances where it may not be possible to wean him off ventilation and the use of such invasive measures will neither restore health or confer any real benefit to the child and will cause him pain and suffering.'

In determining the best interests of the child, Kearns P deemed it necessary to balance the various factors such as

> the pain, suffering that the child could expect if he survives; the longevity and quality of life that the child could expect if he survives; the inherent pain and suffering involved in the proposed treatment and the views of the child's parents and doctors.[23]

Kearns P went on to agree with the comments of Lord Donaldson MR in the English case of *Re J (Wardship: Medical Treatment)*[24] that the 'proper test' is to 'ask what the ward would choose if he were in a position to make a sound judgment'.[25] This introduces the substituted judgment doctrine and makes it a central element in the decision-making framework. Kearns P clarified that in applying this approach 'the decision maker should not impose his own views on whether the quality of life which the child would enjoy would be intolerable, but should determine the best interests of the child subjectively'.[26] The reference to 'intolerability' is somewhat problematic and issues with this concept have previously been highlighted by Holman J in *Re MB*.[27] Kearns P followed *Re J (Wardship: Medical Treatment)*.[28] The question of tolerability was considered by Taylor LJ in *Re J*. where he set out that:

> In an accident case, as opposed to one involving disablement from birth, the child's pre-accident quality of life and its perception of what has been lost may also be factors relevant to whether the residual life would be intolerable to that child.[29]

The approach taken by Kearns P requires a number of assumptions to be made by the Court.[30] On this point, Somers suggests that the approach of the Court looked to the ward's preferences before the accident. This is not entirely in line with *Re J* which suggests that the Court consider 'an imaginary period of contemplation' after the occurrence of the accident. At a minimum, the approach adopted by the High Court suggests a surprisingly advanced level of cognitive development and maturity for a child of less than two years. This approach is further limited by the parents' opposition to the application as they were the only people who could have provided an insight into the child's past preferences.[31] The medical evidence

[23] ibid.
[24] *Re J (Wardship: Medical Treatment)* [1991] Fam 33.
[25] *SR (a Minor and a Ward of Court): An Irish Hospital v RH and J McG* [2012] 1 IR 305, 323.
[26] ibid.
[27] *In re MB (medical treatment)* [1997] EWCA Civ 3093.
[28] *Re J (Wardship: Medical Treatment)* [1991] Fam. 33.
[29] *In re J (a Minor) (Wardship: Medical treatment)* [1991] 2 WLR 140, 158.
[30] C Somers, '"Deciding Obliquely and by a Side Wind": Substituted Judgment and End-of-Life Decisions' (2013) 19(1) *Medico-Legal Journal of Ireland* 11, 21. The assumptions were that the child (i) had reached sufficient cognitive development to understand the concept of incapacity and disability; (ii) took time to consider a future of incapacity and what it would mean for him; (iii) had reached a decision and decided that he would prefer to refuse life-saving treatment and die rather than receive treatment and live a life of incapacity; and (iv) had reached sufficient maturity (*Gillick* competence) so that a judge should be required to give effect to his wishes.
[31] ibid.

presented in *SR* was such that the ward had no prospect of recovery and that intubating and ventilating the ward was not in his best interests.

SR was subsequently followed by *An Irish Hospital v RF*[32] in which a hospital made an application to the High Court for a ruling that it would be in the patient's best interests that medical staff refrain from further aggressive treatment. In coming to a decision, O'Malley J followed the principles set out by Kearns P in *SR* and recognised that 'the overriding obligation on the court is to act in the best interests of the child'.[33] Factors to be taken into account include R's pain and suffering if she were to survive; the length and quality of life to be expected; the suffering inherent in the current course of treatment or in any future aggressive treatment; and the views of the parents and doctors. The Court also considered issues of substituted judgment, intolerability, and the presumption in favour of authorising life-saving treatment. The hospital's application was supported by the child's mother, the Child and Family Agency, and the guardian *ad litem*. The Court ultimately concluded that the hospital's application was in R's best interests and that further aggressive treatment of R was not in her best interests.

VI. The Influence of Professional Standards and Guidelines

Ireland's Clinical Practice Guideline on the Use of Parenteral Nutrition in Neonatal and Paediatric Units includes a section on legislation and other related policies. Tellingly, in the body of the guideline this section is blank.[34] There is no specific legislation to rely on. Instead, central to professional practice are the standards published by the Irish Medical Council (IMC). The eighth edition of the IMC's *Guide to Professional Conduct and Ethics* was published in 2016. Each edition of the Guide has expanded on the preceding document, but the legal status has not changed. In *MR v TR*, McGovern J stated that:

> These ethical guidelines do not have the force of the law and offer only such limited protection as derives on the part of a doctor that he might be found guilty of professional misconduct with all the professional consequences that might follow.[35]

The Guide still has an important role and provides guidance on the treatment of children and young persons as well as the provision of end-of-life care.[36] Section 18.1 of the Guide affirms that the medical practitioner's primary duty is to

[32] *An Irish Hospital v RF* [2015] 2 IR 377.

[33] ibid 383.

[34] Health Service Executive, 'Guideline on the Use of Parenteral Nutrition in Neonatal and Paediatric Units' (HSE, 2018) 3.

[35] *MR v TR* [2006] IEHC 359.

[36] Irish Medical Council, 'Guide to Professional Conduct and Ethics for Registered Medical Practitioners', 8th edn (2016) s 18, Children and Young People; s 46, End of Life Care.

act in the best interests of the child. It also suggests that the medical practitioner 'should involve [the child or young person] as much as possible in discussions about their healthcare, give them information suitable for their age, listen to their views and treat them with respect'.[37] Although it is encouraging that the Guide respects and promotes the involvement of the child in treatment decisions, it provides little guidance on resolving disagreements with family members or determining the threshold for judicial intervention.

Section 46 is also relevant to these decisions as it provides guidance on end-of-life care. The importance of appropriate communication is reflected in section 46.2, which provides that the medical practitioner

> should be sensitive in presenting information, but make sure that patients and their families have a clear understanding of what can and cannot be achieved. You should offer advice on other treatment or palliative care options that may be available to them.[38]

The Guide is clear that there is no obligation to start or continue treatment in certain cases. The medical practitioner must consider whether the treatment would be unlikely to work, might bring about more harm than benefit, or 'is likely to cause the patient pain, discomfort or distress, whether or not you are continuing active treatment'.[39]

The potential for disagreement among the various parties is addressed by section 46.5. It suggests that the medical practitioner 'should make every effort to resolve the issue'.[40] Of course, this is no guarantee that all parties will arrive at an amiable resolution. In the event of disagreement, the IMC does not direct the medical practitioner to the court service but suggests that the practitioner seeks advice from an experienced colleague, gets a second opinion, or involves an independent advocate or mediation service. In sum, the professional code of conduct provides no guidance for doctors on when the courts could or should be engaged.

In addition to standards issued by the IMC, neonatologists and paediatricians in Ireland are also influenced by guidelines issued by the Royal College of Paediatrics and Child Health (RCPCH), such as 'Making decisions to limit treatment in life limiting and life threatening conditions in children: a framework for practice'.[41] This document is intended to serve as an ethical and legal framework for decisions to limit life-sustaining treatments for children. The RCPCH is a UK-based body and the most recent revision to the guideline incorporates relevant case-law and legislation from England and Wales. As such, reliance on this guideline by Irish medical practitioners is problematic as it means that the legal framework for England and Wales is guiding Irish medical practice, which may fail to fully reflect the position of the family and child within the Irish Constitution.

[37] ibid s 18.1.
[38] ibid s 46.2.
[39] ibid s 46.3.
[40] ibid s 46.5.
[41] V Larcher et al, 'Making Decisions to Limit Treatment in Life-Limiting and Life-Threatening Conditions in Children: A Framework for Practice' (2015) 100 *Archives of Disease in Childhood* S1.

In a commentary on the guideline it was stated that: 'The guiding principle remains that of determination of the child's best interests, albeit with greater consideration of the interests of families and of their rights.'[42] The meaning of best interests is expanded on in the framework and is informed by the Children Act 1989, the Mental Capacity Act 2005, and guidance on end-of-life care issued by the General Medical Council. The RCPCH addresses the role of the courts including jurisdiction and factors to be considered. It is well supported by reference to cases, legislation and guidance. However, for the medical practitioner in Ireland it is important to recognise that these are of persuasive authority and that many of these issues have not yet been considered by courts in Ireland.

VII. Conclusion

The Irish legal framework concerning parental rights in the context of medical decision-making for children is fragmented and underdeveloped. The constitutional provisions relating to the family give parents near-absolute discretion to make decisions for their children, which casts a shadow over permissible legislative and medical involvement. This has led to a dearth of professional guidelines for clinicians to use when parents disagree with the recommended medical intervention for their child. The Irish courts have established a clear line of jurisprudence on the appropriate approach in so-called 'exceptional' cases but cases that fall below this threshold remain in murky waters. It is clear that robust professional guidelines are needed to support the medical profession and to clarify the steps needed to ensure that the best interests of the child are maintained at all times.

[42] ibid S4.

16

Decisionally Incapable Children and Medical Treatment Choices in Canada

CONSTANCE MacINTOSH

I. Introduction

Canada's approach to treatment decisions involving children who are decisionally incapable is determined through the interplay of statutory instruments and the common law,[1] the requirements of Canada's Charter of Rights and Freedoms[2] and indirectly through criminal law. Statutory instruments include provincial and territorial legislation that concern consent to treatment and child protection The common law both complements and interprets statutory law and also perpetuates the jurisdiction of provincial superior courts to assume a *parens patriae* role in the case of statutory gaps.[3] The Charter protects a sphere of parental rights and restrains state interventions. Criminal law may impose liability on parents if they fail to provide their children with the 'necessaries of life'.[4] Collectively, these sources recognise the rights of parents to make decisions on behalf of their decisionally incapable children while also recognising that there may be circumstances in which the state has a duty to intervene and overrule parental choice. There are some strong similarities to English and Scottish law, reflecting how Canadian courts have drawn upon British precedents, such as *Gillick v West Norfolk and Wisbech*

[1] *Hepton v Maat* [1957] SCR 606, at 607, 10 DLR (2D).
[2] Canadian Charter of Rights and Freedoms, Part I of the Constitution Act, 1982, being Schedule B to the Canada Act 1982 (UK), 1982, ch 11 (Charter); *B(R) v Children's Aid Society of Metropolitan Toronto*, [1995] 1 SCR 315 at 372, 122 DLR (4th) 1.
[3] *E (Mrs) v Eve* [1986] 2 SCR 388 at 426, 31 DLR (4th) 1; *Beson v Newfoundland (Director of Child Welfare)* [1982] 2 SCR 716, 142 DLR (3d) 20.
[4] Criminal Code, RSC 1985, ch C-46, s 215(1)(a), 215(2)(a)(ii).

Area Health Authority, in early Canadian cases.[5] Canadian law also recognises that if non-emergency healthcare is provided to a decisionally incapable child without either parental consent or pursuant to judicial or legislatively authorised consent, that such treatment constitutes unlawful battery.[6] Aside from criminal law aspects, jurisdiction in this area does not rest with the singular federal government, but rather with each of the provincial and territorial governments and courts. There are strong commonalities across the jurisdictions, with some variations.

This chapter first discusses the recognition of parental rights, then identifies how those rights are predicated on fulfilling certain duties, and samples several provincial regimes[7] to illustrate how state actors may become involved. The chapter then turns to the approaches courts use where there is a conflict between parental choices and physician recommendations, the extent to which parental rights attract constitutional protection, and how the 'best interests of the child' standard rests at the core of judicial decision-making. In discussing the 'best interests of the child' standard, special attention is given to situations involving Indigenous children. This section should be read in light of Gray's chapter in this volume, where he argues that there is no such thing as 'the objective best interests of a child', and that cultural insensitivity can result in devaluing different views and experiences.[8] The chapter closes with a discussion of when criminal liability may arise, and considers cases where doctors believe that following the parents' decision will result in futile treatment.

II. Parental Rights to Make Treatment Decisions

Canadian common law recognises parents as the presumptive substitute decision-makers for their decisionally incapable children, unless another person has been appointed to this role through, for example, guardianship.[9] This principle,

[5] For a discussion of English and Scottish approaches, see I Goold, C Auckland and J Herring, 'Medical Decision-Making on Behalf of Children in England and Welsh Law: A Child-Centred Best Interests Approach'; and A Brown, '"Parental Rights", "Best Interests" and the Withdrawal of Life-Sustaining Medical Treatment of Children in Scotland: A Lack of Authority', both in this book.

[6] J Gilmour, 'Children, Adolescents and Health Care' in J Downie, T Caulfield and C Flood (eds), *Canadian Health Law and Policy*, 2nd edn (Ontario, Butterworths, 2002) 205–50, 206. See also *Toews (Guardian ad litem of) v Weisner*, 2001 BCSC 15 [16].

[7] Canada has thirteen provinces and territories. These are the ten provinces of Alberta, British Columbia, Manitoba, New Brunswick, Newfoundland and Labrador, Nova Scotia, Ontario, Prince Edward Island, Quebec, and Saskatchewan, and the three territories of Northwest Territories, Nunavut, and the Yukon.

[8] B Gray, 'The Relevance of Cultural Competence to Resolving Disputes in Relation to Medical Decisions for Children', in this book.

[9] J Gilmour, 'Death, Dying and Decision Making about End of Life' in J Downie, T Caulfield and C Flood (eds), *Canadian Health Law and Policy*, 4th edn (Ontario, LexisNexis, 2011) 385–436, 403. For the purpose of this chapter, whenever the word 'parent' is used, it should be read to include guardians.

along with its limits, has been articulated several times by the Supreme Court of Canada, and as discussed by Francis in this volume is also a hallmark of the US regime.[10] In the 1957 decision of *Hepton v Matt*, which concerned whether birth parents could revoke their consent, given three months previously, for their twin infants to be given up for adoption, the court described children's welfare as residing 'first, within the warmth and security of the home provided by the parents'.[11] After prioritising the presumption that parents are inherently best placed to advance their children's welfare, the court added the caveat that the state may intervene:

> [W]hen through a failure, with or without parental fault, to furnish that protection, that [child's] welfare is threatened, the community, represented by the Sovereign, is, on the broadest social and national grounds, justified in displacing the parents and assuming their duties.[12]

The Supreme Court of Canada revisited the common law approach in the context of health treatment decisions concerning children in 1995. Once again, they confirmed the legal presumption that parents are to make decisions for their children, while noting that this presumption contains an internal limitation:

> [T]he common law has always, in the absence of demonstrated neglect or unsuitability, presumed that parents should make all significant choices affecting their children, and has afforded them a general liberty to do as they choose.[13]

According to the jurisprudence, parental rights have presumptive primacy due to the assumption that parents will know, and will act to advance, the best interests of their children. Thus these common law rights are inherently embedded in an obligation to faithfully discharge their duties.[14] The Supreme Court of Canada frames these twinned presumptions in terms of parents having a deep personal interest 'in fostering the growth' of their children[15] and being 'more likely to appreciate the best interests of their children', while the state is 'ill-equipped' to make such assessments.[16]

While the common law has long recognised parents as possessing decision-making rights for their children, most provinces and territories have enacted legislation that indicates an age at which that right is displaced, and the youth is presumed to have full capacity and autonomy to make treatment decisions, including declining life-sustaining treatment. This age tends to be below the age

[10] L Francis, J Botkin and D Diekema, 'Decision-Making on Behalf of Children in the Research and Clinical Context: A United States Perspective', in this book.

[11] *Hepton v Maat* (n 1) SCR 606 at 607, 10 DLR (2D) 1.

[12] ibid.

[13] *B(R) v Children's Aid Society of Metropolitan Toronto* [1995] 1 SCR 315 at 372, 122 DLR (4th) 1.

[14] Gilmour (n 6) 225; E Adjin-Tettey, 'Rights and Tort Law: Respecting Children's Decisional Autonomy for Medical Interventions' (2018) 84 *Supreme Court Law Review* (2d) 161, [13].

[15] *B(R) v Children's Aid Society of Metropolitan Toronto* (n 13) [85].

[16] ibid.

of majority. For most jurisdictions, this age varies between sixteen and eighteen. The Yukon, Ontario and Prince Edward Island, which are home to 39 per cent of the Canadian population,[17] take a different approach. Their legislation makes no reference to age. They instead create a rebuttable presumption that every person is capable of making their own treatment decisions.[18] Obviously in the case of young children, they are likely to not be found capable of making any complex treatment decision, but may have capacity for quite simple ones. In the provinces which set out a presumptive age for medical capacity, most also recognise in their legislation that minors under these ages – as young as twelve – may have capacity and be 'mature minors'. If this is the case, parental decision-making rights are ousted or modified.[19]

While the focus of this chapter is young children who are, in fact and law, decisionally incapable such as infants or toddlers, the points above are set out to illustrate the character of the positions taken in Canadian law toward who decides if medical treatment will be given or declined; they place a significant value on maximising autonomy through individualized consent-based decision-making as soon as capacity is found or presumed present.[20] This stands in tension with the approach taken with decisionally incapable children, where parental autonomy stands in for a child's autonomy, but may be tested against the views of presumably disinterested healthcare professionals.

III. State Intervention and Constitutional Restraints

As noted above, the rights of parents to make health treatment decisions on behalf of their decisionally incapable young children is tethered to and limited by their corresponding duties to discharge those rights in the best interests of their children, which includes taking steps to ensure that their children receive necessary medical treatment. If this duty is not met, the state may 'intervene when it considers it necessary to safeguard the child's autonomy or health'[21] and the parental decision-making rights are displaced. These parental duties do not extend to fetuses, which are not legal persons in Canada. A pregnant woman cannot be required to receive

[17] Statistics Canada, 'Canada at a Glance 2018, Population' (27 March 2018) www150.statcan.gc.ca/n1/pub/12-581-x/2018000/pop-eng.htm.

[18] Health Care Consent Act, SO 1996, ch 2, Schedule A, s 4; The Consent to Treatment and Healthcare Directives Act, SPEI 1999, ch C-17.2, s 3(1); The Care Consent Act, SY 2003, ch 21, schedule B, ss 3–6.

[19] Regimes vary. While some jurisdictions recognise the youth as having full decisional capacity, other jurisdictions require that the treatment choice of the youth be in their best interests if there is a parent–youth disagreement.

[20] See eg *Fleming v Reid* (1991) 4 OR (3d) 74, 82 DLR (4th) 298 (CA), ss IV and V, where the court describes the common law right to determine what is done with one's body and the constitutional right to security of the person as coextensive.

[21] *B(R) v Children's Aid Society of Metropolitan Toronto* (n 13) [85].

medical treatment for the purpose of protecting the viability or well-being of a fetus without her consent.[22]

All provinces and territories have enacted legislation setting out a process for determining whether parents have not met their duties and if state intervention is warranted. For all processes, the ultimate decision-maker is a judicial body before whom the recommended treatment (or non-treatment) is debated.[23] The legislation which authorises such processes and interventions will only be lawful if it is compliant with the Canadian Charter of Rights and Freedoms ('the Charter'), which is a part of Canada's constitution.[24] This approach differs from that of Norway, for example.[25] Within the Canadian context, the rubric for assessing constitutionality involves interpreting the situation at hand in light of a set of fundamental rights exercised by all. However, in Norway, as described by Sovig, children's rights have express recognition in their constitution, with the provisions having been drafted to align with the rights recognised in the UN Convention on the Rights of the Child.[26] This results in a more predetermined approach.

In *BR v Children's Aid Society of Metropolitan Toronto*,[27] the Supreme Court of Canada delivered the leading Canadian precedent on how the Charter supports and restrains parental and state roles vis-a-vis decisions about medical treatments for decisionally incapable children. The case concerned an infant whose parents were Jehovah's Witnesses. They refused to consent to their infant receiving blood transfusions on the basis of their religious beliefs. On two occasions, a children's aid society[28] received judicial authorisation to have brief wardships over the infant, based on the finding that receiving a blood transfusion was in the infant's best interests. In each instance, physicians believed the transfusion was necessary to preserve the infant's life. The parents appealed the orders. They claimed that the legislative regime violated their Charter rights to liberty in a manner that was inconsistent with the principles of fundamental justice.[29] In particular, the parents argued that their liberty interests included the right to choose medical

[22] *Winnipeg Child and Family Services (Northwest Area) v DFG* 1997 SCJ No 96, 152 DLR (4th) 193.

[23] *BR*, 10 OR (3d) 321, 96 DLR (4th) 45 (CA).

[24] Charter, Part I of the Constitution Act, 1982, being Schedule B to the Canada Act 1982 (UK), 1982, ch 11.

[25] South Africa raises another interesting contrast, where children's rights to health and life are explicitly incorporated into the constitution; see A Moyo, 'Parental Responsibility and Medical Decision-Making in Southern Africa: A Comparative Analysis of South Africa and Botswana', in this book.

[26] K Sovig, 'Reviewing Medical Decisions Concerning Infants Within the Norwegian Healthcare System – A Public Law Approach', in this book.

[27] *B(R) v Children's Aid Society of Metropolitan Toronto* (n 13).

[28] In Canada, children's aid societies are independent, non-profit, government-funded organisations that are responsible for providing child protection services pursuant to child protection legislation and policies. They are required to investigate and act on reports of abuse or neglect, and to pursue processes to protect children.

[29] Everyone has the right to life, liberty and security of the person and the right not to be deprived thereof except in accordance with the principles of fundamental justice.

treatment for their child,[30] and flaws in the process rendered it inconsistent with the principles of fundamental justice. The parents also argued that their Charter right to practice freedom of religion was unlawfully violated because they were unjustifiably denied the right to make a treatment decision for their child in line with their faith.[31]

Although there was concurrence in the outcome, with all nine judges finding that the legislation should stand, there was disagreement about why the regime withstood Charter scrutiny. There was division over the question of whether parental liberty rights that are protected under the Charter can extend to declining necessary medical treatment for their children, or if such a decision would fall outside the scope of their liberty rights.

In the majority set of reasons, Justice La Forest[32] discussed the meaning of the liberty right in the parental context. He rejected an argument based on US constitutional jurisprudence, which recognises the right to liberty as 'endur[ing] in the family as an entity'.[33] He instead found that in the context of the Canadian Charter, liberty is an individual right of the parent that reflects having personal autonomy, privacy and choice when making fundamental decisions, and to exercise these rights without state interference.[34] La Forest J found 'it plain that the right to nurture a child, to care for its development, and to made decisions for it in fundamental matters such as medical care, are part of the liberty interest of a parent'.[35] The parents' liberty rights were therefore prima facie engaged by a legislative regime which denies their right to have their treatment decision respected. However, La Forest J found that the violation, and in particular the process set out in the legislation for determining if state intervention should be ordered, was consistent with the principles of fundamental justice. He wrote that while 'a deprivation of liberty [must] be in conformity with the principles of fundamental justice, … it does not guarantee the most equitable process of all; it dictates a threshold below which state intervention will not be tolerated'.[36] The regime set out a requirement for reasonable notice to be provided to the parents, permits a judge to summon and compel witnesses, to hear evidence from parents and others, for the parents to be represented by counsel and thus present arguments and cross-examine witnesses and so forth, with the onus of proving that the child is in need

[30] *B(R) v Children's Aid Society of Metropolitan Toronto* (n 13) [70].

[31] s 2(a) of the Charter states that 'everyone has the fundamental freedom of religion'. Where a law violates religious rights, it will fall unless it is proven to be justified pursuant to a legal test known as the *Oakes* test. The *Oakes* test asks whether the law is rationally connected to the objective, minimally impairing, and if the *effect* of the law is proportional to the objective of the law: *R v Oakes*, 1 SCR 103, 26 DLR (4th) 200, ss 65, 73–75.

[32] Justice La Forest's reasons were endorsed by four other judges.

[33] *B(R) v Children's Aid Society of Metropolitan Toronto* (n 13) [72], [81]–[82].

[34] *R v Morgantaler* [1988] 1 SCR 30 at 166, 44 DLR (4th) 385; (n 13) [80].

[35] *B(R) v Children's Aid Society of Metropolitan Toronto* (n 13) [83].

[36] ibid [101].

of protection resting on the applicant.[37] Thus, from the perspective of the majority, the liberty rights of parents stand to be infringed whenever parental treatment choices are denied, but such infringements will stand if the process meets the standards for procedural fairness. Notably, the majority did not discuss the actual conflict at issue – rather the discussion was entirely at the level of principle.

The concurring judgment did discuss the nature of the dispute.[38] They found that the scope of Charter-protected parental liberties do not include a right to make a decision to refuse medical treatment for a child that a medical professional considers necessary where there is 'no legitimate alternative'.[39] They read the majority judgment as ignoring the child's own rights to life and liberty, and expressed concern that La Forest's approach wrongly subsumed the child's right to life within the parental liberty to make decisions about that child.[40] They found it 'counter-intuitive' that parental liberty would extend to denying a child necessary medical treatment unless the state created a procedurally fair method to curtail that right[41]

The Court's reasoning on the religion claim split in a similar fashion. The majority concluded the right to religious freedom includes being able to make treatment decisions that are consistent with religious belief, so a legislative scheme that denies parents the right to choose medical treatment for their child in accordance with their faith violates their religious rights. However, they found the violation to be justified. Drawing on the *Oakes* analysis,[42] the majority found the state interest in protecting children is a pressing and substantial objective, the process for assessment was carefully crafted to avoid arbitrariness, and there were robust procedural protections for parents. As a result of the state sharing an interest in protecting children, and having crafted a legislative regime to exercise that interest that withstood constitutional scrutiny, the Court could rely on the legislation to declare the child a ward of the state for the purpose of consenting to medical treatment. The concurring set of reasons, on the other hand, found parental rights to freedom of religion do not include imposing religious practices on a child that threatens the child's health, safety or life.[43] They once again brought the rights of

[37] ibid [92]–[93].

[38] Concurring reasons were authored by Cory J. They were directly adopted by two judges, and the remaining judge wrote a set of reasons which concluded that s 7 did not extend to parental liberties. In effect, there was a five–four split.

[39] *B(R) v Children's Aid Society of Metropolitan Toronto* (n 13) [215].

[40] ibid.

[41] ibid [217].

[42] The three-part *Oakes* test assesses whether a law is justified in violating the Charter. The first step is whether the law is prescribed by law: *R v Oakes*, 1 SCR 103, 26 DLR (4th) 200, s 65 (*Oakes*). The second step is whether the objective of the law is a 'pressing and substantial' one as to justify being present in a free and democratic society: *Oakes*, s 73. And the third step is whether the means chosen are reasonable and demonstrably justified through a 'proportionality test': *Oakes*, s 74. To satisfy this test, the means must be rationally connected to the objective, they should be minimally impairing, and there must be a proportionality between the *effects* of the law and the *objective*: *Oakes*, ss 74–75.

[43] *B(R) v Children's Aid Society of Metropolitan Toronto* (n 13) [225].

the child forward, arguing that the parents had proceeded as if their infant shared their faith, when in fact the infant had not expressed any view on faith whatsoever. They felt the child's right to freedom of conscience precluded their parents' religious beliefs being imposed on her where this would result in her death, and that she had the right to live long enough to make her own decision on faith.[44] This approach has some resonance with how Goold describes similar disputes being resolved in the English context. Goold notes that decisions are usually made in favour of treatment. She posits that this outcome may reflect courts accepting 'the authority of the medical profession in claiming expertise on children's medical welfare' which stands in contrast with 'no one ha[ving] similar standing in relation to religious issues'.[45]

The two sets of reasons in *BR* share common ground. They both recognise parental decision-making rights as having expression in constitutionalised religious and liberty rights, they both place limits on parental decision-making rights, and presume that these limits are reached if the parents chose to deny medical care which has been found necessary in light of the best interests of the child.[46] In writing the majority set of reasons, La Forest strongly endorsed parental rights bearing constitutional status. He wrote that this status acts to constrain the power of the state to intervene, and ensures that any state interference is subject to monitoring by the courts and thus only permitted when it is consistent with Charter values.[47] The minority judgment, on the other hand, illustrated concerns about parental rights having too great a scope, and concerns that infants' rights risked being downplayed.

The next section describes the child protection regimes that have been enacted in various Canadian jurisdictions. The chapter then turns to the jurisprudence arising from cases where parents and treatment teams held conflicting views as to what would serve the best interests of a child.

IV. Legislated Child Protection Regimes

As noted above, and like the United States,[48] each province and territory has its own child protection legislation. On their face, the statutes are extremely deferential, and reflect the values and principles as described in the jurisprudence. They authorise intervention when there is a failure or refusal by parents to provide or

[44] ibid [231].

[45] Goold et al (n 5).

[46] Justice La Forest added an addendum to his set of reasons to ensure that this view on this point was clear.

[47] *B(R) v Children's Aid Society of Metropolitan Toronto* (n 13) [85].

[48] Francis et al (n 10).

seek access to medical treatment which professionals have concluded is essential or required for the child so as to preserve life or prevent serious impairment. There is deference to parental choice for decisions regarding non-essential treatments (as long as they do not have permanent adverse effects such as non-essential sterilisation), as well as non-therapeutic interventions such as ear-piercing and male infant circumcision.[49]

For example, Ontario's legislation deems a child to be in need of protection where 'the child requires treatment to cure, prevent or alleviate physical harm or suffering' or suffers from a 'mental, emotional or developmental condition that, if not remedied, could seriously impair the child's development' and the child's parent refuses to consent to the treatment.[50] The language of 'required' or 'essential' is common in these statutes. Saskatchewan refers to the refusal to provide care considered 'essential by a duly qualified medical practitioner'.[51] Other provinces seem to contemplate a potentially lower threshold, such as when the care is "recommended" by a qualified health practitioner.[52]

Some provinces require a concurring medical opinion as a threshold for bringing a protection application. In Nova Scotia, the medical care or treatment must be considered 'essential by two duly qualified medical practitioners for the preservation of life, limb or vital organs',[53] and in British Columbia two medical practitioners must be of the opinion that the care 'is necessary to preserve the child's life or to prevent serious or permanent impairment of the child's health'.[54]

Proceedings can be triggered by a report being made to a children's aid society or a court application. The statutes impose obligations on professionals and others who have duties with children to file reports if they have reasonable grounds to believe the child may need protection, and make the failure to report a summary offence that can lead to fines or imprisonment.[55] The statutes override obligations of confidentiality or privilege.[56] No action can be taken against a reporter, as long as they did not report falsely or maliciously,[57] while a false or malicious report is an offence. The statutes contemplate proceedings directed at obtaining a temporary custody order, which would permit a state body to consent in lieu of the parents and reviewing orders to determine if they should be renewed.

[49] Gilmour (n 6) 226.
[50] Child, Youth, and Family Services Act SO 2017. ss 74(2)(e) and (j) (current to 27 April 2019). Prince Edward Island has similar provisions: Child Protection Act PEI Reg EC2003-215, ss 9(o) and (p).
[51] Child and Family Services Act SS 1989–90, ch C-7.2, s 11(a)(iv).
[52] Children and Youth Care and Protection Act SNL 2010, ch C-12.2, s 10(1); Child and Family Services Act CCSM, ch C80, s 17(2)(b)(iii).
[53] Child and Family Services Act SNS 1990, ch 5, s 61(1).
[54] Child, Family and Community Service Act RSBC 1996, ch 46, s 29(1).
[55] See eg Child and Family Services Act SNS 1990, ch 5, s 24(2), (6).
[56] See eg ibid ch 5, s 24(3).
[57] See eg ibid ch 5, s 24(2)–(5).

V. The Best Interests of the Child: Legislation and Litigation

When an application is heard, the question of what is 'essential' or 'required' is canvassed in light of the best interests of the child standard. This is supposed to be an 'objective' standard.[58] Its purpose 'is to provide courts with a focus and perspective through which to act on behalf of those who are vulnerable'.[59] Some jurisdictions rely solely upon the common law to identify the best interests of the child, while others have enacted statutory terms to guide the assessment. Although there is a strong presumption in favour of actions that prolong life,[60] this presumption can be rebutted given the broad circumstances that are canvassed when assessing the best interests of the child.

New Brunswick's legislation defines the best interests of the child as 'the best interests of the child under the circumstances taking into consideration … the mental, emotional and physical health of the child and his [*sic*] need for appropriate care or treatment, or both'.[61] The legislation in Ontario and Manitoba each have a term that flags similar categories of factors, while also identifying some circumstances deemed to be presumptively relevant, including race, culture, gender expression, religion, emotional needs and the value of continuity of care.[62]

A. Parental Refusal to Consent to Life-Sustaining Treatment

The presumption that pursuing life-sustaining treatment is in the best interests of a child has been rebutted in several Canadian decisions where the prognosis had uncertainties, and there were significant concerns about quality of life and/or challenges post-surgery or treatment. In *Saskatchewan (Minister of Social Services) v P(F)*,[63] an infant named K'aila was born with a severe liver disease, from which he would die within the year unless he received a liver transplant. The five-year rate of survival after such transplants was 60–65 per cent.[64] The parents refused to consent to the transplant. The Minister applied to have K'aila declared in need of protection. Expert evidence was presented on both sides. All agreed that a

[58] *Manitoba (Director of Child & Family Services) v C(A)* 2009 SCC 30 [82]. The Supreme Court wrote: 'The application of an objective "best interests" standard to infants and very young children is uncontroversial.'

[59] ibid [81].

[60] Gilmour (n 9) 404.

[61] Family Services Act SNB 1980, ch F-2.2, s 1(a).

[62] Child, Youth and Family Services Act SO 2017 ch 14 schedule 1, s 74(3); Child and Family Services Act CCSM ch 80, s 2(1).

[63] *Saskatchewan (Minister of Social Services) v P(F)* (1990), 83 Sask R 161, 69 DLR (4th) 134 (Sask Prov Ct).

[64] ibid [8].

liver transplant was the only option for sustaining life, and that it was considered standard treatment for end-stage liver disease. The parents' arguments, which were accepted, turned on evidence regarding the likely quality of life for K'aila, including continuous immune-suppressive therapy using a drug which can cause kidney fibrosis and for which the long term side-effects were unknown, specific types of cancer associated with the treatment, risks and quality of life post-surgery, etc. Three of the four testifying physicians felt either treating or not treating were both reasonable courses of action, while one considered the treatment essential.[65] The court contrasted this situation with cases involving Jehovah's Witnesses, commenting on how blood transfusions are commonplace with minimal risks, while an infant liver transplant was a 'difficult, complex, non-commonplace, major surgical procedure' with risks that are both known and unknown.[66] The judge characterised the Minister's position as focused only on the medical component of the best interests assessment, noting that along with medical issues, there were also practical, emotional, social and psychological components for both the child and parents, and the quality of life component for the child.[67] In a few concise paragraphs the court provided considerable insight into how these components are to be weighed. They found the parents had acted consistently with 'the values society expects of thoughtful, caring parents for a terminally ill child',[68] that the decision was acceptable to the majority of the doctors who testified,[69] and that a successful surgery would potentially perpetuate life but with considerable known risks and quality of life issues:

> The surgery option offers a probability of prolonging life for an uncertain period with a reduced quality. The emotional, social, and psychological cost to the child and the family may be high. The decision to be made cannot be reduced to mere mathematical probabilities.[70]

The court concluded that the parental decision did not lack judgement nor was it unreasonable, and the parents had not neglected their duty 'in rejecting a much more invasive procedure and the mandatory immuno-suppressive therapy that follows'.[71] The case illustrates that although the best interests of the child assessment is supposed to be individualised, that the court nonetheless measures the parents' decision against broader societal mainstream values, and medical judgement. Moreover, despite the law focusing on the best interests of the child, and not the parents, relational aspects emerge as the court considers the lives of the child and parents together.

[65] ibid [76] and [77].
[66] ibid [73]. Some of the unknown risks included the long-term effects of using the required drugs, which had only been in use for twelve years, on an infant.
[67] ibid [84].
[68] ibid [92].
[69] ibid [89].
[70] ibid [91].
[71] ibid [90].

A somewhat contrasting outcome was reached in *New Brunswick (Min of Health and Community Services) v RB*.[72] This case concerned a child, Sheena, who was born with encephalocele, which resulted in her being 'severely mentally retarded and neurologically handicapped'.[73] Shenna developed meningitis, and subsequently suffered an infection associated with a shunt that was used to drain fluid from her skull. Her neurosurgeon testified that Shenna 'cannot "be expected to have any quality of life"' and that treatment for the infection would prolong her life and thus prolong her suffering. Her paediatrician contended that she should be treated with antibiotics. The parents refused to consent to Sheena receiving antibiotics. They argued that it was in her best interests to die from the consequences of the infection. The court ordered a wardship and transferred custody to the Minister. They found that the parents' position, and that of the neurosurgeon, would not have been advanced had the child not been disabled, and so violated the child's section 15 Charter right to equality and to be free from discrimination. The court found no one had the right to judge the quality of a disabled child's life, and that given the non-invasive and low-risk character of the proposed treatment, that failing to treat with an antibiotic and allowing death to ensue would offend the section 12 Charter right to be free from cruel and unusual punishment.[74]

Generalities can be drawn from these cases. Where the proposed treatment is life-prolonging without causing significant adverse side-effects or risks, then the best interests of the child are going to rest in treatment. When the prognosis is less certain, and there are considerable risks and adverse side-effects, then physician opinion and societal expectations of what parents ought to do seems to play a significant role in the judicial assessment of the child's best interests. Where children are disabled, courts are very cautious to focus the analysis on the specific treatment decision that is at issue – the outcome in Sheena's case may have been different if the decision had been about replacing her shunt or making other painful interventions.

The assessment of what constitutes an unacceptable risk, an acceptable side-effect, or reasonable parenting decisions is undoubtedly a culturally informed one. With cases involving Indigenous children, this practice has often been buried. More recently cases have addressed this practice head-on.

B. The Best Interests of the Child and Indigenous Children

Child protection regimes, and the best interests of the child standard, have an ugly history in Canada for Indigenous peoples, whose child-rearing practices have

[72] *New Brunswick (Min of Health and Community Services) v RB* [1990] NBJ 404, 70 DLR (4th) 568.
[73] ibid [1].
[74] Charter, s 12. Subsequent decisions have not picked up on the argument about withholding treatment being cruel and unusual punishment.

long been treated with racist disdain by the state. As has been well documented through Canada's Truth and Reconciliation Commission, Indigenous children were historically forcibly removed from their families and placed in residential schools. This was justified on the basis that Indigenous people were 'savages' whose culture rendered them 'unfit to care for their children'.[75] The state hoped that residential schooling would sever family and cultural bonds, and so change the children's modes of thought and assimilate them into non-Indigenous culture.[76] When residential schools closed, child protection regimes continued the project of separating Indigenous children from their families, with widespread removal of Indigenous children from their homes through child protection proceedings which often turned on racist views of what constitutes good parenting or a reasonable decision for a child.[77]

Provinces have attempted to assuage the role of racism and cultural ignorance in child protection proceedings in several ways. As noted above, all provinces include culture and religion as relevant for determining the best interests of a child. Some provinces have taken more directed steps, such as explicitly authorising a representative from an Indigenous parent's First Nation, Inuit or Métis community as having rights as parties in protection proceedings.[78] In some provinces, the best interests test is drafted to require that the decision-maker 'consider the importance, in recognition of the uniqueness of First Nations, Inuit and Métis cultures, heritages and traditions, of preserving the child's cultural identity and connection to community'.[79]

There are two cases of particular note concerning disputes between parents and health treatment teams regarding treatment for Indigenous children who lacked decisional capacity. The first decision was discussed above, *Saskatchewan (Minister of Social Services) v P(F)*. In this case, the court noted that K'aila's parents' decision to decline the liver transplant was consistent with societal values. The fact that both parents were Indigenous, with the mother being Mohawk and the father Dene, was almost invisible in that decision. However, other sources reveal that their cultural positions were strongly reflected in their own decision-making process. The father was concerned with the spiritual aspects of transplanting an organ from one person to another, and given the risks, saw transplants as inconsistent with his beliefs about the Creator's intentions. The mother expressed similar concerns.[80] While these views are in the public record through newspaper articles

[75] The Truth and Reconciliation Commission of Canada, 'Honouring the Truth, Reconciling for the Future: Summary of the Final Report of the Truth and Reconciliation Commission of Canada' (2015) *Library and Archives Canada Cataloguing in Publication* 137.

[76] ibid 2–3.

[77] M Kline, 'Child Welfare Law, "Best Interests of the Child", Ideology and First Nations' (1992) 30 *Osgoode Hall Law Journal* 375.

[78] Child, Youth and Family Services Act SO 2017 ch 14 schedule 1, s 79(1)(4); Child and Family Services Act CCSM ch 80, ss 23(1)(b), (2), (3) and (4).

[79] Child, Youth and Family Services Act SO 2017 ch 14 schedule 1, s 74(3)(b).

[80] J Downie, 'A Choice for K'aila: Child Protection and First Nations Children' (1994) 2 *Health Law Journal* 99, [5]–[8].

and in-depth television shows, these views are nowhere to be seen in the formal decision. The judge upheld their choice, as Jocelyn Downie argues, because it was framed as fitting within accepted medical practice.[81] There is only one mention in the whole decision of the parents being Indigenous, and in context of a comment that negates the relevance of Indigenous culture in the decision-making process:

> 63 The mother is rational, objective, and balanced in her assessment of the situation.
>
> 64 The father of the child is a Dene Indian. The mother is a Mohawk Indian. The parents brought the child to Poundmaker Indian Reserve in the Province of Saskatchewan near Cut Knife, Saskatchewan, in January of 1990 to seek out traditional Indian medicine.
>
> 65 The parents' reasons for withholding consent are clearly personal and not cultural.

These passages are troubling. They suggest that 'rational, objective, and balanced' decisions are not informed by culture – or at least not by Indigenous culture. Downie cautions: 'If K'aila had needed a form of treatment accepted as standard therapy by the medical community but rejected by his parents on cultural grounds, then the Paulettes might not have won their case.'[82]

Downie's conclusion was sound in 1990, but the jurisprudence on the rights of Indigenous peoples has continued to develop. The debate and reasons in *PF*, and in particular its emphasis that the parental decision was reasonable because it did not reflect Indigenous culture, stands in contrast to the recent decision of *Hamilton Health Sciences Corp v DH*[83] where cultural rights were directly on the stand.[84] In this case, the mother (DH) and child (JJ) were Haudenosaunee and members of the Six Nations of the Grand River. JJ was diagnosed with leukemia. The mother initially consented to chemotherapy, but after some sessions she withdrew her consent, and said she wished to try traditional Aboriginal medicines instead. The hospital brought an application to declare JJ in need of protection, for the purpose of returning to chemotherapy. The physicians' testimony was that in JJ's case, chemotherapy would have a 90 per cent likelihood of curing the leukemia, and that they were unaware of any persons with paediatric leukemia who survived without chemotherapy.[85] DH and her First Nation defended her decision as an expression of her constitutionally protected Aboriginal rights.

As well as recognising human rights, Canada's constitution also recognises Aboriginal rights, through a provision that was introduced in 1986.[86] The provision in question shields practices that are integral to an Indigenous people from

[81] ibid [33].
[82] ibid [34].
[83] *Hamilton Health Sciences Corp v DH* 2014 ONCJ 603.
[84] For an in-depth discussion of this case, and its contextualisation within Indigenous health governance generally, see C MacIntosh, 'The Governance of Indigenous Health' in J Erdman, V Gruben and E Nelson (eds), *Canadian Health Law and Policy*, 5th edn (Ontario, LexisNexis, 2017) 135–60, 137–42.
[85] *Hamilton Health Sciences Corp v DH* (n 83) [12].
[86] Constitution Act, 1982, s 35, being Scheduled B to the Canada Act 1982 (UK), 1982, ch 11.

unjustified state infringement,[87] where the question of whether an infringement is justified often turns on the extent to which the state consulted with the Indigenous peoples and sought to minimise any impairment.

The presiding judge, Edward J, declined to find that JJ was a child in need of protection. He wrote that: 'I cannot find that JJ is a child in need of protection when her substitute decision-maker has chosen to exercise her constitutionally protected right to pursue their traditional medicine over the applicant's stated course of treatment.'[88] After the decision was released, it attracted controversy, and concerns about whether the state had vacated the field if Aboriginal children were involved. The family worked with the Ontario government, and expanded the healthcare team to include a new paediatric oncologist, and a traditional healer to develop a plan which was acceptable to all. JJ's cancer relapsed and she returned to chemotherapy, while also continuing to use Aboriginal medicines. The group petitioned Edward J to include a clarification to his set of reasons, which identified the relationship between Aboriginal rights and the best interests of the child. Edward J found that given the respect in Haudenosausne culture for children, 'it does no mischief to my decision to recognize that the best interests of the child remains paramount'.[89] A key passage in the clarification stated:

> [I]mplicit in this decision is that recognition and implementation of the right to use traditional medicines must remain consistent with the principle that the best interests of the child remain paramount. The aboriginal right to use traditional medicine must be respected, and must be considered, among other factors, in any analysis of the best interests of the child, and whether the child is in need of protection[90]

While this unique decision continues to attract controversy, it also calls out for the need for paediatric treatment teams to reflect a multiplicity of perspectives such that Indigenous children can access the best care that Western and Indigenous medicines can offer. With such teams in place, it may be presumed that the cultural competency that Gray identifies as essential will be present, drastically reducing the likelihood of judicial involvement.[91]

C. Parental Refusal to Consent to Withdrawing or Not Providing Life-Sustaining Treatment

This last section on the best interests of the child considers how decisions are made if physicians recommend ceasing or not providing life-sustaining treatment,

[87] Contemporary activities or practices have constitutional protection if they have continuity with precontract activities and practices which were (and are) integral to the people's culture. *R v Van der Peet*, [1996] SCJ No 77, 137 DLR (4th) 289, [44]–[47].

[88] *Hamilton Health Sciences Corp v DH* (n 83) [83].

[89] *Hamilton Health Sciences Corp v DH* 2015 ONCJ 229, [4].

[90] ibid [83(a)].

[91] Gray (n 8).

and parents refuse to consent. The first appellate court decision in Canada to consider whether a physician could order withholding resuscitation without patient consent concerned an infant, *RL*. In this 1997 decision, an infant was in a persistent vegetative state, and the physician sought to write a 'Do Not Resuscitate' (DNR) order on the infant's chart, over the objections of the parents.[92] Drawing on US jurisprudence, the court ruled that physicians had the independent discretion to use their judgement to place a DNR order on an infant's chart, without seeking parental consent or judicial authorisation, because consent is only needed for treatment. All that was required was a judicious exercise of physician judgement. That is, the court characterised a DNR order as not being a form of treatment.[93] This decision has not been favourably received. It assumes consent is given for resuscitation unless it has been expressly refused, it ignores how a DNR order is part of a broader plan of treatment, and it artificially draws distinctions between positive and negative aspects of the plan.[94]

This approach has not been followed in more recent cases, such as the 2014 decision in *Chalifoux v Alberta Health Services*.[95] That case concerned an infant who was born with a presumptively fatal medical condition that required aggressive and continuous painful interventions. Unlike the 1997 case, this infant was not vegetative, and would sometimes respond. However, the doctors saw no benefit in continuing the interventions, and characterised them as harmful. They recommended removing the artificial ventilator and adopting a palliative care plan.[96] The court agreed that moving to palliative care was in the infant's best interests.

The court considered and expressly declined to follow the reasoning in *RL*. It found judicial authorisation was necessary to override the parental choice to continue life-sustaining interventions, and physicians could not lawfully make such a unilateral decision. The court located its authority to intervene in legislation which permits a court to review a parental decision if it is 'likely to have serious long-term consequences for a child',[97] or in the alternative, in the court's *parens patriae* jurisdiction to make an order that is in the best interests of a child.[98]

In *Chalifoux*, and other cases, parents have argued that their child's best interests are not served by treatment choices that lead to their child's death. These arguments have been argued based in love for their child, and in religious belief.[99] When adjudicating such cases, courts refer to there being 'a general societal

[92] *Child and Family Services of Central Manitoba v RL* (1997), 154 DLR (4th) 409 (Man CA). The case is discussed at length in B Sneiderman, 'A Do Not Resuscitate Order for an Infant Against Parental Wishes: A Comment on the Case of Child and Family Services of Central Manitoba v RL and SLH' (1999) 7 *Health Law Journal* 205.

[93] *Child and Family Services of Central Manitoba v RL* (n 92).

[94] Gilmour (n 6) 236. See also Sneiderman (n 92).

[95] *Chalifoux v Alberta Health Services* 2014 ABQB 624.

[96] ibid [33]–[37].

[97] ibid [68].

[98] ibid [74].

[99] eg *Alberta (Child, Youth, and Family Enhancement Act, Director) v DL* [2012] AJ No 949 [64].

understanding that a life without awareness and totally supported by machines is not in accord with the best interests of any patient, including a child', and that invasive medical treatments should only be drawn upon 'where there is at least a potential benefit to the patient'.[100] This sort of reasoning rests on the conclusion that painful medical interventions which merely continue life with no hope of recovery or improvement do not in and of themselves provide a 'benefit', and may instead cause a harm.[101] In cases where the child is not believed to be capable of recovering awareness and is completely supported by machines, judicial decisions seem to favour ending treatment over the objections of parents. This trend appears to be at odds with the approach taken in Israeli courts. The jurisprudence which Gilbar[102] describes illustrates a prioritising of the 'sanctity of life' to the point that 'making judicial decisions not to provide life-prolonging treatment due to the child's pain and suffering would be rare'.

VI. Failure to Provide Necessities of Life

The previous discussions all involve instances where applications are brought to determine the best interests of a child, in the context of a disagreement between healthcare professionals and parents. Criminal charges may be laid if it is found that a parent or guardian 'failed to provide the necessities of life for a child under the age of 16', if a child is in 'necessitous circumstances', or if the failure results in endangering the life of the child or permanently endangers their health.[103] The necessities of life include medical attention.[104] While the majority of prosecutions brought under this provision involve situations where a child has died due to the lack of medical attention, for instance due to untreated infections which became septic[105] or untreated meningitis,[106] the jurisprudence is clear that the child's life does not need to be endangered for criminal liability to arise. The failure to act in the case of 'necessitous circumstances' will suffice, such as significant open wounds that remain untreated but have not endangered the child's life,[107] or not seeking treatment for burns given that the child cannot, on their own, seek treatment.[108] The standard for criminal liability is not perfection, and

[100] ibid [65]. Upheld 2012 ABCA 275. Leave to appeal denied 2012 SCCA No 364.
[101] *Chalifoux v Alberta Health Services* (n 95) [37].
[102] R Gilbar, 'Withholding and Withdrawal of Life-Prolonging Treatment from Young Children in Israel', in this book.
[103] Criminal Code, RSC 1985, ch C-46, ss 215(1)(a), 215(2)(a)(ii).
[104] See *R v Bakker* [2017] OJ No 5152 [137]; *R v J(s)* 2015 ONCA 97 [64] and [66].
[105] See *R v Lovett* 2017 ABQB 46.
[106] See *R v Stephan* 2017 ABCA 380 (overturned due to improper charge to jury, 2018 SCC 21 with the retrial starting in 2019).
[107] *R v J(s)* (n 104) [86]–[88].
[108] *R v Boone* 54WCB (2d) 621, [2002] OJ No 2796 [33].

mere negligence will not suffice.[109] It is an 'objective or community' standard of conduct, which asks if the parental action of not seeking medical attention was a '"marked departure" from what a reasonably prudent person would do' in the circumstances.[110] Once again we see a reference to societal standards being drawn upon.

VII. Conclusion

In Canada, parents are the substitute decision-makers for their decisionally incapable children's treatment choices. While this role attracts constitutional protection, it is not completely shielded, and is restrained by the right and obligation of the state to intervene if a child is in need of protection. Protection assessments, and therefore treatment choices, are evaluated in light of whether the parents' choice is in the best interests of the child. Where the prognosis is good, treatment is likely to be ordered over parental objections. Where prognosis is less clear, and other medical complications and risks are present, the other factors usually receive more weight in determining the best interests of the child. Thus, while physician recommendations carry considerable weight, emotional, religious, cultural and other factors also play a role. The best interests standard has cloaked racist treatment of Indigenous decision-making, a practice that is now challenged by changing legislation and jurisprudence which recognises constitutionally protected rights to use Indigenous medicines.

[109] *R v J(s)* (n 104) [54].
[110] ibid.

17

Offering a Reasonable Future: Withdrawal of Life-Sustaining Treatment from Infants in French Law with Illustrations from a Parisian Neonatal Resuscitation Unit

JEAN-FRÉDÉRIC MÉNARD*

I. Introduction

Less than fifteen years ago, French neonatology could be described as a Weberian ideal type of medical paternalism.[1] Since that time, the French legal landscape has undergone significant transformation, even though physicians continue to wield significant power with regard to the treatment of young children without decision-making capacity.

Protecting our common humanity while enabling individuals to flourish autonomously is, I would argue, the perilous task that French health law has set for itself in the last quarter of a century.[2] The French regime pertaining to withdrawal of life-sustaining treatment from infants and young children must therefore be

* The research for this chapter was funded by a doctoral scholarship from the Pierre-Elliot Trudeau Foundation and doctoral studentships from the Centre for Ethics and Law (UCL) and the Graduate School (UCL). I thank Dr Myriam Hunter-Henin (UCL) for her comments on a previous version.

[1] K Orfali, 'Parental Role in Medical Decision-Making: Fact or Fiction? A Comparative Study of Ethical Dilemmas in French and American Neonatal Intensive Care Units' (2004) 58 *Social Science & Medicine* 2009, 2011.

[2] See generally A Ponseille, 'Le droit de la personne malade au respect de sa dignité' (2003) 11 *Revue générale de droit médical* 159; M Canedo-Paris, 'La dignité humaine en tant que composante de l'ordre public: l'inattendu retour en droit administratif français d'un concept controversé' [2008] *Revue française de droit administratif* 979; D Roman, 'A corps défendant' [2007] *Recueil Dalloz* 1284; M-L Moquet-Anger, 'La dignité et le droit de la santé' [2016] *Revue française de droit administratif* 1075; G Glénard, 'La dignité de la personne humaine: un ordre de valeurs?' [2015] *Revue française de droit administratif* 869.

understood in light of the fundamental tension that runs through French law between upholding an objective conception of human dignity imposing limitations on individual choices and the recognition of the fundamental value of autonomy and self-determination.

In this chapter, I will review the current state of French law on the matter, as well as provide a contextual complement based on fieldwork I conducted between 2014 and 2017 in the neonatal resuscitation unit[3] of a Parisian university hospital exploring the norms (social, ethical and legal) applied by French healthcare professionals (HCPs) with regards to withdrawal of life-sustaining treatment from infants in their care.

II. Parental Authority

The civil law institution of parental authority provides a general mechanism whereby a child's parents are endowed with the right and duty to exercise the rights of their child with a view to furthering the child's interests.[4] It is the background against which more specific provisions relating to withdrawal of life-sustaining treatment arise.

Parents are primarily responsible for the upbringing of their children. The decisions of parents are legally protected as long as they promote the best interests of the child.[5] The Civil Code (CC) defines 'parental authority' as 'an ensemble of rights and duties having the interest of the child as its end' (Article 371-1 al 1 CC). It further adds that 'parental authority is granted to parents until majority or emancipation, for the purpose of protecting the child's safety, health, and morality, securing his education, allowing his development, with the respect owed to a person' (Article 371-1 al 2 CC).

In the medical context, parents have both a duty to seek medical treatment for their sick children and the power to exercise their children's right to consent to such medical treatment on their behalf.[6] The ability of parents to consent to treatment, or conversely to refuse treatment, for their children is limited by their duties toward their children.[7] Protection mechanisms are in place to ensure that

[3] The medical units known as neonatal intensive care units (NICUs) in the English-speaking world are called 'unités de réanimation néonatale' in France. In order to highlight the difference between the two, I will translate the French name as 'neonatal resuscitation unit' (NRU) which emphasises that the purpose of such a unit is to offer life-sustaining treatments rather than referring to such purpose euphemistically like its English counterpart does. More generally, all translations from normative materials are mine.

[4] CB Esper and M Dupont, *Droit hospitalier*, 9th edn (Paris, Dalloz, 2014) 759.

[5] J Carbonnier, *Droit civil 1 – Introduction les personnes. La famille, l'enfant, le couple*, 2nd edn (Paris, Presses Universitaires de France, 2017) para 414.

[6] I Corpart, *L'autorité parentale* (Rueil-Malmaison, Groupe Liaisons, 2002) 37–38.

[7] P Bonfils and A Gouttenoire, *Droit des mineurs*, 2nd edn (Paris, Dalloz, 2014) 442; A Laude, B Mathieu and D Tabuteau, *Droit de la santé*, 3rd edn (Paris, Presses Universitaires de France, 2012) 355.

the child receives necessary care notwithstanding the opinion of his or her parents to the contrary.[8]

The operational criterion in determining if parents are adequately discharging their duties toward their child is that of danger to the health of the child.[9] The Civil Code states that when parents fail to exercise parental authority properly, such that there is a 'danger to the health, safety or morality of a child', educational assistance measures may be ordered (Article 375 al 1 C.C.).[10] Article 375-1 al 1 CC attributes the jurisdiction over educational assistance measures to a magistrate with expertise with regard to matters concerning children, the 'judge of children'.[11] In deciding matters brought before him or her, the judge of children must 'endeavour to obtain the assent of the family to the contemplated measure and must rule exclusively in light of the interest of the child' (Article 375 al 2 CC).[12]

Traditionally, in the context of a disagreement between parents and healthcare professionals as to the appropriate medical care to give to a minor child, an educational assistance measure can be requested by the child's treating physician or by the hospital where the child is being treated (Article 375 al 1 CC; Article R 1112-35 Code of Public Health (CPH)).[13] Parents have a margin of appreciation in making decisions for their children. Parental decisions deemed to be reasonable are therefore out of reach of the jurisdiction of the judge of children, even though healthcare professionals might consider them less than optimal.

In this context, French law explicitly tolerates a certain level of potential harm to the child in order to uphold parental authority. In this regard, it differs from English law where the High Court exercises jurisdiction whenever the best interests of a child are raised before it and purports to identify the objective best answer to the issues raised.[14] In the seminal case of *Mme B ... c B ... I*, the Court of Appeal of Nancy concluded that it was unacceptable for the judge of children to intervene in the absence of any evidence of familial failing (*défaillance familiale*).[15] The Court of Appeal found that the judge of children ought to have refrained from exercising jurisdiction over a case where the child's mother had withdrawn

[8] Esper and Dupont (n 4) 754.

[9] F Capelier, *Comprendre la protection de l'enfance: l'enfant en danger face au droit* (Paris, Dunod, 2015) 114–15; D Duval-Arnould, *Le corps de l'enfant sous le regard du droit* (Paris, LGDJ, 1994) 79–83.

[10] Corpart (n 6) 37–40; Y Favier, 'La défaillance parentale en matiere de sante: protection judiciaire et protection medicale' (2005) *Revue générale de droit medical* 55.

[11] M Eglin, 'La Protection des enfants face à la liberte religieuse des parents, notamment dans le cas d'appartenance sectaire des parents' (2009) 44 *Enfances & psychologie* 130.

[12] ibid.

[13] ibid.

[14] *Re K (A Child) (Withdrawal of Treatment)* [2006] EWHC 1007; see also I Goold, C Auckland and J Herring, 'Medical Decision-Making on Behalf of Children in England and Welsh Law: A Child-Centred Best Interests Approach', in this book.

[15] *Cour d'Appel de Nancy, Chambre Spéciale, 3 Décembre 1982, Mme B c B.* JCP 1983 II 20081; Favier (n 10) 54–55; Capelier (n 9) 114; M King and A Garapon, 'Le juge, l'expert et le controle de la réalite dans les juridictions de la jeunesse en France et en Angleterre' (1988) 10 *Droit et société* 431; Duval-Arnould (n 9) 79; A Gouttenoire and H Fulchiron, 'Autorité parentale' in *Répertoire de droit civil* (Paris, Dalloz, 2017) para 84.

her adolescent daughter from one hospital to take her to another one, despite the claim from the treating team in the first hospital to the effect that the treatment proposed in the second hospital had less chance of saving the life of the child than what they proposed. In that case, the fact that the child's mother had opted for another course of treatment rather than refusing treatments altogether was determinative.

III. The role of physicians

In many of the jurisdictions discussed in this volume, medical decision-making for children is approached through the prism of the *ius commune*, the common law or a general statute on parental authority or responsibility, meaning that rules of general application are adapted to the medical context.[16] For its part, France is an example of a jurisdiction where a regime has been enacted specifically to allocate decision-making between parents and physicians.

Indeed, the respective roles of parents and of the judge of children with regard to health matters sketched out in the previous section needs to be nuanced in light of the specific mechanisms applicable to minors found in the Code of Public Health since 2002.[17] The duty to control the exercise of parental authority in matters of healthcare seems to be moving away from the judge of children to physicians, who are enabled to overlook the position of parents without applying for an educational assistance measure.[18] This decision-making power conferred on doctors is subject to the control of administrative courts. In principle, parents can challenge the decision of doctors to treat their child or to withdraw life-sustaining treatment by invoking a fundamental freedom, either theirs or that of their child – freedom of religion, personal integrity or personal autonomy are likely to form the basis of such claims – using a procedure called 'freedom referral to the court' (*référé-liberté*).[19]

[16] See eg in this book: A Büchler, 'Parental Decisions on their Children's Medical Treatment'; M Dobernig Gago, 'Parental Rights in Mexican Law'; Goold et al (n 14); C McIntosh, 'Decisionally Incapable Children and Medical Treatment Choices in Canada'; M Navarro-Michel, 'Young Children and Healthcare Decisions in Spain: Who decides?'; A Moyo, 'Parental Responsibility and Medical Decision-Making in Southern Africa: A Comparative Analysis of South Africa and Botswana'; D Chunyan, 'Medical Decision-Making on Behalf of Children in China: A Multidimensional Analysis of Parental Authoritarianism', all in this book.

[17] C Delaporte-Carré, *L'articulation des institutions de protection de la personne de l'enfant contre ses parents* (Paris, Dalloz, 2008) 38–39.

[18] A Kimmel-Alcover, 'L'autorité parentale à l'épreuve de la sante des mineurs: chronique d'un declin annonce' (2005) 2 *Revue de droit sanitaire et social* 265; F Dekeuwer-Defossez, 'L'autorité parentale à l'épreuve de la loi Kouchner' (2004) 12 *Revue générale de droit medical* 99, 104.

[19] Code de Justice Administrative, Art L 521-2.

IV. Limitation or Withdrawal of Treatment on the Basis of Unreasonable Obstinacy

Unreasonable obstinacy establishes essentially a severe harm threshold allowing physicians to withdraw or withhold such treatment in extreme circumstances. The bar for overriding parental preferences is therefore placed higher than for educational assistance measures, which can be applied for and obtained if danger to the health of the child is established. However, it is important to highlight that, unlike the reform of English law advocated by Auckland and Goold,[20] under the current French regime, physicians do not need court approval to withdraw or withhold life-sustaining treatment where they conclude that continuing or initiating it would amount to unreasonable obstinacy.[21]

The French legal framework also explicitly puts withdrawal and withholding of treatment in a distinct category, apart from the norm of reasonability that is applied to parents' appreciation of their child's best interests, notably in choosing between treatment plans. This is another important feature that distinguishes the French model from its English counterpart, where this two-tier model has been rejected in favour of applying a holistic interpretation of best interests.[22] The adoption of a regime aimed specifically at regulating withholding or withdrawal of treatment also sets France apart from other jurisdictions, such as Belgium, that provide physicians with authority to override parents in certain circumstances but do not distinguish between providing necessary treatment and withholding or withdrawing treatment against the wishes of parents.[23]

In the French legal regime, physicians hold significant discretion with regard to withdrawal of life-sustaining treatment. This discretion must be understood against the backdrop of the right to appropriate care found in Article 1110-5 CPH. Article 1110-5-1 CPH introduces the notion of unreasonable obstinacy, the cornerstone of the French legal regime. It reads as follows:

> 1110-5-1. The acts mentioned in article L 1110-5 must not be implemented or pursued when they ensue from unreasonable obstinacy. When they appear useless, disproportionate or as having no other effect than artificially maintaining life, they can be suspended or not be initiated in conformity with the will of the patient and, if the latter is incapable to express his will, following the collegial procedure defined through regulation.

[20] C Auckland and I Goold, 'Parental Rights, Best Interests and Significant Harms: Who Should Have the Final Say over a Child's Medical Care?' (2019) 78 *Cambridge Law Journal* 287.

[21] Compare with the Thai position which Tengaumnuay characterises as one of almost complete deference to the wishes of parents and therefore as situated at the other end of the spectrum (T Tengaumnuay, 'Parental Authoritarianism and Medical Decision-Making in Thailand: The Need to Limit Parental Authority', in this book). On the other hand, notwithstanding procedural differences, Western jurisdictions all confer significant authority on physicians.

[22] *Re J* (A Minor) (Wardship: Medical Treatment) [1991] Fam 33.

[23] See eg I Boone, 'Parental Rights, Best Interests and Significant Harm: Medical Decision-Making on Behalf of Children in Belgium', in this book.

> Artificial nutrition and hydration constitute treatments that can be stopped in conformity with the first paragraph of the present article.
>
> When the acts mentioned in the first two paragraphs of the present article are suspended or not initiated, the doctor must preserve the dignity of the dying person and ensure quality of life by providing the palliative care mentioned at article L 1110-10.

Unreasonable obstinacy is, to a large extent, the legal transposition of a vivid expression that was (and still is) broadly used in French public discourse, *acharnement thérapeutique*.[24] This culturally loaded expression can perhaps be translated as 'harmful therapeutic excess'. It refers to unjustified persistence in medical interventions, despite the inevitability of the patient's death or irremediable loss of either consciousness and human relations or quality of life.[25] The expression 'unreasonable obstinacy' was preferred in the legislative text as a way to convey a similar meaning, yet in a more neutral fashion.[26]

The function of unreasonable obstinacy is to point to the limit at which medical treatment becomes counterproductive and comes to be seen as impairing rather supporting the dignity of the patient, either by the patient himself, the patient's entourage or healthcare professionals. By highlighting the type of care that is not appropriate and ought therefore not to be provided, Article 1110-5-1 establishes a clear contrast with the type of medical care that is appropriately provided.[27] Some authors insist that unreasonable obstinacy has never been legal and therefore that there was no need to prohibit it.[28] Nonetheless, it was meant as an answer to the anxiety of the medical profession as to the question whether withdrawing or withholding certain treatments could be in contradiction with their duties to provide care and to provide assistance to a person in danger.[29] Similarly, the legislator insisted on the symbolic importance of reiterating the prohibition.[30]

A. What Constitutes Unreasonable Obstinacy?

The French legislator intentionally left the notion vague, notably to ensure that it would always be applied to the specific characteristics of a given patient's

[24] J-L Misset, 'Cancer en phase avancée et obstination déraisonnable' (2016) 64 *Laennec* 21, 22.

[25] P Le Coz, 'Acharnement thérapeutique: approche éthique', *Dictionnaire de droit de la sante et de la biomedecine* (Paris, Ellipses, 2006) 20.

[26] L Fermaud, 'Les droits des personnes en fin de vie' (2016) *Actualité juridique droit administratif* 2143; E Cadeau, 'Obstination déraisonnable', *Dictionnaire de droit de la santé et de la biomédecine* (Paris, Ellipses, 2006) 228.

[27] A Mirkovic, 'Patient polyhandicapé et obstination déraisonnable' (2017) 5 *Droit de la famille* 64.

[28] G Mémeteau, *Cours de droit medical*, 4th edn (Bordeaux, Les Études Hospitalières, 2011) 431.

[29] ibid 371; D de Saint Affrique, 'Regard sur la loi relative aux droits des malades et a la fin de vie' (2005) 74–75 *Médecine & droit* 133, 141; J Coelho, 'La loi n° 2005-370, du 22 avril 2005, relative aux droits des malades et à la fin de vie' (2005) 17 *Revue generale de droit medical* 335, 340.

[30] Commission spéciale chargée d'examiner la proposition de loi relative aux droits des malades à la fin de la vie, 'Rapport sur la Proposition de loi de M Jean Leonetti et plusieurs de ses collegues relative

predicament and that it would not become too constraining to achieve its purpose.[31]

Even though it does not offer a comprehensive or conceptual definition, Article 1110-5-1 highlights three types of treatment that are susceptible of amounting to unreasonable obstinacy: (1) acts that appear to be useless; (2) acts that appear to be disproportionate; and (3) acts that appear to have no other effect than artificially maintaining life.

These criteria are not cumulative, each of them being susceptible of characterising a treatment as amounting to unreasonable obstinacy.[32] In attempting to unpack their meaning, I will rely primarily on the observations that Jean Leonetti, the spearhead of French legal reforms in relation to end of life for the last quarter century, submitted to the State Council as a part of the 2014 procedure in the Vincent Lambert case.

i. Uselessness

For Leonetti, the utility of a treatment has to be defined in relation to a specific objective. If a proposed treatment cannot be related to a desirable objective *for the patient*, it is useless. Such objectives have to be specific to the actual situation of the patient. Objectives that are too general or determined a priori would not qualify as being useful to the patient, nor would scientific interest alone. Objectives include curing the patient, managing symptoms, alleviating pain and suffering, increasing comfort and so on.[33] On the other hand, even when interventions based on a curative objective are deemed to be useless, interventions aimed at appeasing pain and suffering or increasing the comfort of the patient remain entirely justifiable. Leonetti also suggests that the criterion of uselessness is akin to that of 'futility' as it is used, somewhat controversially, in English-language medical ethics.[34]

ii. Disproportionality

Leonetti distinguishes two categories of disproportionate treatments. In the first are those where the burden of expected secondary and undesirable effects of an intervention exceeds the expected benefits from the intervention. He notes

aux droits des malades et à la fin de vie' (Assemblée Nationale 2004) no 1929, 15–19, www.assemblee-nationale.fr/12/rapports/r1929.asp#P164_27482.

[31] ibid.

[32] J Leonetti, 'Observations de Jean Léonetti' (2014) 4 *Revue française de droit administrative (RFDA)* 696; see also J Leonetti, 'Obstination déraisonnable et droits des patients dans la loi du 22 avril 2005' (2014) https://jeanleonetti.com/sites/default/files/rapport_leonetti_obstination_deraisonnable_et_droits_des_patients.pdf, 2; P Véron and F Vialla, 'Arrêt des traitements: deux premières applications de la loi du 2 février 2016' (2017) 5 *Actualité juridique droit administratif* 301.

[33] Leonetti (n 32) 2.

[34] ibid; LJ Schneiderman, 'Defining Medical Futility and Improving Medical Care' (2011) 8 *Journal of Bioethical Inquiry* 123; see also Navarro-Michel on futility in the Spanish context (n 16).

that 'going ahead with a round of chemotherapy that is not well supported and would only add a few days of survival' is a prime example of a disproportionate treatment.[35]

On the other hand, disproportionality should also be appreciated with regard to the expected effect of the intervention on the patient, not only with regard to its secondary effects. This is the reasoning that allows artificial hydration and nutrition to be characterised as disproportionate when survival is irremediably compromised or when major and irreversible neurological injuries make relational life and self-consciousness impossible, as now codified in paragraph 2 of Article 1110-5-1 CPH.[36]

iii. No Other Effect than Artificially Maintaining Life

Leonetti suggests that the notion of having no other effect than artificially maintaining life refers to the idea of a life that is maintained solely in its biological dimension when the patient cannot experience self-consciousness and relational life. Consequently, this criterion is aimed at capturing the cases of patients diagnosed as being in either a chronic vegetative state or a minimally conscious state who receive life-sustaining therapies. Leonetti distinguishes such situations from those where intensive care is used as a bridge to a cure or an improvement in the patient's condition, those where organ replacement therapy allows patients to continue a meaningful life (eg dialysis in an otherwise healthy patient), and those where despite a cognitive impairment, the patient is capable of expressing desires, to experience pleasure and to relate with others (eg a person suffering from an advanced stage of Alzheimer's disease).[37]

Even though the three criteria found in Article 1110-5-1 provide some useful guidelines that outline the scope of the notion of unreasonable obstinacy, the notion was deliberately left undefined to ensure that its application would be tailored to the specific circumstances of each patient. The crucial task of specification was therefore left to medical teams as part of the collegial procedure, but also to the administrative judges who would inevitably by seized of the controversies arising from the application of the notion to specific situations.

B. The Collegial Procedure

The notion of unreasonable obstinacy is inextricably linked with the collegial procedure, for it is only following the collegial procedure that a determination of

[35] Leonetti (n 32) 2.
[36] ibid.
[37] ibid 3.

unreasonable obstinacy can be made and acted upon by the treating physician and the treating team.

Article R 4127-37-2 CPH sets forth the requirement of the collegial procedure. While collegiality is required in the consultation process, the decision-making power ultimately remains with the treating physician of the patient concerned.[38] The decision to limit or withdraw treatment on the basis of unreasonable obstinacy is made by the treating physician of the patient ('the physician in charge of the patient') following a consultation with the members of the treating team and in light of the reasoned opinion of at least one other physician who is hierarchically independent from the treating physician. If one of the two physicians deems it useful, a third physician can be consulted.

The treating physician must also enquire into the previously expressed will of the patient. The collegial procedure includes a hierarchy of sources from which this can be obtained. Obviously, this is only applicable in cases involving older children who would, at some point, have been able to express their will on such complex matters as end-of-life care or unreasonable obstinacy.

However, the second paragraph of Article R 4127-37-2 III specifies that for minors, the treating physician must also obtain the opinion of the holders of parental authority over that child, except in cases where urgency makes this impossible. As I show below, the interpretation to be given to this requirement remains controversial in French law.

Article R 4127-37-2 IV states that the decision to go ahead or not with a limitation or withdrawal of treatment must be supported by reasons and that such reasons are to be recorded in the patient's medical file, as well as communicated to the patient's trusted person, or if no trusted person has been appointed, to the patient's family or close circle.

C. Factors to Consider in Assessing Unreasonable Obstinacy

The 'affaire Vincent Lambert' as it is known in France, was a major milestone for French health law. The cases arising from it have both influenced the subsequent legislative developments and provide the leading judicial pronouncements on the French legal framework. However, given space limitations, I will take the context and details of the affair as read.[39] I will therefore focus solely on the detailed

[38] F Vialla, 'Penser sa mort ? A propos des decrets du 3 aout 2016' (2016) 32 *Recueil Dalloz Sirey* 1869, 1869–70.

[39] The affair has given rise to more than thirty court decisions at every level. It has recently come to an end with the final decision of the Cour de Cassation and by the death of Mr Lambert following interruption of medically administered hydration and nutrition on 11 July 2019. See Agence France-Presse, 'Man at Centre of French Family's Battle over Life Support Dies' *The Guardian* (11 July 2019)

methodology for assessing unreasonable obstinacy set forth in the 24 June 2014 decision of the State Council.[40]

The methodology adopted by the State Council is premised on the dual nature of unreasonable obstinacy, making its assessment dependent on both objective factors based on the professional appreciation of the patient's medical condition and on subjective factors grounded in the patient's dignity, will and social relationships.[41] As such, it also recognises that unreasonable obstinacy cannot be reduced to the appreciation of medical or scientific elements, even if, ultimately, the treating physician must take the decision.[42] Such assessment calls for being attentive to the ethical dimension of each specific situation and, as such, brings into play the most fundamental deontological obligations of healthcare professionals.[43]

Medical elements must include: (1) the current state of health of the patient; (2) the evolution of the patient from the time of the accident or the inception of the disease; (3) the suffering of the patient; and (4) the patient's clinical prognosis. Such medical elements ought also to cover a sufficiently long period of time and be analysed collegially.[44]

The State Council specifies that if a previously expressed will of the patient is not available, as will be the case for very young children, a desire not to be maintained alive should not be presumed. The treating physician must also consider the opinion of the patient's legal representative (*la personne de confiance*) if one has been appointed, as well as that of the members of his or her family, or failing that, a close associate, with a view to reaching a consensual position. The search for consensus is an obligation of means rather than an obligation of results: while the treating physician must endeavour to achieve it, his or her decision could stand without it, as long as reasonable efforts have been deployed.[45]

Finally, the State Council states that the analysis of a particular situation must, first and foremost, be guided by the highest level of beneficence (*bienfaisance*) toward the patient.[46] As observed by some commentators, the principle of beneficence is primarily an ethical principle, at least presented as such, and there is no obvious legislative grounding for invoking it in such cases.[47]

www.theguardian.com/world/2019/jul/11/vincent-lambert-man-at-centre-of-french-familys-battle-over-life-support-dies; Cour de Cassation, Assemblée Plénière, 28 juin 2019, 19-17330 19-17342, Publié au Bulletin.

[40] Conseil d'État, Assemblée, 24/06/2014, 375081, Publié au Recueil Lebon; D Truchet, 'L'affaire Lambert' (2014) 29 *Actualité juridique droit administratif* 1669.

[41] D Thouvenin, 'L'arrêt "Lambert", miroir des limites de la loi du 22 Avril 2005, dite loi Leonetti' (2014) 6 *Revue de droit sanitaire et social* 1101; F Vialla et al, 'Affaire Vincent L: les maux de la fin' (2014) 129 *Médecine & droit* 135, 139.

[42] F Vialla, 'Acta est fabula?' (2014) 28 *Semaine juridique (édition générale)* 1392.

[43] ibid; B Legros, 'Des clés pour tenter de résoudre les conflits secretés par le dispositif Léonetti aux certitudes du Conseil d'état dans l'affaire Vincent Lambert' (2015) 64 *Revue droit & santé* 188.

[44] Conseil d'État, Assemblée, 24/06/2014, 375081, Publié au Recueil Lebon (n 40) [17].

[45] Legros (n 43).

[46] Conseil d'État 375081 (n 40) [17].

[47] Truchet (n 40); Vialla et al (n 41) 141.

Nonetheless, a duty of beneficence is at the heart of the deontological duties of healthcare professionals, who are bound to 'serve the individual and public health and, in fulfilling their mission, to respect human life, the person and its dignity' (Article 4127-2 CPH).

This methodology has been applied again by the State Council in the case of a young child, a ten-month-old baby who was hospitalised in the paediatric critical care unit of hospital on appeal from the Administrative Tribunal of Marseille. At first instance, the Administrative Tribunal concluded that the conditions allowing a physician to withdraw life-sustaining treatment were not met. The Tribunal observed that, because she was less than one year old, the child was not able to express her will and that, with a view to approach the situation with utmost beneficence, as mandated by the State Council, the opinion of her parents was of special significance. Considering the medical aspects of the case, the Administrative Tribunal noted that the child's condition had evolved slightly between the time of the decision to withdraw treatment and the last observations by the experts it had mandated to evaluate her. The Tribunal recognised that those changes were not sufficient to improve the very unfavourable clinical prognosis of the child. However, the Tribunal saw this improvement of the child's state as revealing that the decision to withdraw treatment had been premature in light of the requirement enunciated by the State Council in Lambert that the medical elements considered cover a sufficiently long period of time to be meaningful.

The decision of the Administrative Tribunal was appealed to the State Council. The State Council confirmed the approach taken by the Administrative Tribunal of Marseille which, in keeping with the Lambert methodology, insisted on the importance of evaluating medical aspects over a long period of time. It introduced the notion that the opinions of the parents of a minor child whose will is inherently impossible to ascertain by reason of her young age should be given 'special importance'.[48]

In relation to the relevant medical elements of the situation, the State Council invoked the high level of uncertainty that endured with regard both to the child's level of consciousness and the suffering and discomfort she experienced to confirm the assessment of the Administrative Tribunal.[49]

In relation to the non-medical elements of the analysis, the State Council endorsed the 'special importance' of the opinion of parents in circumstances such as that of an infant whose will cannot be enquired into in the process of gathering the non-medical elements. However, it remained silent on the connection between the opinions of parents and the duty of beneficence.[50] The State Council went on to conclude that the fact that the child was in an irreversible state of lack of autonomy,

[48] Mirkovic (n 27).
[49] Conseil d'État, Juge des Référés, 08/03/2017, 408146, Publié au Recueil Lebon, [22].
[50] ibid [23].

making her dependent on life-sustaining treatments, did not, on its own, make the treatments she was receiving useless, disproportionate or having no other effect than artificially maintaining life. As such, the situation of the child could not be characterised as amounting to unreasonable obstinacy.[51]

In a comparative context, we can ask whether the French regime is susceptible of yielding outcomes different to those produced by other legal regimes, such as the English one. The position of the hospital in the Evans and Gard cases, even though it was framed in terms of best interests, was close to arguing that continuing with life-sustaining treatments amounted to unreasonable obstinacy. In my view, the results under the French regime would have been the same in both cases.

In the Evans case, I can identify no element that could have been used to counter the conclusion that continuing with life-sustaining treatment amounted to an unreasonable obstinacy argument. For instance, even though transfer to Italy was proposed, it did not purport to add any further chance of a cure.[52] Similarly, notwithstanding the interpretation of his parents, nothing indicated that Alfie Evans's condition was improving, even slightly.

On the other hand, in the case of Charlie Gard, an added difficulty came from the fact that an experimental treatment was proposed by another physician. The very slight chance of improvement, along with the favourable opinion of the child's parents, had to be balanced against continuing and prolonging the burdens of treatment. If the chance of improvement is taken to be less than zero, it cannot be said that life-sustaining treatment is entirely futile or useless. Similarly, if the purpose is to give the child an ultimate chance at a cure, life-sustaining treatment cannot be seen as having no other effect than artificially maintaining life. What we are left with, then, is the issue of whether the burden of treatment, both present and projected, is proportional to the probability that the experimental treatment would improve the child's condition. Again, it appears likely that the concrete evidence of the burden of a prolonged stay in a neonatal intensive care unit would be found to be out of proportion to the slight chances of success of the proposed treatment.

This tentative application of the French regime to the facts of these two controversial English cases is incomplete because it leaves out an important systemic distinction in the organisation of the two regimes. In the French regime, physicians are the default decision-makers, whereas in English law, parents occupy this position.[53] This difference, I would argue, has the potential to influence outcomes profoundly.

[51] ibid.

[52] *In re E (A Child) (Child on Life Support: Withdrawal of Treatment)* [2018] EWCA Civ 550, [21].

[53] On the influence of default rules in non-ideal situations, see eg CR Sunstein and RH Thaler, 'Libertarian Paternalism Is Not an Oxymoron' (2003) 70 *University of Chicago Law Review* 1159, 1174 et seq.

Another crucial aspect to consider in appraising the French regime and contrasting it with other legal solutions is to consider how it is received and applied in context, notably in the vast majority of cases that do not spill over from the wards to the courts.

V. Offering a Reasonable Future to the Child and the Family: An Illustration of the Practical Application of the French Regime

In effect, in an area as fraught as the end of life in paediatrics, where non-jurists wield significant influence over outcomes, attention to 'law on the books' only offers a partial picture.[54] In order to gain a deeper understanding of the law and ethics of neonatology, in the context of my doctoral research I conducted fieldwork in the neonatal resuscitation unit (NRU) of a Parisian university hospital.[55]

In this NRU, whenever the possibility of withdrawing life-sustaining treatment was considered, a meeting of all the staff of the unit was called. Most, and often all, of the unit's neonatologists would attend, as well as some other specialists depending on the specific situation of the child, along with fellows, residents and medical students. Nurses and allied professionals also attended. Parents are never invited to such meetings.

Even though they are not labelled or announced as such, such meetings appear to meet all of the formal requirements of the collegial procedure. The meetings are chaired by the head of the department. As far as physicians are concerned, it functions collegially. The group seeks to reach a consensus on the situation of the child and on the orientation to give the treatment plan, including whether it is appropriate to discuss withdrawal of life-sustaining treatment with parents.

In line with the *Lambert* criteria, the analysis includes medical factors such as the child's diagnosis, prognosis, the potential burdens of treatment throughout the projected life of the child and the potential for meaningful interactions. It also delves deeply into non-medical factors and considers the attitudes and reactions of the parents, the presence of other children in the family, as well as social elements including the socioeconomic status, living arrangements and immigration status of the parents.

[54] See generally RA Macdonald and K Glover, 'Implicit Comparative Law' (2013) 43 *Revue de droit de l'Université de Sherbrooke* 124.

[55] I interviewed several healthcare professionals, from nurses to senior consultant neonatologists, and allied professionals. I observed the functioning of the unit and attended several meetings where the status and treatment plan for severely disabled neonates and infants was discussed. Obviously, as this is qualitative research conducted on a single site, such findings cannot be generalised to all French NRUs.

For physicians, the notion of unreasonable obstinacy is founded on the belief that treatment can be appropriate at one point over the course of a child's illness trajectory, yet persisting with it calls for periodic re-evaluation. The team adheres to the typically French conception of 'standby reanimation', according to which the ethical warrant for offering critical care is to be obtained, or at least revised and confirmed, once the treatment has been initiated.[56] The purpose of standby resuscitation is therefore to ensure that any child who can benefit from critical care receives it and that it is discontinued for those for whom it is deemed to amount to unreasonable obstinacy.[57]

As a result, the question of unreasonable obstinacy is somewhat reversed in the discussion. We can also hypothesise that it is, at least partially, conflated with the broader question of the best interests of the child, traditionally understood as a standard of reasonableness.[58] The overriding question for HCPs in the Parisian NRU is whether continuing with life-sustaining treatment is reasonable, and whether it can offer a reasonable future to the child and their family. Logically, what is reasonable is necessarily not unreasonable, yet it is debatable whether concluding that a treatment plan that is not reasonable according to the analysis described here necessarily leads to unreasonable obstinacy.

In effect, the discussion is often quite broad and includes many of the elements that Ujewe associates with the 'network of communal relationships' that he argues characterises the African ethics outlook. Notably, the social positioning of parents, as well as the projected place of the child within her family, both nuclear and extended, are considered.[59]

However, even if relational aspects are extensively discussed in the context of the collegial procedure, physicians in the Parisian NRU do not see themselves as having the legitimacy to impose their interpretation of what would be a reasonable future on parents. We can speculate that the limited involvement of parents in the process contributes at least part of the explanation why this is. Furthermore, potential overreach in the interpretation of unreasonable obstinacy, and therefore in the jurisdiction of physicians, resulting from the focus on the reasonable rather than on the narrower range of situations that can be characterised strictly as unreasonable obstinacy, appears to be adjusted for in the way physicians approach parents. They indicated that they never actively seek to convince parents. The treating physician presents the conclusion of the collegial procedure as the considered view of the team and leaves it to parents to accept or refuse it.

[56] K Orfali, 'Extreme Prematurity: Creating "Latrogenic Lives"' (2017) 17 *American Journal of Bioethics* 34.

[57] Comité Consultatif National d'Ethique, 'Réflexions éthiques autour de la réanimation néonatale' (2000) 65 www.ccne-ethique.fr/fr/publications/reflexions-ethiques-autour-de-la-reanimation-neonatale#.V_zy25MrLFQ.

[58] LM Kopelman, 'The Best-Interests Standard as Threshold, Ideal, and Standard of Reasonableness' (1997) 22 *Journal of Medicine and Philosophy* 271, 279.

[59] S Ujewe, 'Making Decisions for Children in Healthcare and Medical Research: African Communal Responsibility or Individual Rights?', in this book.

In light of the high esteem in which the expertise of French physicians is generally held and the considerable influence of default options on decision-making, the team recommendation undoubtedly carries significant normative weight.[60] Yet parental authority, notwithstanding its uncertain status in the formal legal regime, seems to be given the last word in determining whether life-sustaining treatment constitutes unreasonable obstinacy in practice. Such deference to parents is in sharp contrast with both the formal French and English legal regimes.

VI. Conclusion: The Articulation of the Power of Physicians to Withdraw Life-Sustaining Treatment and Parental Authority Remains Uncertain

As observed by Mirkovic, the legal regime in virtue of which the treating physician takes the decision to withdraw life-sustaining care following the collegial procedure amounts to depriving parents of their authority on the matter and, therefore, to ignoring the fact that the minor child is legally represented by her parents.[61]

Furthermore, in light of the status of the collegial procedure as a regulation, it is not clear whether it can supersede parental authority. Unlike cases in which parents refuse to consent to care for their child and there is a risk that serious consequences for the child will follow from that refusal, where it is clearly stated that the physician is entitled to provide indispensable care (Article 1111-4 paragraph 6 CPH), there is no indication in the wording of Articles L 1110-5-1 or R 4127-37-2 CPH to the effect that they operate notwithstanding the duty of parents to consent to medical care for their child or the provisions of the Civil Code on parental authority.[62]

Nonetheless, even assuming that minors are not subjected to a different regime by reason of parental legal representation having precedence over the collegial procedure, the role of parents and the weight to be given to their opinion needs to be clarified. While it seems correct to suggest that the opinion of a child's parents is germane to the kind of holistic appreciation of relevant factors that is mandated by the State Council's methodology, the question remains open as to how this 'special importance' is delineated and how much weight it is given in the overall determination.

As already mentioned above, in presenting its methodology in *Lambert*, the State Council insists that the respective weight of each element under consideration

[60] MF Haward and A Janvier, 'An Introduction to Behavioural Decision-Making Theories for Paediatricians' (2015) 104 *Acta Paediatrica* 340.

[61] Mirkovic (n 27).

[62] F Vialla, 'In limine primo (au premier seuil de l'âge)' (2017) 14 *JCP G Semaine juridique (édition générale)* 666.

should not be preordained. It also states quite clearly that the previously expressed will of the patient concerned is of particular importance.[63] Should the will of the child's parents systematically play a similar role in the case of an infant who has yet to acquire the capacity to form and express her own will? Or should the will of the child's parents occasionally be subordinated, for that same reason that the child does not have a clearly articulated will, such that other factors, including the lack of capacity to form meaningful relationships or the potential discomfort, pain and suffering associated with prolonged life-sustaining treatments, can be seen as tilting the balance toward a conclusion of unreasonable obstinacy? To put it differently, should the parents hold a quasi-veto in the context of the collegial procedure, or should their opinion be treated as that of the trusted person or that of family members in adult cases? These are questions to which French law has yet to articulate a definitive answer even if the current practice of physicians points toward deference to the opinion of parents.

[63] Conseil d'État 375081 (n 40) [17].

18

Parental Responsibility and Medical Decision-Making in Southern Africa: A Comparative Analysis of South Africa and Botswana

ADMARK MOYO

I. Introduction

This chapter analyses the reach of the laws governing parental consent to medical and surgical treatment in South Africa and Botswana. The choice of countries is informed by their shared Roman-Dutch and English legal history, their ratification of the Convention on the Rights of the Child (CRC) and the African Children's Charter, and efforts these countries have made – and continue to make – both through judicial interpretation and legislative interventions to regulate parental consent to children's medical treatment. More importantly, these countries have protected children's rights either within their constitutions or national legislation. In addition, both South Africa and Botswana have enacted specific legislation entrenching children's rights and governing, whether directly or indirectly, parental consent to the medical or surgical treatment of their children.

This chapter investigates the extent to which the applicable laws, including case-law, balance parental responsibility, child participation and state intervention in medical decision-making. In order to do so, the chapter explains who has the legal capacity to make specific treatment decisions and under what circumstances; thereby giving details on the circumstances under which parents, children or state functionaries are authorised to consent to children's medical treatment in the two countries under study. In South Africa, parental consent to children's medical or surgical treatment is now comprehensively regulated by the Children's Act.[1]

[1] Act 38 of 2005.

Consequently, this chapter examines the extent to which the relevant provisions of the Children's Act either erode parental responsibility or create an appropriate balance between parental responsibility and state intervention in medical decision-making. The chapter also discusses the values, principles or standards informing medical decision-making in Botswana and South Africa, the threshold for judicial intervention and the tests applied by the courts. It emerges that there are strong overlaps between the relevant principles or standards in the two countries although there is a lot that Botswana can learn from the South African experience.

II. Medical and Surgical Treatment

A. Parental Consent to Children's Medical Treatment in South Africa

Just like ministerial and court-ordered consent to medical or surgical treatment, parental medical decision-making in South Africa should comply with certain standards that are protected in the Constitution. Like everyone else, children have rights to life and health that are explicitly provided for in the Constitution. Protected in section 11 of the Constitution, the right to life is entirely illimitable and non-derogable under South African law, even during public emergencies.[2] The elevation of human life to a non-derogable right has implications for the way in which parents, hospital authorities and the state approach consent to or refusal of treatment on behalf of children. It suggests that refusal of life-saving treatment or acceptance of life-threatening medication by anyone is invalid and should be overridden by the courts as ultimate guardians of the supreme Constitution.

The Constitution also protects every person's right to healthcare services and provides that 'no one may be refused emergency medical treatment'.[3] Since the standard appears to be that the sick must be treated, this provision also has implications for the exercise of parental responsibilities that relate to treatment decisions for both adolescents and the very young, especially during medical emergencies. In addition, the child's right to healthcare services is underlined in section 28(1)(c) and, at that level, its realisation does not appear to be explicitly subject to the availability of resources or progressive realisation.[4] Lastly, the

[2] See the table on derogations during public emergencies in s 37 of the South African Constitution.
[3] See s 27(1) and (3) of the South African Constitution.
[4] For textual comparisons, see s 27(2) of the South African Constitution which provides that the enjoyment of the general right to healthcare services is subject to progressive realisation and resources that are available to the state.

enjoyment of children's rights, including access to treatment or surgery, is governed by the general principle that '[a] child's best interests are of paramount importance in every matter concerning the child'.[5] As will be demonstrated in some detail below, the best interests of the child and the other rights briefly referred to above have shaped the approach taken by Parliament and the courts to parental consent to or refusal of treatment on behalf of children.

In non-emergency situations,[6] parents or guardians have the responsibility for making medical decisions for two groups of children. Section 129(4) of the Children's Act provides that:

> The parent, guardian or care-giver of a child may, subject to section 31, consent to the medical treatment of the child if the child is (a) under the age of 12 years; or (b) over that age but is of insufficient maturity or is unable to understand the benefits, risks and social implications of the treatment.

Similarly, section 129(5) of the Children's Act confers on parents or guardians the responsibility to consent to surgical operations, again subject to section 31, on behalf of the same categories of children. These provisions allow parents or guardians to make medical decisions for children (a) who are either below the age of twelve years or (b) whose capacities have not yet fully developed when they reach the statutory age of consent (twelve years).

Children below the age of twelve years have no legal capacity to give consent to medical treatment and surgical operations. This lack of capacity is statutorily constructed and it matters not that the child in question factually possesses the 'sufficient maturity and mental capacity' required to make independent medical choices. Therefore, treatment and surgical decisions for children below twelve years of age are to be made by parents or guardians.[7] Where there is no parent or guardian, decisions concerning medical treatment may be made by a caregiver.[8] Only when a parent, guardian or caregiver is unable to give consent (or is deceased) or unreasonably refuses to grant consent to treatment will ministerial or court-ordered consent be sought to ensure that the child receives treatment or undergoes surgery.[9] For the very young, the legislative scheme for consent to medical or surgical treatment relies solely on age as a ground for denying them autonomy in decision-making. The Children's Act does not even refer to 'sufficient maturity and mental capacity' in respect of children below the age of twelve years and it does not explicitly say that such children are presumed to lack capacity for rational action.

There is some direction on how courts are likely to handle the issue of parental consent to children's medical treatment. In *Hay v B*,[10] Dr Hay, a paediatrician

[5] s 28(2) of the South African Constitution.
[6] For rules governing emergencies, see s 129(6) of the Children's Act.
[7] s 129(4) and (5) of the Children's Act.
[8] s 129(4) of the Children's Act.
[9] s 129(7) and (9) of the Children's Act.
[10] *Hay v B* 2003 (3) SA 492 (W).

attending to baby R, made an urgent application asking the High Court to authorise an emergency blood transfusion to be administered to the baby. The child's condition was deteriorating and the parents had denied an emergency blood transfusion on the basis of their religious beliefs. Jajbhay J held that in terms of section 28(2) of the Constitution, the best interests principle 'is the single most important factor to be considered when balancing or weighing competing rights and interests concerning children'.[11] Besides, the High Court as the upper guardian of all children had the obligation to protect children.[12] According to the Court, these were the principles that had to be applied in this case.[13] The attending physician did not explicitly allege that parental refusal of consent was unreasonable in the circumstances, but instead emphasised that the administration of a blood transfusion substantially increased the child's chance of survival. Along these lines, the Court would later hold that while the religious beliefs of the parents deserved to be respected and the parents' concerns about the process were understandable, such beliefs were not reasonable and could not override the baby's right to life.[14]

The right to life played an important role in drawing the boundaries of the best interests of the child in *Hay v B*. Following *S v Makwanyane*,[15] the High Court emphasised the 'inviolable' nature of the right to life, insisted that baby R would die imminently if the transfusion were not administered and held that it was in baby R's interests that his right to life be protected.[16] Consequently, the Court held that it was clear that the religious beliefs of R's parents 'negate[d] the essential content of the right' to life as the baby had no chance of survival without the immediate administration of a blood transfusion.[17] Thus, while the parents' concerns were 'understandable', they were 'neither reasonable nor justifiable. Their private beliefs [could] not override baby R's right to life.[18] Applying the English Court of Appeal's decision in *T (a Minor) (Wardship: Medical Treatment)*,[19] the Court reiterated that the 'paramount consideration ... was the welfare of the child and not the reasonableness of the parents' refusal of consent'.[20] The Court held that where it is in the best interests of the child, the High Court as the upper guardian of all minors may order that the child receive medical treatment despite the parents' refusal to

[11] ibid 494I.

[12] ibid 494J–495A.

[13] ibid 495A.

[14] ibid 494–95. See also D McQuoid-Mason, 'Parental Refusal of Blood Transfusions for Minor Children Solely on Religious Grounds – The Doctor's Dilemma Resolved' (2005) 95 *South African Medical Journal* 29, 29.

[15] *S v Makwanyane* 1995 (3) SA 391 (CC) para 144, where the Constitutional Court held that '[t]here can be no more basic value constitutionally protected than the right to life'.

[16] *Hay v B* (n 10) 495B–C.

[17] ibid 495C–D.

[18] ibid 495D.

[19] *T (a Minor) (Wardship: Medical Treatment)* [1997] 1 All ER 906 (CA).

[20] *Hay v B* (n 10) 495G. See also M Katz, 'The Doctor's Dilemma: Duty and Risk in the Treatment of Jehovah's Witnesses' (1996) 85 *South African Law Journal* 484, 484.

consent to such treatment.[21] Ultimately, the Court held that 'the interests of baby R in receiving the blood transfusion outweigh[ed] the reasons advanced by the respondents in opposing the administration of such transfusion'.[22]

While *Hay v B* was decided before the passage of the Children's Act, it stands as authority for the view that the state and courts may override parental decisions that threaten the child's right to life as this right is more important than the parent's religious freedom. Elsewhere, courts have similarly held that a child's well-being outweighs a parent's religious freedom and that there is no liberty so sacred that parents can hide behind it to 'make martyrs of their children'.[23] There is emphasis on child protection over parental autonomy when it comes to life-and-death decisions concerning children.[24] The 'right to life is antecedent to all other rights'[25] and this explains the general reluctance to permit the termination of human life. Thus, courts should override the decisions of parents who reject medical interventions which prevent death or improve the child's medical condition. This approach is consistent with the gradual movement away from the historical portrayal of children as the property of their parents to the recognition of the child as an individual with separate rights that justify state intervention in the private family.[26]

[21] *Hay v B* (n 10) 495H–I.

[22] ibid 496J–496A.

[23] In *Prince v Massachusetts* 1944 321 US 158 (1944), the US Supreme Court held that: 'Parents may be free to become martyrs themselves, but it does not follow that they are free in identical circumstances to make martyrs of their children before they have reached the age of full and legal discretion when they can make choices for themselves.' See also *R v Senior* [1899] 1 QB 283 and *Re O (A Minor) (Medical Treatment)* [1993] 2 FLR 149. In England, courts have also authorised blood transfusions and HIV/AIDS testing of children born of minors in the face of unreasonable refusal of parental consent based on religious values and beliefs. See *Re E: (A Minor)(Wardship: Medical Treatment)* [1993] 1 FLR 386; *Re P (A Minor)(Medical Treatment: Best interests)* 2 All ER 1117 and *Re C (HIV Test)* [1999] 2 FLR 1004.

[24] See also S Woolley 'Children of Jehovah's Witnesses and Adolescent Jehovah's Witnesses: What Are Their Rights?' (2005) 90 *Archives of Diseases in Childhood* 715, where the author generally argues that parents have no right to refuse life-saving treatment or surgery on behalf of their child based on their religious beliefs and values, especially where such refusal places the child's life and survival in danger.

[25] See *S v Makwanyane* (n 15) [326]; see also J Fedler 'Life' in M Chaskalson, J Kentridge, J Klaaren, G Marcus, D Spitz and S Woolman (eds), *Constitutional Law of South Africa* 1 edn, RS 2 (Cape Town, Wetton and Johannesburg, Juta, 1998) 15–1, 15–3; and LS Flicker, 'Acting in the Best Interest of a Child Does Not Mean Choosing the Best Child' (2012) 12 *American Journal of Bioethics* 29, 30.

[26] For instructive readings on the property theory of children's rights, see T Hobbes, *De Cive* [1642], ed H Warrender (Oxford, Oxford University Press,1983) ch 9, [8], stating that while the parent can emancipate the child, such actions merely loosen parental authority, but do not liberate the child; E Brake and J Millum 'Parenthood and Procreation' in EN Zalta (ed), *The Stanford Encyclopedia of Philosophy* (Spring 2012) http://plato.stanford.edu/archives/spr2012/entries/parenthood/ [4.1]; T Hobbes, *The Elements of Law* [1640], ed JCA Gaskin (New York, Oxford University Press, 1994) ch 23, [8]; T Hobbes, *Leviathan* [1651], ed JCA Gaskin (New York, Oxford University Press, 1998) ch 2, [20]; R Filmer, *Patriarcha and Other Political Works of Sir Robert Filmer* [1653], ed P Laslett (ed) (Oxford, Basil Blackwell, 1949) ch 20, [3]–[4]; D Archard and C Collins, 'Introduction' in D Archard and CM Collins (eds), *The Moral and Political Status of Children* (Oxford, Oxford University Press,

B. Medical Treatment in the Context of Emergencies

The requirement of parental consent to treatment is not to be adhered to in cases of emergencies. At common law, a doctor may rely on the defence of unauthorised administration if he or she performs a medical intervention in circumstances where, as a result of shock, delirium, coma or unconsciousness, it is difficult to acquire the patient's consent to such an intervention.[27] For the doctor to rely on this defence, there should be an emergency in the sense of an imminent threat to the patient's life that makes the administration of the intervention urgently necessary to save the patient's life, prevent serious injury or preserve their health. The emergency must be so urgent that it is impossible to delay the intervention for purposes of obtaining consent from the patient or, in the case of incompetent minors, the person authorised to give consent.[28]

Today, emergencies are directly regulated by the Children's Act. Section 129(6) thereof provides as follows:

> The superintendent of a hospital or the person in charge of the hospital in the absence of the superintendent may consent to the medical treatment of or a surgical operation on a child if –
>
> (a) the treatment or operation is necessary to preserve the life of the child or to save the child from serious or lasting physical injury or disability; and
>
> (b) the need for the treatment or operation is so urgent that it cannot be deferred for the purpose of obtaining consent that would otherwise have been required.

Both these requirements should be met for emergency treatment to be lawful under this subsection. In emergencies, the requirements of parental, ministerial or court-ordered consent are bypassed and hospital authorities may treat the child without consent. Not even the consent of the child is necessary in these circumstances.[29] Like its predecessor,[30] the Children's Act ensures that the legal requirement of consent is not applied in a manner that delays the treatment of children in emergency situations. In such situations, waiting for the parent or the guardian to give consent to treatment would defeat the purpose of obtaining such consent.

2002) 1, 1; P King, 'Thomas Hobbes' Children' in SM Turner and GB Matthews (eds), *The Philosopher's Child: Critical Perspectives* (Rochester, NY, University of Rochester Press, 1998) 65, 81–82; and A Borkowski and P Du Plessis, *Textbook on Roman Law*, 3rd edn (Oxford, Oxford University Press, 2005) 113.

[27] *Stoffberg v Elliott*, 1923 CPD 148, 150 and *Castell v De Greef*, 1994 (4) SA 408 (C) 421.

[28] In *Stoffberg v Elliot* and *Esterhuizen v Administrator, Transvaal*, a two-year life expectancy and a one-year life expectancy were respectively held to be insufficient for purposes of an emergency and sufficient for purposes of obtaining the patient's consent.

[29] See also McQuoid-Mason (n 14), where the author argues that 'if medical treatment is necessary to save the child's life, or to prevent it suffering severe physical injury or disability, such treatment will be undertaken without consent'.

[30] s 129(6) of the Children's Act largely reproduces the provisions of s 39(2) of the Child Care Act.

C. The Values or Principles Informing Medical Decision-Making in South Africa, the Threshold for Judicial Intervention and the Tests Applied by the Courts

South African child law entrenches general principles which guide 'all proceedings, actions and decisions by any organ of state in any matter concerning a child or children in general'. Most of these general principles assist decision-makers in drawing the boundaries between parental responsibility, children's rights and state intervention (including the courts) in the medical decision-making context. In terms of section 6(1) of the Children's Act, 'if it is in the best interests of the child, the child's family must be given the opportunity to express their views in any matter concerning the child'. In addition, section 6(5) of the same statute also provides that 'a child and a person who has parental responsibilities and rights in respect of that child, where appropriate, must be informed of any action or decision taken in a matter concerning the child which significantly affects the child'. These provisions imply that the views of parents or those exercising parental responsibility perform a pivotal function in determining what is best for children needing medical care. In other words, courts and medical practitioners should not lightly dismiss the views of parents when making treatment decisions that protect children from significant harms.

While the best interests of the child remains one of the key standards in medical decision-making, courts should interpret the concept in a non-confrontational way that fosters cooperation between parents, children and the state. To this end, section 6(4)(a) of the Children's Act provides that 'in any matter concerning a child, an approach which is conducive to conciliation and problem-solving should be followed and a confrontational approach should be avoided'. A non-confrontational approach to children's medical treatment enables decision-makers to consider the problem not as a clash between the interests of parents and those of children, but as an invitation to decide what a proper parent–child relationship would be in the circumstances of each case.[31] A relational approach to the best interests of the child would accommodate the rights of parents and other family members. A relationship-based approach to children's medical treatment envisages an evaluation of competing interests and seeks to ensure that both parties are heard before determining where the interests of the child lie.[32] While they have not been directly invoked in any case, these legislative guidelines are likely to play an important role in shaping parental medical decision-making in the future.

[31] See generally J Herring, 'Welfare Principle and the Rights of Parents' in A Bainham et al (eds), *What Is a Parent? A Socio-Legal Analysis* (Oxford, Hart Publishing, 1999) 89, 101–02.

[32] See generally J Herring, 'The Human Rights Act and the Welfare Principle in Family Law – Conflicting or Complementary?', (1999) 11 *Child and Family Law Quarterly* 223, 225.

The best interests of the child and the reasonableness of the parent's actions are the key standards that are used to determine the correctness of treatment decisions relating to children. The Children's Act provides that 'in all matters concerning the care, protection and well-being of a child the standard that the child's best interest is of paramount importance, must be applied'.[33] One of the factors to be considered in determining the child's best medical interests is 'the need to protect the child from any physical or psychological harm that may be caused' by adopting a particular course of action.[34] As has been demonstrated by developments in the courts, parental refusal of medical treatment causes physical or psychological harm to, and in extreme cases the death of, the child. Accordingly, the courts will consider parental refusal of life-saving treatment to be harmful to children and therefore inconsistent with the latter's best interests. At that point, courts will intervene in the best interests of the child.

There is some overlap between the best interests principle and the role of reasonableness in shaping the courts' or treating physicians' approaches to parental decision-making in the medical context. Section 129(7)(a) of the Children's Act empowers the Minister of Social Development to consent to medical or surgical treatment for a child if the parent or guardian of the child unreasonably refuses to give consent or to assist the child in giving consent. This provision is relevant where the child is either under twelve years, or is over that age but lacks the capacity for informed consent. Section 127(7)(a) signifies a revolutionary departure from the public–private divide and its characterisation of the parent–child relationship as an essentially 'private' relationship to be insulated against state intervention. It recognises that parents sometimes act in ways that threaten the rights of children and permits the state to intervene in the family to promote children's health rights. This approach increases public accountability for children and correctly portrays parents as fiduciaries to be 'removed' from the office of parenthood if they act in ways that threaten the child's rights, health and well-being.

The High Court and, of late, the Children's Court have residual powers to order that medical interventions be administered on children. Historically, the High Court as upper guardian of all minors had the power to interfere with the exercise of parental authority over the child.[35] This power has now been largely codified

[33] s 9 of the Children's Act. See also s 28(2) of the South African Constitution.

[34] s 7(1)(l) of the Children's Act.

[35] See DSP Cronje and J Heaton, *South African Family law*, 2nd edn (South Africa, LexisNexis, 2004) 265 and B Van Heerden 'How the Parental Power is Acquired and Lost' in B Van Heerden, A Cockrell and R Keightley (eds), *Borberg's Law of Persons and the Family*, 2nd edn (Cape Town, Juta and Company (Pty) Ltd, 1999) 313, 313.

in several legislative instruments, in particular the Children's Act.[36] For instance, section 129(9) of the Children's Act provides that:

> The High Court or children's court may consent to the medical treatment of or a surgical operation on a child in all instances where another person that may give consent in terms of this section refuses or is unable to give such consent.

The courts have the power to override the decisions made by parents, children and the Minister of Social Development should any of these persons refuse to give consent or be unable to consent for any reason. Section 129(9) reinforces the idea that the power to consent to treatment or surgery should be exercised in the best interests of the child and the courts should override any refusal of treatment or surgery which is meant to save the child's life, or prevent injury or permanent disability. Given that several persons may grant consent to medical or surgical treatment for the child, the residual powers of the courts are rarely exercised in practice, but may be important where there is conflict between parents, the child and medical practitioners.

Where, for instance, a medical practitioner believes that treatment or surgery is necessary, but the parent and the child agree otherwise, courts may have to endorse the clinical judgement of the medical profession in order to protect the best medical interests of the child. Courts may also intervene in the child's best interests when there is disagreement between parents, or between parents and health professionals, about the proposed medical intervention.[37] Further, parent–child disputes on whether the child possesses the requisite competence to make certain treatment decisions independently are likely to end up in the courts, which are bound to make decisions that advance the child's best interests and basic right to life, survival and development.

Finally, the courts' powers are not just limited to instances where parents, children or other persons refuse or are unable to give consent to treatment. If the parent or the child consents to a procedure that is to the detriment of the child (eg non-therapeutic sterilisation), courts are entitled to disregard their views.[38]

[36] See s 28(1)–(2) which protects children's rights thereby authorising the courts to determine whether parents, who have an express duty to promote children's right to health in terms of the Constitution, are exercising parental responsibility in the best interests of the child. See also ss 1(1), 2(b)(iii) and 7(1)(l)(i)–(ii) of the Children's Act.

[37] See L Hagger, *The Child as Vulnerable Patient* (Farnham, Ashgate, 2009) 55, 59. See also *R v Portsmouth Hospitals NHS Trust ex parte Glass* [1999] 2 FLR 905.

[38] In *Re D (A Minor) (Wardship: Sterilisation)* [1976] Fam 185, Heilbron J reversed a widowed mother's decision to have her mentally challenged eleven-year old daughter sterilised. In the court's opinion, the procedure was not in the child's best interests, since it involved an irreversible procedure of a non-therapeutic nature, which would entail the deprivation of a basic human right to reproduce. Medical examinations had indicated that her condition was improving and that she might, at some future time, acquire the capacity to make an informed choice about the procedure. In the end, it was not considered a matter which fell within a doctors' sole clinical judgement and the court had to intervene.

The fact that non-therapeutic sterilisation is not intended to cure any medical condition, and may have far-reaching and irreversible implications for the child's capacity to reproduce, partly explains why children have been statutorily denied the legal capacity to undergo sterilisation before attaining majority status.[39] Section 2(1) of the Sterilisation Act provides that: 'No person is prohibited from having sterilisation performed on him or her if he or she is (a) capable of consenting and (b) 18 years or above.' Accordingly, all children are statutorily deemed to lack the capacity to consent to sterilisation procedures under all circumstances. The Act allows parents to consent to sterilisation procedures on their children, provided the sterilisation is meant to protect the health and life interests of the child.[40] The Act provides that: 'Sterilisation may not be performed on a person who is under the age of 18 years except where failure to do so would jeopardise the person's life or seriously impair his or her physical health.'[41] This provision implicitly imposes an absolute ban on parental consent to non-therapeutic sterilisation on their children. Nonetheless, there have been no court cases in which parents requested treatment that medical practitioners or the courts deemed not to be in the best interests of the child, and it is difficult to predict how domestic courts will handle such situations.

D. Child Participation and Best Interests in South Africa

In South Africa, child participation is one of the general principles governing the implementation of children's rights. To this end, section 10 of the Children's Act provides that 'every child has the right to participate in an appropriate way and views expressed by the child must be given due consideration'. It recognises the child's evolving capacities through the twin concepts of 'age' and 'maturity'. The concept of the evolving capacities of the child ground both parental control and the child's relative autonomy. Therefore, the principle of the evolving capacities of the child plays an important role in maintaining the balance between child participation, parental responsibility and state intervention.[42] It recognises that children experience rapid growth in their 'physical, cognitive, social and emotional functioning'; pass through zones of rational autonomy before attaining adulthood; and vary in the ages at which they become capable of making particular decisions.[43]

[39] ss 2 and 3 of the Sterilisation Act 44 of 1998.

[40] ss 2(1) and 3(1)(a) read together.

[41] s 2(3) of the Sterilisation Act.

[42] G Lansdown, *The Evolving Capacities of the Child* (UNICEF Innocenti Research Centre, Florence, 2005) 15.

[43] See CRC General Comment 4, paras 1 and 7; and CRC General Comment 7, para 17, where the Committee on the Rights of the Child authoritatively made the following remarks:

> Article 5 draws on the concept of 'evolving capacities' to refer to processes of maturation and learning whereby children progressively acquire knowledge, competencies and understanding,

As an emancipatory concept, the 'evolving capacities of the child' seeks to broaden youth autonomy and encourage children to assume responsibility for their actions. With age and maturity, the consequences of children's decisions increase and diversify until they reach the age of majority, at which point they will fully exercise the totality of their rights. As the child's capacities evolve, the child plays a central role in defining what is in his or her best interest – authorising courts, for instance, to override parental preferences.[44] Where a child is sufficiently mature to be rationally autonomous in making a particular decision, it would be inconsistent with the concept of the 'evolving capacities of the child' to insist that her views be co-terminal with parental preferences.[45]

The concept of the 'evolving capacities of the child' also grounds parental control and state intervention. The primary responsibility of parents is to protect children from the immaturity of their youth and to help them make difficult decisions in life. The Children's Act recognises children's vulnerability and immaturity as grounds for entrenching the right to special protection. Both the child's

> including acquiring understanding about their rights and about how they can best be realized. Respecting young children's evolving capacities is crucial for the realization of their rights and especially significant during early childhood, because of the rapid transformations in children's physical, cognitive, social and emotional functioning, from earliest infancy to the beginnings of schooling. Article 5 contains the principle that parents (and others) have the responsibility to continually adjust the levels of support and guidance they offer to a child. These adjustments take account of a child's interests and wishes as well as the child's capacities for autonomous decision-making and comprehension of his or her best interests. While a young child generally requires more guidance than an older child, it is important to take account of individual variations in the capacities of children of the same age and of their ways of reacting to situations. Evolving capacities should be seen as a positive and enabling process, not an excuse for authoritarian practices that restrict children's autonomy and self-expression and which have traditionally been justified by pointing to children's relative immaturity and their need for socialization. Parents (and others) should be encouraged to offer 'direction and guidance' in a child-centred way, through dialogue and example, in ways that enhance young children's capacities to exercise their rights, including their right to participation (art 12) and their right to freedom of thought, conscience and religion (art 14).

[44] See L Krappman, 'The Weight of the Child's view (Article 12 of the Convention on the Rights of the Child)' (2010) 18 *International Journal of Children's Rights* 501, 506–09 and CRC General Comment 4, para 17, where the Committee on the Rights of the Child explains that: 'Article 5 contains the principle that parents (and others) have the responsibility to continually adjust the levels of support and guidance they offer to a child. These adjustments take account of a child's interests and wishes as well as the child's capacities for autonomous decision-making and comprehension of his or her best interests.'

[45] R Hart, 'The Evolving Capacities for Children to Participate' in V Johnson, E Ivan-Smith, G Gordon, P Pridmore and P Scott (eds), *Stepping Forward: Children and Young People's Participation in the Development Process* (London, Intermediate Technology, 1998) 27–31. At para 17 of CRC General Comment 7, the Committee on the Rights of the Child observed as follows:

> Article 5 contains the principle that parents (and others) have the responsibility to continually adjust the levels of support and guidance they offer to a child. These adjustments take account of a child's interests and wishes as well as the child's capacities for autonomous decision-making and comprehension of his or her best interests. Evolving capacities should be seen as a *positive and enabling process, not an excuse for authoritarian practices that restrict children's autonomy* and self-expression and which have traditionally been justified by pointing to children's relative immaturity and their need for socialization. Parents (and others) should be encouraged to offer 'direction and guidance' in a child-centred way, through dialogue and example, in ways that enhance young children's capacities to exercise their rights, including their right to participation (art 12).

protection rights and the negative aspect of the basic right to life constitute solid reasons for limiting the child's desire to exercise personal autonomy in the medical decision-making process. The protective dimension of the evolving capacities of the child entails, among others, protection in making personal decisions that directly affect the child's own life, survival and development. In many contexts, the child's undeveloped capacities require the parent and the state to shield the child against unsound personal decisions.[46] In most cases, the child's long-term interests are not promoted by giving effect to his or her present desires and preferences. Yet, the involvement of children capable of expressing their views enriches the medical decision-making process.

III. Parental Consent to Children's Medical Treatment in Botswana

A. Developments in the Tswana Courts

In Botswana, there are few cases concerned with parental consent to children's medical treatment and there are no legislative provisions that directly regulate this field of the law. In *Attorney General v Kealotswe*,[47] the respondent was the mother of a six-month-old baby girl who had been diagnosed of anaemia. The girl was at serious risk of cardiac arrest if a blood transfusion was not administered. The respondent refused to give her consent for the blood transfusion on the ground that blood transfusions offended against her religious convictions as a Jehovah's Witnesses. This prompted the Attorney-General to approach the High Court seeking a declaration that the respondent's refusal to give consent was of no force and effect with respect to the minor child. The Attorney General also applied for an order authorising that a blood transfusion be administered to the infant.

The only reported case on parental consent to medical treatment, *Attorney General v Kealotswe*, was decided more ten years before the passage of the Botswana Children's Act in 2009.[48] Unfortunately, the Botswana Children's Act does not directly regulate parental consent to the medical treatment of their children. However, there are several values or factors that are likely to influence medical decision-making about children in the future. These include the best interests

[46] Developmental psychologists and neuroscientists have made significant strides in demonstrating that children, especially the very young, generally have *limited* capacity to engage in the reasoning process and to make informed decisions in light of the information at their disposal. See T Grisso, 'The Competence of Adolescents as Trial Defendants' (1997) 3 *Psychology, Public Policy and Law* 3, 8; and T Grisso, 'What We Know About Youth's Capacities' in T Grisso and RG Schwartz (eds), *Youth on Trial: A Developmental Perspective on Juvenile Justice* (Chicago, University of Chicago Press, 2000) 267–69.

[47] *Attorney General v Kealotswe* 1998 BLR 632 (HC).

[48] Act 8 of 2009.

of the child as defined in the Children's Act, and the child's evolving capacities and the need to protect children from physical, mental, emotional or any other type of harm, whether occasioned by parents or the state. These values or factors should not be analysed in isolation, but as part of a broader regulatory framework designed to promote child-friendly judicial and government approaches to access to medical care by children. More importantly, however, the factors or values to be considered appear to have been borrowed largely from the South African Children's Act, adopted five years before the Botswana Children's Act.

In determining these issues, the High Court started by noting that the government has a direct interest in the health and welfare of its citizens.[49] Gaefele J proceeded to hold that while the Court respected the respondent's right to exercise her right to freedom of conscience as enshrined in the section 11 of the Constitution of Botswana, the order the Court was being requested to make would neither be inconsistent with nor contravene the relevant provisions of the Constitution because the transfusion was to be done in the interests of the health of the infant.[50] In the circumstances of the case, held the Court, it was reasonably

> justifiable to substitute the respondent's consent to give medical treatment with that of the court. This is because the constitutional right that the respondent may claim to have is not … exercisable in relation to herself. She may have the right of guardianship over the minor but … this court as upper guardian of all minors has the right to intervene in the best interests of the child.[51]

Gaefele J would later insist that while the respondent is entitled to adhere to her religion and opinions, the 'court must speak on behalf of a minor who is unable to speak for herself'.[52] The judge lamented the absence of legislation regulating parental consent to medical treatment in Botswana, but drew inspiration from section 39(1) of the now defunct South African Child Care Act which allowed the intervention of the courts, the Minister of Health and hospital authorities to consent to the medical treatment of a child in the event that the parents unreasonably refuse to give such consent.[53] He observed that at common law, medical emergencies justify the examination and treatment of an infant, a minor or child without the consent of its parent or guardian, or otherwise the High Court as the upper guardian of all minors has the power to make an order authorising such examination, operation or treatment.[54] As such, the applicant was entitled to the order sought as it was 'very urgent to save the life of the infant'.[55] In the final

[49] *Attorney General v Kealotswe* (n 47) 634C.
[50] ibid 634G.
[51] ibid 634H–635A.
[52] ibid 635A.
[53] The provisions of s 39(1) of the Child Care Act are now reproduced, with some variations, in s 129 of the South African Children's Act.
[54] *Attorney General v Kealotswe* (n 47) 635E.
[55] ibid 635E.

analysis, the court declared the respondent's refusal to give consent to a blood transfusion on her minor child to be of no force and authorised medical personnel at the relevant hospital to perform the blood transfusion.[56]

In *Attorney General v Kealotswe*, the Court relied primarily on the child's best interests in health and life to override the parent's refusal of medical treatment on behalf of a young child. As shown above, this approach is consistent with that of South African courts. However, the courts in Botswana have not explained the reach of the best interests of the child and, as in South Africa, they have provided limited guidance on the meaning of the concept in the context of access to medical treatment and surgical operations.

B. The Values or Principles Informing Medical Decision-Making in Botswana, the Threshold for Judicial Intervention and the Tests Applied by the Courts

Botswana's Children's Act entrenches general principles and objects which guide the implementation of children's rights and child law. Among these principles and objects are the duty to advance the child's best interests; the need to protect children from harm; the need to acknowledge the role of parents and to preserve family relationships; and finally, child participation rights. These guidelines were enacted more than a decade after *Attorney General v Kealotswe* and are likely to shape parental consent to medical decision-making in the future. Under the Children's Act, any 'person or court performing a[ny] function or exercising a power under shall regard the best interests of the child as the paramount consideration'.[57] In determining the best interests of the child, parents, courts and the state should take account of the following factors:

- the need to protect the child from harm;
- the capacity of the child's parents, other relative, guardian or other person to care for and protect the child;
- the child's cultural, ethnic or religious identity;
- any wishes or views expressed by the child; and
- any other factor which will ensure the general well-being of the child.[58]

Two points stand out from legislative reach of the best interests of the child. First, this list excludes some factors or values that are either not related, or only remotely related, to parental consent to the medical treatment of children, but are nonetheless listed in section 6(1) of the Botswana Children's Act. Second, the list of factors to be considered is not exhaustive, especially given that the Act both refers to 'any

[56] ibid 635F-G.
[57] s 5(1) of the Children's Act.
[58] See s 6(1)(a)–(i) of the Children's Act.

other factor' and stipulates that section 6(1) of the Act should not be 'construed as limiting the factors that may be taken into account in determining what is in the best interests of the child'.[59]

i. Best Medical Interests as Protecting Children from Harm

The inclusion of 'the need to protect the child from harm' in the list of factors to be considered suggests that parental decisions that deny a child access to medical treatment or surgery cannot be deemed to be in the best medical interests of the child. 'Harm' in relation to a child is defined as, among other things, 'any form of harm or ill-treatment inflicted deliberately on a child' or any conduct that exposes or subjects 'a child to behaviour that may harm the child physically, emotionally or psychologically'.[60] In terms of section 4(c), one of the objects of the Children's Act is to 'protect children from harm'. It is also a guiding principle of the Children's Act that 'every child shall be cared for and protected from harm'.[61] Throughout the Children's Act, the need to prevent harm appears to be a guiding principle in the implementation of children's rights, including the right of access to healthcare.[62]

If the treating physician is of the view that the recommended medical intervention will protect the child from physical injury or psychological harm or from any defect or will save the child's life, the courts or the state are allowed to consent to the medical treatment of a child despite the parent's protestations. In other words, the parent would have demonstrated lack of capacity to care or protect the child as stipulated in the Act and the courts are allowed to intervene to defend or advance the best medical interests of the child. This line of thought is backed by the principle that one of the objects of the Children's Act is 'to provide for the protection and care of children where their parents have not provided, or are unable or unlikely to provide, that protection and care'.[63]

ii. Best Medical Interests as Preserving the Child's Religious Identity

The need to promote the child's religious identity while assessing the child's best medical interests is a difficult exercise, especially if such religious identify is inconsistent with what doctors believe to be medically appropriate for the young patient. On the one hand, if the child in question is both young and immature, it is easy for courts, the state and even hospital authorities to argue that the child has not formed

[59] s 6(2) of the Children's Act.
[60] s 1(d) of the Children's Act.
[61] s 7(b) of the Children's Act.
[62] See generally s 20(1)(b), 23(2)(b), 24(4)(b), 40(1)(j), 42(g)–(h), 43(5), 44(1), 56(2)(d), 62(1)–(4) and 93(1) of the Children's Act.
[63] s 4(b) of the Children's Act.

any religious identity and the treatment decision should be based squarely on the child's best interests of good health and life. On the other hand, difficult issues arise if the child in question is sufficiently mature to be rationally autonomous (*Gillick* competent) and makes an informed refusal of life-saving medical treatment based on their religious identity. In Botswana and South Africa, challenges are likely to arise if the child patient is a devout member of either specific (usually apostolic) sects that do not allow their members to attend hospitals for medical treatment or Jehovah's Witnesses who view blood transfusions as a violation of the basic tenets of their faith. These issues are yet to come before the courts in contexts that require the application of the mature minor doctrine.

iii. Best Medical Interests as Acknowledging the Role of Parents and Preserving Family Relationships

Some of the objects of the Children's Act are to 'promote the well-being of children, families and communities in Botswana', and to acknowledge the primary responsibility of parents and families to care for and protect children and to support and assist them in carrying out that responsibility'.[64] In deciding the child's best interests, decision-makers should take account of 'the capacity of the child's parents, other relative, guardian or other person to care for and protect the child'.[65] In addition, there are guiding principles that speak to the importance of parents in the child's life. For instance, the Act recognises that 'the parents, family and community of a child have the primary responsibility of safeguarding and promoting the child's well-being'.[66] It also provides that:

> [A] child's parents, other relatives, guardian and any other people who are significant in the child's life *shall be given an opportunity and assistance to participate in decision-making processes under this Act that are likely to have a significant impact on the child's life*.[67]

These provisions confer considerable autonomy on parents to make medical decisions on behalf of their children. In the absence of abuse by parents of this autonomy, the state should refrain from interfering with family autonomy in medical decision-making. They emphasise that even the twin concepts of the best interests of the child and parental responsibility have not – as was initially thought – spirited away the parental right to exercise discretion in making clinical decisions on behalf of their children.[68] This is the reason why the Act recognises that parents have the 'primary responsibility of safeguarding and promoting the child's

[64] s 4(a) and (d) of the Children's Act.
[65] s 6(1) of the Children's Act.
[66] s 7(c) of the Children's Act.
[67] s 7(e) of the Children's Act (emphasis added).
[68] For comparative analysis, see A Bainham, 'Is Anything Now Left of Parental Rights' in R Probert et al (eds), *Responsible Parents and Parental Responsibility* (Oxford, Hart Publishing, 2008) 23–42.

well-being'. Whatever content is ascribed to it, the phrase the 'best interests of the child' never implies that the child and its needs be considered in isolation but, on the contrary, envisions the child in the context of a system of relationships – the totality of the familial arrangements in which the child finds herself or himself. The legislative protection of parental or familial interests suggests that it is the parent's right and duty to make decisions that educate children to develop an understanding that their interests and rights are part of a broad scheme of relational rights and responsibilities for the protection of important family or social interests.

The importance of parental involvement in medical decisions is underlined by the fact that they must be afforded 'an opportunity and assistance to participate in decision-making processes that are likely to have a significant impact on the child's life'. It is obvious that medical or surgical treatment, whether these have negative or positive consequences on the child, are likely to have a significant impact on the child's life. In some cases, they constitute matters of life and death and will require the involvement of parents even if the law is silent. More importantly, the Children's Act requires medical staff and the state to ensure that parents are involved from an informed point of view. It provides that the child's parents, relatives or guardians should

> be given adequate information, in a manner and language they understand, regarding – (i) decision-making processes under this Act that are likely to have a significant impact on the child's life, (ii) the outcome and implications of any decision about the child, including an explanation of the reasons for the decision, and (iii) any relevant complaint or review procedure.[69]

These provisions create room for parents to be involved at every stage of the medical decision-making process; to demand a comprehensive explanation of the nature, risks and benefits of proposed medical interventions; and, if not satisfied, to request the courts to review the decisions made by attending physicians.

However, parental rights, involvement or autonomy should not be interpreted in a manner that perpetuates the private–public divide or masks existing unjust power relations that have confronted children for centuries. Nor does family autonomy mean that children are the property of their parents to be abused at their parents' whim. Parental autonomy is subject to permissible legal limits, especially where the child has suffered or is likely to suffer harm as a result of its exercise. In other words, the degree to which parents are entitled to exercise paternalistic oversight over children should reflect the degree to which children, based on their level of maturity, need such oversight.[70] As the child grows up and his or her capacities develop, the interests of the child can be equated with his or her wishes, views and preferences. As shown below, this line of reasoning was foreseen by the drafters of the Children's Act.

[69] s 7(f) of the Children's Act.

[70] See A Moyo, 'Reconceptualising the "Paramountcy Principle": Beyond the Individualistic Construction of the Best Interests of the Child' (2012) 12(1) *African Human Rights Law Journal*, 142, 165.

iv. Best Medical Interests as Giving Due Weight to Children's Views

In assessing a child's best medical interests under the Children's Act, regard must also be had to 'any wishes or views expressed by the child, having regard to the child's age, maturity and level of understanding in determining the weight to be given to those wishes or views'.[71] This provision directly imports the mature minor doctrine into the laws of Botswana and clearly implies that when making treatment decisions affecting children, parents and the courts should attach significant weight to the views of competent children. In addition, and perhaps more importantly, the inclusion of the child's views in the analytical framework of the child's best interests suggests that medical decisions that are made without consulting with the child or eliciting the latter's views are not in the best interests of the child. This is consistent with the codification of child participation in decision-making as one of the basic principles governing the interpretation and application of the Children's Act.[72]

Under section 8(1) of the Children's Act, every child who is mature enough to 'be able to participate in decisions which have a significant impact on that child's life shall have a right to do so'. This broad entitlement is the broken down into key sub-rights that inform meaningful participation. Accordingly, the child is entitled to adequate information that is presented in a manner and language that the child understands. This information should relate to (i) the decision to be made, (ii) the reasons for the involvement of persons or institutions other than the child's parents, other relatives or guardian, (iii) the ways in which the child can participate in the decision-making process, and (iv) any relevant complaint or review procedures.[73] In addition, the child should also be afforded the opportunity to express his or her wishes and views freely, and given any assistance that is necessary for him or her to express those wishes and views; given adequate information regarding how his or her wishes and views will be taken into account; provided with adequate information about the decision made and a full explanation of the reasons for the decision; and finally be given an opportunity to respond to the decision made.[74]

The right to be heard enables competent children to challenge adult authority and imposes on parents and the state the duty to cede control of the medical decision-making process to children when this is justified by the child's age and maturity. Therefore, the Children's Act recognises children as social actors with the ability to participate in matters that have a bearing on their lives. More importantly, the Tswana Children's Act outlines in great detail the components of

[71] s 6(h) of the Children's Act.
[72] s 8(1)–(2) of the Children's Act.
[73] s 8(2)(a) of the Children's Act.
[74] s 8(2)(b)–(f) of the Children's Act.

genuine, non-tokenistic, participation that should be complied with when involving children in decision-making. These components reinforce the child's informed participation in medical decision-making by ensuring that he or she understands what is involved in the proposed medical procedure; the reasons for involving other persons; in what way he or she can be part of the process; how he or she can challenge clinical or parental decisions they do not agree with; what inspired the clinical decision; and how he or she challenge or respond to the decision.

South African law does not necessarily give details on the meaning or components of child participation and the government can share notes with and borrow from its neighbour's experiences. Going forward, the provisions governing child participation under the Children's Act will empower children to make rights-based claims for inclusion and influence in the medical decision-making process. In the event that the child's views regarding medical treatment are not given effect to in order to defend or advance their interests in health and life, the child in question is still entitled to further information on how to confirm or challenge the correctness of the treatment decision allegedly made in their own medical interests.

C. Contextualising the Similarities and Differences between South Africa and Botswana

There are two preliminary or background issues that can help in synthesising the similarities and differences which exist between the two legal systems dealt with in this chapter. The first, which probably explains the scarcity of case-law on the subject, is that both countries are largely inhabited by ethnic groups that are predominantly communitarian and therefore view children as an integral or inseparable part of the family. Communitarian cultures and societies pose a serious challenge to the individualistic nature of rights, particularly those of children. Children's rights potentially clash with African cultural ideology because the latter emphasises collectivism, reciprocal duties of support and restraint on individual rights.[75] Hence, the preservation of group identity is thought to be in the interests of the child and the interests of the family. There is an attempt to limit conflict at all costs, even though this may mean a violation of children's rights to medical treatment and access to healthcare services.

Relationships are constructed along the extended family model. Parenthood is largely social and all decisions concerning children should be taken after consulting other members of the kinship group, not just the child's biological parents.

[75] For a detailed discussion of reciprocal support obligations, respect and restraint, see BA Rwezaura, 'Changing Community Obligations to the Elderly in Contemporary Africa' (1989) 4 *Journal of Social Development in Africa* 5; and A Twum-Danso, 'Reciprocity, Respect and Responsibility: The 3Rs Underlying Parent–Child Relationships in Ghana and the Implications for Children's Rights' (2009) 17 *International Journal of Children's Rights* 415.

The child stands not as an individual but as a family member; she serves the family and the family serves her.[76] Under this conception of social relations, the individual rights or interests of the child and those of the family are symbiotic and inseparably interwoven. This approach stands in sharp contrast to international and domestic laws that emphasise the primacy of the child's rights and interests. Given that the child is not seen as an atomistic individual living outside the realm of relationships with others, the possibility of conflicts between parental interests and children's interests are limited, especially with adolescents who would have been socialised for a reasonable number of years to fully capture social values. As such, despite the existence of laws that enable children to assert autonomy in the medical decision-making context, concrete cases dealing with these issues have been far and between. Unfortunately, especially given the scarcity of case-law on the subject, the truthfulness of these assertions has not been tested before the courts.

The second issue, possibly following from the first and explaining the differences between South Africa and Botswana, is that there is only one major ethnic group in Botswana, the Tswana. Hence, the socialisation of citizens along communitarian lines is highly dominant in Botswana and there is limited room for the clash of diverse values. This could explain why, to date, there are no explicit legislative provisions governing who should consent to the medical treatment of the child and under what circumstances. There is no clear and hierarchical allocation of the responsibility to consent (to children's treatment) among parents, guardians, holders of parental responsibility, children, the Minister and the courts. It could be that the prevailing uniform value system limits the possibility of conflicts between parents themselves; children and parents; parents and medical practitioners; parents and the courts; and medical practitioners and the courts. Against this backdrop, Parliament (which is also dominated by a single political party, further indication of the country's single shared value-system) may not consider extensive regulation of consent to medical treatment as a priority.

In South Africa, the dynamics are a bit different. While there is no doubt that the country is largely inhabited by communitarian ethnic groups, these groups are so many that there are likely to be variations between how each group approaches a particular issue. Furthermore, the country is a vibrant multiparty democracy with strong institutions that make the incorporation of competing interests into the legal system possible. Whilst the African National Congress is always the party to beat in elections, the country also has strong opposition political parties, principally the Democratic Alliance and the Economic Freedom Fighters. In addition, the country is a multiracial society with large and politically powerful pockets of

[76] A Armstrong, *A Child Belongs to Everyone: Law, Family and the Construction of the Best Interests in Zimbabwe*, Innocenti Occasional Papers, Child Rights Series 11 (1995) 5; and T Kaime, *The African Charter on the Rights and Welfare of the Child: A Socio-Legal Perspective* (Pretoria, Pretoria University Law Press, 2009) 114.

remnant white and Indian peoples who have, even among themselves, different origins and value-systems. The ancestors of these groups mainly came from the Netherlands, Britain and India.

For purposes of this chapter, it is important to emphasise that given the historical power dynamics of apartheid South Africa and the fact that these 'minority' groups have political and economic power to influence decision-making at the highest level, it is obvious that they have the power to set the agenda and can easily influence the legislative reform process. Accordingly, there is a possibility that domestic laws governing parental consent to children's medical treatment are way ahead of the ordinary peoples they are meant to govern and that the poor have bread-and-butter issues to contend with instead of 'cracking their heads' over who should consent to the treatment of children who need medical attention. These assertions also have to be empirically explored and do not explain why there are no cases arising from treatment decisions and conflicts within South African families, who come from largely individualistic European backgrounds.

IV. Conclusion

There are strong parallels in the rules governing parental consent to the medical treatment of and surgical operations on children in Botswana and South Africa, especially in the context of judicial reversal of unreasonable parental refusal of treatment on behalf of children. The courts in both countries have reversed decisions, by parents, to refuse emergency blood transfusions on behalf of children on the basis of the parent's religious beliefs (although each country has had one decided case and it is difficult to argue that each of these cases reflect overall judicial practice). In both countries, part of the values or standards justifying such reversal has been the fact that refusal of treatment is inconsistent with the best interests of the child, particularly the child's basic interests in health and life. While the Tswana courts have refrained from declaring that parental refusal of treatment on the basis of religion is unreasonable or unjustifiable, South African courts have explicitly emphasised that it is unreasonable and unjustifiable for parents to make martyrs of their children and to negate the child's inviolable right to life.

There are also overlaps in the broad value-systems that inform parental consent to medical decision-making in the legislation specifically enacted to protect children. First, both pieces of legislation reiterate the centrality of the best interests of the child; the need to acknowledge the role of parents and preserve family relationships when making any decision (including those on medical interventions) that has a significant impact on the child's life; the need to protect children from harm in the (medical) decision-making process; and the centrality of giving due weight to the child's views when making (treatment) decisions in the best interests of the child. These principles or values are designed to guide courts in determining whether the decisions made by parents benefit children. The other similarity between the two countries is that the principles or values stipulated above have never been applied to concrete cases and the cases discussed in this chapter were decided before the passage of relevant legislation. Even then, there is a subtle difference between the two countries in the sense that the values or principles in Botswana are codified at a very general level because the Children's Act does not directly regulate parental consent to children's medical treatment. In South Africa, there are rules that directly govern parental consent to medical treatment and these rules mirror the values and principles stated above.

Even in the absence of decided cases, there are lessons Botswana can learn from South Africa. First, the country should enact rules that specifically regulate, in a hierarchical manner, parental consent to medical or surgical treatment. As is the case in South Africa, the rules should confer on parents the primary responsibility and right to make treatment decisions on behalf of children. Second, the rules should explicitly outline the circumstances under which parental consent to or refusal of medical treatment can either be reversed or by-passed by the courts, hospital authorities and the state, especially through the Minister responsible for health-related matters. The standards or values that should guide the allocation of decision-making powers to different players are already entrenched in the Tswana Children's Act and this should eliminate any challenge in the decision-making process. Third, the rules (which should take the form of an amendment to the Children's Act) should also explicitly authorise hospital authorities to override parental, court-ordered or ministerial consent to children's medical treatment in the context of emergencies. Again, useful guidelines can be found in the South African Children's Act.

19

Young Children and Healthcare Decisions in Spain: Who Decides?

MONICA NAVARRO-MICHEL

I. Introduction

This chapter aims to present the Spanish laws on medical decision-making as regards underage minors, in particular very young children. Spanish media followed the Charlie Gard case, and legal academics published papers and comments analysing how decisions on life-sustaining treatment for children are made in Spain, and whether there was much difference, in theory and in practice, to the manner in which the English case was addressed.[1]

In this chapter, I will explain, firstly, the legislative framework of parental responsibility in Spain, as this is the starting point for all decisions concerning children. Secondly, I will set out the rules that apply in the medical context, in particular when there is refusal of life-sustaining treatments. Thirdly, I will discuss how courts would apply the principle of the child's best interests to requests of medical treatment, and I will conclude with some final remarks on the role both physicians and parents have in this specific area. Conflicts between parents and doctors over appropriate treatment rarely reach the courts in Spain and, so far, there is no equivalent to the Charlie Gard case in Spain. Several criteria exist, however, that allow us to ascertain what the legal response would be in a similar case.

II. Parental Responsibility

Parents have the power to make decisions on behalf of their underage child, based on legal representation (Article 154 of the Spanish Civil Code (SCC)). Parental

[1] Among others, see ML Marín Castán, 'La polémica decisión del Tribunal Europeo de Derechos Humanos sobre el caso Gard y otros contra el Reino Unido' (2018) 43 *Revista de Bioética y Derecho* 261, and T Honrubia Fernández, 'Tratamiento potencialmente inapropiado en oposición a futilidad y otras cuestiones eticas del caso de Charlie Gard' (2018) 43 *Revista de Bioética y Derecho* 245.

authority is linked to a duty of care, a duty that is enshrined in the Spanish Constitution, which states that 'parents must provide all kinds of assistance to their children' (Article 39.3). Therefore, parental responsibility is not about the parent's rights and powers, but about the fulfilment of parental obligations owed to children. Article 154 SCC mentions such parental duties, which include: '1. To watch over them, keep them in your company, feed them, educate them and provide them with an integral formation. 2. To represent them and administer their assets.' If the child is mature enough, the right to be heard before making any decision that affects him or her must be ensured,[2] and the child is considered to be mature for this purpose from the age of twelve.[3]

Parents have the right to determine how to raise their children, but parental responsibility should always be exercised 'in the interest of the children, in accordance with their personality, and with respect for their rights, and their physical and mental integrity' (Article 154 SCC). This specific reference to the best interests of the minor (*interés superior del menor*) was introduced for the first time in 1981 in an amendment to the SCC.[4]

Organic Law 1/1996, 15 January, on the legal protection of minors, strengthened the idea that the child's best interests should be the primary consideration, over any other legitimate interest. In all actions concerning children, whether undertaken by public or private institutions, courts of law, administrative authorities or legislative bodies, the child's best interests should be the paramount consideration. This is in accordance with international conventions, such as the United Nations Convention on the Rights of the Child of 20 November 1989 (CRC), ratified by Spain on 6 December 1990.[5]

There are, however, some exceptions to legal representation, which include 'acts relating to personality rights that the child, in accordance with his maturity, can exercise by himself' (Article 162 SCC). Personality rights, such as bodily integrity, privacy and one's own image, among others, are excluded from legal representation. A minor is entitled to exercise these rights if he or she is sufficiently mature. There are, however, some decisions that require the person to be at least eighteen years old, such as organ donation or assisted reproduction; in these cases, consent given by parents or the underage competent minor is invalid.

The best interests of the minor should, therefore, be the guiding principle in all decisions made concerning minors. This is a binding principle for parents, courts,

[2] Art 154 SCC.

[3] Organic Law 1/1996 at Art 9.2.

[4] By Law 11/1981, 13 May, in matters of filiation, *patria potestas* and economic matrimonial regime. Initially it only made reference to the child's personality; subsequent reforms introduced other criteria such as physical and psychological integrity (2007 amendment) and mention of rights in general (2015 reform).

[5] The United States remains the only country that has not ratified the CRC since Somalia and South Sudan ratified it in 2015. See treaties.un.org/Pages/ViewDetails.aspx?src=IND&mtdsg_no=IV-11&chapter=4&lang=en.

public authorities and any person who plays a role in the child's life, including healthcare practitioners.[6] Once legal provisions are in place to ensure the best interests of the child is the primary consideration, the assessment and determination of the best interests may be difficult to assess in practice.

The concept of best interests of the child falls under the category of undefined legal concepts (*concepto jurídico indeterminado*) and its implementation relies heavily on judicial interpretation. Organic Law 1/1996 was amended in 2015 to include the criteria that need to be taken into account, established by the UNCRC, General Comment No 14 (2013) on the right of the child to have his or her best interests taken as primary consideration (Article 3(1)), 29 May 2013. According to the UN Committee, the child's best interests is a threefold concept, as it is a substantive right, a principle and a rule of procedure.[7] The substantive right dimension is so novel that there are, as yet, no specific references to it in Spanish case-law.[8]

The best interests of the child may vary from child to child, from family to family, so parents have authority to make a variety of different decisions, and each could be in the child's best interests. For example, whether a child goes to church or to synagogue would be a family-specific decision, and any option (to attend or not attend, or which denomination to attend) could be deemed to be in the child's best interests. Parents have extensive discretionary powers in many aspects of their children's upbringing.[9] When parents disagree with each other, they may take the matter to court (although this is rarely done in practice) and the judge will give one of the parents the power to decide (Article 156.2 SCC). The judge will not decide directly on the given matter, but rather will identify the parent who can make the decision on this specific contentious matter.[10]

The limit to parental discretion is when the child is placed at risk of harm.[11] Any person who detects a situation where a child is at risk of harm (ie either a relative, neighbour, teacher, social services personnel, physician) can notify the courts, who have powers to take any appropriate measure to remove a child from danger or to prevent harm to the child (Article 158 SCC). Clearly, a decision that puts a child at risk of harm is contrary to the best interests approach. This provision specifically mentions some of the measures courts may apply, such as a prohibition to go near the child, or the removal of a child's passport when there is a risk of

[6] Art 2.1 Organic Law 1/1996 in accordance with Art 3.1 UN CRC.

[7] At [6].

[8] I Varela Castro, 'El interés del menor como derecho subjetivo' (2016) 2188 *Boletín del Ministerio de Justicia* 1, 22.

[9] F Rivero Hernández, *El interés del menor*, 2nd edn (Madrid, Dykinson, 2007) 292; D Roda y Roda, *El interés del menor en el ejercicio de la patria potestad* (Cizur Menor, Thomson Reuters Aranzadi, 2014) 42.

[10] In a recent decision by the Court of Appeal of Pontevedra, 125/2019, 22 July (JUR 2019/254424), the father was awarded sole decision-making power with regards to his child's vaccination; he was in favour of it while the mother was against it.

[11] For the debate over whether the law should change to include a harm threshold similar to this one, see chapters in this book on the UK, the US, and Belgium.

international child abduction. Courts also apply the latter when there is a risk of genital mutilation if a girl travels abroad, even though this situation is not specifically mentioned in the law.[12] And, finally, there is a general clause to include 'any measure the court deems appropriate', and authorisation of life-sustaining medical treatment falls under this all-encompassing reference.

III. Consent to and Refusal of Medical Treatment

Regulation on informed consent is set out in Law 41/2002, of 14 November, on patient autonomy and the rights and obligations regarding information and clinical documentation (Patient Autonomy Law, for short; hereinafter LAP, for the Spanish acronym). This piece of legislation was passed in order to provide some detail to the Convention for the Protection of Human Rights and Dignity of the Human Being with regard to the Application of Biology and Medicine: Convention on Human Rights and Biomedicine (Oviedo Convention, 4 April 1997), which entered into force in Spain on 1 January 2000.[13]

Any medical act may only be carried out after the patient has given free and informed consent (Article 8.1 LAP). Spanish law combines two criteria to determine a minor's capacity in the healthcare context: age and maturity.[14] From the age of sixteen, a minor is competent to make healthcare decisions and, therefore, there is no need to obtain parental consent (Article 9.4 LAP).[15] However, when the medical procedure involves a serious risk for the minor's life or health, according to the doctor's opinion, then parental consent becomes necessary (Article 9.4 in fine LAP).[16] This curtailment of medical autonomy was introduced in 2015, and while some authors justify this as necessary (or benign) paternalism, others see this as evidence of mistrust of the capacity of adolescents to make healthcare decisions.[17]

Below the age of sixteen, a minor may give valid consent only if he or she is mature enough. For young children, with no capacity to understand the scope of

[12] See the decisions by the Court of Appeal in Girona 152/2007, 2 July (AC 2008/750) and in Barcelona 26/2012, 13 March (JUR 2012/164191).

[13] Prior to this informed consent was set in Law 14/1986, 25 April, on Health, on similar terms (Art 10.6).

[14] The wording of the law was criticised in MA Parra Lucán, 'La capacidad del paciente para prestar válido consentimiento informado. El confuso panorama legislativo español' (2003) 1 *Aranzadi Civil* 1901.

[15] Autonomous communities with their own legislation on this matter establish similar rules for minors' consent, such as Cataluña, Galicia, Extremadura, La Rioja, Navarra, Valencia, Castilla y León, and the Balearic Islands. Aragón considers minors to have capacity from the age of fourteen.

[16] Law 26/2015, 28 July, which modifies the protection system of childhood and adolescence.

[17] D Cadenas Osuna, 'El consentimiento informado y el rechazo a la intervención o tratamiento médico por el menor de edad tras la reforma de 2015: estudio comparado con el Common Law' (2018) 3 *Anuario de Derecho Civil* 789, 823.

the intervention, consent will be obtained from the minor's legal representatives, usually his or her parents ('consent by representation', Article 9.3.c LAP). This will require physicians to provide information about the proposed medical treatment, its risks, possible complications and side effects, to the parents.[18] When parental consent is required, 'the decision should always be made with the greatest benefit to the life or health of the patient in mind' (Article 9.6 LAP).

Competent adults have a right to refuse life-sustaining treatments, and physicians must respect that decision but, as regards young children, physicians do not have to accept the wishes of the parents when these put the child at risk of death or irreversible injury.[19] Even though parents consider such refusal to be in the child's best interests, the decision would not be binding for doctors. Therefore, parental discretion to make decisions for the child is curtailed in the medical context, since refusal of treatment for the child is contrary to the objective interests of the child.[20]

When parents refuse life-sustaining treatment for their child, physicians will seek, and obtain, judicial authorisation. However, if the situation becomes urgent, it would be lawful for physicians to apply life-saving treatment before obtaining judicial authorisation, as this would fall under such justifications as state of necessity or compliance with a duty (doctors in Spain have a duty to provide medical assistance).[21] Therefore, before obtaining judicial authorisation, if the need arises, health professionals may apply the necessary measures to safeguard the life or health of the incompetent patient.

In 2012, the Spanish Attorney General (Ministerio Fiscal) issued some 'Guidelines on the Substantive and Procedural Treatment of Conflicts about Blood Transfusions and other Medical Interventions on Minors in the Event of Serious Risk'.[22] The document starts by highlighting the complexity of situations where doctors and parents disagree in the face of life-sustaining treatments for the child, which is a situation that involves human rights and is fraught with emotional elements. The Guidelines reiterate the legal position: when legal representatives of an incompetent minor do not consent to medical treatment and this refusal poses

[18] Failure to do so may lead to a claim under tort law. For details, see eg J Ribot Igualada, 'La responsabilidad civil por falta de consentimiento informado' (2007) 91 *Revista de Derecho Privado* 29; M Navarro-Michel, 'Responsabilidad médica ante la ausencia de consentimiento informado' (2011) *Revista de Derecho de Daños* 131; and D Cadenas Osuna, 'El estándar de información sanitaria sobre riesgos de los tratamientos e intervenciones médicas en España y el common law: una visión panorámica' (2016) 4 *Indret* 1.

[19] For a case of deaf parents who opposed a cochlear implant for their very young deaf daughter when there was no medical consensus and no urgency, see decision by Court of Appeal Las Palmas 287/2015, 28 December (AC 2016/258) that revoked judicial authorisation granted by the Court of First Instance.

[20] For a discussion on the assessment of objective best interests, see R Ojeda Rivero, 'El rechazo del tratamiento médico por los menores de edad en grave riesgo' (2015) 3 *Indret* 1.

[21] Physicians who fail to offer medical assistance may even be held criminally liable.

[22] Circular 1/2012 de la Fiscalía General del Estado.

a 'serious risk' to the minor's life or health, the need for judicial intervention arises. Once physicians seek judicial authorisation, the process will be dealt with urgently. However, if the situation becomes urgent, physicians may adopt any measure that is necessary to safeguard the life or health of the incompetent patient.

These Guidelines emphasise that incompetent minors are in a process of development and, therefore, no weight should be awarded either to a child's decision (if any) or the parent's decision, when this could lead to the death or serious injury of the child. These Guidelines, however, only address parental refusal of necessary treatment on behalf of the child. They do not address the case of parents who demand life-sustaining treatment against medical opinion, or the scenario where parents want to take the child abroad to receive experimental treatment (as in Charlie Gard's case).

The Spanish Constitutional Court has been called on only once, in 2002,[23] to decide about a minor's refusal of life-sustaining treatment, a thirteen-year-old Jehovah's Witness who died after he vehemently refused a blood transfusion. The Constitutional Court stated that the decision to consent or refuse treatment made by a thirteen-year-old child, when his life is at stake, is not binding. Since this case involved an adolescent, it falls outside the scope of this chapter.[24]

IV. Withdrawal of Life-Sustaining Treatment and Request for Experimental Treatment

Organic Law 1/1996 states that, in the assessment of the child's best interests, first and foremost one must take into account the protection of the child's right to life, survival and development, as well as the satisfaction of his or her material, physical, educational and emotional needs.[25] Given the letter of the law, it would seem that saving a child's life should be the essential decision to make. The CRC establishes that states shall take appropriate measures 'to ensure the provision of necessary medical assistance and health care to all children' (Article 24.2), but this does not include unnecessary medical treatment. When the child's condition deteriorates and saving their life is not possible, palliative care may become an option, perhaps the only one. If treatment becomes futile, physicians may recommend withdrawal of life-sustaining treatment. Even though one could argue that continuation of life-sustaining treatment does not, in fact, harm the child, it is unclear whether it is in the child's best interests.

[23] Judgement 154/2002 of 18 July 2002.

[24] For comments see MJ Santos Morón, 'Sobre la capacidad del menor para el ejercicio de sus derechos fundamentales. Comentario a la STC 154/2002, de 18 de julio' (2002) 7 *Diario La Ley* 1635; and H López Bofill, 'Transfusions, menors i Testimonis de Jehová. La llibertat religiosa en un cas extrem' (2003) 102 *Revista Jurídica de Catalunya* 743.

[25] Art 2.2.a.

When does treatment cease to be in the child's best interests? The answer lies in futility.[26] When there is high certainty that treatment has no benefit, or that harm outweighs benefit, a physician's assessment of futility should prevail over parental decisions.[27] Doctors are entrusted with the protection of vulnerable patients and, as far as children are concerned, there is no substituted judgement to take into account, so best interests are deemed to be objective.[28] However, when the level of uncertainty is high, and the balance of benefits and harms is debatable, best interests may become unclear. In this case, the Catalan Committee of Bioethics recommends giving more weight to parental wishes.[29]

In certain cases, limitation of therapeutic effort can be good medical practice. Admitting patients to intensive care units when this is unlikely to benefit the patient may lead to more invasive and potentially harmful interventions, as well be an inappropriate allocation of resources.[30] So far, parents have not challenged physicians in court.[31] In order to explain why this is so, one must bear in mind that physicians are highly respected in Spain[32] and, in fact, sociological studies show that doctors rank first as the most trusted professionals.[33] Religion, and Christian resignation, on the other hand, may not play a very relevant role here. Even though Spain is usually perceived to be a Catholic country, and indeed society identifies as such,[34] studies have shown that religion carries very little weight for everyday life.[35] Catholicism in Spain is a cultural reference, rather than a doctrine with practical implications.

Parents of children who are severely ill need to understand their child's medical condition and come to terms with it. This may be challenging since their experience

[26] For a discussion on futility, see the chapter on the US in this book.

[27] Castán (n 1) 273 – when the assessment of futility is 'reasonably clear'.

[28] Rivero Hernández (n 9) 197; P De Lora, 'Autonomía personal, intervención médica y sujetos incapaces' (2008) 40–41 *Enrahonar. Quaderns de Filosofi* 128; and J Doplico Gómez-Aller, 'Problemas del consentimiento informado "por representación"' in M Corcoy (ed), *Consentimiento por Representación* (Barcelona, Fundación Víctor Grífols, 2010) 78.

[29] Comité de Bioética de Cataluña, *Recomendaciones Ante el Rechazo de los Enfermos al Tratamiento* (2010) 6.

[30] For the guidelines jointly developed by the Spanish Association of Paediatrics, the Spanish Society of Paediatric Intensive Care, and the Spanish Society of Intensive and Critical Care Medicine and Coronary Units, see P De la Oliva, F José Cambra-Lasaosa, M Quintana-Díaz, C Rey-Galán, J Ignacio Sánchez-Díaz and M Cruz Martín-Delgado, 'Admission, Discharge and Triage Guidelines for Paediatric Intensive Care Units in Spain' (2018) 42 *Medicina Intensiva* 243.

[31] This contrasts with parents in the UK. See *Gard, Evans, Haastrup, Raqeeb.*

[32] In France there is also strong deference to the medical profession.

[33] Study no 2978 *Barómetro de Febrero* (2013) 6, and Study no 3192 *Barómetro Sanitario* (2017) 6; both by the Spanish Sociological Research Centre (CIS, Centro de Investigaciones Sociológicas).

[34] Sixty-six per cent of Spaniards identify as Catholics (22% practising Catholics, 44% non-practising Catholics), 2% as believers in another religion, while the rest are agnostic, indifferent or atheists. See *Barometro Julio* (CIS, 2019) 26.

[35] Of those who identify as believers, 58% never or almost never go to church (or other religious services), 17% attend several times a year, and only 12% go every Sunday. See *Barometro Julio* (CIS, 2019) 26.

with the dying process is usually limited. Physicians have the knowledge and the experience to assess futility,[36] and to ascertain when further treatment is painful and there is no real chance for improvement. Doctors must promote meaningful opportunities for parental involvement in the decision-making process. It does not help, of course, to have promises made by other doctors offering contrary opinions – as seemed to be the case with Charlie Guard.

Children can take part in clinical trials with parental consent,[37] but this does not include experimental treatments outside the framework regulating such trials.[38] The options offered to Charlie Gard were not, it seems, supported by scientific evidence.[39] This leads us to raise the issue of how vulnerable parents perceive their options and the role the media play in raising false hopes and unrealistic expectations. Parents may try to seek treatment elsewhere, and this is possible as long as it is not detrimental to the child's health or well-being. But when decisions put the child at risk of harm, doctors can go to court to prevent this. Courts may intervene and override parental decisions when these place the child at risk (as per Article 158 SCC), and they could even prohibit parents from travelling in order to avoid laws that protect children, as the cases involving female mutilation attest.

Perhaps inevitably, parents will hold on to any chance of a better outcome, and want to try any possible treatment, however experimental, hoping for a miracle. There is no right to demand treatment when doctors do not recommend it, and there is no right to access experimental medication for the terminally ill. The European Court of Human Rights has stated that refusal of experimental treatment may be justified and would not be in violation of the right to life (Article 2 ECHR) or the right to privacy (Article 8 ECHR).[40]

V. Conclusion

Spanish parents do not tend to challenge doctors in court. Disagreements are usually dealt with within the hospital setting. Even in the case brought before the

[36] Perhaps the use of the term 'potentially inadequate treatment' is preferable, as suggested by Fernández (n 1) 253.

[37] Royal Decree 1090/2015, 4 December, which regulates clinical trials with medications, the Ethics Committees for Drug Research and the Spanish Registry of Clinical Studies (Art 5).

[38] For a case on refusal of reimbursement of cost of growth hormone treatment for a child, see Judgment of the High Court Madrid, STSJ 73/2018, 12 February.

[39] The treatment had not even reached the experimental stage on mice, let alone been tried on humans. See *Gard and others v UK* App no 39793/17 (ECHR, 27 June 2017) para 30.

[40] *Hristozov and others v Bulgaria* Apps no 47039/11 and no 358/12 (ECtHR, 13 November 2012); *Durisotto v Italy* App no 62804/13 (ECtHR, 28 May 2014).

Spanish Constitutional Court, of a thirteen-year-old Jehovah's Witness, the parents of the child did not oppose treatment in court.[41]

Relations in the healthcare setting are at their best when physicians and parents reach decisions together, after careful consideration of the medical situation. Parents must be involved in the decision-making process, although that does not necessarily imply that parental wishes will be followed.[42] When the relations between parents and physicians strain, and confrontation ensues, the conflict may be taken to court. In this case, parental responsibility will not be challenged, per se, but specific decisions on healthcare will be scrutinised. Courts have a duty to protect the child's best interests and may override parental wishes in order to protect the child's paramount interests, generally relying on medical evidence to ascertain futility. However, courts are not necessarily the best place to resolve these conflicts. Such an environment encourages confrontation between doctors and parents, fails to promote trust in healthcare professionals, and fails to address the needs of grieving parents.

[41] The case brought before the Constitutional Court dealt with the charges of criminal liability against the parents, who were convicted of murder by omission on the understanding that, as protectors of the minor, they should have prevented his death.

[42] As I mentioned elsewhere, parents do not necessarily want to choose but they do want to have a voice. See M Navarro-Michel, 'The Role of the Family in Healthcare Decisions: The Dead and the Dying' in C Stanton, S Devaney, A-M Farrell and A Mullock (eds), *Pioneering Healthcare Law: Essays in Honour of Margaret Brazier* (London, Taylor & Francis/Routledge, 2016) 140.

20

Who Decides the Best Interests of the Child in the End-of-Life Process? A Look at the Peruvian and Argentine Reality

PAULA SIVERINO BAVIO*

I. Introduction

The dramatic case of Charlie Gard, born in August 2016 with an extremely rare and deadly degenerative disorder, generated global controversy.[1] Having decided to try an experimental treatment, the worsening of the child's condition made it impossible to carry this out, after which the medical team suggested withdrawing life-support measures, providing palliative care and allowing him to die. The parents opposed this and sought judicial support against the Great Ormond Street Hospital in London, with the matter eventually reaching the European Court of Human Rights. All courts supported the position of the medical team.

This chapter considers what solution would be expected in Argentina and Peru if a case of similar characteristics were presented? Relevant factors in answering this question include the degree of development of bioethical reflection, the still-prevailing paternalism in a large part of the medical community, the influence of religious conservative groups, the acceptance of patriarchal schemes and verticality in family relationships, especially in places far from the capital, and their impact on the patient–doctor relationship, as well as on the effective recognition of children as subjects of law. The parents, as legal representatives of the child, are those indicated by law to have authority to make decisions about their life and health, but this authority has limits.

* I thank Patricio Ato del Avellanal for translating this article and Lucia Camacho Gutierrez for her assistance with research.

[1] Myelodysplastic depletion syndrome of mitochondrial DNA of infantile onset (MdDS), which affects the brain and most other organs, causes progressive muscle weakness and shortness of breath, and ultimately causes death.

The purpose of this chapter is to reflect on the limits of parental responsibility against end-of-life decisions in young children in Argentina and Peru, based on the Gard case. In order to do so, I will present the Argentine legal framework, the guidelines on the competence of minors, the scope of consent for representation and the best interests of the child, as well as a brief jurisprudential review and what would be a probable resolution in a similar case to the Gard case. Then I will discuss Peruvian regulations, briefly commenting on the experience of a paediatric reference institute and how the Gard case in Peru would have been resolved. Later, I will mention structural issues that have an impact in addressing these conflicts. Since both countries tend to find intrafamily resolutions with the health team in this type of situation, and only exceptionally is a judicial case involved, I will finally outline a proposal on what strategies can be implemented to improve the quality of decision-making for those potentially involved in situations as critical as the one addressed in this chapter.

II. Argentina's Legal Framework

A. Capacity, Competence and General Principles of the Civil Code

The reform of the Civil and Commercial Code of Argentina (CC&CA), in force since August 2015, adopts the constitutionalisation of private law, incorporating human rights treaties and the Argentinian Constitution ('constitutional block') as parameters of interpretation of the norms and civil law institutions.

As a result, and in line with the provisions of the United Nations Convention on the Rights of the Child, Advisory Opinion 17 of the Inter-American Court of Human Rights (2002)[2] and Law 26.061 on the Integral Protection of the Rights of Children and Adolescents (2005), the reform makes the concept of 'civil capacity' more flexible by incorporating the notion of 'competence' which especially affects the field of decisions taken by minors about their body and their health.

The CC&CA recognises as a rule that every person has the ability to be a holder of rights and obligations (rights capacity) and can exercise these rights themselves (exercise capacity), except for the limitations that the Code determines. Those under eighteen years exercise their rights through their legal representatives, being able to exercise for themselves the acts that are allowed by law, according to the principle of gradual autonomy and the right to be heard. From the age of thirteen the law considers them 'adolescents'.

[2] IACHR, Advisory Opinion OC-17/2002, 'Juridical Condition and Human Rights of the Child', 28 August 2002.

The CC&CA regulates the competence of minors to make medical decisions. While under thirteen years of age, they have the right to be heard and can participate in the decision-making process, but decisions will be entrusted to their parents.

When assessing the situation of children and end-of-life treatments, the CC&CA standards must be integrated with Law 26.061, the Law on Patients' Rights (2009) and its amendment, the Dignified Death Law, No 26,742 (2012) together with its Regulatory Decree 1089/12. This law made public the debate about the scope of parental authority against the decision to interrupt the treatment of their children at the end of their life.

B. Rights at the End of Life, Consent for Representation and Parental Responsibility

The Dignified Death Law was promoted by Melina, a young woman who requested terminal sedation in the face of intolerable physical conditions, and by Sandra, the mother of a three-year-old girl in a permanent vegetative state, given the refusal of the medical centre to suspend vital support. The medical centre feared a complaint and demanded that parents waive any legal claim before a notary – a clear example of doubts about the legal framework and the practice of defensive medicine.[3]

Law No 26,529, on Patients' Rights, contemplated the rejection of medical treatment, but there were doubts about the legality of limiting life-support measures, especially hydration and nutrition for persons lacking the ability to decide. Its modification was Law No 26,742 the rejection of futile treatments or those that produce 'excessive suffering', including hydration or food 'when they produce as a sole effect the prolongation in time of that irreversible or incurable terminal stage'. The rejection of, and withdrawal from, hydration and feeding was one of the most controversial points raised by religious conservatism.[4] The purpose of the norm is to avoid therapeutic excess in the face of futile interventions at the end of life and to humanise death.

Regarding minors, this law sets three guidelines: (a) they have the right to be assisted in the care of their health as a priority; (b) they have the right to intervene in making decisions about therapies or procedures that involve their health under the terms of Law 26.061;[5] (c) they can give their consent by representation, according to the requirements and priority order of the Transplant Law (parents, siblings over eighteen years of age, grandparents, blood relatives up to the fourth degree, relatives related up to including the second degree, legal representative).

[3] JC Tealdi, 'Bioética de los derechos humanos en muerte digna' in G Domínguez (ed), *Muerte digna* (Buenos Aires, La Ley, 2013) 107–120.

[4] JP Alonso, 'De medios ordinarios y extraordinarios: la Iglesia Católica y los debates sobre la "muerte digna" en Argentina' (2014) 34 *Religão e Sociedade* 122.

[5] Ley 26.061 de Protección Integral de Niños Niñas y Adolescentes (2005).

In relation to children, consent by representation is a derivation of the exercise of parental responsibility and is defined by the C&CCA as the set of duties and rights that correspond to those the parents have in relation to the person and property of the child, for the protection, development and comprehensive training of children while they are minors and have not been emancipated, according to the following principles: (a) the best interests of the child; (b) gradual autonomy (according to psychophysical characteristics, aptitude and development); and (c) the right of the child to be heard and to have their opinion taken into account according to their age and degree of maturity.

Regulatory decree 1089/12 of the Dignified Death Law regulates the consent of minors in Articles 2 and 5. Article 2 indicates that the will of children and adolescents must be taken into account according to their competence and discernment and, in case of disagreement with their legal representatives, or among them, the physician must submit the case to the ethics committee of the institution or another if necessary, to give an opinion, in accordance with Law 26.061. This opinion is not legally binding.

If the child is young or lacks the capacity to decide, Article 5 permits consent by representation, and indicates that, if there is opposition to the course of action to be taken from only one of the persons in the same legal degree of priority (e.g. between the parents), intervention by the hospital's ethics committee is necessary. The committee will require a judicial intervention only 'as difficulties arise to discern the most favourable situation for the patient'. The law prioritises agreement between parents, seeking independent and interdisciplinary resolution in cases of conflict, rather than referring the matter to a judge, but it does not contemplate what happens if the conflict is between the parents and the medical team; likewise, the norm gives the doctor the possibility, not the family, of bringing the case to the ethics committee.

On the other hand, a decision by the parent that accords with that of the medical team is presumed to be the most favourable, discarding in principle judicial intervention. By contrast, the Federal Supreme Court of Switzerland has understood that when a medical recommendation is indicated in a specific case, it is presumed to be compatible with the best interests of the child.[6]

As noted above, the CC&CA introduces the rule of consideration of the best interests on the basis of medical opinion regarding the consequences of taking medical action, in the event of conflict between the desire of the adolescent and that of the parents, about non-invasive procedures or treatment that put the adolescent's life at risk. However, in the face of a more complex situation, the Dignified Death Law requires the participation of an ethics committee, whose task is to ensure the rights of the patient and which, with the best interests of the child as its goal, will weigh legal, medical considerations and ethics, including the family context, to recommend a course of action.

[6] A Büchler, 'Parental Decisions on their Children's Medical Treatment', in this book.

For its part, the C&CCA prohibits any act that physically or psychologically harms children or adolescents and foresees the possibility that the judge may order interdisciplinary intervention measures in case of repeated disagreements between the parents or events that hinder the exercise of parental authority.

In judicial processes that involve them, children and adolescents can participate through legal representatives and have a lawyer if they are opposing the position held by their parents or the process affects their interests; the Public Prosecutor's Office intervenes on their behalf and for their protection.[7] In addition, Law 26.061 introduces the notion of the child's lawyer, although there is no consensus in the doctrine or jurisprudence on the scope of this individual's competence, and creates the Ombudsman for the Rights of Girls, Children and Adolescents, who is elected by Congress and will be in charge of ensuring the protection and promotion of the rights of the child.

C. The Best Interests of the Child and End of Life: Legal Principles and Judicial Criteria

In the face of a conflict, what are the guiding guidelines?

Any decision (medical, administrative or judicial) should have the best interests of the child as a guiding principle, which functions as a right, principle of interpretation and procedural norm.[8] As a procedural norm, when making a medical decision that affects the life of the child, one must specify how this right has been respected in the decision, on what criteria it has been based and how the interests of the child have been weighed against other considerations. There is consensus that dignity is the cardinal value that gives content to the best interests of the child, who experiences multiple vulnerabilities in the end-of-life process and, before the inevitable end, cannot be treated 'as an object or merchandise of an autonomous technological domain'.[9] Children have rights derived from their condition, to which correspond specific duties of the family, society and the state.[10]

Acting in the best interests of the child functions as the guiding principle. This is not an abstract consideration,[11] but involves assessing specific parental behaviours and any adverse effects these may have on the well-being and

[7] JP Olmo y N Mendiondo, 'Actuación principal y complementaria del ministerio público: el artículo 103 CCyCN' in *Ministerio Público de la Defensa. Estudios sobre Jurisprudencia. Secretaria Especial sobre Capacitación y Jurisprudencia* (2016) jurisprudencia.mpd.gov.ar/Estudios/2016.3.%20Actuaci%C3%B3n%20principal%20y%20complementaria%20del%20Ministerio%20P%C3%BAblico%20el%20art%C3%ADculo%20103%20CCyCN.pdf.

[8] General Comment 14 (2013) from the Committee on the Rights of the Children CRC/C/CG/14.

[9] Tealdi (n 3).

[10] IACHR, OC17/2002, [54].

[11] IACHR *Atala Riffo y Niñas vs Chile*, Fondo, Reparaciones y Costas, Judgment of 24 February 2012. Serie C, no 239, [108].

development of the child, and, depending on the case, consideration of proven damages or real risks, and not speculative or imaginary ones.[12] For the Argentine Supreme Court, the best interests principle serves two basic purposes: to become a guideline for decision-making in the face of a conflict of interest; and to be a criterion for institutional intervention aimed at protecting the child. Likewise, the best interests principle conceptually separates the interest of the child as a legal subject from the interests of other subjects and even that of the parents themselves, however legitimate these may be; it then operates as a limit to consent by representation if the welfare of the child is jeopardised, enabling judicial intervention. As is the case in Spanish law, parental responsibility must be exercised for the benefit of the child, and regarding medical decisions there is a smaller margin of discretion, limited to medical criteria that enable physicians to go before a judge if they consider that the welfare of the child is in danger,[13] a principle similar to the 'escape clause' of the Belgian law on patient rights.[14]

This has been the criterion followed in cases of children whose parents are Jehovah's Witnesses,[15] as well as in cases of children whose parents refuse to vaccinate them,[16] on the understanding that parental responsibility must be exercised in accordance with the guiding principles of the C&CCA (i.e. the best interests of the child, gradual autonomy and the right to be heard).[17]

The Supreme Court has ruled about the authority of parents to refuse to vaccinate their children, deciding that family privacy is permeable to state intervention in the best interest of the child, prioritising their right to health over all other considerations.[18]

In decisions at the end of life, drawing lines becomes more complex. The Dignified Death Law prioritises humanised death by avoiding futile measures that generate excessive suffering or only serve to prolong a terminal and irreversible state, and regulates consent for representation.

Analysing the scope of consent by representation, Büchler distinguishes between absolute and strictly personal rights. Most medical situations involve the exercise of strictly personal rights, where consent by representation is applied, having as a limit and guiding pattern the best interests of the child.[19]

[12] Ibid [109].

[13] M Navarro-Michel, 'Young Children and Healthcare Decisions in Spain: Who Decides?', in this book.

[14] I Boone, 'Parental Rights, Best Interests and Significant Harm: Medical Decision-Making on Behalf of Children in Belgium', in this book.

[15] R de Vía Mendoza, 'Desde el notti explicaron por qué le hicieron una transfusión al bebé Testigo de Jehová' Noticia del 13 de Noviembre de 2017, viapais.com.ar/mendoza/258849-desde-el-notti-explicaron-por-que-le-hicieron-la-transfusion-al-bebe-testigo-de-jehova/?page=2.

[16] CSJN *NN o, U, V s/ protección y guarda de persona*, Judgment of 12 June 2012. In the case, the parents alleged that compulsory vaccination violated family beliefs, violating family privacy and autonomy.

[17] JM, DL s/ ley 4109 (Reservado) Expte N° 24299/17, Juzgado de Familia N° 7, San Carlos de Bariloche, Sentencia del 16/11/17.

[18] CSJN (n 16).

[19] Büchler (n 6).

Those rights who are absolute and strictly personal are excluded from consent by representation. The tendency is to consider that an intervention that is not urgent, or of imperative therapeutic need, and is irreversible, implies the exercise of an absolute and strictly personal right.[20] This is the case of genital interventions on intersex babies, which radically impact the child's life, affecting their right to sexual identity, integrity and the free development of their personality, also understood as the right to an open future.[21] It has also been raised whether consent for representation is acceptable before circumcision and cochlear implants.

The safeguard of the exercise of absolute strictly personal rights assumes that children will eventually be competent to be able to determine very personal matters for themselves. This will not happen in young children with pathologies that prevent them from having discernment.

In the same vein, from an integrated reading of the Argentine Supreme Court doctrine[22] it can be deduced that while the protection of the principle of self-determination governs decision-making about persons without autonomy, the protection of the best interests of the child is the guiding principle in children under thirteen years of age. In both situations, the aim is to guarantee the respect of the interests of the patient who cannot decide for himself, above the interests of third parties, including his own parents. In the case of children, their dignity and general context should be considered in terms of the preservation of the family environment and the maintenance of relationships, as well as weighing the advantages, risks and effects of medical treatments.[23]

In adolescents under the age of sixteen, a balance should be made between the principles of self-determination and protection of their best interests; between the ages of sixteen and eighteen, the principle applicable to those would be the one for persons of legal age., Even though the Dignified Death Law does not authorise advance directives to those under eighteen years of age, the Civil Code recognises full autonomy for medical acts at age sixteen.

The law presumes that the family –especially parents, to whom it gives the authority to decide for their children – will naturally ensure the welfare of children. However, consent for representation must be exercised within the limits of parental responsibility and, in case of conflict, it must be proven that the parents' decisions meet the best interests of the child, in accordance with ethical, legal and medical considerations.

Nevertheless, the jurisprudence of lower courts presents disparate criteria and reasoning, sometimes at odds with logic.

[20] ibid.

[21] ibid.

[22] CSJN,(n 16) and CSJN 373/2013 *DMA s/ declaración de incapacidad*, Judgment of July 7 2015. The case was about an adult who had been in a vegetative state for twenty years. It was considered that dying with dignity is a very personal and non-transferable right and that the role of legal representatives in such cases is to testify to the patient's will.

[23] CRC/C/CG/14 (n 8).

In the cases scrutinised, some judges understand that the right to a dignified death can only be exercised by the owner of that right and, these rights being non-transferable, the judges refer to 'medical self-limitation' according to whether the treatment is considered proportionate or disproportionate. Even if they cannot decide for the child, the parents and the medical team would be in a better position to make decisions than 'a stranger' (i.e. the judge). Another judge declared that a legal representative could only request that treatments – the application of which cannot be presumed to be cruel treatment – considered disproportionate not to be carried out, then argued that legal representatives could demand medical equipment and even the use of disproportionate measures.[24]

In one complex case, parents asked the judge to require the doctors treating their daughter to avoid mechanically ventilating her in a respiratory crisis. For the judge, the refusal of the parents was fully effective and there was no need for judicial intervention. The doctors appealed the measure and insisted that mechanical ventilation would prevent the girl from dying in agony, without artificially prolonging her life. While the parents were in a hearing about the case, the girl had a crisis and was intubated. After her death, the judge sanctioned the doctors' lawyer and the doctors for going against the will of the parents. The Court of Appeals revoked the sanctions on the doctors, but reaffirmed that the decision rests with the parents, despite the questionable request.[25]

The disparity of criteria, typical of a system involving diffuse constitutional review, makes it difficult to foresee how a case in Argentina similar to the Gard case would be resolved. If such a case were to reach the Supreme Court, and the medical criteria and the opinion of one or more ethics committees were to coincide in terms of the futility of life support, the suspension of life support would probably be authorised.

Now we turn to the legal scenario in Peru.

III. Peruvian Legal Framework

The Peruvian Constitution protects the dignity of the person as the supreme purpose of society and the state (Article 1), as well as the integrity, privacy, free development and welfare (Article 2) of the person. The Civil Code (CC) stipulates in Article 5 that the rights to life and integrity are inviolable and inalienable and, in general, their exercise cannot be subject to voluntary limitation. Article 5 (CC) is usually alleged to call into question the legality of the adequacy of therapeutic

[24] *SME y otros s/ se oficie s/ su situación* (Expte N°791/08), Civil and Commercial District Court of First Instance of the 9th Nomination of Rosario, August 2008 ruling.

[25] *Benítez, MR, y otros c/ GCBA*, Chamber of Appeals in Administrative and Tax Litigation of the Autonomous City of Buenos Aires, room I, judgment of 11/16/2001, LA LEY2002-C, 201 – DJ2002-2, 135, AR/JUR/1971/2001.

effort measures – considering the abstention or withdrawal of life-support measures as euthanasic practices –, making it very difficult to respect the rights of patients at the end of life.

The Code of Children and Adolescents (CCh&A) contemplates the right to the integrity of children and adolescents, the protection against cruel, inhuman or degrading treatment, the right to integral health and enumerates the duties and rights of parental authority,[26] without mentioning an age of majority for medical treatment[27] or giving guidelines for situations of conflict. According to the CCh&A and the CC, adulthood is acquired at the age of eighteen years and from the age of sixteen years, when competence is acquired for acts that the law authorises, one is considered to be 'relative factual incapable'[28] (*incapaz relativo de hecho*), and able to accept or renounce patrimonial rights if their parents authorise or tacitly ratify the act, and able to work with parental authorisation. From the age of fourteen the minor can request the removal of his or her guardian, and a minor capable of discernment can exercise strictly personal rights,[29] which are not susceptible of representation.

While there is not yet an articulated bioethical position in Peru and because the CC reflects patrimonial bias, we do not find normative solutions for a subject under treatment, and the latest CC reform project has not introduced changes either.[30] However, from an integrated reading of the quoted legislation, in accordance with the principles of progressive development and the right to be heard, it is possible to claim the minor has competence from the age of fourteen to intervene and consent to medical decisions[31] – with parents' assent in life-threatening situations[32] – and from the age of sixteen can be considered competent to decide autonomously about their life and health.

In Peru, the rights of patients are described in the General Health Law No 26842 (1997) and its amendment, Law No 29414 (2009). Articles 4 and 15.2(g) allow people of legal age to refuse medical treatment. In the case of a minor, it is foreseen that if the legal representative denies consent for medical treatment, the attending doctor or the health establishment must notify the competent judicial authority to order to expedite actions to safeguard the life and health of the minor. This norm, which has the case of Jehovah's Witnesses in mind, does not foresee conflicts between the parents, or between parents and their minor child, nor does

[26] Peruvian Civil Code (Art 418) and the Code of Children and Adolescents (Art 74) use the term 'parental authority'.

[27] R Mejia Rosasco, *Estipulaciones de autotutela para la propia incapacidad: la penúltima voluntad* (Lima, Grijley, 2009).

[28] C Fernández Sessarego, *Derecho de las personas*, 10th edn (Lima, Griljey, 2008) 172–173.

[29] C Fernández Sessarego, *Los veinticinco años del Código civil peruano de 1984* (Lima, Motivensa, 2009) 43.

[30] Anteproyecto de Reforma del Código Civil, gacetajuridica.com.pe/boletin-nvnet/ar-web/AnteproyectoReformaCodigoCivil.pdf.

[31] R Rabinovich, *Actos jurídicos y documentos biomédicos* (Buenos Aires, La Ley, 2004) 63–73.

[32] C Fernández Sessarego, *La responsabilidad civil del médico* (Lima, Motivensa, 2011) 440.

it consider the minor's will if they wish to refuse treatment. Nor does it foresee that the medical team could be the party who proposes the minor should abstain from treatment.

Nor are there clear guidelines in the scarce jurisprudence.[33] In the case of *P R*,[34] it was discussed whether a tutelary investigation should be initiated to deprive parents who were Jehovah's Witnesses of their parental rights when they refused to allow a blood transfusion to be given to their son, who was undergoing chemotherapy. The case reached the Supreme Court and it concluded that the tutelary investigation does not proceed, since parents have the right to choose the appropriate treatment for their children. However, the Court clarified that, despite the religious beliefs of the parents, the child's right to life prevails and that, if necessary, in the future, such a child should be given a transfusion. One judge dissented, considering that refusal to provide a necessary treatment to save a child's life constitutes moral abandonment

A. An Experience in the Peruvian Health System

In line with what has been reported in Thailand[35] and Chile,[36] there is in Peru a legally consecrated social context in which the fundamental role of the family and a certain 'parental authoritarianism' leads us to assume that it is the parents' responsibility to decide for their children as they know what is better for them. Doctors generally avoid conflicts with parents, not least because of legal fears.

Peru has several centres specialised in child care, with the National Institute of Children's Health (NICH) being the centre of reference. In the absence of published data, I contacted several of these centres, obtained a response from the NICH, and conducted an extensive telephone interview with the head of the Palliative Care Unit (PCU) at the NICH to gather information on the treatment of children at the end of their life.

I was informed that around 25 per cent of NICH patients are potential beneficiaries of palliative care. The PCU can only intervene when summoned by interconsultation, which happens in 10 per cent of the cases. The PCU evaluates the patient and if it is concluded that life-support measures are not to proceed, the patient's parents must sign two documents: one for acceptance of palliative care and one giving Consent for Adequacy of Therapeutic Effort (CATE). About 80 per cent of the parents are single women.

[33] We asked for information from the Commission of Vulnerable Persons, Children and Adolescents of the Supreme Court, whose Chair sent us the case *PR*.

[34] *PR*, Transitory Civil Chamber, Supreme Court, CAS 1822-02 Lima, Investigación Tutelar, Expediente 234-2002, Judgment of 26 July 2002.

[35] T Tengaumnuay, 'Parental Authoritarianism and Medical Decision-Making in Thailand: The Need to Limit Parental Authority', in this book.

[36] F Lathrop Gómez, 'Decisions About Their Body: Children's Rights and Parental Responsibilities in Chile', in this book.

The NICH does not have general directives describing the level of therapeutic effort and relies on the criteria of the various departments, although there is a tacit rule of not confronting parents to avoid any legal issues, especially in the accident and emergency department and in the intensive care unit (ICU). It is reported that the accident and emergency department tend to respect the will of parents if a CATE is signed, whereas in the ICU, in general, the level of therapeutic effort is not accepted, and there have even been cases of conscientious objection to the CATE because it is considered euthanasia. Sixty per cent of ICU patients have chronic conditions; these patients do not receive palliative care; the criterion is to do what the parents decide, without confronting them.

Given the doubts generated by the legal framework on measures at the end of life, it is reasonable to question the quality of information provided to parents by the medical team. Children often die in the ICU, in an environment lacking in warmth, company and comfort.[37]

The experience reported by the NICH leads us to believe that physicians continue to associate the level of the therapeutic effort with euthanasia, ignoring the ethical and legal framework for treatment at the end of life, influenced by religious prejudice,[38] ignorance of bioethical principles and the practice of defensive medicine,[39] to the detriment of the rights and dignity of sick children.[40]

If the Gard case had happened in Peru, and the parents had been able to afford the treatment, their wishes would have been fulfilled. It is unlikely that the medical team would have opposed, let alone legally fought to achieve, the withdrawal of life support.

IV. Analysis of the Scenarios in Argentina and Peru

In both Argentina and Peru, judicialisation of cases of treatment at the end of children's lives is very low, being mostly due to health professionals who turn to justice – usually in the case of Argentina requesting judicial authorisation to take or not take a specific course of action – and to a lesser extent, the patient's family.[41] Sometimes, urgency determines the judicial ruling be made by telephone, making it difficult to record the process.[42]

[37] P Lago et al, 'Life Support Limitation at Three Pediatric Intensive Care Units in Southern Brazil' (2005) 81 *Jornal de Pediatria* 111.

[38] P Siverino Bavio, 'Bioética y derechos humanos. La 'bioética' confesional como estrategia' in JM Vaggione and J Mujica (comp), *Conservadurismos, religión y política. Perspectivas de investigación en América latina* (Ferreyra, 2013) 195–235.

[39] ibid nn 2, 162.

[40] Lago (n 37) nn 36, 116.

[41] JP Alonso, 'Derechos en el final de la vida: el rechazo de tratamientos médicos en los tribunales argentinos' (2016) 12 *Revista Salud Colectiva* 383–396.

[42] A Kemelmajer de Carlucci, 'El derecho del niño a su propio cuerpo' in Bergel and Minskersky (coord), *Bioética y derecho* (Rubinzal Culzoni, 2003) 162.

I share the perspective of Alonso, who believes that these low levels of litigation are due to (a) an unclear legal framework, (b) the absence of legal support structures and associations that defend the rights of terminally ill patients, and (c) the lack of perception by some citizens that rejection of treatment is a right.[43] An example of the above is that the two emblematic cases that led to the enactment of the Dignified Death Law in Argentina, which involved a girl and a teenager, were discussed in the media and the National Congress, but were not judicialised.[44]

On the other hand, the hospital care of paediatric patients with terminal illnesses differs between institutions and it is difficult to access relevant information.[45] A 2003 study warns of the widespread practice of the 'middle way' (*vía de medio*) by which treatment is maintained without intensification until death is inevitable, due to legal fears, social, religious and cultural factors, and ambiguous institutional policies, combined with very poor training in bioethics.[46]

Both in Argentina and in Peru, it is possible to verify – to varying degrees depending on the bioethical and legal training of health teams – the influence of these factors. In Peru, a decision to limit treatment usually results in fear of participating in an illegal practice, whether this is a euthanasic act or an abandonment of person. Medical staff may resort to dilatory practices or defensive medicine[47] due to divergences in the applicable legal criteria.

The lack of clarity on what protects the right to life has led to the belief that the legally protected right is biological life, the material substrate on which the existence of the individual unfolds. Although the right to life protects biological life, it is also inextricably linked to 'biographical life', i.e. the wider existence of the individual.[48] The lack of a right to this 'biographical life' implies ignoring the individual and protecting only the corporeality that sustains him, stripping him of his human dignity.

This lack of clarity about what protects the right to life is related to the belief about the sacredness, inviolability and inalienability of human life, widespread in places of strong religious influence and vigorous medical paternalism.

[43] Alonso (n 41) 390.

[44] 'La chica que peleó por la muerte digna' *Página 12* (2 March 2011) www.pagina12.com.ar/diario/sociedad/3-163303-2011-03-02.html; 'Camila, nuestro ángel, pudo partir' *Página 12* (8 June 2012) www.pagina12.com.ar/diario/sociedad/3-195907-2012-06-08.html.

[45] E.g. the lawyer of one Argentinian paediatric hospital denied access to the information, alleging that it could only be used for academic purposes by the medical team.

[46] M Althabe et al, 'Dying in the Intensive Care Unit: Collaborative Multicenter Study About Forgoing Life-Sustaining Treatment in Argentine Pediatric Intensive Care Units' (2003) 4 *Pediatric Critical Care Medicine* 164.

[47] C Gherardi and N Gherardi, 'La judicialización del acto médico y la generación de nuevos conflictos' (2007) 67 *Medicina* 502.

[48] P Siverino Bavio and J Mujica, 'Vivir y morir según la ley. Reflexiones teóricas interdisciplinarias sobre la vida de la persona y el derecho a la vida' (2012) 69 *Derecho PUCP* 81.

The sacredness of life and the medical mission of protecting biological life through the Hippocratic oath is alleged to be an ethical impediment. There is a confusion between 'procuring death' and accepting the decline of life when the process has reached a point of no return.

In recent years, action by conservative groups has increased to span from the exclusion and defence of social stratification, to the appropriation of 'naked life' (*nuda vida*) (and its relation to sexuality and the body) as the core of a discourse of absolute truths,[49] coupled with a change in the organisation of religious discourse based on 'strategic secularisms', substituting references to God and dogmas with scientific and bioethical arguments, and replacing ecclesiastical actors with members of civil society.[50] In the debate on the Dignified Death Law in Argentina, academics and directors of Catholic bioethics centres led the defence of the conservative position. In Peru, the collective Con Mis Hijos No Te Metas maintains an active offensive against any attempt to expand rights.[51]

Even though Argentina is undergoing a process of secularisation, Alonso warns that the role of the Catholic Church as a leading actor is part of a long history, and parliamentary 'defeats' on issues such as equal marriage or decent death should not be read as a 'withdrawal' of the Church; rather, its active participation in these debates clearly mark it as a political actor in the democratic dynamic.[52] In Peru, conservative groups have been present throughout the country's history, maintaining a close relationship with the Catholic Church, elites of the economic system, government structures,[53] and more recently, with evangelical churches and political parties.

In the Peruvian case, and to a lesser extent in the remoter parts of Argentina, the strong medical paternalism that still prevails in these societies with young democracies and a strong totalitarian imprint makes it difficult to accept and recognise autonomy, enshrined in the constitutions of both countries, and allowing the democratisation of family relationships to be recognised, giving the rights of children and adolescents real substance. As Lathrop Gomez warns in the context of Chile, although the paradigm shift towards the recognition of the rights and the gradual competence of children and adolescents is palpable, in practice, the logic of parental authority as the seat of decision-making still prevails.[54]

[49] J Mujica, *Economía política del cuerpo. La reestructuración de los grupos conservadores y el biopoder* (Lima, Centro de Promoción y Defensa de los Derechos Sexuales y Reproductivos, 2007).

[50] Alonso (n 4).

[51] Con Mis Hijos No Te Metas is an ultraconservative social movement that fights against LGBTQ rights, abortion, sexual education, gender policies, etc; it is very strong in Peru and in many other Latin American countries.

[52] ibid.

[53] Mujica (n 49) 33.

[54] Lathrop Gomez (n 36).

V. Conclusion: Protect the Best Interests of the Child by Improving the Quality of Decisions

Considering the scenarios described here, it is observed that most situations that involve decisions about the end-of-life treatment of children are taken within the family and/or with the medical team. In the event of conflict, it will be the judge who must decide. As we can see, it is not just about who decides, but how to ensure the best possible quality of the decision to ensure that the best interests of the child are really respected. I believe that strategies in this regard should be considered, such as promoting the teaching of bioethics and human rights for both health teams and lawyers, and providing in training in emotional management.

In the Peruvian case, attention should be paid to the health system, not just the judicial apparatus. Many doctors do not protect the rights of dying children, because they believe they will be exposed to claims for imaginary crimes (euthanasic practices or abandonment of person, which are not crimes).[55] The child's best interests give way to defensive medicine.[56] There is an urgent need to clarify the laws on capacity, competence and health issues, and to train health providers.

In other parts of the world, it has been questioned whether it should be the parents or the medical team who decide in cases of children at the end of their lives, an attitude that challenges the concept of 'joint consent' and places too much weight on the role of the judiciary.[57] However, in several judgments on which we comment, judicial action is frankly deficient. Is it a good idea to leave the rights of the dying children only in the hands of the judges? In Latin America, in general, the answer is no. Not yet.

Why do judges make mistakes? Because they have no training in legal bioethics. Health teams have little grounding in bioethics, and the training of lawyers and judges in bioethics is therefore non-existent. Judges lack conceptual tools and theoretical frameworks to address complex and interdisciplinary issues, and in general make their decisions based on a rigid civil law education (ignoring the constitutionalisation of private law and the parameters of conventionality) that does not have appropriate categories to address bioethical issues.

The best interests of the child is a category of international human rights law. How can bioethical dilemmas be solved within a rigid and infra-constitutional discipline such as civil law? 'Competence', for example, is a category of bioethics, which has been accepted by some civil codes, such as that of Argentina, and is

[55] KL Weise, AL Okun, BS Carter et al, 'Guidance on Forgoing Life-Sustaining Medical Treatment' (2017) 140 *Pediatrics* e20171905.

[56] Gherardi and Gherardi (n 47); J Pedro Piva et al, 'Dilemmas and Difficulties Involving End of Life Decisions and Palliative Care in Children' (2011) 23 *Revista Brasileira de Terapia Intensiva* 78.

[57] G Birchley, 'Deciding Together? Best Interests and Shared Decision-Making in Paediatric Intensive Care' (2014) 22 *Health Care Analysis* 203.

required to make effective the right of children to be heard and to participate in decisions concerning their health.

'Legal bioethics' is a concise term to describe bioethics dealing with and arising from human rights, training in which should be mandatory not only for members of the health system but for any lawyer and, especially, for family judges; it is a tool that allows analysis of complex cases, and offers an axiological platform (that of international human rights) and a concrete and flexible legal scaffolding[58] (categories, procedures, standards). Bioethics is linked to the very core of human rights.[59] Comment No 14 of the CRC describes proposed rules of procedure very similar to those that govern a bioethics committee.

In every procedure that involves decision-making about the health of a child, there must be, at the very least, and compulsorily, participation of a lawyer specialised in the rights of the child who legally represents him and a bioethics committee that functions as an independent, interdisciplinary body, whose guiding principle is the best interests of the child and who fights for the rights of the paediatric patient, following the guidelines proposed by Comment No 14. The committee is a space that parents and the medical team can access to present their points of view and attempt to remove any doubts (legal, ethical or procedural). Apart from the committee's own task, nothing prevents any of its members from collaborating in the task of 'translating' to the parents and/or the medical team the intention of the other party in order to alleviate conflict.[60]

It is essential that those whose work involves bioethical conflicts – lawyers, judges, doctors, nurses – learn to manage their own emotions to avoid projecting their fears and values, so as to be able to guide and give emotional support to parents. It is necessary to understand when we are facing a real conflict and when we are facing an unresolved duel. In my experience, the human factor makes all the difference. Facing a suffering child is not about being right, much less about making jurisprudence; it's about being at peace and transmitting that peace to the child.

Faced with an urgent case where there is dissent between parents and the treating team, or between parents, the judge, the child's lawyer and the bioethics committee should be called in. The bioethics committee should be the main expert reference, enabling the judge to reach a decision that takes account of the bioethical imperative: not everything technically possible is ethically recommendable.[61]

[58] P Siverino Bavio, 'La bioética jurídica ante el reto de las tecnologías reproductivas' in J Cieza, *Las técnicas de reproducción humana asistida. El impacto y la necesidad de una regulación en el Perú* (Lima, Instituto Pacífico, 2017) 9–32.

[59] JC Tealdi, *Bioética de los derechos humanos. Investigaciones médicas y dignidad humana* (México, UNAM, 2008).

[60] J Piva et al, 'Dilemmas and difficulties involving end of life decisions and palliative care in children', 2011, *Revista Brasileira de Terapia Intensiva* 78–86.

[61] I Pereira et al, 'Directivas de adecuación del esfuerzo terapéutico en niños. Experiencia de la unidad de cuidados paliativos pedíatricos del Centro Hospitalario Pereira Rossell (2009–2015)' (2017) 33(1) *Revista Médica del Uruguay* 17.

If it becomes necessary to change the therapeutic regime, the dignity of the child is the main consideration. The child has the right not to suffer anguish or pain, to receive palliative care,[62] to be comfortable and accompanied by his or her loved ones and meaningful objects; to have a smooth, placid transit, surrounded by love;[63] the parents should be give an appropriate environment to be able to transmit peace.[64] Any measure towards the child must take into account the need to alleviate any conflict that might affect him; legal conflicts are a disgrace for the sick child. Offering quality of life to patients and their families is consistent with the best approach from medicine, considering their values and needs.[65] Non-maleficence, unrestricted respect for dignity – which forces us always to see the child as an end in itself, beyond paternal suffering – compassion, honesty, integrity, solidarity – all these are cardinal values in decision-making.[66]

To achieve this, training in legal bioethics and emotion management are essential basic requirements for lawyers, judges and medical teams to prevent and defuse conflicts, in order to allow a real respect for the rights of children at the end of their lives.

[62] S Negri, 'Cuidados paliativos y derecho internacional de los derechos humanos: el derecho universal a no sufrir' in T Zamudio (ed), *Bioética, herramienta de las políticas públicas y de los derechos fundamentales del siglo XXI* (Buenos Aires, UMSA, 2012).

[63] O Orlandi, 'El paciente y su familia ante el proceso de muerte digna' (2012) *Revista Derecho de Familia* 133.

[64] D Black, 'The Dying Child' (1998) 316 *British Medical Journal* 1376.

[65] J Piva et al, 'Dilemmas and difficulties involving end of life decisions and palliative care in children', 2011, *Revista Brasileira de Terapia Intensiva* 80.

[66] A Royes, 'Principios y aplicación de los principios' in M Casado (comp), *Sobre la dignidad y los principios. análisis de la Declaración Universal sobre Bioética y Derechos Humanos de la UNESCO* (Madrid, Thomas Reuters/Civitas, 2009) 431.

21

Reviewing Medical Decisions Concerning Infants within the Norwegian Healthcare System: A Public Law Approach

KARL HARALD SOVIG*

I. Introduction – Overview of the Legislation Relating to Health

Norway is a constitutional monarchy and the Constitution from 1814 is still in force. Norway is situated in the north of Europe, on the western part of the Scandinavian peninsula, and is a middle-sized country (ranked as no 67 of the world's countries in terms of area) with a small population (ranked no 118 in the world).[1] It has a population of 5.3 million people (5,295,619 persons were registered as living in Norway as of 1 January 2018).[2]

Norway was a founding member of the Council of Europe. Cooperation within the Council is still important and Norway has ratified the Convention on Protection of Human Rights and Dignity of the Human Being with regard to the Application of Biology and Medicine (the Oviedo Convention, 4 April 1997). Norway's relation to the European Union has been a politically controversial topic. In two referendums (1972 and 1994) the public turned down draft agreements to enter the Union. Norway is affiliated to the European Union and its Member States through the European Economic Area (EEA) agreement.[3] Based on the EEA agreement,

* I thank my research assistant Kristine Skorpen for collecting material and for assistance with the references.

[1] wikipedia.org/wiki/List_of_countries_and_dependencies_by_area#cite_note-47 (Svalbard and Spitsbergen are excluded) and wikipedia.org/wiki/List_of_countries_and_dependencies_by_population.

[2] For a presentation of a selection of vital statistics in English, see Statistics Norway, www.ssb.no/en.

[3] For an in-depth analysis of this agreement, see C Baudenbacher (ed) *The Handbook of EEA Law* (Cham, Springer, 2015) and F Arnesen et al, *Agreement on the European Economic Area: A Commentary* (Oslo, CH Beck, Nomos/Hart, Universitetsforlaget, 2018).

the three European Free Trade Association countries (Iceland, Liechtenstein and Norway) participate extensively in the EU's internal market.

The Parliament (Stortinget) is the legislator.[4] A major health law reform took place in 1999, introducing four new acts relating to healthcare. Three of these were replacements of older legislation but the reform also introduced a separate Patient's Rights Act (PRA, 2 July 1999 No 63).[5] For the purpose of this chapter, the latter is of importance, together with the Specialised Health Care Services Act (SHCSA, 2 July 1999 No 61) and the Health Personnel Act (HPA, 2 July 1999 No 64). Additionally, the Act relating to Children and Parents (CPA, 8 April 1981 No 7) is of relevance. The Norwegian healthcare sector is to a large extent publicly funded,[6] and citizens are entitled to 'emergency healthcare' and 'necessary healthcare' (cf PRA section 2-1). The Norwegian legal system has for historical reasons many similarities with the Danish legal system, and both are inspired and influenced by continental legal thinking, especially from Germany.[7] It is a matter of discussion whether the Nordic countries belong to a separate law family, or are to be considered part of the continental family.[8] Within health law, there is a close collaboration within the Nordic countries and law revisions are often inspired by the neighbouring countries.[9] As demonstrated by the chapter on Sweden, there are many similarities between these two neighbouring countries when it comes to the issues addressed in this book.[10]

The Constitution underwent a major reform in 2014 as part of the country's bicentennial.[11] Human rights protection was strengthened, and the language was updated from old-fashioned Norwegian (with similarities to Danish) to modern Norwegian. The Constitution is now articulated in both versions of the written Norwegian language, which are equally authentic. Although the right to health was not guaranteed (a proposal in this respect did not achieve the sufficient majority),

[4] A selection of legislation translated into English is available at app.uio.no/ub/ujur/oversatte-lover and lovdata.no/register/loverEngelsk. Please note that not all legislation is translated and that the translation is not always updated.

[5] For an overview of Norwegian health law in English, see KH Søvig, 'Medical Law – Norway' in H Nys (ed), *International Encyclopaedia for Medical Law*, 2nd edn (Alphen aan den Rijn, Wolters Kluwer, 2019).

[6] For an overview of healthcare funding, including a country report of Norway, see W Sauter, J Boertjens, J van Manen and M Mikkers (eds), *The Law of Healthcare Financing: An International Comparison of Models and Outcomes* (Cheltenham, Edward Elgar, 2019).

[7] For analysis and discussion of Norwegian legal methods, see S Koch and I Helland (eds), *Nordic and Germanic Legal Methods: Contributions to a Dialogue between Different Legal Cultures, with a Main Focus on Norway and Germany* (Tübingen, Mohr Siebeck, 2014).

[8] K Zweigert and H Kötz, *Introduction to Comparative Law*, 3rd edn (Oxford, Clarendon Press, 1998) 276; 85 re the Nordic legal systems as a separate law family.

[9] E Rynning and M Hartlev (eds), *Nordic Health Law in a European Context: Welfare State Perspectives on Patients' Rights and Biomedicine* (Leiden, Martinus Nijhoff, 2012).

[10] *cf* P Leviner, 'Who Has the Final Word? On Trust and Legal Uncertainty Within the Swedish Health Care System', in this book.

[11] See K Gammelgaard and E Holmøyvik (eds), *Writing Democracy: The Norwegian Constitution 1814–2014* (New York, Berghahn, 2014).

children's rights are now secured by section 104. Children have the right to respect for their human dignity. They have the 'right to be heard in questions that concern them' and 'due weight' shall be attached to their views 'in accordance with their age and development' (first paragraph). For actions and decisions that affect children, the 'best interests of the child shall be a fundamental consideration' (second paragraph). Children have 'the right to protection of their personal integrity' (third paragraph). Section 104 is drafted with the UN Convention on the Rights of the Child (CRC, 20 November 1989) in mind, and part of the wording is similar to the text of the CRC, see in particular Articles 3 and 12. The CRC is incorporated into Norwegian legislation by the Human Rights Act (21 May 1999 No 30), with supremacy over concurring domestic legislation.[12]

II. The Competence to Decide on Behalf of the Minor Patient

Given the topic of this book, the rules concerning minor patients in general will not be examined and the focus will be on infant patients. The general age of majority in Norway is eighteen years (see Guardianship Act, 26 March 2010 No 9, section 8). Parents will act as guardians for their children unless they are deprived of their parental responsibility.[13] In general, both parents have to consent, with some exceptions (see below).

The PRA has a separate chapter stipulating 'special rights for children' (see Chapter 6). However, these are of limited interest since they regulate the conditions during hospital stay, e.g. the right to be accompanied by parents and the right to access to education. The only provision to be mentioned in this context is section 6-1, second paragraph which states that parents are 'obliged' to contribute to the health checks of their children.

A guiding principle for all decisions concerning children, both when interpreting the legislation and when making decisions on behalf of children, is that the best interests of the child should be a primary consideration, anchored both in the Constitution (section 104), binding international human right's instruments (CRC Article 3) and various national legislation (CPA section 30).

PRA section 4-4 regulates consent on behalf of children under the age of sixteen who are not competent to give their own consent. Since the core issue is infant children with severe conditions, the provisions regarding daily and ordinary healthcare will not be examined.

[12] See M Langford, M Skivenes and KH Søvig (eds), *Children's Rights in Norway: An Implementation Paradox?* (Oslo, Universitetsforlaget, 2019).

[13] See HS Aasen, 'Barns rett til selvbestemmelse og medbestemmelse i beslutninger om helsehjelp' (2008) 6(1) *Tidsskrift for Familierett, Arverett og Barnevernrettslige Spørsmål* 4, 4–27.

Previously, it was an absolute requirement that if parental responsibility was shared, both parents had to consent to healthcare on behalf of their children. PRA section 4-4 was revised in 2010, in order to secure children necessary medical treatment. It is sufficient that one of the holders of parental responsibility consent to healthcare that qualified health personnel find 'necessary' to avoid the child being harmed (see section 4-4, third paragraph). Before such healthcare is provided, both parents or holders of parental responsibility shall as far as possible be given the opportunity to express their views. In the preparatory work, the ministry of Children and Equality emphasised that what would be 'harmful' for the child depended on an individual assessment of the case and included medical discretion.[14] Relevant factors will be the severity of the child's condition, the need for an instant intervention, the consequences of postponing the decision and the risk connected with providing healthcare.

A decision to provide healthcare according to this provision can be appealed to the county governor by the parent who opposes the treatment. The county governor is a state body, and works to ensure that decisions of the Parliament and government are implemented correctly. Health cases before the county governor will be dealt with by the county medical officer, who is a physician under the direct order of the Norwegian Board of Health Supervision (see Act 15 December 2017 No 107, section 3). The county governor has full competence to review the case. He or she decides that the healthcare shall cease until a final decision is made based on the complaint by the other parent or other holders of parental responsibility. There are few reported complaints concerning this provision.

The remedies of intervention according to the Child Welfare Act (17 July 1992 No 100) will not be dealt with in general here, but two provisions are of special interest. According to section 4-10, the county board for child welfare and social affairs can issue orders for medical examination and treatment. The county board is an independent state body serving as a tribunal and normally composed of a chair (lawyer), an expert (often a psychologist) and a layperson. If there is 'reason to believe' that a child is suffering from a 'life-threatening or other serious illness or injury', and if the parents fail to ensure that the child is examined or receives treatment, the county board may decide that the child, with the assistance of the child welfare service, shall be examined by a doctor, or be taken to a hospital for examination. The county board may also decide that such an illness shall be treated at a hospital or at home in accordance with a doctor's instructions. Section 4–11 provides the county board with the competence to issue treatment orders for children with special treatment and training needs. Such an order may be issued if the parents fail to 'ensure that a child who is disabled or in special need of help receives the treatment and training required'. The county board may then decide that the

[14] Ot prp nr 104 (2008–2009) *Om lov om endringer i barnelova mv (flytting, delt bosted, samvær, vold mv)*, 63.

child shall receive treatment or training with the assistance of the child welfare service. Orders according to sections 4-10 and 4-11 are in practice seldom issued.

HPA section 7, first paragraph, states that – with some exceptions that are not relevant here – emergency healthcare is to be given even if the patient is incapable of granting his consent, and even if the patient objects to the treatment. The latter part of the provision is an explicit legal foundation for coercive measures. The starting point for the assessment of whether to provide emergency treatment is the severity of the patients' health condition. If there is a risk of loss of life or severe deterioration of the health condition, then physicians may be entitled to intervene, especially if the risk of death or significant harm is high. A core element is when the negative consequence may occur, and the term 'emergency' indicates that the situation must be acute. When the acute phase is passed, healthcare can only be provided based on the ordinary conditions (normally informed consent).

The assessment must include an evaluation of the probable effect of the intervention, and there should be a reluctance to intervene if it is doubtful whether the treatment will prevent loss of life or basic functions. Possible side effects of the interventions must also be included in the assessment.

HPA section 7, first paragraph is mainly discussed in the preparatory works and in the literature with the adult patient in mind, but the competence to intervene will also apply to minor patients. It should be emphasised that HPA section 7 does not contain any procedural requirements. The competence to carry out emergency treatment can therefore be made by the individual physician, without consulting a colleague. However, if there is time for consultations and the interference is especially intrusive (high risk for the patient and/or the use of force), the requirements for professional responsibility and diligent care in HPA section 4 may warrant such a consultation. In any case, the obligation to keep patients' records applies (cf. HPA chapter 8) and the physician may be obliged to document the assessment that has been made.

It should be added that both PRA section 4-4 and HPA section 7 are concerned with the situation where there is a need of a legal foundation for the intervention, either based on consent by one the parents accompanied by a medical assessment (PRA section 4-4), or a medical assessment alone (HPA section 7). The decision not to continue medical treatment, like in the cases of Charlie Guard or Alfie Evans, is not regarded as an intervention. Hence, consent from the parents is not needed, and therefore there is also no need for an alternative legal foundation to remedy a lack of consent. The situations where medical treatment is discontinued will be dealt with below.

The patient, and parents on their behalf, are entitled to choose the institution to carry out the examination or treatment. The patient can either choose a public institution, also outside the region where the patient is residing, or a private provider. The patient can only choose private providers that have an agreement with the regional health enterprise, or private providers that are appointed and approved by the Directorate of Health and that are providing services according to fixed prices. The directive on the application of patients' rights in cross-border healthcare[15] is considered EEA relevant and is implemented in Norway by a separate regulation insofar as it concerns health services provided in another EU/EEA Member State. The basic requirement is that healthcare provided in another EU/EEA Member State is only covered insofar as the patient would have been entitled to care according to national legislation. The patient can in such cases either have the expenses reimbursed or require a prior authorisation regarding whether the treatment would be covered and the maximum amount that will be reimbursed.

If necessary healthcare cannot be provided due to lack of adequate treatment within the country, the patient is entitled to treatment abroad within the time limit set for 'necessary healthcare'. Such treatment is covered by the regional health enterprises. It is a condition that the healthcare can be given abroad according to established standards. In exceptional cases the patient can also be given experimental treatment abroad.

III. The Kristina and Ove Cases

There are no reported Supreme Court cases concerning disputes about healthcare for infant children, but there are two cases from the lower courts. The Kristina case received a lot of attention in the national mass media in the winter of 2006. Kristina was almost five years old in September 2005 when her home was hit by a landslide in which her mother lost her life. Her father and two siblings were unharmed. Kristine was brought to hospital without respiration and heart activity. She was resuscitated and placed on a respirator. After a period of treatment, the doctors concluded that Kristina had severe brain damage which made her unable to store and process information and she had no sense of being. She was not able to breath or swallow and had spasms. The doctors found that she was perhaps able to feel pain and that it would be unethical to continue treatment. The hospital decided to end treatment in November 2005. Her father brought an appeal to the county governor who confirmed the hospital's decision to discontinue treatment. Subsequently, the father instituted proceedings at the City Court. Besides the ordinary lawsuit claiming that the decision was void, he filed an application for an interim court order to postpone the execution of the decision to end treatment. The City Court held an oral hearing before deciding the interim court order.[16]

The City Court rejected the claim for an interim court order. According to the relevant provision, such a claim would only be successful if it is necessary to make 'a temporary arrangement in a disputed legal issue in order to avert considerable loss or inconvenience'.[17] An interim measure cannot be granted if the loss

[15] Directive (EU) 2011/24 on the application of patients' rights in cross-border healthcare [2011] OJ L88.

[16] Judgment 18 January 2006 (case 06-000665TVI-BBYR/02).

[17] *cf* the Act relating to mediation and procedure in civil disputes 17 June 2005, no 90, s 34-1(1).

or inconvenience to the defendant is clearly disproportionate to the interests of the claimant in the interim measure being granted.[18] If delay poses a risk, the court may grant an interim measure even if the claimant's claim is not proven.[19]

The court took PRA section 2-1 on the 'right to necessary healthcare' as a starting point and stated that is was doubtful that the provision, read in light of the preparatory works, established a right to judicial review regarding ongoing treatment. The patient has a legal entitlement to specialised healthcare when the conditions in the legislation are fulfilled, but the court held that the content of the treatment and its execution is not suitable for judicial review, except the right to have medically sound treatment. Even though the ethical considerations were more present in the given case than in most other situations, the court held that a decision to end treatment is to a large extent a matter of medical expertise. The core element of the reasoning is that the judge held that the decision seemed reasonable and was within 'the margin of appreciation' of the medical discretion. The conditions of the patient and the consequences of further treatment must be assessed, which the courts could hardly review in a meaningful manner.

The father had also challenged the decision over procedural errors, including assessment of the facts. He experienced that Kristina responded when he talked to her by opening her eyes or moving her limbs. Two external medical doctors had examined Kristina, one appointed by the hospital and one appointed by the Norwegian Board of Health Supervision. They both agreed with the main findings of the hospital doctors. Kristina's father had engaged a medical doctor who had observed Kristina and her father but not examined her. This doctor issued a memorandum where he described communication between Kristina and her father and where he stressed that as a child Kristina had potential for development. The hospital found that her movements were associated with spasms. The court held that the arguments put forward by the plaintiff gave no reason to doubt the reasonableness of the medical assessment by the hospital.

The decision was appealed to the High Court by the father. As mentioned above, the case gained a lot of media attention. A part of the story was the behaviour of representatives of the hospital visiting the father at home in the evening trying to convince him to withdraw the appeal. A bishop acted as a mediator and the father withdrew his appeal shortly before the oral hearing of the High Court. The life-prolonging treatment was terminated at the beginning of February 2006 and Kristina died shortly thereafter.

An investigation was carried out by Norwegian Board of Health Supervision.[20] The board divided the case into separate parts. The first related to the communication between the hospital and father. The second related to the issue at stake here.

[18] *cf* ibid s 34-1(2).
[19] *cf* ibid s 34-2(2).
[20] A summary of the report is available at the homepage of the Norwegian Board of Health Supervision. See helsetilsynet.no/historisk-arkiv/avgjoerelser-i-tilsynssaker-og-rapporter-etter-alvorlige-hendelser/ingen-reaksjon-helseforetak-forsvarlighet-kommunikasjon-samtykke.

Before assessing the treatment of Kristina, the board appointed two international experts. The board concluded that she had been given sound medical treatment during her hospital stay.

The case was also discussed in Parliament by a written answer by the Minister of Health to a question put forward by a Member of Parliament.[21] The Minister held that the final decision should be up to professional personnel but emphasised the need for a proper procedure in order to assess the viewpoints of the parents. However, the discussion in Parliament was not followed up by legislative amendments.

Shortly after the Kristina case, the regional health enterprises were instructed according to the steering documents to establish clinical ethics committees. This reform was not a reaction to the Kristina case but was part of a general debate within the healthcare sector. The clinical ethics committees are not a formal body with the competence to issue orders but can be a support in the decision process. Cases concerning termination of treatment of children are regularly being dealt with by the clinical ethics committees, as illustrated by the subsequent case.

The Ove case concerned a child born with trisomy 18. This is a congenital genetic disease where the patient has a third copy of all parts of chromosome 18 (Edwards' syndrome).[22] It occurs in around one in 5,000 live births. Ove was initially diagnosed during pregnancy, and the disease was confirmed after birth, first by blood samples and subsequently by extended genetic testing. He had a 'complete' trisomy 18 affecting nearly all cells in the body. Ove was not unconscious in the sense of being in a coma, but he did not respond with eye contact, sounds or movements. It could not be out of the question that he could feel pain. He had probably massive brain damage. Ove frequently stopped breathing and he was routinely bagged to prevent suffocation. The doctors wanted to end treatment, which was supported by his mother but opposed by his father. The hospital brought the case to the clinical ethics committee which held an oral hearing where the father and his lawyer expressed their viewpoint. The committee stated that there were 'more than sufficient medical grounds to decide that further life support in the form of manual ventilation should not be given, and indeed is not in the best interest of this child'. Furthermore, the committee held 'that it is not ethically acceptable or defensible to continue intermittent bag and mask ventilation until such time as the father recognises that stopping this is the right thing to do'. The hospital then decided to end treatment and the father brought the decision to the county governor. The county governor came to the conclusion that the child had received 'necessary healthcare' according to PRA section 2-1. According to the county governor, it was not up to the relatives to claim a certain treatment or method. Subsequently, the hospital confirmed their decision to end treatment.

[21] The question and the answer is available at the website of the parliament, stortinget.no/no/Saker-og-publikasjoner/Sporsmal/Skriftlige-sporsmal-og-svar/Skriftlig.

[22] en.wikipedia.org/wiki/Edwards_syndrome.

The father instituted proceedings at the City Court and filed an application for an interim court order to postpone the execution of the decision to end treatment. The City Court rejected the application without holding an oral hearing. The father appealed to the High Court which decided the case after an oral hearing.[23] The High Court rejected the claim. The primary submission of the hospital was that the claim should be dismissed. The hospital held that the court lacked jurisdiction to decide a dispute that was not of legal nature but concerned medical and ethical considerations. The court took as a starting point that the all kinds of administrative decisions are subject to judicial review. This is a core element of the rule of law and exceptions must be well founded. This also applies to decisions within the healthcare sector where there has been a development in recent years towards a strengthening of the legal position of patients. The court also found that such an approach had support in the preparatory works of the PRA. However, the court emphasised that even if the claim is subject to judicial review, the courts would be careful in their assessments. The judicial review would foremost be connected to the procedural aspects.

Turning to the material issue, the court supported the findings of the City Court, and held that the hospital had made a careful assessment and had consulted the clinical ethics committee. If the court approved the claim, it would contribute to a continued treatment that was not medically sound and that was not in the child's best interests and that was opposed by his mother. The father had held that even if the claim was not proven, an interim measure should be awarded since a delay would pose a risk.[24] This provision requires an overall assessment of the case, where the risk is one element, but where other factors also had to be taken into account. Even if an interim measure was granted, the child would probably not live until a final judgment was given and, in the meantime, he would probably live in pain. The father, and the hospital, appealed the decision to the Supreme Court. The appeals committee of the Supreme Court refused to grant appeal.[25]

IV. Reflections

This overview of the legislation and case-law indicates the public law orientation of the legal structure of Norwegian health law, in line with the funding of these services. Cases concerning end of treatment of infants are not dealt with as a matter of family law but as a health law issue. Consequently, the legal disputes are dealt within the public law framework.

The PRA provides a rather detailed regulation of consent and information, that also applies to children. It also regulates disagreement between the parents in this

[23] Decision 2 February 2007 (RG-2007-1441).
[24] *cf* DA s 34-2(2).
[25] Decision 6 June 2007, HR-2007-1238-U.

respect. Foremost among the provisions in the PRA is intervention, and the Act provides a legal basis for treatment where the patient is not able to consent on their own behalf. Issues relating to end of treatment are not directly addressed, apart from certain aspects concerning adults, such as blood transfusions, etc (see PRA section 4-9). This means that disputes between medical personnel and the parents have to be solved based on more general principles of health law. The starting point – both for adults and children – is that patients are not entitled to choose which treatment shall be offered and the methods, as long as they are provided with necessary healthcare that is medically sound. The viewpoints of the parents – acting as guardians – have rather weak legal protection as long as the child is in hospital care and the question is not whether an intervention should take place but whether an ongoing treatment should be discontinued.[26]

The issue of moving a child to another country has not yet been an issue before the Norwegian courts. The legal questions will then be somewhat different since medical personnel in a different jurisdiction may consider it to be medically sound to allow a life-sustaining treatment to continue. Nevertheless, this will still be regarded as an administrative legal issue. The crux of the matter will probably be whether the treatment abroad can be regarded as 'necessary healthare' which cannot be provided in Norway due to a lack of adequate domestic treatment options. Questions regarding free movement within the EU/EEA can also arise, but it should be kept in mind that cross-border healthcare is only covered insofar as the patient would have been entitled to care according to national legislation.

The reported cases were all solved within an administrative law framework. The hospitals are publicly funded and decisions within the healthcare sectors can be appealed to the county governor. In cases concerning judicial review of administrative cases the courts are reluctant to substitute their own discretion with that of the administrations as long as the basic requirements of equal treatment and proportionality are satisfied. The courts can fully review the procedural aspects and the interpretation of the legislation. The reported cases both show that the courts are hesitant to review the medical assessments as long as the patients are provided with 'necessary healthcare'.[27]

Possible development of the Norwegian approach might include paying greater attention to the assessment of the best interests of the child. Inspiration for such an approach could be found in England and Wales.[28] The domestic courts would still rely heavily on the assessment by the hospital doctors or other experts but the courts will normally be more willing to engage in a review of the best interests of the child than simply reviewing what can be considered as a medically sound treatment.

[26] See as a contrast the approach in Ireland, where parents have stronger legal protection, J Lombard and L Bracken, 'Medical Decision-Making on Behalf of Children in Ireland', in this book.

[27] The reluctance of the courts to overrule the medical expertise has similarities to Spain, *cf* M Navarro-Michel, 'Young Children and Healthcare Decisions in Spain: Who Decides?', in this book.

[28] *cf* I Goold, C Auckland and J Herring, 'Medical Decision-Making on Behalf of Children in England and Welsh Law: A Child-Centred Best Interests Approach', in this book.

22

Children and Medical Decision-Making in Australia Post-*Gard*: A Possible Reformulation

CAMERON STEWART

I. Introduction

This chapter examines the Australian law of consent to the treatment for children, with a particular focus on disputes between parents, doctors and the courts. Australia is a federated constitutional monarchy where disputes concerning the medical treatment children may be resolved by state and federal courts. There are six states and two major territories, each with their own Supreme Court that is empowered with *parens patriae* jurisdiction over children. Additionally, there is a federal Family Court of Australia, which has a statutory version of the *parens patriae*.[1] This court has jurisdiction over children from all of Australia, barring Western Australia (which has its own Family Court). All of these courts are subject to the appellate jurisdiction of the High Court of Australia. Australian law is heavily influenced by the common law of England and Wales but there are some significant points of departure both concerning the limits of parental decision-making and the nature of the jurisdiction to review.

This chapter begins with an introduction to the primary case on the Australian law of consent to medical treatment: *Secretary, Department of Health and Community Services v JWB and SMB* ('Marion's case').[2] The chapter goes on to describe how Marion's case adopted the therapeutic/non-therapeutic distinction and the notion of the court as an *uber*-parent. The chapter maps out the problems that Australia has experienced with these ideas and then proceeds to look at the Australian approach to *Gard*-like disputes.[3] The chapter then concludes

[1] *Family Law Act* 1975 (Cth) S 67ZC.

[2] *Secretary, Department of Health and Community Services v JWB and SMB* (1992) 175 CLR 218.

[3] See *Great Ormond Street Hospital v Yates and Gard* [2017] EWHC 972 (Fam) (*Gard*); *Great Ormond Street Hospital for Children NHS Foundation Trust v Yates Court of Appeal (Civil Division)*

with recommending a modified form of the 'significant risks' approach, specially adapted to Australian conditions and based on principles of judicial review.

II. Marion's Case

Marion's case is the leading Australian case on consent to treatment for children.[4] The case was concerned with a 14-year-old girl with cognitive disabilities, Marion, and whether she should undergo a sterilisation procedure. Marion's parents believed that it would be in her best interests to be sterilised as they were concerned about her ability to deal with menstruation and they were also concerned about the risks of her falling pregnant. The primary question to decide was whether Marion's parents had the power to consent to a sterilisation or should such decisions be made by the courts?

The majority of the High Court of Australia (Mason CJ, Dawson, Toohey and Gaudron JJ) found that Marion's parents did not have the power to consent to the sterilisation. In so finding, the majority distinguished between treatment which has the 'purpose of curing some disease or malfunction of the body' ('therapeutic treatment') and that which is proposed for other reasons ('non-therapeutic treatment').[5] The majority determined that, in cases where non-therapeutic treatment is proposed for minors, parents had no power to consent and some form of court or tribunal consent was mandatory before the treatment could be provided. The majority recognised that the therapeutic/non-therapeutic distinction was imprecise (noting that the House of Lords had already rejected it) but they employed the principle anyway.[6]

The High Court majority considered a number of factors to be in favour of mandatory court authorisation including the seriousness of the proposed treatment and the risks involved in parents making such decisions, that facts that sterilisation was invasive and irreversible, the gravity of the operation and the risk of making a wrong decision.[7] There was also the tendency for the medical profession to 'medicalise' decisions and a risk of conflict between parental interests and concerns and the interests of the child.[8]

[2017] EWCA Civ 410 (*Gard 2*); *Alder Hey Children's NHS Foundation Trust v Mr Thomas Evans, Ms Kate James, Alfie Evans (A Child by his Guardian CAFCASS Legal)* [2018] EWHC 308 (Fam) (*Evans*), [2018] 2 FLR 1223; *Kings College Hospital NHS Foundation Trust v Ms Thomas, Haastrup and Haastrup* [2018] EWHC 127 (Fam), [2018] 2 FLR 1028 (*Haastrup*); *Raqeeb v Barts NHS Foundation Trust* [2019] EWHC 2531 (Admin) and [2019] EWHC 2530 (Fam).

[4] *Secretary, Department of Health and Community Services v JWB and SMB* (1992) 175 CLR 218.

[5] *Secretary, Department of Health and Community Services v JWB and SMB* (n 2) 259–50.

[6] *Re B (A Minor)(Wardship: Sterilisation)* [1988] AC 199, 203–05, 211.

[7] *Secretary, Department of Health and Community Services v JWB and SMB* (n 2) 259–50.

[8] ibid.

The majority's approach is very different from that of the English and Welsh courts which had decided to reject the therapeutic/non-therapeutic distinction and not require mandatory court authorisation, instead encouraging recourse to the courts for such matters as 'highly desirable as a matter of good practice'.[9]

Outside of the majority in Marion's case, Brennan J also adopted the therapeutic/non-therapeutic distinction and found that a treatment was therapeutic if it had the 'chief purpose of preventing, removing or ameliorating a cosmetic deformity, a pathological condition or a psychiatric disorder, provided the treatment is appropriate for and proportionate to the purpose for which it is administered'.[10] However, Brennan J found, unlike the majority, that the courts and parents had no power to authorise a non-therapeutic sterilisation.

Deane J took a practical approach to the issue of consent. His Honour found that parents could consent to sterilisation when there was obvious need for surgery in the interests of the welfare of the child, according to general community standards.[11] Deane J also allowed for parental consent when:

- the child was 'never going to be capable of being a party to a mature human relationship involving informed sexual intercourse, of responsible procreation or of caring for an infant';
- the surgery was 'necessary to avoid grave and unusual problems and suffering which are or would be involved in menstruation' such as an 'inability to comprehend or cope with pain; a phobic aversion to blood; a complete inability to cope with problems of hygiene with psychiatric or psychological consequences';
- the surgery was a treatment of 'last resort' and 'no alternative and less drastic treatment' was available; and
- the parents had consulted with 'competent medical advice from a multidisciplinary team, acting on the basis of appropriate paediatric, social and domestic reports'.[12]

Deane J also stated that it was still within the power of parents to consent to 'plastic surgery … for purely cosmetic purposes' and 'male circumcision for perceived hygienic – or even religious – reasons'.[13]

McHugh J, clearly in dissent, found that parents had an unsupervised right to consent to medical treatment and that there was no community consensus on whether sterilisation decisions should be mandatorily reviewed. The court's role

[9] *Re F* [1990] 2 AC 1, 56, 79. The findings have been repeated over the years: *Airedale NHS Trust v Bland* [1993] 2 WLR 316; *Frenchay NHS Trust v S* [1994] 1 All ER 403, 409; *An NHS Trust and others (Respondents) v Y* [2018] UKSC 46.

[10] *Secretary, Department of Health and Community Services v JWB and SMB* (n 2) 269.

[11] ibid 305.

[12] ibid.

[13] ibid 297.

was only to review decisions of parents which failed to advance and protect the welfare of the child.

This review of Marion's case illustrates that its primary effect was twofold – it cemented the therapeutic/non-therapeutic distinction as the foundation of the law of consent for children, and it created a shift in the court's jurisdiction towards the notion that the court had greater power than parents to consent to treatment. We will now examine each of these effects.

III. The Problems of the Therapeutic/ Non-Therapeutic Distinction

In the decades since Marion's case the distinction between therapeutic and non-therapeutic treatments has proved to be extremely difficult to apply and has created enormous uncertainty.[14] As I have argued elsewhere, the cases that came after Marion's case failed to employ the distinction logically, and instead a pattern emerged where the decision over mandatory court authorisation had less to do with a rational employment of the therapeutic/non-therapeutic distinction and more to do more to do with a 'general feeling of judicial unease'.[15]

As non-therapeutic sterilisations became rarer (possibly due to the advent of less invasive and effective contraceptives) the courts began to require court consent to sterilisations that should have been viewed as therapeutic (under either the majority or Brennan J's definition of the term). For example, in *Re Edith*[16] the Family Court found that a proposed partial hysterectomy of a girl, who mutilated herself when she menstruated, was said to be non-therapeutic. Similarly, in *Re Lesley*[17] court approval was said to be necessary for a gonadectomy to be performed on an infant with 17-β/HSD deficiency, a disorder of sexual development rendering a child genetically male but insensitive to androgens while gestating, resulting in the appearance of being female.[18] The Family Court also required approval in *Re Sally (Special Medical Procedure)*[19] for the surgical removal of male gonads from a 14-year-old girl with an intersex condition. Murphy J said:

> Despite the fact that all parties are in agreement about a proposed course of action, and those who agree include the child, the parents and the relevant medical agency, this court nevertheless retains an independent obligation to consider all of the matters

[14] C Stewart, 'Cracks in the Lintel of Consent' in I Freckelton and K Petersen (eds), *Tensions and Traumas in Health Law* (Sydney, Federation Press, 2017).

[15] ibid.

[16] *Re Edith* [2014] FamCA 908.

[17] *Re Lesley* [2008] FamCA 1226.

[18] See *Re Carla (Medical Procedure)* [2016] FamCA 7 where the Family Court found, in an almost identical case to *Re Lesley*, that sterilisation was therapeutic. See also *Re Sean and Russell* [2010] FamCA 948, for another example of a therapeutic sterilisation.

[19] *Re Sally (Special Medical Procedure)* [2010] FamCA 237.

directly relevant to Sally's best interests in arriving at a conclusion about whether this invasive and irreversible procedure ought be permitted.[20]

With respect to Murphy J, it is hard to see how such a conclusion could be justified by Marion's case. This is the clearest example of a therapeutic sterilisation that one could find.

Similar irrational decisions can be found on abortion[21] and tissue donation.[22] But worst of all were a series of tragic decisions from the Family Court regarding treatments for gender dysphoria. Originally, the Family Court took the view that treatments for gender dysphoria were non-therapeutic[23] and later decisions continued to require court approval.[24] In 2013 the Family Court recognised that stage 1 of treatment (puberty blocking) was therapeutic but still required mandatory testing of the child's capacity for stage 2 (hormonal therapy for secondary sexual characteristics), and if that capacity was proven the child, parents and doctors could then move forward without further court review.[25] Eventually, that position also was discarded, given an explosion in the number of applications that were being made to the court.[26] In *Re Kelvin*[27] the Full Family Court decided that consent to treatment could be given by the parents and child as properly advised by medical practitioners, a final recognition that the treatments for gender dysphoria were therapeutic and not required to be court approved.[28]

[20] ibid 71.

[21] According to *Queensland v B* [2008] QSC 231 and *Central Queensland Hospital and Health Service v Q* [2016] QSC 89, abortions are non-therapeutic, but under the criminal law of Queensland (at the time of the decisions) no abortions could be performed unless they were therapeutic.

[22] In *GWW and CMW* (1997) FLC ¶ 92-748, bone marrow donation was said to be non-therapeutic but in *Re Inaya (Special Medical Procedure)* (2007) 38 Fam LR 546, the court found that it was within parental responsibility.

[23] *Re Alex* [2004] FamCA 297.

[24] *Re Brodie (Special Medical Procedures: Jurisdiction)* [2007] FamCA 776; *Re Brodie (Special Medical Procedure)* [2008] FamCA 334; *Re Rosie (Special Medical Procedure)* [2011] FamCA 63; and *Re O (Special Medical Procedure)* [2010] FamCA 1153.

[25] *Re Jamie* (2013) 50 Fam LR 369. See the excellent arguments of Felicity Bell, 'Children with Gender Dysphoria and the Jurisdiction of the Family Court' (2015) 38 *University of New South Wales Law Journal* 426.

[26] *Re Matthew* [2017] FamCA 74; *Re Lincoln (No 2)* [2016] FamCA 1071; *Re Dallas* [2016] FamCA 1131; *Re Gleeson* [2016] FamCA 998; *Re Tony* [2016] FamCA 936; *Re Quinn* [2016] FamCA 617; *Re Sara* [2016] FamCA 405; *Re Oliver* [2016] FamCA 423; *Re Tara* [2016] FamCA 406; *Re Marco* [2016] FamCA 187; *Re Logan* [2016] FamCA 87; *Re Lucas* [2016] FamCA 1129; *Re Anita* [2016] FamCA 1137; *Re Lincoln (No 2)* [2016] FamCA 1071; *Re Kerry* [2016] FamCA 970; *Re Shay* [2016] FamCA 998; *Re Jason* [2016] FamCA 772; *Re Darryl* [2016] FamCA 720; *Re Mackenzie* [2016] FamCA 610; *Re Sara* [2016] FamCA 405; *Re Harley* [2016] FamCA 334; *Re Emery* [2016] FamCA 240; *Re Celeste* [2016] FamCA 503; *Re George* [2016] FamCA 136; *Re Martin* [2015] FamCA 1189; *Re Jacinta* [2015] FamCA 1196; *Re Cameron* [2015] FamCA 1113; *Re Marley* [2015] FamCA 878; *Re Karsen* [2015] FamCA 733; *Re Kate* [2015] FamCA 705; *Re Flynn* [2015] FamCA 629; *Re Julian* [2015] FamCA 562; *Re Sasha* [2015] FamCA 785; *Re Dale* [2015] FamCA 473; *Re Christopher* [2015] FamCA 454; *Re Jamie* [2015] FamCA 455; *Re Darcey* [2015] FamCA 409; *Re Ashley* [2015] FamCA 373; *Re Drew* [2015] FamCA 784; *Re Janson* [2015] FamCA 499; *Re Xanthe* [2015] FamCA 116; *Re Sarah* [2014] FamCA 208; *Re Shane (Gender Dysphoria)* [2013] FamCA 864.

[27] *Re Kelvin* [2017] FamCAFC 258.

[28] See also *Re Matthew* [2018] FamCA 161 where stage 3 (surgical treatment) was therapeutic so there was no need for the court's approval; *Re Eddie (No 2)* [2017] FamCA 1001 (child competent for stage 2); *Re LG* [2017] FCWA 179 (child was competent for stage 3 – breast reduction).

Overall, the therapeutic/non-therapeutic distinction has been a poor indicator of when the courts will require a decision to be mandatorily court reviewed, but it remains as the core Australian test. It would be wonderful if the High Court could provide us a with a review of the test and how it should be applied as we approach the 30th anniversary of Marion's case, but until that time the test is likely to be applied unpredictably.

IV. The Court as an *Uber*-Parent – A New Development

The second feature of Marion's case that I wish to discuss is the case's departure from the traditional understandings of the role of the court. In the past the court's power was one of supervision and review of parental decision-making or, in cases where the child was a ward of the state, of acting as a parent.[29] The High Court in Marion's case fundamentally altered this role by making the court an *uber*-parent – a parent who can decide issues that other parents cannot.[30]

If we wish to probe this notion of the *uber*-parent we need to examine the history of *parens patriae* jurisdiction. As with the courts in England and Wales, the power of Australian superior courts is often said to be based on the *parens patriae* power, but in reality, the courts' modern powers are an amalgamation of the *parens patriae* jurisdiction and the wardship jurisdiction, which developed separately as concepts but which today are often treated as interchangeable.[31]

The wardship jurisdiction developed earlier than the recognition of *parens patriae* over children.[32] Its purpose was to regulate the administration of the property of infant heirs. When an adult died leaving an infant heir there was an obvious need to regulate the control of the heir's assets. This was especially the case given the feudal structure of tenure in medieval England, with its incumbent need to exact military and financial dues from tenants. When a tenant under military tenure died leaving an infant heir, the mesne lord took wardship over the heir and had the right to enjoy the profits and rents from the land as well as control the whereabouts of the heir and their choice of marriage partner. The position was somewhat different for non-military or 'socage' tenures, as the guardian could not take the profits and had to account to the heir.[33]

[29] J Seymour (1992) 'The Role of the Family Court of Australia in Child Welfare Matters' 21 *Federal Law Review* 1.

[30] Stewart (n 14) 223. Similar statements can also be found in English cases: see *Re R (a minor) (wardship: treatment)* [1991] 4 All ER 177, 186 (Donaldson MR).

[31] See J Seymour (1994) '*Parens Patriae* and Wardship Powers: Their Nature and Origins' 14 *OJLS* 159.

[32] ibid 162.

[33] ibid 163–64.

The Court of Wards was established in 1540, in response to the rapid expansion in the number of wards created by the Statute of Uses.[34] It was abolished in 1660, the same year that the concept of tenure and traditional wardship was dealt a death blow by the Tenures Abolition Act.

When the jurisdiction moved to Chancery a rather fundamental change occurred in the nature of wardship. It appears that Equity courts remodelled the philosophy of wardship from a concern with the property of infants to a more general 'parental' preoccupation with the well-being of children. This was justified on the basis that Chancery had originally held the jurisdiction of *parens patriae* over children as it had over adults, and had merely surrendered this jurisdiction to the Court of Wards during its operation.[35] Seymour has argued that a more sceptical but historically valid understanding of the court's power sees it as having emerged independently and later than the wardship jurisdiction.[36] Because the *parens patriae* jurisdiction is considered to be the primary source of the court's power, it is exercisable over children whether or not they have been made a ward of the court.[37]

V. Disputes between Parents, Doctors and the Courts – When Should the Court Act as a De Novo Decision-Maker?

The brief historical summary shows that, as originally conceived, the role of the court was to act as a parent (or to find a 'replacement' parent) in cases where the natural parents were missing, or where it could be shown that the natural parents had acted inappropriately. There was no suggestion in these cases that the *parens patriae* could do more than what an ordinary parent could do. To that degree Marion's case does represent a major shift in the concept of role of the court as *parens patriae* in Australia. The Australian courts were now able to make decisions about matters that ordinary parents could not. This has a practical effect of splitting the court's role into two functions: a *review function*, where the decisions

[34] The reasons for this are complicated and outside the terms of the discussion. Put simply, the 'use' or 'trust' as it is now known was a device used to avoid the financial burdens of wardship. It was, inter alia, used to defer a heir's rights until he obtained majority, thereby avoiding the need for wardship and the costs associated with it. Henry VIII, in an effort to re-establish his tax base, collapsed the use relationship in the Statute of Uses (1540). The effect of the Act was to transfer ownership to the infant heir, so recreating the need for a wardship, with the result that revenues were restored. To administer this rapid increase in wardship, Henry set up the Court of Wards in the same year. See J Baker, *An Introduction to English Legal History*, 3rd edn (London, Butterworths, 1990) 288–89; Seymour (n 31) 166.

[35] *Falkland v Bertie* (1696) 23 ER 814; *Eyre v Saftesbury* (1722) 24 ER 659.

[36] Seymour (n 31).

[37] *Re W (a minor)(medical treatment)* [1992] 4 All ER 627, 631; *K v Minister for Youth and Community Services* [1982] 1 NSWLR 311, 323.

of parents can be assessed in cases of disputes to see whether they accord with the child's best interests; and an original *uber-parental function* to make orders regarding non-therapeutic interventions which were nevertheless in the child's best interests.

In situations where the court is being asked to exercise its jurisdiction to make decisions regarding non-therapeutic treatment, it makes sense for the court's power to determine a child's best interests to be exercised in an original way, as there are no other decision-makers with power to decide. In the case of disputes regarding therapeutic treatment, one would assume that the court's role is the opposite – the history of the *parens patriae* jurisdiction is for the court to review the decision of the parents and 'step-in' to a parental role when the parents had failed to act in the child's best interests.

Nevertheless, it is undeniably clear that the modern role of the court in determining the best interests of a child (in both England and Wales and Australia) is that of an original decision-maker, meaning that the court hears the matter de novo and does not sit in review of the parental decision.[38] In that sense even a reasonable parental decision can be overturned by the court if it believes that it would be in the best interests of the child to do so.[39] I believe that the problems raised by *Gard* and subsequent cases can be understood as ones about whether the court's jurisdiction to review parental decision-making for therapeutic interventions should properly take the form of a decision de novo or of a judicial review.

VI. Post-*Gard* and the 'Risk of Significant Harm' Test in Australia

I will not repeat the excellent summaries of *Gard* and subsequent cases made by others and instead will rely on the summary supplied by Goold, Auckland and Herring in Chapter 11 on the position in England and Wales.[40] They summarise the problems of these cases as ones where the best interests are finely balanced – in *Gard*, *Evans*, *Evans*, *Haastrup* and *Raqeeb* the central issue was whether the child could be transferred to a hospital overseas to be subjected to unconventional interventions, and in all of them, barring *Raqueeb*, the courts disagreed with the assessment of the parents that the move was in the child's best interests. They also

[38] *Re A (children)(conjoined twins)* [2000] 4 All ER 961, 1008 (Ward LJ).

[39] *In re T (a minor)(wardship: medical treatment)* [1997] 1 All ER 906; *Re Z (A Minor) (Identification: Restrictions on Publication)* [1996] 2 WLR 88; *Re MM (Medical Treatment)* [2000] 1 FLR 224.

[40] I Goold, C Auckland and J Herring, 'Medical-Decision Making on Behalf of Children in English and Welsh Law: A Child-Centred Best Interests Approach', in this book. See also C Auckland and I Goold (2019) 'Parental Rights, Best Interests and Significant Harms: Who Should Have the Final Say Over a Child's Medical Care?' 78 *CLJ* 287; C Auckland and I Goold, 'Defining the Limits of Parental Authority: Charlie Gard, Best Interests and the Risk of Significant Harm Threshold' (2018) 134 *LQR* 37.

describe the attempt to carve out a space for parental freedom through the use of a threshold test which would only permit a judicial determination when the parents' decision puts the child at risk of significant harm. Goold, Auckland and Herring express a degree of agnosticism about the adoption of this test.[41] According to the authors, it may not operate that differently from the current approach (as parental views are listened to already by the courts) and it may force the courts to render a negative judgment about the parents' decision-making abilities.[42] On the other hand, the authors recognise that a more open and honest assessment of the parents' decision may be helpful, and a threshold test may encourage more acceptance of divergent views.[43]

The only Australian case involving a parental decision to take a child overseas for experimental interventions is *Re Baby A*.[44] Baby A had been born with a rare and fatal metabolic disorder that had no known treatment. Both the parents and treatment team wished for her to be treated with an experimental drug known as Drug X. The drug had not been tested on humans but had shown promise in mice. The judge doubted whether approval was necessary as a 'special treatment' under Marion's case. The treatment was clearly the only option for the child even though no one could say what its effects would be with certainty. Nevertheless, Dessau J proceeded on the basis that the treatment did require approval as the judge wished for there to be no doubt that the parents had the power to consent to the treatment. The treatment was approved and a declaration was made that the parents were empowered to consent to it. The *Baby A* decision has none of the disputed issues that we see in *Gard* but it firmly establishes that the decision to seek experimental treatment for a fatal condition falls within the category of therapeutic treatment. This, in turn, means that the courts should exercise their review function over any such dispute.

Another more recent case before the Family Court of Western Australia is more illustrative of what happens in cases of disputes between parents and medical staff about standard treatments as opposed to unproven approaches. The case concerned Oshin Kiszko, a five-year-old with a medulloblastoma.[45] Oshin underwent surgery for the tumour but a dispute arose between his parents and the treatment team about radiotherapy and chemotherapy. Oshin's mother and father preferred for Oshin to be treated with alternative therapies and expressed

[41] ibid.

[42] ibid.

[43] ibid.

[44] *Re Baby A* [2008] FamCA 417

[45] *Director Clinical Services, Child & Adolescent Health Services v Kiszko* [2016] FCWA 19 (*Kiszko 1*); *Director Clinical Services, Child & Adolescent Services v Kiszko* [2016] FCWA 34 (*Kiszko 2*); *Director Clinical Services, Child & Adolescent Services v Kiszko* [2016] FCWA 75 (*Kiszko 3*). See also I Freckelton, 'Parents' Opposition to Potentially Life-Saving Treatment for Minors: Learning from the Oshin Kiszko Litigation' (2016) 24 *Journal of Law and Medicine* 61; I Freckelton and S McGregor, 'Refusal of Potentially Life-Saving Treatment for Minors: The Emerging International Consensus by Courts (2016) 23 *Journal of Law and Medicine* 813.

how his diagnosis was placing them under pressure. Oshin's mother had studied 'bodyworks' which involved some knowledge of natural remedies such as herbal medicine and iridology. The dispute was mediated by the hospital ethics committee which stated that it thought more active treatment would be in Oshin's overall benefit, while recognising that palliative chemotherapy was also an ethical option given Oshin's condition.

The relationship between the parents and the treatment team later deteriorated to the point that the team sought a court order for treatment. At the time Oshin had a 50–60 per cent chance of survival after five years with combined radio- and chemotherapy, and a 30 per cent survival rate after five years with just chemotherapy. In the first trial Thackray CJ ordered chemotherapy to be commenced with the possibility of radiotherapy later as the chance for having radiotherapy at the hospital had since passed.[46] A second hearing occurred after two courses of chemotherapy. Oshin's parent were alleged to have become more obstructive, and a treating doctor believed that Oshin's chances of survival on chemotherapy alone were falling, mandating that high-dose radiotherapy was now necessary. However, an independent specialist gave evidence that he thought high-dose radiotherapy was not reasonable given Oshin's chances, and that chemotherapy should be continued. At the end of the second hearing Thackray CJ decided that the main issue was the balance to be struck between maintaining life and having quality of life.[47] Given the medical opinion was split, Thackray CJ felt he should not override the parental decision. His Honour said:

> I have already observed that there appears to be no other case where a medical intervention has been imposed on parents in circumstances where there is a reputable, independent expert who considered that the views of the parents were supportable based on an assessment of the relative benefits and burdens of the proposed treatment. …
>
> Decisions must now be made for Oshin against the background of conflicting opinions from eminently qualified medical specialists. Both opinions are carefully considered, and neither can be said to be wrong. The medical specialists have respect for the opinion of the other, but they disagree as to the central issue of whether radiotherapy treatment, with all that entails, both positive and negative, is the best option for Oshin. In the absence of a consensus of qualified medical opinion, there is, in my view, no role for the state in directing the parents to act in accordance with one entirely valid opinion in preference to another. My view is reinforced by the fact that at least in Professor Kellie's clinical experience, although it is not the experience of the doctors at P[rincess] M[argaret] H[ospital], a substantial minority of parents would follow the course adopted by Oshin's parents.[48]

[46] *Kiszko 1* (n 45).
[47] *Kiszko 2* (n 45) [65].
[48] ibid [67]–[68].

Three months later the matter was back in court before a third judge, O'Brien J. The chemotherapy had led to improvements and the treating team wished to try three further cycles of consolidation chemotherapy, stem-cell rescue and cranio-spinal radiation therapy, or, in the alternative, consolidation chemotherapy and/or craniospinal radiation therapy. The treating team's estimates of successful cure were about 30–40 per cent. The independent expert assessed the treatment's chance of success as remote, and expressed concerns that the delays in treatment had contributed to a worsening of Oshin's chances. Oshin's parents instead wished to commence palliative care. They believed that 'the quality of Oshin's life should be prioritised over the duration of his life'.[49]

O'Brien J ordered that palliative care be commenced. O'Brien J repeated that statement by Thackray CJ that the court 'should not interfere in the exercise of parental responsibility unless there is some clear justification for doing so'.[50] O'Brien J also expressed doubts over an argument from Counsel that the rejection of palliative care was a decision only the court could make, but in the end made no final decision on the matter, after deciding that palliative care was in Oshin's best interests.[51]

On reflection, Thackray CJ's statement of non-interference is very close in flavour to the principle of 'risk of significant harm'. It suggests primacy for parental decision-making and a preference for the court not exercising power in cases when the parental decision is clearly not incorrect or badly made. This principle most certainly seems to conflict with the notion that the court sits de novo when deciding best interests and it is more reflective of the notion that the job of the court in these cases is to review the decision of the parents. If analysis is correct, it raises the question of what approaches to judicial review might be applied to the assessment of a parental decision concerning therapeutic treatment?

VII. Judicial Review of Parental Decisions Regarding Therapeutic Treatments

I believe that the adoption and adaptation of judicial review principles might help to clarify the court's role in the post-*Gard* world. The general grounds of judicial review are split into two main camps: the doctrine of ultra vires and the doctrine of procedural fairness.[52] An ultra vires decision can be reviewed when the decision was made beyond the power of the decision-maker (narrow ultra vires) – for

[49] *Kiszko 3* (n 45) [65].
[50] ibid [72].
[51] ibid [77]–[78].
[52] See C Stewart, 'Judicial Review of Treatment Decisions: A Further Role for the Courts?' (1999) 7 *Journal of Law and Medicine* 212.

example, when a decision is made by a body who does not have the power to make it.[53] In parental decision-making in Australia this would include any decision to consent to a non-therapeutic treatment.

A decision can also broadly ultra vires if there are defects in the way the power was exercised. Such defects include abuses of power such as bad faith on the part of the decision-maker, decisions made for an improper purpose, or decisions where the decision-maker took account of an irrelevant consideration or ignored a relevant one. These concepts seem to also be applicable to parental decisions and could easily be adapted to review of parental consent when errors and misassessments have taken place regarding the child's best interests.

Irrationality and unreasonableness are also abuses of power. In administrative law a decision may be reviewed if it is so irrational or unreasonable that no reasonable body could have come to make it, under the so-called *Wednesbury* test.[54] *Wednesbury* unreasonableness might also conceivably play a role in reviewing parental decisions – for example, in reviewing decisions to refuse treatment for children based on irrational distrust of modern medicine, or unusual religious beliefs.

The notion of procedural fairness as a grounds of review seems less relevant to parental decisions regarding consent. Traditionally this ground of review allows decisions to be found illegal if the decision-maker breaches requirements of procedural fairness involving the right of a person to be heard and treated impartially by the decision-maker.[55] In the medical context, a right to natural justice may be conferred on someone who has a legitimate expectation that they will be treated in a particular way.[56] Such expectations might arise from a representation that a patient will receive treatment from a hospital or that a health service will not be closed. Once a patient is found to have a legitimate expectation the decision-maker needs to give the patient a chance to respond to the proposed change. Moreover, the decision must be considered in light of the patient's legitimate expectation. But while we can employ these concepts to health services, they seem less apposite to parental decision-making, which is done informally and outside legal expectations of service provision.

On reflection, there is obvious potential in the use of these notions of judicial review, although some principles appear to be less suited than others. What is clear is that these principles establish that the court's rule is only to override the parental decision when that decision suffers from a recognised legal defect. This approach would place the parental decision at the centre and establish clear grounds for the court's decision to override it.

[53] *Fitzgerald v Muldoon* [1976] 2 NZLR 615.

[54] This requirement is often referred to as *Wednesbury* unreasonableness, after the case which established the principle: *Associated Provincial Picture House Ltd v Wednesbury Corporation* [1948] 1 KB 223.

[55] Stewart (n 52) 218.

[56] ibid 218–19.

VIII. Conclusions

This chapter has outlined the jurisdiction of Australian courts to review disputes concerning the medical treatment of children. Following Marion's case, the courts have two functions: a function to consider consent questions for non-therapeutic treatments (the *uber*-parental function), and a function to review decisions concerning therapeutic treatment (the review function). Traditionally, the courts have treated both functions as ones where the court sits de novo and makes its own assessment regarding the child's best interests. This chapter has argued it is time to revisit this approach post-*Gard*. The *Gard* type of cases suggest that it would be better to afford parental decisions regarding therapeutic decisions with more respect. The court's function should be to truly review the parental decisions on therapeutic treatments rather than decide matters de novo. This requires the court to assess the parental decision and only overturn it when there has been some defect discovered in the assessment of the child's best interests. I have suggested that, following the *Kiszko* litigation, there is some judicial support for this notion and that the principles of judicial review may be helpful in articulating some of the ways a parental decision might be overridden. Much work needs to be done. These types of changes would be easier to implement legislatively, but it is not impossible to envisage some reforms coming from the courts themselves.

23

Parental Authoritarianism and Medical Decision-Making in Thailand: The Need to Limit Parental Authority

THITINANT TENGAUMNUAY

I. Introduction

The value of 'autonomy' constitutes a fundamental principle in medical law, shifting away from the idea that 'doctor knows best' to respecting the patient's autonomy in making his or her own decisions about medical treatment.[1] 'Informed consent' is generally required under medical law in most nations, including Thailand, before conducting any medical treatment. To produce consent that serves the value of patient autonomy, the competence of a patient usually needs to be demonstrated by showing that the patient can understand the information provided, analyse it and then make a decision.[2] The medical treatment of a child therefore concerns the issue of the competence of a child, as he or she might not be sufficiently mature to make the serious decisions associated with a complex medical process. The lack of competence is more obvious in the case of an infant, who is too young to have or express his or her own views. As with any other patient, an infant's autonomy is to be respected, but because it is not possible to know his or her decisions on preferred treatment, others are required to make such decisions on their behalf.

The question of who should make decisions on behalf of children is usually answered by giving this authority to the family, or more precisely the parents. As the family is closest to the patient and should know best about his or her

[1] L Furst, *Between Doctors and Patients: The Changing Balance of Power* (Charlottesville, VA, The University Press of Virginia, 1998); see further discussion in *Re B (Consent to Treatment: Capacity)* [2002] EWHC 429, [2002] 1 FLR 1090.

[2] See M Donnelly, 'Capacity Assessment under the Mental Capacity Act 2005: Delivering on the Functional Approach?' (2009) 29 *Legal Studies* 464.

preferences, most scholars support the idea of the parents as decision-makers with certain limits.[3] Laws in various countries, both with civil law and common law jurisdictions, respect parents' rights in decision-making on medical matters affecting their children. However, in several countries, as discussed and explored in other chapters in this book, medical professionals and the courts still retain the role of protecting the best interests of children, and judicial intervention is allowed in cases where the interests of children are not optimised by relying on parental decisions. As an Asian country with a culture that attaches great importance to family and parental authoritarianism, an attitude that is reflected in various laws, Thailand provides an interesting case study for exploring medical law and ethics concerning the parental authority in medical decision-making on behalf of children.

The chapter begins by describing the legal conditions of medical treatment of children in Thailand where parents play a significant role in making medical decisions on behalf of their children, reflecting the concept of parental authoritarianism. Then, the role of medical professions and the court in counterbalancing parental authority in order to protect the best interests of children is explored. This chapter argues that although parents are in the best position to acknowledge the values and preferences that their children would choose if they had sufficient competence to make a decision, parental authority should have certain limits so as to serve the purpose of the law, namely preserving the interests of a child. This chapter therefore suggests the establishment of a counterbalancing system in Thai law by allowing the court to review parental decisions through the application of the 'harm principle' approach, rather than the 'best interests' approach.

II. Medical Treatment of Children: Autonomy versus Parental Authoritarianism

Before 2007, 'consent to treatment' was not required by any statutory laws of Thailand but was recognised as a general principle of law that constituted a defence for doctors and medical professionals involved in medical treatment from criminal and civil liabilities under Thai law.[4] The requirement of 'informed consent' before conducting any medical treatment was officially established by the enactment of the National Health Act 2007; section 8 imposes the duty on public health personnel to provide necessary information concerning health services to the patient and requires the patient's consent before the provision of health services. This provision of the law reflects the principle of autonomy and respect for self-determination, for

[3] See AE Buchanan and DW Brock, *Deciding for Others* (Cambridge, Cambridge University Press, 1990) 136; L Gillam, 'The Zone of Parental Discretion: An Ethical Tool for Dealing with Disagreement between Parents and Doctors about Medical Treatment for a Child' (2015) 11 *Clinical Ethics* 1.

[4] Decision of the Supreme Court of Thailand no 1403/2508.

a patient is the one to decide the way he or she would be treated; and if he or she refuses to receive any medical treatment, his or her decision must be respected.

However, in cases where a patient is not 'in the state enabling him or her to acknowledge the information', section 8(2) mentions persons whom the health service provider must consult. This state of incompetence includes the case where a patient is still a child and might not be sufficiently mature to fully understand the seriousness of his or her health conditions and the medical procedure. In such cases, the medical professionals have to consult the parents or legal guardians of the child instead. The provisions in the National Health Act do not explicitly authorise the parents or legal guardians to give consent to treatment on behalf of children, but only require the rendering of information to parents. The scope of parental authority with regards to decision-making for the treatment of children has not been specified as such in any healthcare laws or medical laws of Thailand but is based on the Civil and Commercial Code which establishes the rights and duties of parents. Under section 1564, parents are bound to take care of their children during their minority. Generally, under Thai law, a person becomes sui juris when he or she reaches the age of 20.[5] This means that parents remain responsible for their children until they turn 20, and the children are still subject to parental power as long as they are not sui juris.[6]

As the cultural context of Thailand respects the significant role of the family in raising children and the hierarchy of seniority in instructing children, the provisions of the law reflect parental authoritarianism, stating that parents are responsible for deciding on behalf of children who are still too young to make beneficial decisions for themselves. However, this does not mean that parental power is unlimited. In cases where parents abuse their powers over their children, such as cruelly punishing or starving their children or forcing them to take part in committing a crime, eg pickpocketing, the court may order the deprivation of power,[7] and appoint a new legal guardian to exercise such parental power instead of the parents.[8] As long as children are not sui juris, they remain under the power of adults, either their parents or legal guardians. A minor can, in any case, make basic life decisions on his or her own without approval from parents.[9] These 'basic life decisions' refer to everyday life activities about which a child can make a decision on their own without asking permission from parents, as such activities do not cause any significant risks to their own benefits; for example, a child can buy reasonable amounts of stationery at school. The provisions under the Civil and Commercial Code are the basis for the involvement of parents in medical

[5] s 19 of the Civil and Commercial Code of Thailand. (There is an exception that a minor can become sui juris before reaching twenty years old. In cases that a minor gets married in accordance with marriage laws, he or she will be sui juris even though he or she is not twenty years old yet.)

[6] s 1566 of the Civil and Commercial Code of Thailand.

[7] s 1582 of the Civil and Commercial Code of Thailand.

[8] s 1585 of the Civil and Commercial Code of Thailand.

[9] s 24 of the Civil and Commercial Code of Thailand.

decision-making on behalf of children. In practice, health service providers in Thailand usually request the parents to sign the standard consent form for medical treatment on behalf of their children to prevent any future liabilities. Nevertheless, the competence of a child to consent to treatment does not need to rely on the status of sui juris, since section 24, as mentioned above, allows a minor to make basic life decisions; if a minor is not too young to understand the implications of the medical treatment, then informed consent from such a minor is legally acceptable as it qualifies as a 'basic life decision' that a child can legally make without requiring the approval from parents or legal guardians. Necessary or non-complex medical treatment, such as first-aid services or treatment for minor illness, could be decided by children themselves under section 24.[10] However, this does not apply to the case of a newborn child or an infant who cannot consent at all. In this case, parents or legal guardians have sole authority to make any decisions concerning medical treatment for their children. Although the law establishes certain limits to parental power in order to prevent abuse of powers over children, such legal provisions are interpreted to apply in a case that parents physically or mentally harm their children in an active way or intentionally abandon their children, placing them at significant risk of harm. There is no explicit provision that allows the court to intervene or review parental decisions on medical treatment for their children.

It is usual in most countries that parents are assigned to take care of their children, and such responsibilities include making decisions on their behalf; however, there are different thresholds for intervention, and various approaches are taken to review parental decisions in order to protect the best interests of children. Belgium is an example of a country where children's rights are explicitly protected and parents are primarily entitled to make decisions for their children. Nevertheless, unlike Thailand, Belgium has a special act on patients' rights that permits medical intervention to overrule parental decisions in cases where medical professionals disagree with the parents.[11] A doctor can request the public prosecutor to bring an objection against parental wishes before the court, whereas in Thailand there is no law specifically addressing conflicts between doctors and parents, and furthermore neither doctors nor the public prosecutor have authority to petition the court under Thai law.

[10] However, the criteria on which treatment a child could decide on his or her own are still unclear. The court has mentioned in the case of liposuction of a child that liposuction was a complex procedure for which a child, as a minor, was still too young to thoroughly consider the consequences. The consent of a child in this case was not sufficient to protect the doctor from liabilities; the consent of the parents was still needed. (See decision of the Supreme Court of Thailand no 8156/2555.) It has been perceived from this case that if the medical treatment or health services at issue concern complex procedures or high risks, and there is no immediate need for them to take place, the parents of the child should be consulted and their consent is required. See W Threesuntornrat and T Suthibordee, *Thai Medical Laws: Informed Consent* (กฎหมายการแพทย์ ความยินยอมภายหลังได้รับการบอกกล่าวแล้ว) (Bangkok, Nititham Publishing, 2018) 87.

[11] See I Boone, 'Parental Rights, Best Interests and Significant Harm: Medical Decision-Making on Behalf of Children in Belgium', in this book.

In 2015, the Medical Council of Thailand introduced the Declaration of Patients' Rights and Guidance. Although this Declaration does not have the status of legislation, it reflects the mutual agreement of medical professionals on how to conduct proper treatment for patients. Article 9 of the Declaration suggests that parents or legal guardians can exercise the patient's rights on behalf of a child whose age does not exceed 18. Although this Declaration specifies eighteen years as the maximum age for a child to be subject to parental power in medical decision-making, which is lower than the age of twenty required for becoming sui juris, this provision is merely a guideline for practice and does not have any legal effect. Parental authority under the Civil and Commercial Code still exists; as long as such medical decisions are not considered a 'basic life decision', and in cases where the children are too young to have their own views, parents still retain their responsibilities to decide on medical treatment on behalf of their children.

As explored above, all legal provisions of Thailand concerning medical treatment of children indicate the significant role of parents in managing their children's lives, reflecting the concept of parental authoritarianism. It is true that the family is in the best position to recognise the preferences of a patient, especially a minor patient, since the family normally implants their thoughts and values into their children through the responsibility of raising and taking care of them.[12] It is, therefore, sensible to assume that children will share their parents' perception about their medical treatment, and parents are in the best position to represent their children. However, the strong dominance of parental authoritarianism, despite aiming to address the lack of competence of children in making decisions associated with complex medical procedures or the serious risks of treatment, might adversely affect children if the parental powers have no limits, and could dilute the concept of autonomy and self-determination. The 'best interests' of children would not be served if these decisions are simply left to the parents due to the mere presumption that a family knows the best. This leads to the question of the role of doctors and the courts in protecting the best interests of children under Thai law.

III. The Role of Medical Professionals and Judicial Intervention for Preserving the Best Interests of Children

As a medical professional who has expertise and the most detailed information regarding the health of, and treatment options for, a patient, a doctor is supposed to have a legal duty to provide health services that benefit the patient, not simply treating as the patient asks. The 'best interests' of the patient has been the fundamental principle of medical practice and ethics since the age of Hippocrates,[13]

[12] Buchanan and Brock (n 3) 233–34.

[13] RM Veatch, *Hippocratic, Religious, and Secular Medical Ethics* (Washington, DC, Georgetown University Press, 2012); S McLean, *Autonomy, Consent and the Law* (London, Routledge-Cavendish, 2010).

and provides the foundation of the legal duties of medical professionals in a number of national laws in both common law and civil law countries. In Thailand, under section 15 of the Medical Council Regulations on Medical Ethics Preservation, 'A medical practitioner shall maintain the highest standard of medical practice in a particular setting, within the scope of competence and the limits of objectivity and circumstance surrounding.'[14] Even though the term 'best interests' of the patient is not explicitly applied, the provision is interpreted to require a doctor to follow best practice in treating the patient. However, the criteria for qualifying best practice under the law have not been specifically defined, leaving the court discretion to determine what the best medical practice is on a case-by-case basis.

The duty to follow best practice, as required by section 15, aims to prevent medical negligence and, at the same time, protect a medical practitioner from liabilities arising from failures of medical treatment if the medical practitioner follows best practice for that situation.[15] The provision has been interpreted to establish the standard of care for medical practitioners and might not be completely equal to the explicit requirements to provide health services in the 'best interests' of a patient. A question could be raised, with regards to this provision, whether a doctor in Thailand could refuse to follow parental decision-making on behalf of their children if their decisions are not in the best interests of the patients. In other words, could a doctor in Thailand refuse to conduct a medical treatment that he or she considers not beneficial for the infant patient despite conflicting with the patient's parents by referring to section 15 that providing such health services will not be the best practice the doctor can offer in that situation?

In the Charlie Gard case in the United Kingdom,[16] the medical service providers insisted that their opinions on treatment better served the best interests of Charlie than the wishes of his parents, creating a conflict between professional duty and parental duty. The judicial intervention that overrode the parents' decision in this case, despite the widespread criticisms of the 'best interests' approach, indicates the limits of parental authority in deciding on behalf of children, and determines that the fate of children does not wholly rely on their parents' decisions but on their own best interests, which supports the principle of integrity of the patient, rather than the concept of parental authoritarianism. In Thailand, there have been no cases of judicial intervention in medical decision-making. The concept of parental authoritarianism has deep roots in the Thai cultural context, meaning that doctors usually remain passive and do not offer or provide health treatment against the wishes of the parents. With the terms setting the standard of care for medical practitioners, it might be too extensive to interpret the duty to perform the best practice under section 15 as a ground for doctors to act against parental

[14] The Medical Council of Thailand, *The Medical Council Regulations on Medical Ethics Preservation* (2006) www.tmc.or.th/download/The_Medical_Council_Regulations_on_Medical_Ethic.pdf.
[15] See decision of the Supreme Court of Thailand no 6906/2554.
[16] *Great Ormond Street Hospital v Yates* [2017] EWHC 1909 (Fam).

decisions; section 15 does not override the requirement of informed consents. On the other hand, the terms contained in section 15 leave rooms for doctors to claim that they have done their duties of best practice under the scope of the parents' consent to treatment. This is different from French law, which explicitly explains the situation called 'unreasonable obstinacy' and establishes the process to decide for the proper treatment of a patient who is incapable of expressing his or her will. Thai laws do not provide any particular provisions that allow reviews of decisions concerning medical treatment for children; the laws only serve to protect medical practitioners from liabilities.[17]

Further, if a doctor disagrees with the parents because their decisions do not serve the best interests of children, neither the doctor nor the healthcare service provider has any legal standing to bring a case to court seeking judicial intervention in parental decisions. The only thing a doctor can do if he or she disagrees with the option the parents choose for treating their children is to refuse to provide the treatment as requested and to provide proper advice.[18]

The role of doctors in Thailand in protecting the best interests of children is considerably limited, compared to other jurisdictions, such as the United Kingdom, where doctors can perform a more active role in petitioning for judicial intervention in cases that the treatment requested by parents does not conform to the best interests of the child. In Thailand, the near impossibility of judicial intervention and the limited role of doctors in arguing for infant patients cause an imbalance between parental authority and professional judgement, since the dominance of parents' decision over their children's welfare is undoubtedly significant, leaving too much discretion for parents to decide on behalf of their children. As the intention of section 8(2) of the National Health Act is to ensure that a patient has the competence to comprehend the medical procedure as well as the consequences of his or her medical treatment before making a decision,[19] the protection of the children's interests is the key reason for authorising parents to make decisions on behalf of their children. However, giving all of the decision-making power to parents without establishing counterbalancing powers might put the children's welfare at stake and cannot ensure the children's best interests.

While the exercise of parental powers in entering into certain juristic acts associated with the management of a minor's property requires permission of the court,[20] there is no provision in Thai law authorising a court to review decisions

[17] See J-F Menard, 'Offering a Reasonable Future: Withdrawal of Life-Sustaining Treatment from Infants in French Law with Illustrations from a Parisian Neonatal Resuscitation Unit', in this book.

[18] It must be noted that the doctor can refuse to provide medical treatment only on the condition that the patient is not in an emergency or a fatal condition (s 28, Medical Council Regulations on Medical Ethics Preservation, 2006).

[19] W Threesuntornrat and T Suthibordee, *Thai Medical Laws: Informed Consent* (กฎหมายการแพทย์ ความยินยอมภายหลังได้รับการบอกกล่าวแล้ว) (Bangkok, Nititham Publishing 2018) 76.

[20] s 1574 of the Civil and Commercial Code of Thailand.

made by parents or guardians. The only intervention the court can make to prevent an abuse of parental powers is simply to deprive the parents of their powers and appoint a new legal guardian for a minor, as previously mentioned. However, this is the only possible legal basis for the court to counterbalance the extensive scope of parental powers in deciding about their children's medical treatment. So far, there have been no cases in which the court has made such an intervention.

In some jurisdictions, judicial intervention is allowed when there is disagreement on what is the 'best interests' of a child. The court's decision can override the parental decision, as happened in the case of Charlie Gard. Doctors' opinions, as the opinions of professional experts, are recognised by the court and can be balanced against parental decisions. Although parents are in the best position to represent their children's preferences, due to their intimacy and family bonding, it is not completely certain that their decisions will always conform to the best interests of their children. Doctors, with their professionality and experience, can understand the health conditions of their patients and might have different opinions on what the best interests of the children are. Such opinions should not be ignored simply by relying solely on parental decisions. Due to the cultural context of Thailand that parental authoritarianism is influential and the role of doctors remains passive, there is a need for legal provisions that confer legal standings to doctors to petition the court to review parental decisions regarding medical treatment if they are not in the best interests of children.

Culture and norms have significant influence in the weight given to parents' decisions on behalf of their children. As can be seen in Sweden, which is a welfare state, the responsibilities for protecting children's interests are not ultimately rendered to the family; it is the state that preserves the duty to protect its citizens. Social welfare committees can intervene in parents' acts in order to protect the interests of children.[21] Norway and Denmark, welfare states like Sweden, regard the issue of children's health as a matter of healthcare rather than family law. While Thailand does not separate issues concerning children's treatment from parental authorities under the Civil and Commercial code, Sweden, Norway and Denmark consider such issues a matter of child welfare and give little weight to parental wishes. As can be seen in the 'Kristina' and the 'Ove' cases, medical expertise is highly respected; the children's best interests, rather than parental wishes, are privileged.[22]

By contrast, in countries that acknowledge the special relationship between the family and children, decisions made by parents carry significant weight and the threshold for judicial intervention is very high. Similar to Thailand, the Irish legal framework assigns the principal responsibilities for taking care of children

[21] See P Leviner, 'Who Has the Final Word? On Trust and Legal Uncertainty Within the Swedish Healthcare System', in this book.

[22] See K Sovig, 'Reviewing Medical Decisions Concerning Infants Within the Norwegian Healthcare System – A Public Law approach' in this book.

to the family. Further than Thailand, the Irish Constitution even explicitly recognises the family as an important social institution and guarantees the rights and duties of the parents to take care of their children, while in Thailand the authorities and responsibilities of the parents are simply stated in the Civil and Commercial Code. However, although Irish law gives great weight to parental decisions, the Constitution nevertheless provides for 'exceptional' cases where a court can overrule parental decisions if these significantly threaten a child's life or welfare.[23] This is different from Thailand in that, in Ireland, medical professions can seek judicial intervention (although Lombard and Bracken note in Chapter 15 that the Irish professional standards and guidelines still require more details), while in Thailand, the Thai Constitution does not include any particular sections to protecting the interests of children when their parents or legal guardians fail in their duties towards their children's welfare. There is only Article 25 which generally allows any persons whose rights are affected to bring a case to the court. This Article does not address the problem of a child whose rights to life or health are potentially affected but who is incapable of thinking and deciding properly on his or her own; there is no standing provided for other actors, namely medical professionals, to request an intervention or review of parental decisions. Thailand, therefore, requires development in its legal framework concerning child patients' rights by establishing a counterbalancing mechanism to minimise the risks of giving too much discretion to the parents.

Nonetheless, in a jurisdiction where there is such a counterbalance to the powers of parents, a number of people protested against judicial intervention, as could be seen in the case of Charlie Gard, and demanded respect for parental decision-making.[24] The 'best interests' approach was challenged, and the prolonged judicial process was criticised for causing suffering to the patient and family rather than benefiting them.[25] It could be argued that deciding the best interests of children is a moral judgment, not a medical judgment, and that doctors, despite possessing greater expertise and medical knowledge than the parents, do not have the moral relationship or intimacy with the patient that the family possess.[26] The Gard case greatly upset many people and suggested that the 'best interests' approach should be reconsidered. However, it should be kept in mind that judicial intervention and the opinions of medical professionals should not be completely neglected. The Gard case, to a certain extent, indicates an imbalance of power: parental authority on behalf of children carries less weight than medical opinions, and parents'

[23] See J Lombard and L Bracken, 'Medical Decision-Making on Behalf of Children in Ireland', in this book.

[24] See 'Reality Check: Why Don't Charlie Gard's Parents Have the Final Say?' *BBC Health News* (14 July 2017) www.bbc.co.uk/news/uk-40600932.

[25] See J Bridgeman, 'Gard and Yates v GOSH, the Guardian and the United Kingdom: Reflections on the Legal Process and the Legal Principles' (2017) 17 *Medical Law International* 285.

[26] Buchanan and Brock (n 3) 139–40.

views could be simply ignored if these conflicted with the views of the majority of physicians. The sad case of Charlie Gard does not simply suggest the extreme approach that parents' rights and powers must be respected without any intervention or check.

Considering the case of Thailand, the laws and medical practices reflect the concept of parental authoritarianism, with a limited role for medical professionals representing children's best interests and little possibility of judicial intervention in parents' decision-making on behalf of their child. While the concept of checks and balances is fundamental to preventing excessive or mistaken use of power, there are no legal provisions setting particular checks or reviews on parental decisions concerning their children's medical treatment. Compared to the management of children's property, although parents are granted powers to manage their children's property, they are required to apply to the court for permission to undertake certain legal transactions that can significantly affect their children's interests.[27] While the children's interests in property are protected by requiring a review from the court, parental authority in medical decision-making on behalf of children, which could cause harm or impair children's health and certainly affects their interests, has no counterbalancing powers to check or review whether such decision would serve the children's interests. The fact that the decision-making powers in this regard are totally conferred on parents leaves children's welfare at stake. The establishment of counterbalancing systems to review parental decisions is therefore required to protect children. The Gard case would be an excellent case study for establishing a better balanced system since, contrary to Thailand where parental powers have few restraints, the court in the Gard case has been criticised for its intervention in the parents' decisions by relying on medical opinions that went against the parents' wishes.

The lessons from the Gard case infer the need to reconsider the 'best interests' approach because this approach offers very vague standards and could cause problems arising from disagreements in determining what is 'best' for children. On the other hand, prioritising parental decision-making on behalf of their children without establishing counterbalancing powers does not guarantee that the best options of treatment will be chosen for the children and could risk impairing their health. The better solution is to strike a balance between respecting the opinions of parents and medical professionals on the optimal treatment.

The harm principle has been argued for as an alternative to the 'best interests' test as the point of judicial intervention. The application of this approach would respect the parental decision-making on behalf of children as long as such a decision does not cause harm to children. While the best interests approach requires the optimal treatment for children, which is difficult to define since various values and factors are involved, including not only medical and professional opinions

[27] For example, mortgaging or selling the children's real property, or loaning in the name of children. See s 1574 of the Civil and Commercial Code of Thailand.

but also moral values and family attachments, the harm principle only considers whether such parental decision-making would cause harm to the children. If not, the parents' decisions are to be respected. This approach does not require the 'best' or 'optimal' treatment for children but only sets a threshold that the parents' decision should not to be detrimental to the children.[28] However, the indeterminacy of what is considered harm does not address the problem of judicial intervention in determining the best interests of children.[29] Clear guidelines with details of a step-by-step process should be developed to solve the problem of indeterminacy. Gillam suggests the application of 'the Zone of Parental Discretion', which sets the range of potential treatments from the optimal to the suboptimal options that still do not cause harm to the patient.[30] This approach would strike a good balance between parental authority and the duty of medical professionals to provide health services to patients according to the best practices the situation allows. Parental wishes are recognised and respected but at the same time limited to the point that will not harm the children. The adoption of the harm principle with the clear settings of parental discretion will provide better guidelines for the court to intervene in parental authority only in a case where the parents' decisions will harm their children. This approach will serve the context of Thailand in terms that the law still respects parental authority in representing their children's benefits but sets certain limits to ensure that the children will not be physically or mentally impaired by such decisions, thereby striking a better balance for protecting the children's interests.

IV. Conclusion

Medical laws and practices in Thailand reflect the significant influence of parental authoritarianism. The role of parental decision-making is obviously dominant while the role of medical professionals remains passive and possesses no legal standing to bring a case to protect the children's best interests where there is disagreement over the children's treatment between parents and doctors. Judicial intervention to review parental decisions regarding medical treatment of their children is rarely possible. Parental authority in medical decision-making has no substantial limits, and their decisions – even when made with the best of intentions for their children – could impair or harm their children's health. The sad case of Charlie Gard in the UK has caused widespread criticism of the best interests test and caught public attention to demand the respect of parental wishes. Meanwhile, in Thailand, parental authority has minimal limits with no counterbalancing power from

[28] Gillam (n 3).

[29] G Birchley, 'Harm Is All You Need? Best Interests and Disputes about Parental Decision-Making' (2015) 42 *Journal of Medical Ethics* 111.

[30] Gillam (n 3).

other institutions such as medical professionals and even the courts. Such extensive power of decision-making granted to parents could be detrimental to their children's health if it turns out that parental decisions unreasonably conflict with suggestions from expert medical professions. Reviews of parental decisions are required to protect children's interests; the fact that children cannot express their own views does not mean that their rights and autonomy are entirely under the authority of their parents. This chapter suggests establishing a counterbalancing system in this regard by granting legal standing for doctors and healthcare service providers to request from the courts reviews of parental decisions. This chapter, then, supports the application of the harm principle test, with detailed guidelines for preventing problems of indeterminacy, as a tool for solving disputes where there is a clash of medical decisions between parents and medical professionals.

24

Medical Decision-Making on Behalf of Critically Ill Minors in Greece

THEODOROS TROKANAS

I. Introduction

Medical-decision making on behalf of critically ill minors is a challenging and emotionally complicated issue. It involves decisions for patients who have never achieved decision-making capacity, such as newborns and older infants with genetic disorders or physical disabilities, as well as cases of extreme prematurity or low birth weight.[1] Their medical treatment may generate disagreements not only between healthcare staff and parents, but also among healthcare personnel or within a child's family. Cases such as those of Charlie Gard[2] and Alfie Evans,[3] which have recently monopolised media and academic interest worldwide, have tested the ethical and legal limits of whether physicians may justifiably withhold (if not commenced) or withdraw or limit (if commenced) life-sustaining treatments (LSTs).[4] LSTs have the potential to prolong life and encompass conventional treatments (cardiopulmonary resuscitation, mechanical ventilation, antibiotics, renal dialysis, etc) as well as experimental treatments, which may not be validated by research.[5] With the Greek Civil Code (CC) and the Greek Code of Medical Deontology (CMD) as key reference points, this chapter explores the legal framework for such medical decision-making on behalf of critically ill minors in Greece.

[1] See American Academy of Pediatrics, 'Ethics and Care of Critically Ill Infants and Children' (1996) 98 *Pediatrics* 149.

[2] See *Gard and others v The United Kingdom*, 27 June 2017, ECtHR.

[3] See *Evans v The United Kingdom*, 28 March 2018, ECtHR.

[4] T Beauchamp and J Childress, *Principles of Biomedical Ethics*, 7th edn (New York and Oxford, Oxford University Press, 2013) 173. V Larcher, F Craig, K Bhogal et al, 'Making Decisions to Limit Treatment in Life-Limiting and Life-Threatening Conditions in Children: A Framework for Practice' (2015) 100 *Archives of Disabled Childhood* s1, 6.

[5] Larcher et al (n 4).

II. The Regime of Parental Responsibility in Greek Family Law

Following a standard European tradition of codified civil law instruments (see the chapters by Boone, Büchler and Menard in this volume), Greek legislation features a Civil Code,[6] Articles 1346–1709 of which constitute a fifth book entitled 'Family Law'. According to Article 1510 §1 CC, parental responsibility of minors is a functional right, ie it is both a right and a duty, and it is exercised in principle jointly by both parents. The content of parental responsibility is subdivided into three functions: (a) custody of the person, which is the primary function; (b) property administration; and (c) representation in every affair, legal act or trial. According to Article 1511 §1 CC, every decision of the parents regarding the exercise of parental responsibility shall aim at the welfare of the child. After all, parents are the persons best suited and most inclined to act in the best interest of their children (see the chapter by Botkin/Diekema in this volume). According to Article 1511 §3 CC, depending on his or her maturity, a child's opinion shall be requested and taken into consideration before each parental decision is made.[7] According to Article 1512 CC, if parents disagree over the exercise of parental responsibility and the welfare of the child necessitates making a decision, a court decides. The provision implies Navarro-Michel's consideration (in this volume) that the 'best interests of the child' is an undefined legal concept whose implementation relies heavily on judicial interpretation.[8] All the aforementioned provisions of the Greek Civil Code also apply to parents who have concluded civil partnership (Article 10 of Law 3719/2008[9] or Article 11 of Law 4356/2015[10]) as well as to adoptive parents (Articles 1566–1567 CC). Likewise, parental responsibility concerns children under guardianship (Article 1603 CC). In these ways, Greek law shares features of other jurisdictions, such as the duality of parental rights and duties (see the chapters by Leviner, Menard, Navarro-Michel and Bracken in this volume) and the joint exercise of parental responsibility (see the chapters by

[6] Preparatory works on drafting a Civil Code began in the 1930s and the Greek Civil Code finally came into force on 23 February 1946. It consists of 2035 Articles and is organised in 5 books.

[7] Several international treaties require that in any judicial or administrative proceedings a child be consulted and be allowed to freely express his or her views, which should be given due weight in accordance with his or her age and maturity. See indicatively Art 12 of the UN Convention on the Rights of the Child. See also Arts 3 and 6 of the European Convention on the Exercise of Children's Rights.

[8] M Navarro-Michel, 'Young Children and Healthcare Decisions in Spain: Who Decides?', in this book.

[9] This was the first Greek civil partnership law, which was passed in 2008 and was limited to heterosexual couples.

[10] This is the second Greek civil partnership law, which was passed in 2015 and was extended to homosexual couples. It should be clarified, though, that unlike heterosexual couples, homosexual couples cannot exercise parental responsibility rights, since homoparenthood is not recognised in the law.

Boone, Büchler and Menard in this volume); yet, it stands in marked contrast to the African setting, where the extended family prevails over the nuclear family and communal responsibility towards minors is elevated to a status similar to that of individual rights (see the chapter by Ujewe in this volume), as well as to East Asia, where, under the influence of Confucianism, the family retains a key role in decision-making for family members (see the chapter by Cheung in this volume).

The child's best interests is an overarching principle, which is enshrined in supranational legal texts, such as Article 3 of the UN Convention on the Rights of the Child[11] and Article 1 of the European Convention on the Exercise of Children's Rights.[12] The Greek Parliament ratified both Conventions, the former with Law 2101/1992[13] and the latter with Law 2502/1997,[14] and by virtue of Article 28 §1 of the Greek Constitution[15] their provisions prevail over any other contrary Greek law, including the Greek Civil Code. It is noteworthy that a Declaration contained in a Note Verbale of the Greek government limited the scope of the aforementioned European Convention on the Exercise of Children's Rights in Greece to cases concerning the custody of children, the communication between parents and children, and adoption. In doing so, Greece may have fulfilled the minimum triple family case requirement of Article 1 §4 of the Convention,[16] but it has excluded several other crucial family law issues, notably medical treatment.[17] Similarly, the child's best interests as a guiding principle has been established in Article 24[18] of the EU Charter of Fundamental Rights.[19]

[11] The UN Convention on the Rights of the Child was adopted and was opened for signature, ratification and accession by General Assembly Resolution 44/25 of 20 November 1989. It entered into force on 2 September 1990.

[12] The European Convention on the Exercise of Children's Rights (ETS No 160), which was elaborated by the Council of Europe, was opened for signature and for accession on 25 January 1996 and was brought into force on 1 July 2000.

[13] Greek Law 2101/1992, OJ vol A no 192 of 2 December 1992, 4101 et seq.

[14] Greek Law 2502/1997, OJ vol A no 103 of 28 May 1997, 4111 et seq.

[15] Greece has a written codified Constitution, Art 28 §1 of which stipulates: 'The generally recognised rules of international law, as well as international conventions as of the time they are ratified by statute and become operative according to their respective conditions, shall be an integral part of domestic Greek law and shall prevail over any contrary provision of the law.'

[16] See Art 1 §4 of the European Convention on the Exercise of Children's Rights: 'Every State shall, at the time of signature or when depositing its instrument of ratification, acceptance, approval or accession, by a declaration addressed to the Secretary General of the Council of Europe, specify at least three categories of family cases before a judicial authority to which this Convention is to apply.'

[17] This is one of the several family case categories enumerated in the Explanatory Report to the European Convention on the Exercise of Children's Rights, under Art 17.

[18] Art 24 of the EU Charter of Fundamental Rights: '2. In all actions relating to children, whether taken by public authorities or private institutions, the child's best interests must be a primary consideration.'

[19] According to Art 6 §1 of the Treaty on the European Union: 'The Union recognises the rights, freedoms and principles set out in the Charter of Fundamental Rights of the European Union of 7 December 2000, as adapted at Strasbourg, on 12 December 2007, which shall have the same legal value as the Treaties.'

III. Parental Consent to Medical Acts in Greek Law

A. Greek Civil Code

Greek family law theory[20] deems that medical decision-making on behalf of children falls within the scope of the custody of the person, which is the primary function of parental responsibility. Parents are responsible for the physical and mental health of the child, and monitoring his or her health, and they have the authority to consent to medical acts performed on the child. Neglecting a child's health indicates poor, or even failed, exercise of parental responsibility. Here a contrast can be drawn with, for instance, Argentinian legislation, which not only allows minors above sixteen to decide alone on the care of their body and health, but also allows minors aged between thirteen and sixteen to decide on their own for non-invasive treatments (see the chapter by Siverino-Bavio in this volume).

In the exercise of parental responsibility various forms of disagreements may arise. A primary source of sharp disagreement may present itself between health-care professionals and parents. A frequently recurring issue are Jehovah's Witness parents who refuse to consent to a required blood transfusion for their sick child due to strong religious beliefs. The Greek legislator attempted to resolve this legal impasse with Article 1534 CC, which provides that in case of overwhelming urgency for medical intervention on a minor whose parents refuse to consent, the Public Prosecutor may immediately grant permission upon request from the treating doctor, in order to avoid the risk of death or for the health of the child.

On the other hand, Article 1516 CC allows each parent to perform by himself or herself acts relative to the exercise of parental responsibility, such as common acts of custody or acts of urgency. Greek theory[21] interprets this provision as allowing for the consent of one parent to medical acts, such as regular visits to a physician, as well as emergency hospital admissions.

Nevertheless, part of Greek jurisprudence[22] maintains that some serious medical acts, which endanger or are vital for human health, require decision-making beyond the scope of custody and remain within the hard core of parental responsibility. Consequently, if both parents have parental responsibility, but only one of them has been awarded custody of the child (eg in cases of a divorce or

[20] See generally: E Kounougeri-Manoledaki, *Family Law*, vol II, 7th edn (Athens, Sakkoulas Publications, 2018) 321; A Georgiadis, *Family Law*, 2nd edn (Athens, Sakkoulas Publications, 2017) [31], under 7, 599–600.

[21] K Fountedaki, 'The Consent of the Informed Patient According to the New Code of Medical Deontology' in M Kaiafa-Gbandi, E Kounougeri-Manoledaki and E Symeonidou-Kastanidou (eds), *The New Code of Medical Deontology, Publications of Medical Law and Bioethics* (Athens, Sakkoulas Publications, 2006), 20.

[22] G Koumantos, *Family Law*, vol II (Athens, Sakkoulas Publications, 2009) 207, § 3.4.1.3.8; T Papachristou, *Family Law* (Athens, P.N. Sakkoulas Publications, 2014) 341, § 3.1.3; P Filios, *Family Law*, 4th edn (Athens, Sakkoulas Publications, 2011) 324, [126].

factual separation of the spouses), the consent of the latter does not suffice, but a co-decision by both parents is required. This jurisprudential view has also been endorsed in the case-law of the Greek Supreme Court.[23] Most recently, hearing an interim measures dispute between two spouses living in factual separation, a lower Greek court[24] provisionally awarded full custody of the child to its mother, excluding healthcare issues in general and inoculations in particular, which shall be co-decided by both parents, because the mother had been refusing to consent to their child being vaccinated up to the age of two.

B. Oviedo Convention

Greek Law 2619/1998 ratified the Convention for the Protection of Human Rights and Dignity of the Human Being with regard to the Application of Biology and Medicine: Convention on Human Rights and Biomedicine (the Oviedo Convention).[25] The Convention was designed to preserve principles, rights and freedoms against the misuse of biological and medical advances and it was the first legally binding international text of its kind to have been incorporated into Greek law. It should be pointed out here too that by virtue of Article 28 §1 of the Greek Constitution, Oviedo Convention provisions take precedence over any other contrary Greek law.[26]

Chapter II of the Oviedo Convention is dedicated to the notion of 'consent', with Article 6 focusing on the protection of persons unable to consent due either to their age (minors) or their mental incapacity.[27] Apart from the authorisation of the legal representative of the minor (or of an authority or other body), which is prescribed in Article 6 §2, Article 6 makes any medical intervention[28] carried out on minors conditional upon the existence of a direct benefit for him or her. At the same time, Article 6 §2 lays down that the opinion of the minor shall be taken into consideration as an increasingly determining factor in proportion to his or her age and degree of maturity, obviously with the view to preserving his or her autonomy.[29]

[23] See Greek Supreme Court (Areios Pagos) decisions: 1321/1992 (Armenopoulos 1994, 340 et seq), 1700/2001 (Dikaiosyni 2002, 1619/Chronika Idiotikou Dikaiou B/2002, 35 et seq), 1005/2006 (Dikaiosyni 2006, 1352 et seq).

[24] Court of First Instance of Athens 4029/2019, Applications of Civil Law and Civil Procedure 1/2020, 61 et seq, annotated by Trokanas.

[25] Preparatory works of the Council of Europe began in 1992 and the Oviedo Convention (CETS no 164) was opened for signature on 4 April 1997. To date, thirty-five out of forty-seven Member States of the Council of Europe have signed it. Greece signed the Oviedo Convention on 4 April 1997, ratified it on 6 October 1998 with Law 2619/1998 and brought it into force on 1 December 1999.

[26] n 15.

[27] See Explanatory Report to the Oviedo Convention, [41].

[28] The term is to be understood in its broadest sense in order to include all medical acts of preventive care, diagnosis, treatment, rehabilitation or research (See Explanatory Report to the Oviedo Convention, [29] and [34]).

[29] See Explanatory Report to the Oviedo Convention, [45].

The rule of the existence of a 'direct benefit' is subject to two exceptions:[30] the first exception is research on minors without the capacity to consent. According to Article 17 §2 research with no potential to produce results of direct benefit to the health of the person concerned may be authorised if the following additional[31] conditions are met: (i) the research is capable of conferring benefit to other persons in the same age category or afflicted with the same disease or disorder or condition; and (ii) the research entails only minimal risk and minimal burden for the individual concerned.[32] The second exception is the removal of regenerative tissue (eg bone marrow) from a compatible minor donor to his or her brother or sister (Article 20 § 2).

The element of 'direct benefit' that was inserted in the Oviedo Convention adds a new dimension to our parental decision-making discussion. In the high-profile Charlie Gard case the judge granted the request of the treating clinicians to withdraw the child from artificial ventilation and to continue only palliative care, sharing the view that nucleoside therapy, which a neurology professor at a medical centre in the United States recommended for the affected minor, could not reverse his structural brain damage. The judge concluded that the proposed treatment would be of no benefit to the child and therefore it would be futile.[33] In addition, the same judge clearly distinguished the subjective benefit of the experimental treatment for the minor patient from the objective benefit of it for medical science, which does not merit protection.[34] In fact, the judge seemed to brook no contradiction that the said experimental treatment might be worth trying, on the basis that medicine cannot advance without experimentation.[35] One might wonder whether in a similar case a Greek judge would base a position in favour of an experimental life-sustaining treatment on a systematic interpretation of Articles 6 § 1 and 17 § 2 of the Oviedo Convention.

C. Greek Code of Medical Deontology

Greek Law 3418/2005 integrates the Code of Medical Deontology, which is of a dual nature: at the same time, a code of professional ethics and a positive law.[36] Despite the best of intentions a few of its provisions create legal ambiguities, some of which begin to surface when parents disagree with each other on a medical course of action and there exists a division between parental responsibility and

[30] Article 6 §1 Oviedo Convention: 'Subject to Articles 17 and 20 below …'.

[31] Additional to the general conditions of research laid down in Art 17 §1 Oviedo Convention.

[32] The 'burden' test evokes the notions of pain, suffering and distress, which were repeatedly mentioned in the Charlie Gard and Alfie Evans decisions.

[33] *Great Ormond Street Hospital v Yates & Ors* [2017] EWHC 972 (Fam) (11 April 2017), [93].

[34] ibid [21].

[35] ibid [119].

[36] P Ravdas, 'Article 1' in T Vidalis et al (ed), *Medical Deontology, Article-by-article Analysis of Law 3418/2005* (Athens, Sakkoulas Publications, 2013) 2.

custody (eg in cases of divorce, marriage annulment or factual separation, where parental responsibility belongs to both parents, but custody is awarded to one of them).

To begin with, legal ambiguity is generated within the ambit of Article 12 § 2 (b) (aa) CMD, which stipulates that for minor patients consent is given by persons having parental responsibility *or* custody.[37] The interchangeable use of the two terms ('parental responsibility or custody') cannot help resolve clashes of opinion between parents and, needless to say, is incompatible with the Greek system of family law, whereby parental responsibility is the general term, whereas custody is the specific term, except if the phrase were interpreted as 'parental responsibility or at least custody'.

The issue is further clouded, because Article 12 § 1 (b)(aa) CMD, in conjunction with Article 11 § 3 CMD, strictly requires the consent of persons having parental responsibility (ie both parents) for certain categories of medical acts:[38] transplant,[39] medically assisted reproduction,[40] gender change or restoration interventions, and cosmetic interventions. Both articles may reflect the aforementioned Greek theory that some serious medical acts remain at the hard core of parental responsibility,[41] but Greek family law theorists[42] underline that the same articles (by *argumentum a contrario*) could support the conclusion that for any other than the enumerated medical acts the consent of the person having the custody of a minor suffices.

Any disagreement between parents on the exercise of parental responsibility about a medical course of action is resolved with recourse to the court by virtue of the general provision of Article 1512 CC.[43] It is conceivable that the same legal

[37] Art 12 § 2 (b)(aa) CMD continues: 'The opinion of a minor is taken into consideration, insofar as, at a physician's discretion, a minor has age-related, mental and emotional maturity to understand his health condition, the content of the medical act as well as its consequences, its results and its risks.'

[38] Contrary to an expected inclusion of abortion in the list, Art 11 § 3 CMD is actually silent on the issue. It is significant that the old Art 304 of Greek Penal Code made a minor's decision to terminate an unwanted pregnancy contingent on the consent of one parent or of the parent having the custody of the minor pregnant woman. By contrast, the new Art 304 Greek Penal Code (after its amendment with Law 4619/2019) unsuccessfully harmonises with the ambiguous wording of Art 12 § 2 (b)(aa) CMD ("parental responsibility *or* custody").

[39] Paradoxically, Arts 12 § 1 (b)(aa) and 11 § 3 CMD conflict with Art 9 § 1 of Greek Law 3984/2011 'Organ donation and transplant and other provisions', which permits the removal of an organ or organs from deceased minors with the consent of the parents or the parent who has the custody of the minor or of the guardian, provided they have been given appropriate information according to Art 7 § 2 of Law 3984/2011. The same provision applies to the removal of tissue and cells from deceased minors by virtue of Art 49 § 1 of Law 3984/2011. This conflict will be resolved with the roman maxim *lex posterior derogat (legi) priori*, ie the newer law of 2011 repealed the older law of 2005 (CMD).

[40] Unambiguous on the matter is Art 7 § 6 of Greek Law 3305/2005: 'Application of Medically Assisted Reproduction', which stipulates: '[I]f persons who cryopreserve their reproductive material are minors, both parents consent to it, even if only one parent has the custody. In addition, a minor who has reached the age of 15 consents himself or herself to cryopreservation.'

[41] See section III.A.

[42] Fountedaki (n 21).

[43] See section II.

path be followed for disagreements between parents and the medical personnel (eg if the opinion of only one parent coincides with the opinion of the medical personnel).

Nevertheless, if there is a need for immediate intervention, in order to avert a risk to the life or health of the minor patient, Article 12 § 3 CMD[44] allows the doctor to override the parents' refusal to consent to a medical act. Interestingly, by contrast in China hospitals and medical practitioners cannot deviate from a guardian's proxy medical decision, even if the latter appears prejudicial to the child (see the chapter by Chunyan in this volume). In parallel, the article is deemed[45] to impose a specific legal obligation (duty) on physicians to perform any act necessary to eliminate a risk to the life or health of a child, even if his or her parents do not consent. In comparison to Article 1534 CC,[46] Article 12 § 3 CMD reveals a point of legal uncertainty over whether the latter has tacitly partly amended the former. The prevailing opinion among Greek jurisprudence[47] holds that in overwhelming urgency a doctor faced with a parental refusal can intervene even against their wishes without any reference at all to a public prosecutor.

IV. End-of-Life Decisions for Terminal Illnesses

A. Greek Penal Code

Until the entry into force of the Greek CMD in 2005, end-of-life decisions for adult terminally ill patients were only viewed as a penal law issue within the ambit of the Greek Penal Code and in particular its Articles 300 and 301, which criminalise 'consensual homicide'[48] (euthanasia) and 'suicidal complicity',[49] respectively.

[44] Art 12 [3] CMD: 'Exceptionally, consent is not required … (c) if the parents of a minor patient or family members of a patient who is for any reason unable to consent or other third parties who have the power to consent for the patient, refuse to provide the necessary consent and there exists a need for immediate intervention, in order to prevent the risk for the life or health of the patient.'

[45] E Symeonidou-Kastanidou, 'Neonatal "Euthanasia" as a Problem of Penal Law' in M Kanellopoulou-Bottis, E Protopapadakis and F Panagopoulou-Koutnatzi (eds), *Bioethical Issues*, vol III: *The Child* (Athens, Papazisi Publications, 2018) 238.

[46] See text section II.

[47] Fountedaki (n 21) 25; Kounougeri-Manoledaki (n 21) 321; A Pelleni-Papageorgiou, 'Consent of a Minor to the Performance of Medical Interventions' (2017) *Applications of Civil Law and Civil Procedure* 1110, 1114. Against: Papachristou (n 22) 352.

[48] New Art 300 of the Greek Penal Code (after its slight amendment with Law 4619/2019): 'Consensual homicide. A person who conceived and committed homicide after the serious and persistent demand of the victim and out of compassion for him who suffered from an incurable illness shall be punished with imprisonment', translation based on the *American Series of Foreign Penal Codes*, vol 18: *The Greek Penal Code*, trans NB Lolis, intr G Mangakis (South Hackensack, NJ, Fred B Rothman and London, Sweet & Maxwell, London, 1973) 147.

[49] New Art 301 of the Greek Penal Code (after its slight amendment with Law 4619/2019): 'Suicidal complicity. A person who persuaded another to commit suicide, if suicide was committed or attempted, and a person who aided in its commission, which otherwise would not be possible, shall be punished with imprisonment', translation based on the *American Series of Foreign Penal Codes* (n 48).

B. Greek Code of Medical Deontology

Article 29 CMD delineated medical action regarding end-of-life decisions for terminally ill patients. According to Article 29 § 1 CMD:

> At the final stage of an incurable illness, even if all treatment margins have been exhausted, a doctor shall ensure the psychosomatic pain relief of the patient. The doctor offers palliative care and collaborates with his or her close members in this direction. In any case, the doctor shows compassion to the patient until the end of his life and ensures that the patient maintains his dignity until this point.

This provision indirectly introduced the ethical notion of 'futile treatment' (or 'therapeutic obstinacy'[50]) to Greek positive law, especially for terminal diseases in their final stages.[51] It is stressed that the determination of the 'futility' element should be grounded on scientific facts and be independent of any subjective judgements on the part of the doctor.[52] Furthermore, the criterion of 'benefit' of medical treatment should be totally unrelated to its economic cost or, more generally, to healthcare system resource allocation.[53] Obviously, Greek jurisprudence implies that only a treatment may be futile and not the very same life of a patient.

The underlying idea of Article 29 § 1 CMD is that even when every therapeutic benefit has been excluded with certainty, the doctor–patient relationship is still maintained.[54] The determination of the 'futility' element only alters the aim of medical act, which is now oriented towards palliative care provision. In broad terms,[55] palliative care for adults with life-threatening illnesses intends neither to hasten nor to postpone death; it affirms life and regards dying as a normal process. It provides relief from pain and other distressing symptoms, integrating the psychological and spiritual aspects of patient care. It aims to enhance the quality of life of patients, helping them to live as actively as possible until death, and to support their families.

Admittedly, Article 29 § 1 CMD accepts the occurrence of death, without hastening it. However, it does not treat the patient by 'allowing to die' or 'letting die', which entails an intentional avoidance of causal intervention, so that disease, system failure or injury causes death.[56] For this reason, Article 29 § 1 CMD does not clash with Articles 300 and 301 of the Greek Penal Code, which criminalise acts of 'killing'.

[50] This alternative terminology is used in Council of Europe, *Guide on the Decision-Making Process Regarding Medical Treatment in End-of-Life Situations* (May 2014) 11.

[51] T Vidalis, 'Article 29' in Vidalis et al (n 36) 335.

[52] T Vidalis, *Biolaw*, vol I: *The Person*, Publications of Medical Law and Bioethics vol 6 (Athens, Sakkoulas Publications, 2007) 120.

[53] ibid 121.

[54] National Bioethics Commission, Opinion on Artificial Prolongation of Life of 27 January 2006, under A. Γ. A.

[55] For a comprehensive definition of palliative care, see Worldwide Palliative Care Alliance/World Health Organization, *Global Atlas of Palliative Care at the End of Life* (January 2002) 5.

[56] Beauchamp and Childress (n 4), 175.

Within the true meaning of Article 29 § 1 CMD the collaboration of the doctor with the close family members of a patient is confined to palliative care. This means that they cannot demand the continuation of a futile treatment[57] or, conversely, that its interruption is not contingent on their consent according to the previously described Article 12 CMD.[58] The consent of the close family member of a patient would be meaningful only if they were faced with alternative medical choices and not when there is a one-way street.[59]

It is further argued by Greek jurisprudence[60] that a doctor who continues futile treatment breaches Article 29 § 1 CMD and is subject to penal (ie for bodily harm), civil and disciplinary liability. In fact, it is held that the same conclusion would be reached, even without Article 29 § 1 CMD, insofar as the continuation of futile treatment constitutes medical fault.[61]

Finally, Article 29 § 1 CMD does not distinguish between terminally ill adults and terminally ill minors, which leads to the conclusion that it is equally applicable. Palliative care for children is defined as the active total care of the child's body, mind and spirit, in order to alleviate his or her physical, psychological and social distress.[62] It also involves giving support to the family (parents, siblings) and providing access to therapies which are likely to improve the child's quality of life (eg education, grief and family counselling, peer support, appropriate respite care).[63]

V. Beginning-of-Life Decisions on Behalf of Minors

In practice, strong disagreements between parents and medical personnel may arise over resuscitating or not babies born at borderline viability and with little chance of survival,[64] instituting or not full intensive care and support for extremely premature babies, and providing or not nutrition and hydration[65] to infants in a life-threatening condition.[66]

[57] Vidalis (n 51).

[58] ibid.

[59] ibid.

[60] ibid.

[61] ibid.

[62] For a definition of palliative care for children see Worldwide Palliative Care Alliance/World Health Organization (n 55) 5.

[63] See American Academy of Pediatrics, Committee on Bioethics and Committee on Hospital Care, 'Palliative Care for Children' (2000) 106 *Pediatrics* 351.

[64] See Nuffield Council of Bioethics, *Critical Care Decisions in Fetal and Neonatal Medicine: Ethical Issues* (2006) 5.13. Up to twenty-two weeks and six days of gestation, survival to discharge from intensive care is widely regarded as highly unlikely and resuscitation is usually rejected as futile.

[65] It should be pointed out here that it is open to dispute whether artificial nutrition and hydration are forms of treatment, which may therefore be limited or withdraw, or forms of care, meeting individual basic needs, which cannot be withdrawn (see Council of Europe (n 50) 13).

[66] For instance, according to the the US Child Abuse Prevention and Treatment Act (s 111 Definitions): '[T]he term "withholding of medically indicated treatment" means the failure to respond to the infant's

It should be established from the outset that since Article 29 § 1 CMD is destined for terminally ill patients, beginning-of-life disputes over forgoing[67] life-sustaining treatments for minor patients are prima facie outside its scope.

Moreover, 'non-viability' (eg babies at borderline viability, extremely premature babies) cannot be a decisive factor in such beginning-of-life decisions in the Greek legal system. The Greek Civil Code delimits the existence and the demise of a person in Article 35, which sets forth that: 'The person begins to exist as soon as he is born alive and ceases to exist by his death.' Evidently, the Code confers personhood on the one and only condition that a natural person is born alive. By contrast, it does not require 'viability' as an additional precondition for personhood, as is the case in some other European civil codes. On the other hand, the end of a natural person is determined by the notion of death, namely the criterion of brain death. Naturally, the criterion of non-viability does not equate with the criterion of brain death. Consequently, any newborn enjoys the same status of personhood and a right to the protection of his or her life.

Another important consideration is that a decision on forgoing life-sustaining treatments would violate the Greek CMD. A possible consent of the legal representatives of a baby or infant (usually parents) to non-resuscitation or non-commencement of full intensive care or non-provision of nutrition or hydration may not be taken into account by a doctor, insofar as Article 12 § 3 CMD[68] obliges him to continue LST to prevent the risk to the life or health of the baby or infant patient.[69]

From a penal law perspective, a decision for non-resuscitation for a borderline viability baby or for non-commencement of full intensive care for a premature baby or for non-provision of nutrition or hydration for an older infant would not be distinguished from any other type of homicide in the Greek legal system.[70] An omission by a physician to take all necessary life-sustaining measures following a parental decision forms a criminal offence, just as in the case of Jehovah's Witness

life-threatening conditions by providing treatment (including appropriate nutrition, hydration, and medication) [*'appropriate' being the operative word here*] which, in the treating physician's or physicians' reasonable medical judgment, will be most likely to be effective in ameliorating or correcting all such conditions, except that the term does not include the failure to provide treatment (other than appropriate nutrition, hydration, or medication) to an infant when, in the treating physician's or physicians' reasonable medical judgment – A. the infant is chronically and irreversibly comatose; B. the provision of such treatment would – i. merely prolong dying; ii. not be effective in ameliorating or correcting all of the infant's life threatening conditions; iii. otherwise be futile in terms of the survival of the infant; or C. the provision of such treatment would be virtually futile in terms of the survival of the infant and the treatment itself under such circumstances would be inhumane.'

[67] The term 'forgo' should be understood to refer to both stopping a treatment already begun as well as not starting a treatment: see American Academy of Pediatrics, 'Guidelines on Forgoing Life-Sustaining Medical Treatment' (1994) 93 *Pediatrics* 532.

[68] See n 44.

[69] K Fountedaki, *Natural Person and Personhood in the Civil Code* (Athens, Sakkoulas Publications, 2012) 26.

[70] E Symeonidou-Kastanidou, 'Euthanasia in the Domestic Legal System of Greece' (2006) 59 *Revue Hellénique de Droit International* 495, 508.

parents who refused to consent to required blood transfusions for their sick child due to strong religious beliefs: the physician would be charged with intentional homicide (by omission) according to Article 299 of the Greek Penal Code,[71] whereas the parents would be charged as inciters to the intentional homicide (by omission) committed by the physician.[72] It is further supported[73] that such criminal acts could not be excused, even if the 'choice of evils defence' (or lesser-evils or necessity defence) was asserted, ie the sacrifice of life in question balanced against other goals served. Such balancing would be precluded here, since the person affected is unaware of what constitutes a life worth living.[74]

Needless to say, the conflict-of-duties clause, which is safeguarded in Article 15 CMD,[75] could not absolve a physician of either his penal or civil responsibility either, for the provision gives absolute precedence to human life.

Part of Greek jurisprudence[76] exceptionally recognises that in cases of critically-ill minors a physician's legal obligation to take all necessary life-sustaining measures ceases to exist, when this appears futile. This jurisprudential view derives its main argument from Article 29 § 1 CMD.[77] Additionally, the same view might be premised on the conception of medical treatment which is conducive neither to considerable life prolongation nor to patient health amelioration as medical fault.[78] Nonetheless, even the proponents of this position acknowledge that it is extremely difficult to determine a specific point in time of 'futility'. The difficulty is compounded by the absence of a set of criteria, on the basis of which physicians could decide to withhold or withdraw (or limit) life-sustaining treatments as well as by the non-appointment of competent, decision-making medical boards.

VI. Conclusion

It is manifest that physicians in Greece are legally constrained to provide LSTs, even when their medical judgements and the views of the parents are that forgoing them is preferable. To the best of the author's knowledge, no decisions about forgoing life-sustaining medical treatment for minors have been heard before Greek courts, with the exception of cases of Jehovah's Witness parents, who decline to

[71] New Art 299 of the Greek Penal Code (after its amendment with Law 4619/2019): 'Intentional homicide. A person who killed another shall be punished with life imprisonment or a determinate prison sentence of at least 10 years.'

[72] Symeonidou-Kastanidou (n 45).

[73] Symeonidou-Kastanidou (n 70) 508–09.

[74] ibid.

[75] Art 15 CMD: 'Conflict of duties. A doctor who is faced with a conflict of duties addresses the conflict on the basis of his scientific knowledge, the comparison of legal goods at stake, the utmost respect for human life and dignity and his conscience in the framework of principles of article 2.'

[76] Symeonidou-Kastanidou (n 45) 244.

[77] Fountedaki (n 69) 26.

[78] ibid.

consent to a required blood transfusion to their sick child. This does not mean that beginning-of-life decisions are foreign to Greek medical practice, but rather, that they might be taken as a grey area. The Greek legal system does not establish a clear set of criteria and institutional procedures (eg bioethics mediation, ethics committee reviews, judicial reviews) to resolve potential legitimate disagreements.[79] It is therefore interesting to contrast the Israeli legislation, which authorises an institutional ethics committee to have the final say over disagreements over withholding or not treatment from children who are terminally ill and have six months or less to live (see the chapter by Gilbar in this volume). If a Greek court, within its general competence to settle parental responsibility disputes, were called upon to decide on the lawfulness of forgoing life-sustaining treatment, the child's best interests would be of paramount importance, as in all family law cases involving minors. In contrast, no one can prejudge whether the futility element, as proposed by part of Greek jurisprudence, would ever play a role in future court decisions on forgoing life-sustaining medical treatment for critically ill minors.

[79] Beauchamp and Childress (n 4) 170.

25

Making Decisions for Children in Healthcare and Medical Research: African Communal Responsibility or Individual Rights?

SAMUEL J UJEWE

I. Introduction

This chapter situates Charlie Gard-type cases in African communal contexts and provides contextual analyses from an African ethical outlook, where the emphasis is on the ethics of communal responsibility, as opposed to the predominant ethics of individual rights. The use of the terms 'communal' or 'community' in this chapter goes beyond the physically locatable community, as may be found in rural African settings.[1] It also includes the concept of the 'cultural community', where the natural sociability of the human being is recognised, and a sense of community is acknowledged as relevant to total well-being and full realisation of human potential.[2] The Charlie Gard case[3] revives deep conversations about the ethical and legal place of parents, children and physicians in making decisions about the healthcare or treatment options for a sick child. The chapter situates the African communal responsibility principle within the context of healthcare for children,[4] and prescribes a medical decision-making process underpinned by responsibility,

[1] SJ Ujewe, 'Ought-Onomy and Mental Health Ethics: From "Respect for Personal Autonomy" to "Preservation of Person-in-Community" in African Ethics' (2018) 25 *Philosophy, Psychiatry, & Psychology* 4.

[2] K Gyekye, *Tradition and Modernity: Philosophical Reflections on the African Experience* (Oxford, Oxford University Press, 1997).

[3] 'The Story of Charlie Gard' *BBC* (27 July 2017) www.bbc.com/news/health-40554462.

[4] See I Boone, 'Parental Rights, Best Interests and Significant Harm: Medical Decision-Making on Behalf of Children in Belgium'; A Buechler, 'Parental Decisions on their Children's Medical Treatment'; K Sovig, 'Reviewing Medical Decisions Concerning Infants Within the Norwegian Healthcare System – A Public Law Approach', all in this book.

solidarity and harmony, which are key attributes in African decision-making processes.

The decision-making process in the case of Charlie Gard is underpinned by *the best interests of the child* argument,[5] which mostly presents the physicians' perspective and seemingly ignores the perspective of the parents. The rights-based ethics outlook is predominant among cultures that emphasise the place of individual persons, an approach typical of much of Europe and North America.[6] In African contexts, however, community is highly valued, and persons are conceptualised in terms of their place within it. The underlying ethical outlook is that of communal responsibility towards the well-being of every individual member, and children are prioritised, as they represent the future of the community.

Charlie Gard-type cases in African communal contexts of healthcare would see the decision-making process take a different shape from what transpired in the United Kingdom.[7] For instance, the decision to deny Charlie an existing experimental treatment did not recognise the crucial place of family in the life of the child, which would grant them the moral grounds to make final decisions on the child's healthcare. Underlying the doctors' decision is the dominant trend in the current literature on decision-making for children in healthcare and medical research that leans on the principle of the rights of the child.[8] It would be problematic to attempt to apply the rights approach to healthcare decision-making

[5] N Hammond-Browning, 'When Doctors and Parents Don't Agree: The Story of Charlie Gard' (2017) 14 *Journal of Bioethical Inquiry* 4.

[6] For specific applications of children's rights in Switzerland and Belgium, see Buechler (n 4) and Boone (n 4).

[7] This chapter uses the United Kingdom to represent Western contexts generally.

[8] M Bluebond-Langner, JB Belasco and MD Wander, '"I Want to Live, Until I Don't Want to Live Anymore": Involving Children with Life-Threatening and Life-Shortening Illnesses in Decision Making About Care and Treatment' (2010) 45 *Nursing Clinics* 3; EA Lipstein, WB Brinkman, AG Fiks, KS Hendrix, J Kryworuchko, VA Miller, LA Prosser, WJ Ungar and D Fox, 'An Emerging Field of Research: Challenges in Pediatric Decision Making' (2014) 35 *Medical Decision Making* 3; I Coyne, DP O'Mathúna, F Gibson, L Shields, E Leclercq and G Sheaf, 'Interventions for Promoting Participation in Shared Decision-making for Children with Cancer' [2016] *Cochrane Database of Systematic Reviews* 11; I Coyne, A Amory, G Kiernan and F Gibson, 'Children's Participation in Shared Decision Making: Children, Adolescents, Parents and Healthcare Professionals' Perspectives and Experiences' (2014) 18 *European Journal of Oncology Nursing* 3; I Coyne and M Harder, 'Children's Participation in Decision-Making: Balancing Protection with Shared Decision-Making Using a Situational Perspective' (2011) 15 *Journal of Child Health Care* 4; M Hyde, R Punch and L Komesaroff, 'Coming to a Decision About Cochlear Implantation: Parents Making Choices for Their Deaf Children' (2010) 15 *Journal of Deaf Studies and Deaf Education* 2; KM Ruhe, T Wangmo, DO Badarau, BS Elger and F Niggli, 'Decision-Making Capacity of Children and Adolescents – Suggestions for Advancing the Concept's Implementation in Pediatric Healthcare' (2015) 174 *European Journal of Pediatrics* 6; P Grootens-Wiegers, IM Hein, JM van den Broek and MC de Vries, 'Medical Decision-Making in Children and Adolescents: Developmental and Neuroscientific Aspects' (2017) 17 *BioMed Central – Pediatrics* 1; A Aarthun and K Akerjordet, 'Parent Participation in Decision-Making in Health-Care Services for Children: An Integrative Review' (2014) 22 *Journal of Nursing Management* 2; GP Quinn, D Murphy, C Knapp, DK Stearsman, KL Bradley-Klug, K Sawczyn and ML Clayman, 'Who Decides? Decision Making and Fertility Preservation in Teens with Cancer: A Review of the Literature' (2011) 49 *Journal of Adolescent Health* 4.

universally, especially in African contexts.[9] There are various established perspectives and approaches to decision-making developed and practised in other parts of the world that are not underpinned by a framework of individual rights. In African contexts, the decision-making process is underpinned by the principles of responsibility, solidarity and harmony.[10] Decision-making for children in healthcare or medical research is not viewed as a conclusive act or outcome driven; rather, it is process oriented and arrived at harmoniously.[11] The underpinning principle is the community's responsibility towards preserving the health and well-being of the child, which also protects the child's rights to live.

To adequately ground the kinds of issues that arise from Charlie Gard-type cases in African contexts, the chapter proceeds by first contrasting the African ethics of communal responsibility with the ethics of individual rights, and determine how this makes a difference in healthcare decision-making for children. A deeper understanding of the place and value of children in African contexts is crucial to grasping the place of communal responsibility in medical decision-making on their behalf. The chapter provides a descriptive analysis to this effect. It presents medical cases involving decision-making on behalf of children and explores the implications for addressing cases similar to Charlie Gard's in African healthcare contexts. This situates Charlie Gard-type cases in African contexts, showing how important the issue is, providing explanations underlying the frequent oppositions to medical interventions for children in Africa.

[9] A Moyo, 'Parental Responsibility and Medical Decision-Making in Southern Africa: A Comparative Analysis of South Africa and Botswana', in this book.

[10] K Gyekye, 'African Ethics' in EN Zalta (ed), *The Stanford Encyclopedia of Philosophy* (Standford, Metaphysics Research Lab, Stanford University, 2011) plato.stanford.edu/archives/fall2011/entries/african-ethics/; B Bujo, *Foundations of an African Ethic: Beyond the Universal Claims of Western Morality* (New York, Crossroad Publishing Company, 2001); SJ Ujewe, 'Just Health Care in Nigeria – The Foundations for an African Ethical Framework' (thesis, University of Central Lancashire, 2016); Ujewe (n 1); D Tutu, *No Future without Forgiveness* (London, Random House, 2000); E Imafidon, 'On the Ontological Foundation of a Social Ethics in African Traditions' in E Imafidon and AI Bewaji (eds), *Ontologized Ethics: New Essays in African Meta-Ethics* (New York, Lexington Books, 2013); K Gyegye, *Tradition and Modernity: Philosophical Reflections on the African Experience* (Oxford, Oxford University Press, 1997); N Mkhize, 'Ubuntu and Harmony: An African Approach to Morality and Ethics' in R Nicolson (ed), *Person in Community: African Ethics in a Global Culture* (Scottsville, University of KwaZulu Natal Press, 2008); JS Mbiti, *African Religions & Philosophy* (Gaborone, Heinemann, 1990); MJ Tosam, PC Chi, NS Munung, OOM Oukem-Boyer and GB Tangwa, 'Global Health Inequalities and the Need for Solidarity: A View from the Global South' (2018) 18(3) *Developing World Bioethics* 241; P Ikuenobe, *Philosophical Perspectives on Communalism and Morality in African Traditions* (Lanham, MD, Lexington Books, 2006).

[11] See the following chapters in this volume: I Goold, C Auckland and J Herring, 'Medical-Decision Making on Behalf of Children in English and Welsh Law: A Child-Centred Best Interests Approach' and L Francis, J Botkin and D Diekema, 'Decision-Making on Behalf of Children in the Research and Clinical Context: A United States Perspective', on divisiveness of adversarial system; D Chunyan, 'Medical Decision-Making on Behalf of Children in China: A MultiDimensional Analysis of Parental Authoritarianism', and D Cheung, 'Medical Decision-Making on Behalf of Minors: The Hong Kong Context' on communal decision-making; Moyo (n 9) on communal approach; and T Tengaumnuay, 'Parental Authoritarianism and Medical Decision-Making in Thailand: The Need for Limiting the Parental Authority' on parental authority dominance, all in this book.

II. Communal Responsibility versus Individual Rights in Children's Healthcare

To better appreciate the significance of Charlie's case in African healthcare contexts, it is important to gain some insight into the sociocultural principles and values that inform decision-making processes in sub-Saharan Africa, generally speaking. The decision-making process in Charlie's case was underpinned by a social and cultural outlook embedded in Western Europe, which emphasises the value and place of individual rights and society's obligation to protect them. However, in African contexts, the emphasis is on the value of communal wellbeing and the responsibility of the community to protect the welfare of individual members.[12] These would inform decision-making in Charlie Gard-type cases in African healthcare settings,[13] in a similar way that individual rights inform Charlie's case in England/Europe.

A. African Ethics of Communal Responsibility

In African ethics, communal responsibility takes centre stage, and the moral frame of reference is underpinned by the network of communal relationships.[14] This compares to some extent to what obtains in family decision-making in Hong Kong and China.[15] The ethic of communal responsibility emphasises a preoccupation with the well-being of whole communities or societies; not simply of individuals constituting them. It motivates individual members to seek the good of the community or society as a whole, in virtue of which they also seek their own good and build a firm basis for a sustained well-being.[16] Four pillars constitute this kind of ethic, including: *ubuntu*, which defines the social context; *personhood*, which specifies the mode of meaningful engagement; *vital participation*, which provides the conceptual frame of reference; and *harmony*, which is the essence of dialogic or decision-making process.[17] The idea of *ubuntu* presents every individual person within a community or society as inevitably existing in relationships with others around them. The main thesis remains: *a person is a person through other persons*,

[12] SJ Ujewe, 'Moral Residue and Health Justice for the Global South: Addressing Past Issues Through Current Interventions and Research' [2019] *Developing World Bioethics*, doi.org/10.1111/dewb.12238; Ujewe (n 1); GB Tangwa, *African Perspectives on Some Contemporary Bioethics Problems* (Newcastle upon Tyne, Cambridge Scholars Publishing, 2019); GB Tangwa, *Elements of African Bioethics in a Western Frame* (Bamenda, Langaa Research & Publishing CIG, 2010).

[13] Moyo (n 9).

[14] Gyekye (n 10), Ujewe (n 10), Ujewe (n 1).

[15] See Chunyan (n 11) and Cheung (n 11).

[16] K Gyekye, *African Cultural Values: An Introduction* (Accra, Sankofa Publishing Company, 1996).

[17] Ujewe (n 10)

and the individual person is inevitably involved in varied social and moral duties and commitments that focus on the well-being of others around them.[18] This relational coexistence derives from the African communitarian structure that emphasises imperatives for social relationship and vital interdependencies.[19] The ethic emphasises reciprocal or dual responsibility,[20] where individuals are drawn by shared obligations towards each other and to the communities to which they belong.

Upholding individuals' dignity and sustaining communal harmony are crucial underpinnings of decision-making processes in African ethics contexts.[21] Having a sense of belonging to a certain community is essential to how individuals define themselves:[22] '[T]he individual becomes a person only through active participation in the life of the community.'[23] One's possession of personal dignity is largely determined by various commitments to others within the community. This kind of commitment is not limited to a geographically locatable group, as community transcends geographical boundaries and is understood in terms of 'cultural community'.[24]

Decision-making processes in African contexts are, thus, informed by a sense of communal harmony. Accordingly, healthcare decisions are evaluated not only in terms of their potential consequences for the affected person(s), but also for those who share vital relationships with them. South Africa and Botswana have already enacted children healthcare laws that recognise and protect the place of parental and familial responsibility in medical decision-making on behalf of children; they require physicians to enter into a non-confrontational engagement with parents to foster a relationship-based approach.[25]

B. Ethics of Individual Rights/liberty

The ethics of individual rights prominently inform the decision-making process in Charlie Gard's case. The *best interests of the child* is highlighted as the global standard for ethical decision-making for children in healthcare or medical research, as reflected in current international ethics guidelines including the Declaration

[18] M Munyaka and M Motlhabi, 'Ubuntu and its Socio-Moral Significance' in M Murove (ed), *African Ethics: An Anthology of Comparative and Applied Ethics* (Scottsville, University of KwaZulu Natal Press, 2009).

[19] Ujewe (n 10) and Gyekye (n 10).

[20] Gyekye (n 2).

[21] Tutu (n 10).

[22] SJ Ujewe, *Ought-Onomy and African Health Care: Beyond the Universal Claims of Autonomy in Bioethics* (Dunedin, University of Otago, 2012).

[23] Bujo (n 10), 97.

[24] Gyekye (n 20).

[25] Moyo (n 9) ss 2 and 3.

of Helsinki,[26] among others. The physicians' decision to discontinue treatment for Charlie was established against the best interests principle in favour of palliative care to uphold his right to a dignified end of life.[27] Although Charlie's parents pressed for an alternative experimental treatment,[28] their decision equally rested on the best interests principle, ie upholding Charlie's rights to accessing a potential life-saving treatment. The two competing claims can both appeal to the United Nations' Convention on the Rights of the Child: 'In all actions concerning children, whether undertaken by public or private social welfare institutions, courts of law, administrative authorities or legislative bodies, the best interests of the child shall be a primary consideration.'[29]

The discourse in current literature about healthcare decision-making for children largely follows this trend. There is a movement towards shared decision-making involving physicians, parents and older children.[30] Yet, much of the discourse focuses on protecting the rights for child. Coyne and Harder, for instance, argue 'for a situational perspective of children's participation to act in the child's best interest and to balance protection with shared decision-making, according to children's rights and desires'.[31]

C. Responsibility versus Rights

One issue with the rights approach is that it prescribes precise decision-making methods that do not always respect the positions or outlooks of one or more legitimate parties in the decision-making process. This presents shared decision-making as a conclusive act, where absolute decisions are reached based on approved logical representations that the law speaks to as protecting the child's best interests or rights. It does not provide a resolution strategy for a situation where cogent claims are made for the child's best interests by opposing decisions, as observed in Charlie's case.[32] This kind of opposition can be absorbed in the African communal decision-making process, which is 'primarily process driven, incorporating diverse as well as shared values, and working by dissensus as well

[26] World Medical Association General Assembly, *Declaration of Helsinki: Ethical Principles for Medical Research Involving Human Beings* (Fortaleza, 2013).

[27] JJ Paris, J Ahluwalia, BM Cummings, MP Moreland and DJ Wilkinson, 'The Charlie Gard Case: British and American Approaches to Court Resolution of Disputes over Medical Decisions' (2017) 37 *Journal of Perinatology* 12.

[28] ibid

[29] United Nations, *Convention on the Rights of the Child* (New York, United Nations Human Rights Office of the High Commissioner, 1990).

[30] Bluebond-Langner et al (n 8). Coyne et al (n 8, 2014). Coyne and Harder (n 8) Ruhe et al (n 8). Coyne et al (n 8, 2016). Grootens-Wiegers et al (n 8). Aarthun and Akerjordet (n 8). Quinn et al (n 8).

[31] Coyne and Harder (n 8); C MacIntosh, 'Decisionally Incapable Children and Medical Treatment Choices in Canada', in this book.

[32] Hammond-Browning (n 5); Paris et al (n 27).

as consensus'.[33] Specifically, the relationship-based approach engrained in the Botswanan Children's Acts provides that:

> [A] child's parents, other relatives, guardian and any other people who are significant in the child's life shall be given an opportunity and assistance to participate in decision-making processes under this Act that are likely to have a significant impact on the child's life.[34]

The process-driven approach ensures that all significant parties play a role in the healthcare decision-making for the child, especially family members.

III. The Place and Value of Children in African Healthcare Contexts

How can we mitigate controversies in decision-making for children in healthcare and medical research, where legitimate but opposing views to the same claim exist? An African communitarian approach to decision-making provides a viable resolution. This is informed by the significant place and value of children within families and communities. Situating the ethics of responsibility as the moral compass for healthcare decision-making for children in Africa becomes clearer once we grasp their place and value within these contexts. This section provides a brief clarification on the place of children and the value of family or community in the care of children in African settings. African settings, as referred to in this chapter, would include the sub-Saharan Africa region where cultural similarities exist among the various ethnicities.

In African settings, the family is recognised as a fundamental and highly valued institution, and family ties are close, important and cherished.[35] Family has much wider set of members than a typical European or North American family, constituting everyone who may be referred to as 'extended family' in the latter.[36] This means that when a child is born, she or he automatically belongs to an extended network of family members, and she or he influences the place of every family member. On the day a child is born, the parents' siblings begin to view themselves as uncles and aunts, extending to all other members who begin to view themselves as taking new roles within the family.[37] A decision made about or for the child bears on the entire network of family members. This is somewhat reflected in the

[33] CW van Staden and KWM Fulford, 'The Indaba in African Values-Based Practice: Respecting Diversity of Values without Ethical Relativism or Individual Liberalism' in D Crepaz-Keay, K Fulford, W van Staden and J Sadler (eds), *The Oxford Handbook of Psychiatric Ethics* (Oxford, Oxford University Press, 2015) 307.

[34] Moyo (n 9)

[35] Gyekye (n 16).

[36] Mbiti (n 10).

[37] Ujewe (n 10).

discourses on the centrality of parents and the nuclear family in some Western contexts.[38] The premium placed on children is such that everything the family works for or possesses is for their benefit. Wealth is said to be sought primarily for the sake of the children, as wealth has no meaning or value within a family where there are no children.[39] For instance, it is uncommon for teenagers to be asked to leave their parents' houses once they reach the age of eighteen years, as is common practice in Western societies:

> Growing adults are generally expected to live at home – in the family house – even if they are over eighteen, and they may leave only after they marry … there is no time in a person's life when his or her parents cease to show interest in his or her affairs.[40]

This indicates a sense of holistic responsibility that parents and other members of the family bear for the children within the family. One cannot choose to abstain from the expected roles that define family responsibility towards children. When children grow into adulthood, the process is reversed, so that parents and grandparents, for instance, become responsibilities of their children and grandchildren.[41] And now as adults, children cannot choose to abstain from this responsibility either.

What this means for healthcare decision-making is that it is underpinned by communal responsibility. The ethic of responsibility requires each individual to demonstrate genuine concern for the interests of other family members. It is imposed by the ethical values of compassion, solidarity, reciprocity, cooperation, interdependence, and social well-being, which are counted among the principles of communitarian morality. These considerations elevate the notion of responsibility to a status similar to what is given to the notion of rights in Western ethics.[42] The place and value of children so described have been codified in both the South African and Botswanan Children's Act in relation to healthcare decision-making on their behalf.[43]

IV. Children in Healthcare and Medical Research: Some African Examples

The decision-making process in Charlie's case was underpinned by individual rights, including those of the parents and the doctors, with the courts balancing these. In African healthcare settings, the approach is different. Families and

[38] See Goold et al (n 4)
[39] Gyekye (n 16).
[40] ibid 85.
[41] Gyekye (n 16) and Mbiti (n 10).
[42] Gyekye (n 10).
[43] Moyo (n 9).

communities are more directly involved as vital components of the decision-making process. Healthcare issues are treated as family or communal issues, from which communal responsibilities for health ensue. When a family member is in need of urgent medical attention that they cannot afford, family members with financial ability are expected to provide support. There is a sense in which everyone feels obligated to participate in the healing process of the individual member. Restoring the health of the family member, especially if they are a child, 'cannot be a matter for doctor and patient alone: it demands the participation of the entire community'.[44]

In what follows, I present three case examples of how communities get involved in decision-making for the healthcare of young children. The cases are slightly different from that of Charlie Gard in the sense that they involve decision-making in the context of public health; yet, they are all clinical in nature, as was Charlie's. Reference is made to these cases to demonstrate the underlying nature and reason for the dispute, which would apply in a typical Charlie Gard-type case in an African context. I highlight cases from three countries. Moyo provides clinical case examples that correlate with that of Charlie from an African legal outlook with court orders favouring decision on behalf of providing treatment for the child, rather than withdrawing treatment as with Charlie's case.[45]

In 2018, Uganda suffered measles outbreaks that affected many districts.[46] Although Uganda earlier passed a law on mandatory immunisation for some vaccine-preventable diseases, including measles,[47] the health authority did not take any legal action against non-compliant parents. Rather, they mobilised a mass community engagement and vaccination campaign to get parents to voluntarily vaccinate their children.[48] In 2008, a mass drug administration programme for treating schistosomiasis in school-age children was suspended in Tanzania following violent resistance from one community against the administered drug.[49] The reaction was partly motivated by past experiences of similar disputes.[50]

[44] Bujo (n 10) 46–47.

[45] Moyo (n 9).

[46] 'Major Outbreak of Measles in Uganda' *BBC* (20 December 2016) www.bbc.co.uk/programmes/p06w46w1.

[47] A Fallon, 'Uganda Rolls Out Compulsory Immunization to Dispel Anti-Vaccine Myths' *Inter Press Service* (29 June 2016) www.ipsnews.net/2016/06/uganda-rolls-out-compulsory-immunization-to-dispel-anti-vaccine-myths/.

[48] PE Alebtong, 'Government Declares Measles Outbreak in 26 districts' *Daily Monitor* (11 May 2018) www.monitor.co.ug/News/National/Govt-declares-measles-outbreak-26-districts/688334-4555976-11x0e4nz/index.html.

[49] J Hastings, 'Rumours, Riots and the Rejection of Mass Drug Administration for the Treatment of Schistosomiasis in Morogoro, Tanzania' (2016) 48 *Journal of Biosocial Science* 1.

[50] M Parker, T Allen and J Hastings, 'Resisting Control of Neglected Tropical Diseases: Dilemmas in the Mass Treatment of Schistosomiasis and Soil-Transmitted Helminths in North-West Uganda' (2008) 40 *Journal of Biosocial Science* 2. S Muhumuza, A Olsen, F Nuwaha and A Katahoire, 'Understanding Low Uptake of Mass Treatment for Intestinal Schistosomiasis among School Children: A Qualitative Study in Jinja District, Uganda' (2015) 47 *Journal of Biosocial Science* 4.

Additionally, in 2003, a mass polio immunisation programme was halted in Northern Nigeria following a boycott.[51] This protest was linked to a previous dubious clinical trial that had killed several children.[52] The programme was halted and community engagement processes were undertaken to resolve the situation. This represents a quasi-mandatory programme on polio immunisation that attempts to balance the government's obligation to protect the health of children with the parental and communal responsibilities for the same children. It is different from the kind of mandatory child vaccination in Belgium, as described by Boone.[53]

Underlying these three disputes is the African outlook that the health issue of one person concerns everyone within their household and extended family. By extension, a healthcare issue affecting several children involves whole communities in the decision-making process. By implication, a typical Charlie Gard-type case in an African context would require participation of the child's immediate family in the decision-making process. Sometimes, the extended family may be involved, where the parents choose to involve them to provide clarity.[54] For instance, South Africa's Children's Act provides that:

> If it is in the best interests of the child, the child's family must be given the opportunity to express their views in any matter concerning the child … [and] a child and a person who has parental responsibilities and rights in respect of that child, where appropriate, must be informed of any action or decision taken in a matter concerning the child which significantly affects the child.[55]

While Charlie's case presents health authorities as opposing parents' participation in the healthcare decision-making for their child, the African examples present an inverse outlook of health authorities mediating on behalf of the children. Health authorities, practitioners and family members engage in a harmonious decision-making process on the health of the child. This is also reflected in the centrality and value placed on families in medical decision-making in East Asia.[56]

V. Decision-Making for Children in Healthcare

In the Charlie Gard case, decision-making was undertaken against a background of individual rights, following the dominant trend in healthcare decision-making for children. Yet, the African outlook presents a decision-making process

[51] AS Jegede, 'What Led to the Nigerian Boycott of the Polio Vaccination Campaign?' (2007) 4 *PLoS Medicine* 3. JR Kaufmann and H Feldbaum, 'Diplomacy and the Polio Immunization Boycott in Northern Nigeria' (2009) 28 *Health Affairs* 4.

[52] M Yahya, 'Polio Vaccines – "No Thank You!" Barriers to Polio Eradication in Northern Nigeria' (2007) 106 *African Affairs* 423.

[53] Boone (n 4).

[54] van Standen and Fulford (n 33).

[55] Moyo (n 9)

[56] Chunyan (n 11) and Cheung (n 11).

underpinned by communal responsibility, involving parents and whole families, towards the child's healthcare. The process is informed by the familial duty to protect and preserve the life of the child, who is the future of the family; as well as a corresponding obligation of the physician to protect the life of the child and the community's health.

One party or individual does not solely make any serious decision on the child's health without involving other relevant members of the family. Healthcare decision-making for children is, thus, an *unpredetermined* process that involves familial *indaba*:[57]

> The African concept and practice of Indaba entails a substantive communicative process. 'Indaba' is a word from isiZulu, the meaning of which includes 'meeting,' 'matter,' and 'story.' An indaba is a way of doing that entails an attitude, an orientation, an understanding, an insight into the process, and even a personal and a societal identity. Thus we might say that *an indaba is a meeting to discuss a matter where people have a voice and generate a common story to tell about the matter.* ... Although the word comes from isiZulu, indabas are also common in many parts of Africa .... [It is] a substantive communicative process of ... decision-making in which all the parties co-construct and co-produce a decision.[58]

Since the healthcare of children typically also involves physicians, and sometimes the health authorities, the health *indaba* naturally extends to these parties and decisions are reached through a harmonious process. The principle of harmony in healthcare decision-making for children in engrained in both South African and Botswanan Children's Acts.[59] The harmonious decision-making process in healthcare is underpinned by the African outlook of health and illness that recognises a duality of natural and existential causations, and espouses harmony with oneself, community and the metaphysical world as a key determinant of good health.

Accordingly, the search for a child's best interests in healthcare is also a quest for the restoration of harmony for the children, and their family and entire networks of relationships. A child's illness disrupts the harmony within a family, and restoring the child's health positively impacts on the family's well-being. If the child dies, for instance, restoration is sought through the mourning process. Medical decision-making on behalf of the child would involve key members of the child's family in a healing *indaba*, beginning with the parents.

The healing *indaba* plays a crucial role in healthcare decision-making for children, as they are unable to represent themselves in the *indaba* process, and must be jointly represented by family members and/or third-parties. In Charlie's case, the decision-making process was concluded through logical argumentation in the law courts; yet, the African health *indaba* proceeds by means of dialogue,

[57] van Standen and Fulford (n 33) 306–07.

[58] PF Omonzejele, 'African Concepts of Health, Disease, and Treatment: An Ethical Inquiry' (2008) 4 *Explore: The Journal of Science and Healing* 2.

[59] Moyo (n 9).

presenting a communicative rather than an argumentative process.[60] In a typical Charlie Gard-type case in an African setting, the healing *indaba* would trigger a family (or perhaps, community) *indaba*, where key family members engage in a communicative process with the healthcare practitioners. This may result in a compound-*indaba*, where the family engages in a communicative dialogue within and between its members, and the physicians, about the child's health condition. This communicative healing dialogue is not result oriented or predetermined, but is process driven and open-ended. A decision is arrived at in the form of harmony, rather than through precise logical or argumentative means. Rather than the doctors, solely making a conclusive decision, families would be involved in reaching that decision. Through the health *indaba*, a decision is reached to determine whether to terminate treatment or explore further medical options.

A. Seeking Harmony (Through Solidarity) in Decision-Making for Children's Healthcare

The healthcare decision-making process for children is a search for harmony, underpinned by an appreciation of shared responsibility. The imperative to pursue healthcare *indaba* is legitimised by the imperative of communal solidarity to participate in the health and well-being of children. I provide a brief analysis of the concept of solidarity and harmony, and their implications in African contexts, in this section. The next section shows how these bear in healthcare decision-making for children.

Solidarity, as understood and practised in African contexts, is different from the dominant academic outlook.[61] Generally, solidarity is understood in terms of charity, altruism, reciprocity and trust, where there is a unity of feeling or action between individuals or groups to respond to a common problem or take a common course of action. The African outlook of solidarity extends beyond the acts or feelings so described; it is an attribute, underpinned by shared values between individuals, within families, and among communities, which is guided by the imperative towards otherness:[62]

> Solidarity in African context is based on reciprocity, motivated by the desire to live a compassionate, generous and interdependent life. … [For] our humanity is not defined by our biological composition or capacity for rationality, but by our capacity to identify, commiserate and share with other members of the community.[63]

[60] van Standen and Fulford (n 33).

[61] See Goold et al (n 10); A Brown, '"Parental Rights", "Best Interests" and the Withdrawal of Life-Sustaining Medical Treatment of Children in Scotland: A Lack of Authority' and P Leviner, 'Who Has the Final Word? On Trust and Legal Uncertainty Within the Swedish Healthcare System', both in this book.

[62] Ujewe (n 10)

[63] Tosam et al (n 10).

Harmony is the predominant principle in African contexts and ethics, as exemplified in current literature: 'Social harmony is for us the *summum bonum* – the greatest good. Anything that subverts or undermines this sought-after good is to be avoided like a plague';[64] and: 'An action is right insofar as it is a way of living harmoniously or prizing communal relationships, ones in which people identify with each other and exhibit solidarity with one another; otherwise, an action is wrong.'[65]

The idea of harmony subsists in a *we-thinking* social context, where individuals' existence is defined by shared values, obligations and roles; it is underpinned by vital interdependencies by which individuals recognise a loyalty and commitment to each other and to the community.[66] Communal harmony means that individuals within a community have an identifiable sense of belonging with each other; they are united by networks of social relationships through which they accept shared obligations towards each other and to the whole community. Ethical harmony is attained when, through open-ended deliberation, parties involved can understand, view and/or appreciate issues from others' moral outlooks.

In the context of healthcare decision-making for children, solidarity and harmony motivate the communicative or *indaba* process, so that the outcome is not predetermined by the stronger voice or actor. The final decision remains indeterminate and harmoniously reached through appreciation of the shared responsibilities of all parties in upholding the best interests of the child. This resonates with the considerable parental weight given to medical decision-making in Thailand, and the limited role of the courts and healthcare practitioners.[67] The path towards ensuring this best interest is establishing harmony in and through the decision-making process. It presupposes the inclusiveness of all relevant voices in healthcare decision-making for children, as an overarching attribute.

B. Responsibility, Solidarity and Harmony in Decision-Making for Children's Healthcare

In the cases presented above, healthcare authorities in all three countries have the power to enforce compulsory administration of treatments to the affected children. As noted earlier, Uganda has an established law on mandatory immunisation for some vaccine-preventable diseases, including the one in question. Yet, health authorities did not pursue legal enforcement means towards protecting children.

[64] Tutu (n 10) 35–36.

[65] T Metz, 'African and Western Moral Theories in a Bioethical Context' (2010) 10 *Developing World Bioethics* 1.

[66] Ujewe (n 22).

[67] See T Tengaumnuay, 'Parental Authoritarianism and Medical Decision-Making in Thailand: The Need to Limit Parental Authority', in this book.

Rather, community engagement processes were sought to initiate healthcare *indaba* with the affected communities.

The ultimate aim of healthcare *indaba* is to attain harmony in the decision-making process. This determines what or how the decision is reached, especially for children who are unable to self-represent. The communitive process is first established against the background of familial responsibility. The communicative process in the Ugandan case ensures that while the government meets its responsibility for children's healthcare, the decision-making process is in harmony with familial and communal responsibilities for the health and well-being of these same children. Both government and families or communities engage in a communicative process to harmonise their shared responsibilities for the children's health and well-being. The approach taken by Ugandan authorities reflects the non-confrontational and relational approach to healthcare decision-making espoused in South African and Botswanan laws.[68]

In the Nigerian polio case, community leaders assumed responsibility for the affected children and their families. The point of disagreement in this case is the prior absence of a healthcare *indaba* before a decision was made to initiate the mass immunisation programme. It may appear easy to suggest that the government should simply enact a law, as with Uganda, to make polio immunisation compulsory, and then enforce it. However, the resolution process shows the adoption of the healthcare *indaba*, where government and communities/families engaged in a dialogic process to communicate their shared responsibilities for the health of the children. This is exemplified in the community engagement processes that eventually reinstated the polio immunisation programme.

The Tanzanian case follows a similar pattern as above. The community's resistance is underpinned by communal responsibility for the healthcare of the children; likewise the government's decision to initiate the programme. The point of dispute is, however, the absence of a prior communitive process or healthcare *indaba* between the two parties. This presents a disharmony in the decision-making process, which misrepresents the aims of the mass drug administration programme to the community. The role of the healthcare *indaba* in this case would be to restore harmony in the decision-making process, and resolve the situation. This may not necessarily change the decision or alter it significantly, as seen in the Nigerian case, but would ensure that the shared responsibilities for the healthcare of the children are communicated and harmonised.

From an African communal perspective, a review of Charlie Gard's case would show that there is disharmony in the healthcare decision-making process, and the eventual decision endorsed by the British courts. In what should be a shared responsibility for Charlie's healthcare, the doctors assumed absolute responsibility and made the final decision. One thing we do not absolutely know is whether Charlie's life might have been prolonged by the experimental treatment in the

[68] Moyo (n 9).

United States. There are numerous examples of expert evidence in medicine that have been proven wrong by the upward or downward trajectory of the patients' health conditions. A communicative process or healthcare *indaba* leading to the final decision stands a better chance of attaining a decision that all parties involved would endorse.

As a sequel to Charlie's case, in October 2019, the British High Court ruled in favour of a decision by the parents of a five-year-old girl to take her to Italy for treatment, after British doctors ruled that further medical intervention would be futile and attempted to block it.[69] Even if the new treatment does not succeed, it would account for familial responsibility in the health and well-being of the child. The road to health should not simply be about gaining physical well-being, but also crucially a search for harmony in the lives of the children and their entire networks of relationships, starting with their parents.

VI. Conclusion

In the final analysis, the communal responsibility and individual rights approaches to healthcare decision-making for children, as presented in this chapter, may not necessarily be in conflict. The sociocultural context of healthcare in which a child is situated becomes a determining factor for choosing one against the other, but not necessarily. The decision-making process to block further treatment for Charlie Gard would be viewed from the African ethical outlook as taking individual rights as absolute in healthcare. Similarly, it could be argued that there are numerous cases in African healthcare settings where family decisions on behalf of children take communal responsibility too far, and which may not be best for the child. This chapter goes beyond the tension between communal responsibility and individual rights in medical decision-making for children. It points towards adopting harmony as the moral compass in healthcare decision-making for children. This would serve to balance potential extremities in asserting either of the values, and prioritise what should be the best interests of the child in the first instance.

[69] 'Tafida Raqeeb: "Law Should Be Revisited", Say Parents' *BBC News* (5 October 2019) www.bbc.com/news/uk-england-london-49944602.

26

The Relevance of Cultural Competence to Resolving Disputes in Relation to Medical Decisions for Children

BEN GRAY

I. Introduction

The way in which the cases of Charlie Gard and Alfie Evans played out was a tragedy for everyone involved. Both boys were going to die no matter what the legal process, but that process created considerable stress and took up resources in parental time, clinician time and court time, let alone the financial cost, without demonstrable benefit.

Whilst these two cases involved parents wanting to continue treatment and doctors wanting to stop treatment, the issues the cases raise are similar to those where parents are refusing medically recommended treatment.[1]

II. Best Interests is Culture Bound

Central to these cases is the question of 'best interests'. In this chapter I will argue that there is no such thing as the objective best interests of the child. The best interests of the child is culture bound and a better way to approach these processes is by applying the concept of cultural competence.[2] If there is no such thing as the objective best interests of the child, then a declarative judgement will rarely by helpful. Some form of mediation will be needed to find the best way forward, either at the level of parents/clinicians, through referral to a clinical ethics support

[1] B Gray and F Brunger, '(Mis)understandings and Uses of "Culture" in Bioethics Deliberations over Parental Refusal of Treatment: Children with Cancer' (2017) 13 *Clinical Ethics* 55.

[2] JR Betancourt et al, 'Defining Cultural Competence: A Practical Framework for Addressing Racial/Ethnic Disparities in Health and Health Care' (2003) 118 *Public Health Reports* 293.

service, or through court-directed mediation. A judgment by the courts should only be used as a last resort.

I will first define culture and then look at the concept of cultural competence as applied to the practice of medicine. Next I will consider the literature on how we think and argue that unconscious bias is the result of an upbringing within a culture.

III. Definition of Culture

Two definitions of culture that are helpful are those given by Ramsden:

> Being a member of a culture surrounds a person with a set of activities, values and experiences which are considered to be real and normal. People evaluate and define members of other cultural groups according to their own norms.[3]

And by Matsumoto:

> [A] dynamic system of rules – explicit and implicit – established by groups to ensure survival, involving attitudes, values, beliefs, norms, behaviours, shared by a group, but harboured differently by each [individual] within the group communicated across generations, relatively stable but with the potential to change across time.[4]

These highlight that values beliefs and norms are shared but harboured differently, that those who do not share norms are from another cultural group, with the implication that ethics are a feature of a culture.

Hofstede et al[5] have done extensive surveys documenting differences between the cultures of countries. They see the 'moral circle' as being central to culture. Those within our moral circle are part of our culture; those without are 'other'. They also describe culture as existing in many layers and that we may all belong to several different cultures; at a national level, regional, ethnic or linguistic affiliation, gender, generation, social class, work organisational and many others.

A good illustration of the way different cultures have responded to the same case is *Raqeeb v Barts NHS Trust*.[6] This case was about a British-born Bangladeshi girl, Tafida Raqeeb, who suffered an intracranial bleed that left her severely disabled but not in a vegetative state, being artificially fed and ventilated. The British doctors were of the view that treatment was futile and recommended moving to palliative care. However, the family consulted with an Italian hospital who were prepared to take the case on. The doctors there commented: 'As Tafida does not

[3] I Ramsden, 'Teaching Cultural Safety' (1992) 85 *New Zealand Nursing Journal* 21.

[4] DR Matsumoto, *Culture and Psychology*, 2nd edn (Pacific Grove, CA, Brooks Cole Publishing, 2000) 24.

[5] GH Hofstede, GJ Hofstede and M Minkov, *Cultures and Organizations: Software of the Mind – Intercultural Cooperation and its Importance for Survival*, 3rd edn (New York, McGraw-Hill, 2010).

[6] *Raqeeb vs Barts NHS Foundation Trust* CO/2767/2019.

fulfil the criteria for brain-stem death, Italian law does not allow active withdrawal of care.'[7]

In addition, information was provided by the Bangladesh High Commissioner: '[A]ny Bangladeshi national, including doctors, who consented to, or participated in the withdrawal of treatment from Tafida would be guilty of a criminal offence under the law of Bangladesh.'

The weight given to sanctity of life differs from culture to culture. The British doctors felt on balance that continuing active treatment was not appropriate in this case; that her life should end. The Italian and Bangladeshi view was that this would amount to illegal killing. In the chapter in this book from Israel[8] it is noted that 'the bioethical principle of sanctity of life is highly influential in Israeli law'.

In the final judgment Justice MacDonald ruled on a fine balance that the family could take Tafida to Italy to continue active care at the family's own expense. Had some of the detail been different he may have ruled the opposite way. If there is such a thing as objective best interests, how can the test be different in different jurisdictions?

IV. Is there a Common Morality

The idea that there is such a thing as objective best interests is based on the bioethical and legal orthodoxy that there is a Common Morality.[9] The answers to legal/ethical problems are reached by analysis, weighing up the different competing principles. In the case of Tafida Raqeeb, this involved balancing, among other matters, the sanctity of life against any suffering she might endure, and the likelihood of improvement.

A discussion of a common morality without a significant understanding of culture is deficient. Hofstede provides a discussion based on extensive research into the nature of culture, and notes: 'The Universal Declaration of Human Rights adopted in 1948 is based on universalist, individualistic Western values that clearly are not shared by the political leaders nor by the populations of all other parts of the world.'[10]

From a philosophical point of view, Parekh provides a detailed critique of monism and says:

> Human beings are culturally embedded, and a culture not only gives a distinct tone and structure to shared human capacities but also develops new ones of its own. Since cultures mediate and reconstitute human nature in their own different ways, no vision

[7] ibid para 15.
[8] R Gilbar, 'Withholding and Withdrawal of Life-Prolonging Treatment from Young Children in Israel' in this book.
[9] TL Beauchamp and JF Childress, *Principles of Biomedical Ethics*, 7th edn (Oxford, Oxford University Press, 2013).
[10] Hofstede et al (n 5) 429.

> of the good life can be based on an abstract conception of human nature alone … moral life is necessarily embedded in and cannot be isolated from the wider culture. A way of life cannot be judged good or bad without taking full account of the system of meaning, traditions, temperament and the moral and emotional resources of the people involved.[11]

There is, of course, considerable agreement with some moral principles, but it is which priniciples that are included and the relative weighting of different principles that varies. In describing the harm principle, Diekema[12] has argued that best interests sets the bar too high. He lists eight criteria that should be assessed in determining whether the threshold of harm is breached. His eighth criterion is: 'Would most parents agree that the state intervention was reasonable?'

In British law the idea of reasonableness is epitomised by 'the man on the Clapham omnibus'.[13] This expression first appeared in law in 1903[14] and has been continued to be appealed to right up to Brexit,[15] although the Europeans were somewhat bemused by the concept. Madigan[16] reports getting on board a Clapham bus and discovering a racially and economically diverse group of passengers, who of course were not all men, and who did not agree on the meaning of life.

Recourse to 'most parents' or 'the man on the Clapham omnibus' is an appeal to a wide acceptance of the views espoused by either the bioethicist or judge: a proxy for a common morality. The people whose views are most important are the parties to the case, and if they agree that the finding is reasonable, then the case will be resolved. If the parties disagree, then appealing to most parents or 'the man on the Clapham omnibus' is a very weak justification to say the bioethicist or judge is right and the parents are wrong.

Reference to either of these standards is more tenable in a homogeneous society, where indeed most parents do agree and the mythical man (*sic*) on the Clapham omnibus espouses views that are widely agreed. This aligns with the situation described, for example, in Thailand[17] in this book, where there is such agreement that parents should make all these decisions, that such a case has not appeared before the courts.

However, in more diverse societies, what most parents think is reasonable will reflect the culture of the person making the judgement and may diverge significantly from other cultural groups. Such a criterion will inevitably disadvantage those from minority communities.

[11] BC Parekh, *Rethinking Multiculturalism: Cultural Diversity and Political Theory* (Cambridge, MA, Harvard University Press, 2002) 47.

[12] D Diekema, 'Parental Refusals of Medical Treatment: The Harm Principle as Threshold for State Intervention' (2004) 25 *Theoretical Medicine and Bioethics* 243.

[13] N Poole, 'In Praise of the Man on the Clapham Omnibus' (2017) nigelpooleqc.blogspot.com/2017/09/in-praise-of-man-on-clapham-omnibus.html.

[14] *McQuire v Western Morning News Company* [1903].

[15] A Barker, '"Man on the Clapham Omnibus' Rides in to Brexit Talks"' *Financial Times* (7 March 2019) www.ft.com/content/f10bcf8a-40d7-11e9-9bee-efab61506f44.

[16] T Madigan, 'The Man on the Clapham Omnibus Revisited' [2001] no 33 *Philosophy Now*.

[17] T Tengaumnuay, 'Parental Authoritarianism and Medical Decision-Making in Thailand: The Need to Limit Parental Authority', in this book.

As MacIntosh documents in Chapter 16,[18] the Canadian courts provide a clear example of disadvantage to First Nations people. The view of the government was that First Nations people were savages and that their culture rendered them unfit to care for their children. As a result, their children were forcibly removed. First Nations people understandably have little trust in government agencies deciding the best interests of their children. She describes the ways in which the interests of First Nations people have been included in modern legislation, exemplified by the case of JJ where the courts upheld the parent's right to access indigenous treatments and declined to give custody to the hospital.

The contributions to this book on how different countries interpret 'best interests' illustrate the absence of a common morality. In Israel (as in Bangladesh and Italy) the sanctity of life is dominant.[19] In Botswana:

> [T]he best interests of the child never implies that the child and its needs be considered in isolation but, on the contrary, envisions the child in the context of a system of relationships – the totality of the familial arrangements in which a child finds herself or himself.

In China, impacts on the family are included:

> In making such decisions, parents not only consider the interests of the child but also those of the family as a whole, including financial burdens of the family, the interests of other children in the family, the impact on the career of adult family members, the implications for family life, etc.[20]

In sub-Saharan Africa:

> [T]he search for a child's best interests in healthcare is also a quest for the restoration of harmony for the children, and their family and entire networks of relationships. A child's illness disrupts the harmony within a family, and restoring the child's health positively impacts on the family's wellbeing. If the child dies, for instance, restoration is sought through the mourning process. Medical decision-making on behalf of the child would involve key members of the child's family in a healing *indaba*, beginning with the parents.[21]

If it is accepted that there is no common morality, then the views of clinicians, bioethicists and judges can be seen for what they are: the assessment of experienced and wise people of what they think the right thing to do is. It does not suggest that their views lack value but that they are inevitably influenced by their cultural background. The recognition of the importance of cultural background in determining outcomes in healthcare led to the development of cultural competence. This may

[18] C MacIntosh, 'Decisionally Incapable Children and Medical Treatment Choices in Canada', in this book.

[19] Gilbar (n 8).

[20] D Chunyan, 'Medical Decision-Making on Behalf of Children in China: A Multidimensional Analysis of Parental Authoritarianism', in this book.

[21] S Ujewe, 'Making Decisions for Children in Healthcare and Medical Research: African Communal Responsibility or Individual Rights?', in this book.

be a useful framework to address disputes on the care of children between clinicians, parents and courts.

V. Cultural Competence

Cultural competence as a concept of providing care respectful of cultural difference has been widely adopted within Western medicine.[22] It developed because of acknowledgement of the worse health outcomes that minority cultural groups suffered: New Zealand Māori;[23] ethnic minorities in the UK;[24] people with disabilities; lesbian, gay, bisexual and transgender people; and racial and ethnic people in the United States.[25] I will discuss this from my experience in the New Zealand setting.

In New Zealand the Health Practitioners Competence Assurance Act[26] requires registration authorities to do three things: to set standards of clinical competence, cultural competence and ethical conduct.

Whilst cultural competence is not defined within the act, each of the registration authorities has developed statements on cultural competence/cultural safety. The New Zealand Medical Council Statement on Cultural Safety has a number of pertinent sections:

> 8 When considering the needs of your patients, cultural safety requires you to reflect on, take ownership of, and consider in your practice:
>
> a. The effect of your own culture, history and attitudes.
>
> b. The ongoing development of your own cultural awareness and an understanding of how your social-cultural influences inform biases that impact your interactions with patients, whānau, and colleagues.
>
> c. Consciously not imposing your cultural values and practices on patients.
>
> 9 Cultural Safety requires you to engage in ongoing self-reflection and self-awareness. This includes: …
>
> d. A respect for your patients' cultural beliefs, values and practices.

[22] Medical Council of New Zealand, 'Statement on Cultural Safety' (Wellington, New Zealand, 2019) available from www.mcnz.org.nz/assets/standards/b71d139dca/Statement-on-cultural-safety.pdf; Queensland Government, 'Organisational Cultural Competency Framework' (2012) www.health.qld.gov.au/multicultural/contact_us/framework.asp; JR Betancourt, AR Green and JE Carrillo, 'Cultural Competence in Health Care: Emerging Frameworks and Practical Approaches' (Commonwealth Fund, 2002) 576.

[23] G Disney et al, 'Changing Ethnic Inequalities in Mortality in New Zealand over 30 Years: Linked Cohort Studies with 68.9 Million Person-Years of Follow-Up' (2017) 15 *Population Health Metrics* 15.

[24] P Bentley et al, 'Cultural Diversity Training for UK Healthcare Professionals: A Comprehensive Nationwide Cross-Sectional Survey' (2008) 8 *Clinical Medicine* 493.

[25] M Butler et al, 'Improving Cultural Competence to Reduce Health Disparities' (Agency for Healthcare Research and Quality, 2016).

[26] New Zealand Health Practitioner's Competence Assurance Act (2003).

e. Understanding that your patients' cultural beliefs, values and practices influence their perceptions of health, illness and disease; how they respond to and manage their health; and their treatment decisions and interactions with doctors, other health care professionals and the wider health system.
f. Understanding that culture is dynamic and evolves over time, extends beyond ethnicity, and that patients and their whānau may identify with multiple cultural groupings at any one point in time.

10c Develop diagnoses and formulate treatment plans in partnership with patients that fit within their cultural contexts, and are balanced by the need to follow the best clinical pathway.

Central to good cross-cultural care is the development of an agreed management plan as described in the Calgary Cambridge guide to the consultation that we use to teach medical students.[27] This gives detailed instruction on how to reach such a plan based around the principles above. Where there is disagreement between clinician and doctor, then negotiation is needed to find a way forward that may continue over several consultations. The ability to do this well is predicated on the clinician having the humility to accept that their view of what might be the right course is not the only view. It is inevitably distressing for parents if clinicians (or ethicists or judges) tell them that their understanding of the best interests of their child is wrong. By comparison, being able to acknowledge that there are two views as to what might be best, and that this will require ongoing discussions to find the way forward, will go a long way towards maintaining trust and a working relationship.

An important part of developing that humility is understanding the flaws in our thinking and the way in which we all have both conscious and unconscious biases.

VI. Thinking Fast and Slow: Cognitive and Unconscious Biases

In his book *Thinking Fast and Slow* Kahneman[28] challenges the underlying presumption of court deliberation that it is possible to reach an objective unbiased opinion on the facts presented. He argued that:

> [I]n the 1970s the social sciences shared basic assumptions about human nature; that people are generally rational and their thinking is normally sound, and that emotions … explain most of the occasions when people depart from rationality.[29]

[27] JD Silverman, SM Kurtz and J Draper, 'Calgary Cambridge Guide to the Medical Interview – Communication Process' (1998) www.gp-training.net/training/communication_skills/calgary/calgary.pdf.
[28] D Kahneman, *Thinking, Fast and Slow*, 1st edn (New York, Farrar, Straus and Giroux, 2011).
[29] ibid 8.

In talking of an objective best interests standard, the courts[30] appear to be reflecting the assumption that people are rational, and in the decision on *Great Ormond Street Hospital v Yates & Ors*[31] the paragraph

> the parents' … views may have particular value because they know the patient and how he reacts so well; although the court needs to be mindful that the views of any parents may, very understandably, be coloured by their own emotion or sentiment

appears to reflect the second assumption.

Kahneman's thesis is that the way in which we think is far from these assumptions and falls into two systems, the fast and the slow. The fast system is what we do most of the day 'without thinking' and is inevitably affected by many inbuilt biases. Slow thinking is when we consciously address problems that do not have 'obvious' (fast thinking) solutions. He argues that it is hard to sustain slow thinking and that most of our judgements are affected by the biases that come from fast thinking.

A useful definition of unconscious bias is:

> Implicit or unconscious bias happens by our brains making incredibly quick judgments and assessments of people and situations without us realising. Our biases are influenced by our background, cultural environment and personal experiences. We may not even be aware of these views and opinions, or be aware of their full impact and implications.[32]

These biases apply to judges. A study of 1,112 judicial rulings from parole boards in Israel recorded the rulings in relation to the two daily food breaks. The percentage of favourable rulings dropped gradually from 65 per cent to nearly zero within each decision session and returned abruptly to around 65 per cent after the break.[33]

It is also the foundation of the extensive literature on unconscious bias that documents the pervasive biases that we all have as a result of our upbringing … our culture. This has been applied particularly to sexual and racial inequalities. In a study of interruptions of Justices of the American Supreme Court, Jacobi and Schweers concluded that: 'In the last 12 years, during which women made up, on average, 24% of the bench, 32% of interruptions were of the female justices, but only 4% were by the female justices.'[34] There is no rational reason why women should be interrupted more often.

A further rarely discussed source of bias is the emotional life of judges. Implicit in the statement that parents' views may be coloured by emotion is that the judge's

[30] *Great Ormond Street Hospital v Yates & Ors* [2017] EWHC 972 (Fam) (11 April 2017) 11; *Manitoba (Director of Child & Family Services) v C(A)* 2009 SCC 30 [82] [*AC*]. The Supreme Court wrote: 'The application of an objective "best interests" standard to infants and very young children is uncontroversial.'

[31] *Great Ormond Street Hospital v Yates & Ors* [2017] EWHC 972 (Fam) (11 April 2017) 39ix.

[32] Advance Higher Education, 'Unconscious Bias' (2019) www.ecu.ac.uk/guidance-resources/employment-and-careers/staff-recruitment/unconscious-bias.

[33] S Danziger, J Levav and L Avnaim-Pesso, 'Extraneous Factors in Judicial Decisions' (2011) 108 *Proceedings of the National Academy of Sciences of the USA* 6889.

[34] T Jacobi and D Schweers, 'Justice, Interrupted: The Effect of Gender, Ideology, and Seniority at Supreme Court Oral Arguments' (2017) 103 *Virginia Law Review* 1379.

views are not coloured by emotion. Whilst it is a work of fiction, Ian McEwan in *The Children Act*[35] describes the way in which the emotional life of a judge impacts on her decision in a case of an adolescent Jehovah's Witness boy who is refusing a blood transfusion. Of course, judges are human and have emotional lives and their judgments will inevitably be affected by this, even if only unconsciously.

An important further reason against the value of the concept of a common morality is that even if there were a common morality, the nature of unconscious biases are such that anyone trying to espouse such a morality would inevitably reflect the morality of their own culture.

VII. Uncertainty

Another reason to approach these decisions with humility is the often significant level of uncertainty about the 'facts' of the case.

There is always uncertainty around prognosis. For Charlie Gard and Alfie Evans the medical evidence had a high degree of certainty that treatment was futile, although the parents did not entirely agree with this assessment. In cases of parental refusal of treatment the issues around prognosis are more critical. The issue of the need for acute transfusion in a child of Jehovah's Witness parents is exceptional in that there is often high certainty that in the absence of transfusion the child will die. In New Zealand this situation is no longer the subject of court deliberation because of an amendment to the Care of Children Act (2004) that expressly gives authority to transfuse in this acute setting. In most cases of parental refusal of treatment the decision is based upon a percentage likelihood of survival with or without treatment, based on published literature. In our study of parental refusal of treatment in children with cancer, nearly all of the children had been partially treated, and therefore information on likely outcome was much less reliable.

Whilst there is significant information about the effectiveness of treatments, the treatment of each child is likely to be unique; an iterative process that is dependent on measured response to treatments already given, the presence or absence of side effects from the treatment and the level of trust the parents have in the treating team. In his resource for training in these scenarios Curran[36] highlights many of these complexities. Treatment in most cases continues over a long period of time and requires significant cooperation from the parents (attending for treatments and testing) and the child (assenting to management such as insertion of intravenous lines, lying still for imaging, etc).

[35] I McEwan, *The Children Act: A Novel*, 1st US edn (New York, Nan A Talese/Doubleday, 2014).

[36] TR Curran, '"Our Son's Cancer Is Gone. Why Can't We Stop Treatment?"' in AE Caruso Brown, TR Hobart and CB Morrow (eds), *Bioethics, Public Health, and the Social Sciences for the Medical Professions: An Integrated, Case-Based Approach* (New York, Springer, 2019).

The second area of uncertainty is how the parents will respond to the court judgment. In our study of parental refusal of treatment of cancer where cultural or religious reasons were mentioned in relation to the refusal, nine of the twenty-four cases fled as a result of the court order and received no treatment.[37] A fifteen-year-old Hmong child in California whose parents did not agree with the proposed treatment for her ovarian cancer forcibly resisted:

> When police first removed the girl from her parents' custody for an initial round of chemotherapy, they were pelted with stones and had to wrest a knife from the father, who threatened to kill himself.[38]

In the case of Oshin Kiszko, a six-year-old boy with a rare brain tumour, a court order was made mandating treatment and the family passports were retained to prevent them leaving. His first round of chemotherapy was delivered after the first court order, and during that treatment 'the parents hung a "forced chemotherapy" sign over his bed and refused to help the treatment team to comfort him when he became upset'.[39]

Optimal success of the treatment is impossible without at least some cooperation. As a result there is compounding of the uncertainty of prognosis and uncertainty of how the parents respond. In theory a lack of cooperation could be overcome by the court granting guardianship to the treating team, but this would only work with infants, and the resulting friction is likely to affect the outcome.[40] Either the parents are not present at all, which is likely to affect the emotional health of the child, or if they are present, treatment will be made more difficult by the impaired relationships.

The outcome of treatment is likely to be worse if it is provided against the wishes of parents and/or children.

The third area of uncertainty is those factors that are unmeasurable. How can we predict or quantify suffering? Any such prediction is likely to be significantly affected by the suffering experience of the person making the judgement. Dignity is another concept that is acknowledged as important, for example in the Council of Europe's Convention on Human Rights and Dignity of the Human Being, but is unmeasurable and varies with culture. Justice MacDonald traversed these issues in *Raqeeb v Barts NHS Foundation Trust*:

> The concept of human dignity as an element of the best interests analysis is however, not without difficulty. The term 'human dignity' does not lend itself to precise definition

[37] Gray and Brunger (n 1).

[38] M Arax, 'Cancer Case Ignites Culture Clash: Medicine: Hmong Parents Refuse to Agree to Court-Ordered Chemotherapy for Teen-Age Daughter. They Fear Treatment by Doctors Will Make Her Infertile and Unmarriageable' *LA Times* (21 November 1994) articles.latimes.com/1994-11-21/news/mn-65509_1_hmong-community.

[39] BJ Richards and ME Okninski, 'The Best Interests of a Child: A Tragedy in Three Parts (CAHS v Kiszko & Anor [2016] FCWA 19, CAHS v Kiszko & Anor [2016] FCWA 34 and CAHS v Kiszko & Anor [2016] FCWA 75)' (2017) 25 *Medical Law Review* 138, 146.

[40] ibid.

> and there is no universal agreement as to its meaning. The concept of human dignity must, accordingly, contain a significant element of subjectivity and thus be influenced by, for example, the religious or cultural context in which the question is being considered.[41]

The term human dignity may not lend itself to precise definition, but that does not make it unimportant, and the parents are likely to be the most reliable judge of what dignity might mean for their child.

If a judgment is based on uncertain facts then whether the judgment is right is inevitably uncertain. The inherent uncertainty in these cases is another reason for humility

VIII. Approaches to Dispute Resolution

A review by Austin and Huxtable 'revealed five key processes for resolving disagreements about the care of critically ill children: discussions between families and clinicians; second opinion experts; clinical ethics committees; mediation; and court proceedings'.[42]

Successful resolution of these disputes through any of these processes depend on functional relationships and trust.

Weinstock's work on the ethics of compromise[43] is broader than decisions in medicine, but the principles he outlines apply well. He contrasts 'modus vivendi' or negotiation decision-making and compromise decision-making. A modus vivendi[44] decision comes about as a result of the balance of forces; each side exerts power to get their own way. In the cases of Charlie Gard and Alfie Evans, the doctors tried to use the power of the law to force the parents to accept their view, and the parents used the power of social media to counter this. Such a process is low on respect and trust. By contrast, a process seeking a compromise requires a relationship of trust:

> Compromise will be made easier where trust exists between the deliberating parties. Trust exists where all parties believe that those with whom they are negotiating are not ill-disposed toward them, or their core interests and values. If I feel as if someone is favourably disposed and respectful toward my most important commitments, I may be

[41] *Raqeeb v Barts NHS Foundation Trust* CO/2767/2019 [176].

[42] L Austin and R Huxtable, *Resolving Disagreements about the Care of Critically Ill Children: Evaluating Existing Processes and Setting the Research Agenda* (Oxford, Hart Publishing, 2019).

[43] D Weinstock, 'The Ethics of Compromise' in C Rostbøll and T Scavenius (eds), *Compromise and Disagreement in Contemporary Political Theory* (New York, Routledge, 2018); D Weinstock, 'On the Possibility of Principled Moral Compromise' (2013) 16 *Critical Review of International Social and Political Philosophy* 537.

[44] D Weinstock, 'Compromise, Pluralism, and Deliberation' (2017) 20 *Critical Review of International Social and Political Philosophy* 636.

> disposed to define those core commitments more parsimoniously than if I feel that my deliberation partners are not well-disposed toward me.[45]

The value of abandoning the idea of a common morality and objective best interests is underlined here. If there is no objective best interests the way forward will be found through compromise of both parties, rather than further analysis to find the best interest. That discussion will be more successful if clinicians approach it with humility that their view of what might be best cannot be the only answer.

> Now, trust is easier to achieve with respect to a given disagreement where there is already a history of trust between deliberating parties. Conversely, where prior deliberations have given rise to suspicion on the part of the deliberating parties, subsequent deliberations may be more difficult to set on a course favourable to compromise.[46]

A good illustration of the importance of trust is in Brown's case study of an Amish boy with leukaemia.[47] The main opponent of treatment was the maternal grandfather who had had a previous unsatisfactory experience with doctors who had insisted on treatment of a relative that they later admitted was futile. If deliberations are proving difficult, then addressing how to improve trust and relationship may enable parties to find a way forward. The best people to find that way are those most intimately involved with the detail; the parents and the responsible clinicians. As Austin and Huxtable[48] discuss, one process for resolving disagreement is formal mediation. The other processes that they describe could be used either for mediation or for declarative judgement. A clinician giving a second opinion could either see the role as reanalysing what is in the child's best interest, or they could instead function as a mediator, understanding what had undermined trust and relationship and facilitating the finding of a compromise. Similarly the role of clinical ethics support services vary as to how they approach their task. In 2007 a significant minority always recommended a best course of action.[49] Conversely, Zaner describes his role as a mediator:

> [T]he whole point of any such consultation … is to help those who must decide come to understand what it is they face when they have to make decisions, which decisions will be faced in given circumstances, and then learn to live with the aftermath of whatever they eventually decide to do. At most, it has seemed to me, the consultant's job is to help individuals whose situation it is think through their circumstances as thoroughly as possible, then help them understand what must be decided and what aftermath can be expected. It is not to make a recommendation, neither to the physician nor to the

[45] Weinstock (n 44) 42.

[46] Weinstock (n 44) 72.

[47] AE Caruso Brown, 'At the Intersection of Faith, Culture, and Family Dynamics: A Complex Case of Refusal of Treatment for Childhood Cancer' (2017) 28 *Journal of Clinical Ethics* 228.

[48] Austin and Huxtable (n 46) 222.

[49] E Fox, S Myers and RA Pearlman, 'Ethics Consultation in United States Hospitals: A National Survey' (2007) 7 *American Journal of Bioethics* 13.

> patient or family. Deciding (ie, learning which decision or recommendation is best for them) is not my business; it is theirs, just as is the situation theirs and the problems and issues theirs.[50]

In this quote he raises the important question of when these issues are anyone else's business other than those intimately involved. Clearly, if there is any question of whether the parents are abusive in relation to any other issue apart from the critical illness, the state has an important role. In the absence of these concerns, if there is no such thing as an objective best interest, when should the responsibility for making a decision be with anyone other than the parents and clinicians? Ujewe's description of the importance of achieving harmony align well with this approach:

> Ethical harmony is attained when, through open-ended deliberation, parties involved can understand, view and/or appreciate issues from others' moral outlooks. … In the context of healthcare decision-making for children, solidarity and harmony motivate the communicative or *indaba* process, so that the outcome is not predetermined by the stronger voice or actor. The final decision remains indeterminate and harmoniously reached through appreciation of the shared responsibilities of all parties in upholding the best interests of the child. The path towards ensuring this best interest is establishing harmony in and through the decision-making process. It presupposes the inclusiveness of all relevant voices in healthcare decision-making for children, as an overarching attribute.[51]

IX. What Role Should the Courts Play?

Several commentators have noted that these decisions are moral rather than legal and that the courts are no better placed in making these judgements than those intimately involved with the case. In discussing the case of Oshin Kiszko, Richards observed that:

> What makes these questions particularly troubling for a court is that they are properly characterised as social, moral, or ethical questions as opposed to legal ones. When the traditional tools of the court are legal, the decision-maker must adapt these tools to a job for which they are, potentially, poorly suited.[52]

In the 2019 Reith Lectures, Jonathan Sumption observed in relation to the Gard case:

> Although the decision whether to continue treatment was a matter of clinical judgement the clinicians involved were unwilling to make that judgement on their own as I suspect that they would have done a generation before. They wanted the endorsement of a judge. This was not because judges were thought to have any special clinical

[50] RM Zaner, 'A Comment on Community Consultation' (2007) 7 *American Journal of Bioethics* 30.
[51] Ujewe (n 21).
[52] Richards and Okninski (n 43).

> or moral qualifications that the doctors lacked, it was because judges have a power of absolution. By passing the matter to the Courts, the doctors sheltered themselves from legal liability.[53]

The option of appealing to the courts will always remain. In Brown's case study,[54] when the grandfather asks what would happen if they refused treatment, the clinician replied gently that they would seek a court order to enforce treatment. Similarly, Gillam in describing the Zone of Parental Discretion, describes 'doctors standing firm and forcefully stating what they believe must be done for the child's sake (with institutional support, where available), relying on the considerable influence they have over parents'. As discussed above, such an approach has the risk of undermining trust and disrupting the relationship, but can contribute to achieving a better outcome.

If the case appears before the courts the tradition has been predominantly to make a judgment as to the best interests of the child. An alternative approach is to encourage mediation. As Justice Francis said in *Gard*:

> I have already expressed the opinion that I believe that it would, in all cases like this, be helpful for there to be some form of Issues Resolution Hearing or other form of mediation where the parties can have confidential conversations to see what common ground can be reached between them. I believe that that type of hearing, be it Judge led or some other form of private mediation, would have led to a greater understanding between the parents and the clinical team in this case.[55]

X. Conclusion

Justice Francis[56] has argued that the court's task is 'exercising its independent and objective judgment in the child's best interests'. In arguing that ethics is culture bound and given our understanding of human thinking, my view is that this is an impossibility; there is no such thing as an objective best interest. The judgment is inevitably influenced by the unconscious biases of the judge. Many, if not most, of the matters included in the judgment (prognosis, likely side effects, the extent of suffering) are not objective facts; they are opinions held by those expressing them, again influenced by their cultural and unconscious biases. Implicit in making a judgment is the presumption that the proposed course of action will be carried out and will have the predicted outcome. As discussed above, this presumption is far from valid.

[53] J Sumption, 'Law's Expanding Empire' *BBC Radio* (2019) downloads.bbc.co.uk/radio4/reith2019/Reith_2019_Sumption_lecture_1.pdf.

[54] Caruso Brown (n 50).

[55] *Great Ormond Hospital v Yates, Gard and Gard* [2017] EWHC 972 (Fam) Case No FD17P00103 (2017) High Court of Justice Family Division, [130].

[56] ibid [11].

The question the court should be addressing is not what the right course is but how to resolve the dispute between the clinicians and the parents. There are significant risks in trying to impose a way forward that were well illustrated by both of these cases. All efforts should be put towards improving the relationship and trust between the clinicians and the parents, and finding a compromise that is acceptable to all. As Justice Francis said:

> I am not saying that it [some form of mediation] would necessarily have led to a resolution, but I think in many such cases it would and I would like to think that in future cases like this such attempts can be made.[57]

[57] ibid [130].

27

Legal and Cultural Differences in Medical Decision-Making on Behalf of Very Young Children

IMOGEN GOOLD AND CRESSIDA AUCKLAND

This collection brings together analyses of disputes between parents and doctors over the treatment of seriously ill young children from more than twenty-five jurisdictions across six continents. While it is impossible to do justice to all of the themes or patterns that emerge from the contributions in this book, in this chapter, we hope to draw out some of the key themes, and to contextualise these within the social and cultural background of the countries discussed. We begin by exploring the reasons for the lack of reported case-law in many of the jurisdictions, which may be explained both by some countries' values being less likely to give rise to conflict in the first place, and by the existence of alternative mechanisms for resolving such disputes which avoid an adversarial court process. We go on to consider how the role of parents in such decisions is conceptualised, and the differing limits placed of parental authority in the countries examined, with different thresholds to be met before the court can become involved and override a parent's decision. Finally, we examine differences in how the courts in different countries are applying common standards such as 'best interests', and the challenges they face in doing so.

I. Lack of Case-Law

Writing in a jurisdiction where there is regular, high-profile and highly fraught litigation on these issues, one very notable feature from our perspective was the reported *lack* of cases coming to court in many jurisdictions.[1] Indeed, some

[1] Contributors from Greece, Hong Kong, Scotland, Botswana, Sweden and Ireland, amongst others, noted that it is rare (in some cases almost to the point of no litigation at all) for such disputes to be taken before the courts.

contributors reported that there were few, if any, notable cases involving disputes between parents and medical practitioners that ended up requiring court intervention to resolve them. England and Wales stood apart as a jurisdiction in which conflicts between doctors and parents regularly find their way to court in a manner quite alien to other jurisdictions, to such an extent that in some there is not even the mechanism for bringing disputes before the court. For example, there are no legislative provisions that directly regulate parental consent to medical treatment of children in Botswana at all, which Admark Moyo suggests partly explains the scarcity of case-law on the subject.[2] Pernilla Leviner, writing on the Swedish approach, made similar observations, noting that:

> The simple answer to these questions is that we really do not know much more than the little anecdotal information that healthcare providers relate. No similar cases have been tried in a Swedish court and as will become clear in this chapter, it is also unlikely that such cases would be brought to court due to the lack of such mechanisms in our legal system.[3]

Only Australia and the United States appeared to have similar levels of judicial treatment of such conflicts.

This naturally poses the question of why there should be such differences, the answer to which is offered to some degree by the chapters in this collection. While some regional trends can be discerned, other explanations are quite jurisdiction specific. Nonetheless two explanations for the differing levels of litigation can, broadly speaking, be discerned, which will be examined in the following sections. Firstly, disputes of this kind may be less likely to arise in the first place because the cultural context of the jurisdiction is less likely to give rise to conflict. Secondly, even if disputes do arise, the onus (either culturally or legally) of some jurisdictions is on other mechanisms for resolving it, rather than relying on an adversarial legal system as in England and Wales.

A. Lower Levels of Conflict

Explanations for this absence of litigation often revealed much about how background cultural and social context shapes relationships between lay people, medics and the state. We might speculate that the level of value-pluralism varies between jurisdictions, and where there is greater cultural homogeneity, and arguably a higher chance of shared values, then there is less likelihood of conflict over the right course of action for a child, and so such disputes are less likely to emerge in the first place. Moyo makes this observation in regard to Botswana, where he suggests that the presence of only one major ethnic group (the Tswana),

[2] A Moyo, 'Parental Responsibility and Medical Decision-Making in Southern Africa: A Comparative Analysis of South Africa and Botswana', in this book.

[3] P Leviner, 'Who Has the Final Word? On Trust and Legal Uncertainty Within the Swedish Healthcare System', in this book.

combines with 'the socialisation of citizens along communitarian lines' to leave only 'limited room for the clash of diverse values'. Hence he suggests, 'it could be that the prevailing uniform value system limits the possibility of conflicts between parents themselves'.[4] By contrast, value-pluralism is a feature of countries such England and Wales and the United States, as well as a much stronger commitment to individualism and individual liberty, and this might go some way to explaining the levels of conflict in those jurisdictions. This tendency is likely exacerbated by the relative lack of focus on communal or collaborative decision-making in the adversarial court system once the matter passes beyond a hospital's own mechanisms for mediating conflicts between doctors and parents.

A more clearly discernible correlation that emerges from the chapters in this collection is that highly communal cultures often had low levels of litigation. For example, both contributors from African countries noted a communitarian approach to decision-making in the jurisdictions considered, which, coupled with a commitment to resolving disputes by avoiding conflict, meant disputes rarely found their way into the courts. This was bolstered by the central position occupied by the family in some African countries. For example, as Moyo comments, both South Africa and Botswana

> are largely inhabited by ethnic groups that are predominantly communitarian and therefore view children as an integral or inseparable part of the family. Communitarian cultures and societies pose a serious challenge to the individualistic nature of rights, particularly those of children. Children's rights potentially clash with African cultural ideology because the latter emphasises collectivism, reciprocal duties of support and restraint on individual rights. Hence, the preservation of group identity is thought to be in the interests of the child and the interests of the family. There is an attempt to limit conflict at all costs, even though this may mean a violation of children's rights to medical treatment and access to healthcare services.[5]

Samuel Ujewe suggests that this communitarianism is a feature of the 'African ethics outlook' wherein

> communal responsibility takes centre stage and the moral frame of reference is underpinned by the network of communal relationships. The ethic of communal responsibility emphasises a preoccupation with the well-being of whole communities or societies; not simply of individuals constituting them. It motivates individual members to seek the good of the community or society as a whole, in virtue of which they also seek their own good and build a firm basis for a sustained well-being.

Consequently, he explains, '[r]restoring the health of the family member, especially if they are a child … cannot be a matter for doctor and patient alone: it demands the participation of the entire community'.[6]

[4] SJ Ujewe, 'Making Decisions for Children in Healthcare and Medical Research: African Communal Responsibility or Individual Rights?', in this book.

[5] ibid.

[6] ibid, quoting from B. Bujo, *Foundations of an African Ethic: Beyond the Universal Claims of Western Morality* (New York, Crossroad Publishing Company, 2001) 46–47.

Sweden, too, showed a commitment to consensus-building, but the foundation for this differed somewhat. Leviner explains that in Sweden, the focus is on the responsibility of the healthcare provider, rather than on individual rights, but that this sits against a background of a 'high degree of trust' of individuals for one another and for public institutions.[7]

How central a role the family played in a culture also affected levels of litigation. High levels of litigation were reported in England and Wales, the United States and Australia, all of which give cultural (as well as legal) prominence to individualism. By contrast, setting aside Sweden (where the individual is very much the key figure), for the most part, lower levels of litigation correlated with the family unit holding a vital place in the jurisdiction's culture. Numerous contributors discussed the role of family in making such decisions, and this often explained the lack of cases, albeit for different reasons.

Thailand, Peru and China are countries which attach great importance to the family culturally, and this manifests itself as 'parental authoritarianism', where the parents' decision about a child generally holds sway, even where medical professionals disagree. As Thitinant Tengaumnuay argues, in Thailand this explains the lack of judicial intervention in parents' decision-making, and the lack of 'legal provisions setting particular checks or reviews on parental decisions concerning their children's medical treatment'.[8] Thai doctors often remain passive in the face of parental decisions with which they do not agree, and in the view of Tengaumanuay 'would not provide health treatment that opposes the parents' decision'. Similarly in China, medics largely defer to parental decisions, hence avoiding court battles, because those decisions are, as Ding Chunyan argues,

> often made based on familism or 'family-paternalism' … [where] in making such decisions, parents not only consider the interests of the child but also those of the family as a whole, including financial burdens of the family, the interests of other children in the family, the impact on the career of adult family members, the implications for family life, etc.[9]

She goes on to explain that 'Chinese parents often see their children as property that they own, and this view is even shared by judges in adjudication', and this results in parents having a high degree of control in situations where there would otherwise be conflict and disagreement. Medics tend to yield rather than oppose parental wishes. Similarly in Peru, Paula Siverino Bavio reported that doctors tend to avoid conflict and defer to parental desires to continue treatment for fear of being regarded as having illegally failed to treat. This, she suggests, has led to medical staff practising 'defensive medicine'.[10]

[7] Leviner (n 3).

[8] T Tengaumnuay, 'Parental Authoritarianism and Medical Decision-Making in Thailand: The Need to Limit Parental Authority', in this book and D Chunyan, 'Medical Decision-Making on Behalf of Children in China: A Multidimensional Analysis of Parental Authoritarianism', in this book.

[9] Chunyan (n 8).

[10] P Siverino, 'Who Decides the Best Interests of the Child in the End-of-Life Process? A Look at the Peruvian and Argentine Reality', in this book.

In some jurisdictions, the primacy of the family in such decisions is protected via its legal provisions, which likely has an effect on how these disputes proceed in practice. In addition to Thailand noted above, where the doctor does not have any legal standing to bring a case to court if they disagree with the parents' assessment of their child's best interests,[11] in Belgium, the medical professionals 'must in principle respect the decision of the parents', and where parents refuse a proposed treatment, the physician may face prosecution for performing it. It is also the case that a physician who refuses to perform a treatment that the parents request, particularly one that may potentially prolong or save life, may face criminal prosecution (as well as potential civil liability and sanctions). Only in exceptional cases where parents refuse a life-saving therapy can a doctor fail to accept that decision.[12] In Ireland, meanwhile, the centrality of the family is recognised through its constitutional provisions. The Irish Constitution declares the family to be 'the natural primary and fundamental unit group of Society, and as a moral institution possessing inalienable and imprescriptible rights, antecedent and superior to all positive law',[13] and this, explain John Lombard and Lydia Bracken, creates a presumption that the best interests of the child will be met by the marital family. This presumption can be displaced only in 'exceptional cases', with the result that, in practice, parental decisions are generally followed. As Lombard and Bracken comment, the strong protection of parental decision-making

> means that where there is a dispute between the medical profession and the parents as to the treatment of the child, the medical profession will often have little choice but to bow to the parent's decision or to seek judicial intervention. In line with the constitutional framework, court orders are only sought in the most serious of cases, where there is a dispute as to the best course of action for the child.[14]

It is important to note, however, that this presumption applies only where the parents are *married*; where the child's parents are unmarried, the primary consideration is the child's best interests, rather than the parents' marital status.

The centrality of family has different implications in other jurisdictions. According to Ujewe, '[i]n African settings, the family is recognised as a fundamental and highly valued institution', yet as we have seen this leads to a communal, consensus-driven approach, rather than parental authoritarianism.[15] Where in Chinese and Thai culture, this family-centrism affords the family final decision-making power to achieve what is best for the family, in African nations such as South Africa, Moyo suggests it avoids conflict (and hence litigation) because

> the individual rights or interests of the child and those of the family are symbiotic and inseparably interwoven. This approach stands in sharp contrast to international and

[11] Tengaumunauy (n 8).

[12] I Boone, 'Parental Rights, Best Interests and Significant Harm: Medical Decision-Making on Behalf of Children in Belgium', in this book.

[13] Art 41.1.1° of the Irish Constitution.

[14] J Lombard and L Bracken,'Medical Decision-Making on Behalf of Children in Ireland', in this book.

[15] Ujewe (n 4).

> domestic laws that emphasise the primacy of the child's rights and interests. Given that the child is not seen as an atomistic individual living outside the realm of relationships with others, the possibility of conflicts between parental interests and children's interests is limited.[16]

Daisy Cheung describes the approach in Hong Kong, with its obviously strong Chinese influences, as a 'moderate' familist position. While the family does take a central role in decision-making in Hong Kong, and decisions are taken by the family as a whole, the emphasis is on 'harmonious interdependence'. 'The preferred arrangement in Hong Kong is', she explains, 'for the patient and the family to make a decision as one unit'. The key role of the family discourages physicians from challenging decisions made by the family, particularly given the desire to promote and maintain familial harmony and integrity.[17]

In other jurisdictions, meanwhile, contributors explained that there was little conflict because of a tendency for parents to defer to the opinions of the medical profession. In Spain, for example, Monica Navarro-Michel suggests there have been no cases of parents challenging physicians in court because of the very high degree of respect and trust that physicians enjoy there.[18] A tendency for parents to defer to medical professionals in Malaysia was similarly offered as an explanation for the lack of case-law in that jurisdiction. Calvin Ho and Sharon Kaur comment that:

> Malaysian parents may be reluctant to challenge decisions made by healthcare providers. There is some evidence that parents in most instances defer to recommendations of doctors. A 1999 study on withdrawal and limitation of life-support in paediatric intensive care at the University of Malaya Medical Centre found that families often requested paediatricians to do what was best for their children. A more recent multinational study on resuscitation decisions for extremely preterm infants reported that 72 per cent of Malaysian respondents felt that physicians should make the final decision.[19]

That said, when parents *do* disagree with doctors, Ho and Kaur suggest that:

> Healthcare providers are generally respectful of parental autonomy in deciding for their children and of familial integrity, which court intervention will disrupt. On exceptional occasions when healthcare providers do threaten to take legal action due to real concerns that their paediatric patient will suffer serious harm, our experience has been that parents have tended to relent on their decision.[20]

However, they observe that there have in fact been very few formal legal challenges to medical disagreement with the parents' wishes. They explain this by reference to the 'combination of … ethics committees and complementary arrangements

[16] Moyo (n 2).
[17] D Cheung, 'Medical Decision-Making on Behalf of Minors: The Hong Kong Context', in this book.
[18] M Navarro-Michel, 'Young Children and Healthcare Decisions in Spain: Who Decides?', in this book.
[19] CWL Ho and S Kaur, 'Parental Rights, Best Interests and Significant Harms: Singapore and Malaysia perspectives on Medical Decision-Making on Behalf of Children', in this book.
[20] ibid.

including the active facilitation of obtaining a second opinion and a mediation mechanism', which they suggest 'appear to have been effective in preventing a disagreement from escalating into a full-scale legal battle'.[21] Therefore it seems in this jurisdiction, the cultural factors cut in a number of directions, protecting familial decisions, but also supporting deference to the medical profession, combining with a system geared towards collaborative decision-making and consensus-building.

Deference to the medical profession is also once again reflected in the legal position in some jurisdictions. For example, Swiss law supports deference to medical opinion, with the Federal Supreme Court of Switzerland taking the view that medical opinion is presumptively compatible with the best interests of the child.[22] Jean-Frédéric Ménard meanwhile notes that in contrast to English law (where parents are default decision-makers), in the French system 'physicians are the default decision-makers' – a difference that, he argues, 'has the potential to influence outcomes deeply'.[23] While parents in France do have a 'margin of appreciation in making decisions for their children', and their decisions can be less than optimal in the view of the medical professional before they are open to legal challenge, these decisions need to be 'reasonable'. Thus, Ménard, notes, 'French law explicitly tolerates a certain level of potential harm to the child in order to uphold parental authority', but physicians retain considerable authority where parents' decisions amount to 'unreasonable obstinacy'. French physicians do not require court approval to withdraw or withhold life-sustaining treatment if they conclude parents are acting with 'obstinacy', and hence the margin of appreciation is actually limited more to the choice of treatment plans rather than the whole gamut of decision-making. This, he concludes, leaves doctors with a considerable degree of authority to withdraw care,[24] which may then affect how disputes are managed in practice.

There are, therefore, a number of ways in which the background cultural and social context of a country might result in fewer conflicts arising over the appropriate medical treatment of a seriously ill child. Greater homogeneity of values; a more communitarian outlook; greater cultural significance attached to the family unit; and more deference paid to medical professionals may all reduce levels of conflict between parents and doctors, which may in turn explain the sparsity of litigation in these countries.

B. Alternative Mechanisms for Dispute Resolution

Even where disputes do arise, the onus (either culturally or legally) will not always be on legal avenues for resolution. Indeed, in some jurisdictions, mechanisms for

[21] ibid.

[22] A Büchler, 'Parental Decisions on their Children's Medical Treatment in Switzerland', in this book.

[23] JF Ménard, 'Offering a Reasonable Future: Withdrawal of Life-Sustaining Treatment from Infants in French Law with Illustrations from a Parisian Neonatal Resuscitation Unit', in this book.

[24] ibid.

resolving such disputes judicially simply do not exist. In Thailand, for example, even where doctors strongly disagree with the parents' view of what should be done, and consider their decision does not serve the best interests of the child,

> the doctor or the healthcare service provider does not have any legal standings to bring a case to the court for judicial intervention of parental decisions. The only thing the doctor could do if he or she disagrees with the option the parents choose for treating their children is refusing to provide the treatment as requested and providing proper advice.[25]

This, Tengaumanuay notes, stands in stark contrast to the English system, where doctors can request judicial determination of whether a treatment (or withdrawal thereof) conforms to the best interests of the child. Chinese law similarly does not establish procedural rules to facilitate dealing with conflicts where the child's best interests are clearly not being met. As Chunyan explains:

> Although the CPL provides a number of special procedures that do not involve adversarial parties, a proper procedure is lacking that enables either doctors or other relevant parties to file an action to challenge the parents' medical decision on behalf of children in China's civil procedure law.[26]

However, Thailand and China are not the only jurisdictions without a clear means for resolving conflicts through the courts. For example, although Sweden has legal avenues by which at-risk children can be taken into care where parental care is lacking, Leviner reports that 'this does not extend to a facility for medics to request intervention'. Doctors simply 'do not have the opportunity to petition for the authority to decide on the medical care initiatives that are to be carried out or not'. This, she notes, is exacerbated by the fact that mechanisms for taking children into care cannot generally be used to manage such conflicts as the threshold for taking over parental decision-making and removing the child is very high (essentially a significant risk of harm threshold). Consequently, she concludes that 'to take a child into involuntary custody "simply" to provide short-term medical care that the guardians oppose' is 'questionable' and Swedish law is not adapted for conflicts between doctors and parents. This, she posits, may rest in part on the high level of trust placed in doctors, but also because

> in line with Swedish state individualism and the described mutual trust between individuals and public institutions, a 'consensus paradigm' exists, whereby authorities also have confidence that parents, with government support (parental courses, etc), should be able to make the best decisions for their children.[27]

Some jurisdictions, such as Chile, Argentina and Israel, allow doctors to refer conflicts to an ethics committee which can determine which course of action is

[25] Tengaumunauy (n 8).
[26] Chunyan (n 9).
[27] Leviner (n 3).

in the child's best interests.[28] In fact, many systems have some sort of internal hospital mechanism for managing disagreement, with varying levels of authority. In Argentina, doctors can raise the matter with the hospital ethics committee if there is a conflict, but families do not have similar recourse. The law supports finding 'independent and interdisciplinary resolution, rather than referring the matter to a judge', but 'does not contemplate what happens if the conflict is between the parents and the medical team'.[29] In Israel, disagreements may also be brought before the hospital's ethics committee, which has the power to make decisions in cases where the child is not dying. These committees comprise doctors, nurses, bioethicists, lawyer, social workers, psychologists and relevant clergy. The goal of this system is to avoid conflicts being taken before the court, and to facilitate rapid decision-making that is 'not subject to rigid legal procedures', according to Roy Gilbar.[30] While conflicts can in some cases also be brought before the Family Court, the involvement of an ethics committee offers a way of facilitating a less adversarial approach that enables shared decision-making rather than putting parents and medics in opposition to one another within the court system. Similarly, Switzerland reports successful resolution of conflicts within the hospital setting, where disagreements are dealt with via interdisciplinary child protection groups that promote cooperation. If disagreements cannot be resolved, doctors are still permitted to report the situation to the child protection authority. Büchler posits that given 'the small number of court decisions in this area, it can be assumed that, in practice, many conflicts can be resolved within the hospital with the parents'.[31]

The approach of some African jurisdictions also offers an alternative to the adversarial approach, and those that defer to one party or the other, via processes that aim to promote harmonious decision-making. As noted above, the focus in some such jurisdictions is on solidary and harmony, and this, in the view of Ujewe, motivates

> the communicative or *indaba* process, so that the outcome is not predetermined by the stronger voice or actor. The final decision remains indeterminate and harmoniously reached through appreciation of the shared responsibilities of all parties in upholding the best interests of the child.[32]

Such processes stand in contrast to rights-based decision-making, and the approach 'is not viewed as a conclusive act or outcome driven; rather, it is process oriented and arrived at harmoniously'.[33] The core principle is responsibility

[28] F Lathrop Gomez, 'Decisions About Their Body: Children's Rights and Parental Responsibility in Chile', in this book.

[29] P Siverino, 'Who Decides the Best Interests of the Child in the End-of-Life Process? A Look at the Peruvian and Argentine Reality', in this book.

[30] R Gilbar, 'Withholding and Withdrawal of Life-Prolonging Treatment from Young Children in Israel', in this book.

[31] Büchler (n 22).

[32] Ujewe (n 4).

[33] ibid.

on the part of the community towards the health and well-being of the child. Ujewe argues that:

> [I]t is important to gain some insight into the sociocultural principles and values that inform decision-making processes in sub-Saharan Africa, generally speaking. The decision-making process in Charlie's case is underpinned by a social and cultural outlook embedded in Western Europe, which emphasises the value and place of individual rights and society's obligation to protect them. However, in African contexts, the emphasis is on the value of communal well-being and the responsibility of the community to protect the welfare of individual members. Decision-making processes in African contexts are, thus, informed by a sense of communal harmony. Accordingly, healthcare decisions are evaluated not only in terms of its potential consequences to the affected person(s), but also those who share vital relationships with them.[34]

The value of such a responsibility-led approach that aims for harmony is that it encourages governments to engage communities in dialogue and develop solutions that gain broad societal support. He points to the community engagement processes that led to the reinstatement of a previously opposed polio immunisation programme. While this does not, of course, directly apply in individual cases about children, there may be something to be said for jurisdictions considering more active approaches to address the kind of community feeling that ran high during the *Gard* and *Evans* cases.

These approaches can all be contrasted with Australia, the United States, Greece, England and Wales and others where the focus is primarily on legal avenues for resolution. For example, in Greece disagreements between parents are resolved by recourse to the courts, and Theodorus Trokanas posits that 'it is conceivable that the same legal path [would] be followed for disagreements between parents and the medical personnel'.[35] Similarly in Botswana and South Africa, physicians may petition for judicial intervention to make a determination on which course of action is in the child's best interests, and this can, in South Africa, extend to setting aside parental consent to a procedure (such as non-therapeutic sterilisation) that will promote the child's welfare.[36]

Regardless of the approach of the jurisdiction, it is clear from this collection that much can be learnt from the approaches of other countries to managing parent–doctor conflicts. One theme that came out time and again in contributions was dissatisfaction with 'murky' legal frameworks, where there was a lack of clear, principled guidance about how parent–doctor conflicts should be resolved. While supporting the communitarian approach in general, Moyo comments that jurisdictions such as Botswana can learn from those countries like South Africa that offer a clear hierarchy for decision-making.[37] Further, he argues that:

> [T]he rules should explicitly outline the circumstances under which parental consent to or refusal of medical treatment can either be reversed or bypassed by the courts,

[34] ibid.
[35] T Trokanas, 'Medical Decision-Making on Behalf of Critically Ill Minors in Greece', in this book.
[36] Moyo (n 2).
[37] ibid.

> hospital authorities and the state, especially through the Minister responsible for health related matters.[38]

Ho and Kaur comment that in Singapore and Malaysia

> more could certainly be done to clearly set out considerations that help to identify relevant values and interests for the purposes of decision-making and communication in difficult cases. There are already some initiatives to this effect outside of Singapore and Malaysia, although not yet adapted to our local and institutional needs.[39]

Lombard and Bracken similarly make some criticism of the 'fragmented and underdeveloped' nature of the legal framework in Ireland concerning parental rights in the context of medical decision-making for children. In their view:

> The constitutional provisions relating to the family give parents near-absolute discretion to make decisions for their children, which casts a shadow over permissible legislative and medical involvement. This has led to a dearth of professional guidelines for clinicians to use when parents disagree with the recommended medical intervention for their child. The Irish courts have established a clear line of jurisprudence on the appropriate approach in so-called 'exceptional' cases but cases that fall below this threshold remain in murky waters. It is clear that robust professional guidelines are needed to support the medical profession and to clarify the steps needed to ensure that the best interests of the child are maintained at all times.[40]

Others were critical of where the balance of decision-making power lay. For example, Tengaumnauy argues that conferring so much decision-making power on parents in Thailand leaves the children's welfare at stake and suggests that there is a need to establish a counterbalancing system where a balance is struck 'between respecting the opinions of parents and medical professionals on the optimal treatment'.[41] Other authors concluded that in their jurisdiction greater attention needed to be paid to the assessment of the best interests of the child, with Karl Sovig suggesting that England and Wales provide an inspiration in this respect. In his view, the Norwegian domestic courts

> would still rely heavily on the assessment by the hospital doctors or other experts but the courts will normally be more willing to engage in a review of the best interest of the child than reviewing what can be considered as a medical sound treatment.[42]

But while there is much to be said for a collaborative and harmonious approach, Leviner argues that at least in Sweden the consensus model might mask problematic measures taken to ensure agreement is achieved:

> It may be that parents are deferring to healthcare providers, or alternatively, that decisions about treatment are made 'in consensus' without doctors presenting other

[38] ibid.
[39] Ho and Kaur (n 19).
[40] Lombard and Bracken (n 14).
[41] Tengaumunauy (n 8).
[42] K Sovig, 'Reviewing Medical Decisions Concerning Infants Within the Norwegian Healthcare System – A Public Law Approach', in this book.

> justifiable options for parents to consider. If justifiable treatment options are not presented to parents, ie doctors misuse their knowledge and power advantage, consent to treatment cannot be considered informed, which of course is a problem in itself. Conversely, it may also be the case that healthcare providers defer to the will of parents without necessarily having the best interests of the child at stake. The consensus paradigm consequently can conceal coercion that should possibly be tested legally, or a child's right to care in accordance with science and well-tested experience may take second place in situations where parents claim that their child should receive other treatment. … Under the Swedish legal system today there is both the undesirable risk of concealed coercion by healthcare providers, where parents are simply persuaded or 'highly motivated' to defer to the doctors as to what treatment is most appropriate and reasonable in a difficult situation. This could often give rise to such a restriction on the rights of parents and children to private and family life that it should require judicial review.[43]

This comparative analysis of these many jurisdictions offers examples and approaches from which useful lessons for improving practice might be drawn.

II. The Limits of Parental Authority

Another key point for comparison is how the role of the parent is conceptualised in different countries. In essentially all jurisdictions, parents have the authority to make decisions on behalf of their children. This derives from the need for someone to stand in the decision-making role for a child lacking in capacity, but in some jurisdictions it also reflects the belief that the family is best placed to know what is in the child's interests. The parental role was almost universally conceived of as one of authority and responsibility, even though the language of rights is used in some jurisdictions. For example, in France parental authority endows parents with both rights and duties that must be exercised with a view to furthering the child's interests, and these are to be constrained if the parents put the child's health in danger.[44] In some, those parental rights are afforded legislative protection, as in Canada, where the Charter protects a sphere of parental rights and restrains state interventions.[45] In Canada, as in the United States, parents are presumed to be best placed to determine what is in the child's best interests.[46] In no jurisdictions were parental 'rights' conceived as absolute, although it emerged that in some jurisdictions parental views will rarely be overridden.

[43] Leviner (n 3).

[44] Menard (n 23).

[45] C MacIntosh, 'Decisionally Incapable Children and Medical Treatment Choices in Canada', in this book.

[46] L Francis, J Botkin and D Diekema, 'Decision-Making on Behalf of Children in the Research and Clinical Context: A United States Perspective', in this book; Belgium also takes a similar view: Boone (n 12).

What varied considerably between the jurisdictions examined in this collection was the *extent* of parental authority. This is so despite the fact that all (or almost all) jurisdictions considered here have ratified the United Nations Convention on the Rights of the Child[47] and the Convention for the Protection of Human Rights and Dignity of the Human Being with regard to the application of Biology and Medicine. In most jurisdictions, tolerance of parental discretion gives way at *some* point. The question was where this point was.

The bar is set perhaps highest in practice in China where, Chunyan reports, the courts 'have never intervened in a guardian's medical decision for a child', even in cases of parental refusal of treatment for conditions that are curable. Indeed, in one widely publicised case, of a father who refused treatment for his baby's imperforate anus, judicial intervention was not sought even after offers to pay for and arrange the surgery were made to him. This is unsurprising given the high level of deference to familial decisions, and the lack of procedural rules for dealing with conflicts where the child's best interests are clearly not being met.

Lower bars are set in most jurisdictions, with some favouring what is often referred to as a 'significant harm' threshold. In Chile, for example, the threshold is one of risk of serious harm or death. Cameron Stewart suggests that the Australian approach proposed by Thakeray CJ 'is very close in flavour to the principle of "risk of significant harm"', suggesting as it does 'primacy for parental decision-making and a preference for the court not exercising power in cases when the parental decision is clearly not incorrect or badly made'.[48] Francis et al suggest the approach in the United States, in some states at least, is similar,[49] while Mexico takes a related approach. Under Mexican law, parental authority to make decisions for children has been held by the Supreme Court to be limited when the rights of the child are put at risk, or their health threatened. For example, the court does try to enable parents' religious freedom, but this is limited, as in the case of blood transfusion refusals, which have been permitted only when a feasible alternative treatment for the child has been available.[50] As we have seen, the threshold in Ireland is also high, with the court making a determination only in exceptional cases where the parents' failure in their responsibilities is likely to prejudicially affect the safety or welfare of any of their children.[51] For example, a parental refusal for their child to receive a heel prick test to screen for disorders at birth was not sufficient.

Swiss law also operates a high bar for authorising courts to override parental wishes – serious endangerment to the child's health, although if the doctors treating the child consider that this poses a significant risk to the child's welfare, they

[47] UN Convention on the Rights of the Child, 20 November 1989.

[48] C Stewart, 'Children and Medical Decision-Making in Australia Post-Gard – A Possible Reformulation', in this book.

[49] Francis et al (n 46).

[50] M Dobernig, 'Parental Rights in Mexican Law', in this book.

[51] Lombard and Bracken (n 14).

can involve the child protection authority.[52] Ho and Kaur note that the threshold in Singapore is effectively a significant harm threshold, and the courts have consistently reflected in their judgments the view that judicial intervention 'should be an avenue of last resort'.[53] That said, while the bar has been set high, Ho and Kaur comment that it is not generally seen as prohibitive or inaccessible.

Other jurisdictions, such as England and Wales, have a lower threshold, intervening wherever the child's 'welfare' is at issue or their 'best interests' are not being met (used interchangeably in the case-law). Belgium, Spain and Hong Kong, amongst others, also use 'best interests' as a threshold; and given the likelihood that the Scottish courts may follow the English example, a similar threshold is likely operate under Scots law.[54] This is particularly likely as the English dicta align fairly easily with 'welfare test', set out in section 11(7)(a) of the Children (Scotland) Act 1995, which covers disputes regarding all aspects of 'parental responsibilities' and 'parental rights'.[55] In Australia and other jurisdictions, decision-making authority differs depending the *type* of treatment. Parents may make decisions on therapeutically indicated treatment, but following *Re Marion*, where non-therapeutic treatment is proposed for minors, parents have no authority to consent, and instead a court or tribunal must provide consent for the procedure to go ahead. Stewart notes that 'the distinction between therapeutic and non-therapeutic treatments has proved to be extremely difficult to apply and has created enormous uncertainty' and suggests that this leaves open the possibility that 'even a reasonable parental decision can be overturned by the court if it believes that it would be in the best interests of the child to do so'.[56]

While it is clear that different thresholds for intervention exist between jurisdictions, it is important to note that how such disputes proceed in practice is not just a question of when the courts *can* (legally) intervene in a dispute between parents and doctors, but also how likely the dispute is to come before the courts at all. As seen above, the social and cultural values of certain countries may lead to the court rarely intervening in such disputes, even if they have the legal authority to do so, because of, for example greater deference on the part of doctors to parents, or on the part of the parents to the medical profession. Even if the court does become involved, as the following section demonstrates, there may be substantial variation in the ways in which the courts of different countries manage disputes, even where, on the face of it, the legal standards that apply are the same.

[52] Büchler (n 22).

[53] Ho and Kaur (n 19).

[54] A Brown, '"Parental Rights", "Best Interests" and the Withdrawal of Life-Sustaining Medical Treatment of Children in Scotland: A Lack of Authority'; I Goold, C Auckland and J Herring, 'Medical-Decision Making on Behalf of Children in English and Welsh Law: A Child-Centred Best Interests Approach', both in this book.

[55] S 11 of the Children (Scotland) Act 1995 sets out the court's powers in relation to parental responsibilities and rights; in particular s 11(2) provides that: 'The court may make such order … as it thinks fit.'

[56] Stewart (n 48).

III. How Does Best Interests Operate?

While the authority (legal or de facto) for making decisions for children differs across cultures, many of those considered in this collection are guided in some form by the principle of deciding in the best interests of the child. This raises a series of questions for all jurisdictions, including who is best able to determine a child's best interests; what weight should be given to parental wishes when making this assessment; and how should value difference and cultural variance be accommodated within the best interests assessment? It is clear from this collection that different countries have answered these questions differently, with the result that despite seeming convergence in the law, there is substantial variation in the way that this is being applied in practice by the courts in different jurisdictions. While it is not possible to do justice to all of the ways in which differences emerged, in the final section of this chapter we hope to draw out some of the ways in which countries have varied in their approach to best interests decision-making, many of which have been touched on in the preceding sections. Cultural and religious factors understandably shape differences in approach to decision-making on behalf of children, and one way in which this emerged was through differing attitudes to the weight given to the sanctity of life in assessments of best interests, A number of contributors drew out the strong commitment to the sanctity of life, and explained how this influenced the position of all parties. Israel and Greece were two such examples, while Ho and Kaur comment that as Islam is the recognised religion of Malaysia

> the legal system is often referred to as being a hybrid system, being made up of both secular and syariah laws. … It would thus appear that in matters which touch on issues relating to religious sensitivities (Islam in particular), the civil courts are unlikely to challenge any position taken by the religious authorities.[57]

It would therefore seem likely, they conclude, 'that conservative religious positions such as sanctity-of-life arguments would be afforded great weight by the courts'.

But a commitment to preserving life goes well beyond religious perspectives, with most jurisdictions evidencing a general preference for life-sustaining treatment where it was in the best interests of the child. Nonetheless we can discern some differences in the ways in which jurisdictions have approached this aspect of decision-making. In South Africa, the right to life has been referred to as 'inviolable', with the court in one case ordering that transfusions be given to save a baby's life, despite the parents' religious beliefs that led them to refuse the treatment. In most jurisdictions, the right to life (or at least the child's interest in continuing to live) is, however, weighed against other factors. This often operates as a rebuttable

[57] Ho and Kaur (n 19).

presumption in favour of the sanctity of life. For example, MacIntosh notes that in Canada

> the presumption that pursuing life-sustaining treatment is in the best interests of a child has been rebutted in several Canadian decisions where the prognosis had uncertainties, and there were significant concerns about quality of life and/or challenges post-surgery or treatment.[58]

Courts now take the view that life without awareness may not be in the child's best interests, and so judges have begun to support the withdrawal of medical treatment without benefit (and where it may, in fact, be harming, such as causing pain) where there is no chance that the child will regain awareness, despite the objections of parents.[59] English law takes a somewhat similar approach. While in both *Gard* and *Evans* the court supported applications by hospitals to withdraw life-sustaining treatment against the wishes of the parents, as the recent *Raqeeb* decision suggests, where the child is unlikely to suffer harm, life-sustaining treatment may be permitted to continue if the parents wish it, even though the treating medical team does not consider it in the child's best interests.[60] In fact, one interesting dimension to this case was that the parents wished to have Tafida moved to Italy precisely because it was felt that the Italian courts attached greater weight to the inherent good of continuance of life when assessing best interests, with the result that life-sustaining treatment would not be withdrawn from her unless she suffered brain stem death, demonstrating the differences in the way the best interests standard is applied across jurisdictions.

By contrast with Canada and England, in Israel, where the commitment to sanctity of life holds particular sway, courts will override the wishes of parents who wish for life-sustaining treatment to be stopped because

> sanctity of life (or the legal right to life) is given preference over prevention of pain and suffering. … Israeli law … promotes sanctity of life as the dominant consideration, particularly when the child is not terminally ill but suffers from an incurable condition. This violates the right of a child to avoid a life full of pain and suffering when the proposed treatment is futile and prolongs life artificially. Only when the child is terminal does the law provide a mechanism to respect requests by the parents to withhold treatment though there is no obligation on the courts or institutional ethics committees to accept these requests.[61]

Pain and suffering will not therefore necessarily override sanctity-of-life considerations. Malaysia, Peru and Argentina also evince a strong commitment to sanctity of life, in part due to religious influences prevalent in those jurisdictions.

One particular issue that has emerged is what ought to happen where parental views conflict with the doctor's assessment of their child's best interests. In these

[58] MacIntosh (n 45).
[59] ibid.
[60] *Raqeeb v Barts NHS Foundation Trust & Anors* [2019] EWHC 2531 (Admin).
[61] Gilbar (n 30).

circumstances, the weight given to parents' views varies. In some countries the deference to parents is so great that parental views are likely to take precedence notwithstanding the best interests standard. In China, for example, Chunyan notes that:

> [T]he best interests of the child principle laid down in Article 35(1) of the GPCL has hardly restricted how guardians make proxy medical decisions for children. Hospitals and medical practitioners always follow the guardian's proxy medical decision even though it appears prejudicial to the child where the guardian refuses a treatment proposed by the treating doctor.[62]

There are also judicial statements in a number of jurisdictions that evidence the courts' commitment to respecting parental choice insofar as is possible. For example, in Australia in *Director Clinical Services, Child & Adolescent Services v Kiszko*,[63] O'Brien J reiterated the assertion made by Thackray CJ in an earlier decision that the court 'should not interfere in the exercise of parental responsibility unless there is some clear justification for doing so'.[64] Parental discretion is given similar levels of respect by the courts in the United States; as Leslie Francis et al point out, 'the state generally respects parental decisions except when they place a child's health, well-being, or life in jeopardy'.

In Switzerland, meanwhile, the best interests of the child 'must be based on objective criteria', with 'the starting point for the assessment of the child's welfare [being] the medical indication'. Parental religious views 'may not endanger the welfare of the child', with the prime example of parental refusals of blood transfusions for religious reasons being considered contrary to the objective welfare of the child.[65] Mexico takes a similar position, holding that parental rights 'do not confer authority over the life and death of their children. Parents would then have no right to affect the health of their children by virtue of their beliefs or customs.'[66]

In the preponderance of English cases, the medical view has been supported by the courts, but as Jo Bridgman's work demonstrates, this may be because it is only those cases in which the parents' views are very likely to harm the child (or, as she puts it, cannot be followed by the doctors as they conflict with their conscience).[67] For example, while the parents' Muslim beliefs were upheld in *Raqeeb*, much of the judgment focused on the lack of harm to Tafida, who would not experience pain or have any awareness of her situation. This can be contrasted with *Gard*[68]

[62] Chunyan (n 9).
[63] *Director Clinical Services, Child & Adolescent Services v Kiszko* [2016] FCWA 75.
[64] ibid [72]. Stewart (n 48).
[65] Büchler (n 22).
[66] Dobernig (n 50).
[67] J Bridgeman, 'Parental Responsibility, Professional Conscience and the Protection of the Court?' in I Goold, J Herring and C Auckland (eds), *Parental Rights, Best Interests and Significant Harms: Medical Decision-Making on Behalf of Children Post-Great Ormond Street Hospital v Yates* (Oxford, Hart Publishing, 2019).
[68] *Gard* (n 4).

and *Evans*,[69] which both involved children who may have been able to experience pain and discomfort, which was crucial in the court's determining that, contrary to their parents' wishes, it was not in their best interests to be kept alive.

This raises a final point, that while many jurisdictions do apply a best interests standard, this may not reflect the reality of how these disputes are governed in practice. In England, as noted above, the touchstone for the court overriding the parent's decision may in practice be closer to a risk of harm threshold. Francis et al suggest the approach in the United States, in some states at least, is similar,[70] while Cameron Stewart suggests that the Australian approach proposed by Thakeray CJ 'is very close in flavour to the principle of "risk of significant harm"', suggesting a 'primacy for parental decision-making and a preference for the court not exercising power in cases when the parental decision is clearly not incorrect or badly made'.[71] In China, the threshold for interfering with parental decisions is even higher. When evaluating the approach of different countries to managing disputes, therefore, the legal position is only part of the story. While the concept of the child's best interests has proven to be important across many of the jurisdictions, this collection reveals substantial variation in the way that the courts have applied a 'best interests' test in practice, with decision-making ranging from utilitarian and centred on the well-being of the family, to highly child-focused.

IV. Cultural Competence

One final theme that comes out in a number of chapters in this collection is the need for cultural competence, and sensitivity to the beliefs, practices and interests of minorities and indigenous peoples; this represents a challenge for courts applying a 'best interests' standard. MacIntosh's chapter traces some of the deeply problematic treatment of Indigenous people in the Canadian context, and Ben Gray urges us to understand 'the value of abandoning the idea of a common morality and objective best interests'.[72] So much of what we see in the way jurisdictions have approached decision-making for children rests on trying to determine the one, best way for that child – what is purported to be their 'best interests', or what best promotes their welfare (or that of a wider family). But as Ros McDougall's chapter demonstrates, such an understanding of welfare is flawed.[73] It is this very notion, that there is one best approach, that has led to a failure to be sensitive to cultural differences. It is also to some degree the foundation stone of conflict; not

[69] *Evans* (n 5).

[70] Francis et al (n 46).

[71] Stewart (n 48).

[72] B Gray, 'The Relevance of Cultural Competence to Resolving Disputes in Relation to Medical Decisions for Children', in this book.

[73] R McDougall, 'Identifying Who and What, then How: Attending to the Role of the Decision-Maker in the Normative Debate About the Best Interests Standard', in this book.

all conflict, but some. Gray argues that accepting that there are no objective best interests shows us that 'the way forward will be found through compromise of both parties, rather than further analysis to find the best interest'. We should, he argues, be developing approaches that facilitate trust and communication, and support relationships in which these can be fostered. How each jurisdiction achieves that will differ, but we hope that the chapters in this collection offer some insights into ways forward.

V. Conclusion

What can we take from this comparative analysis? Should we, in fact, take any lessons from it at all? In our view, looking across jurisdictions, contextualised by their social and cultural differences, we can all gain from learning about the strengths of other jurisdictions' approaches. Some are less combative, and arguably this might be a good thing. Others are more adversarial, but then having open, clear debate about where decision-making authority lies may also be a valuable approach. Perhaps the most important thing to take from this analysis, however, is the need for cultural sensitivity; recognising that there will be differences within communities, and that these need to be respected and accommodated in the way our legal systems deal with decision-making on behalf of children. We might think that there should be few lessons to draw from a comparative analysis precisely because our differences mean that different approaches suit different contexts and cultures, and we should not then seek to transpose the approach developed for one jurisdiction on to another. However the very conclusion that there is more than one way to think about what is best for a child, and that we do not all share the same values, is in itself important. Once we accept this, we should then see that we need to make space for differences of view and allow for this within the way decisions are made. This does not need to mean allowing any decision, but it does mean approaching disputes with an open mind and a willingness to engage with those differences and work towards creating a system that can accommodate value disagreements while still protecting these most vulnerable members of our community. Arguably, an approach that aims to bring different perspectives together – courts, doctors, parents and the wider family – in a way that all are heard, in a manner aimed at informed and culturally sensitive consensus-building, should be the goal in this area of law in any jurisdiction.

INDEX

www.ingramcontent.com/pod-product-compliance
Ingram Content Group UK Ltd.
Pitfield, Milton Keynes, MK11 3LW, UK
UKHW020231290926
15470UKWH00002B/480

9 781509 928569